FRIENDS
FAMILIES
& FORAYS

This 1904 photograph of Henry Ford was his first official
Ford Motor Company portrait. It was taken by A. G. McMichael, whose
studio was at 212 Woodward Avenue in Detroit.

FRIENDS FAMILIES & FORAYS

Scenes from the
Life and Times of

HENRY FORD

by Ford R. Bryan

FORD BOOKS
Dearborn, Michigan

This book is dedicated to my very good friend Winthrop Sears, Jr., (1918–2000), who in 1963 as a librarian in the Ford Motor Company News Department, by means of a 100-page detailed written memorandum, convinced Ford management that rather than disperse portions of the vast Ford archival holdings to various institutions, the archives should remain intact and made available to the public at one location. As a result, in 1964, both company and personal papers of Henry and Clara Ford were given to Henry Ford Museum & Greenfield Village, where they are now available to the public and form the nucleus of the Benson Ford Research Center.

06   05   04   03   02   1   2   3   4   5

ISBN 0–8143–3108–4

Designed by Mary Primeau

Contents

Introduction

This work contains fifty-five short stories describing people and pursuits that colored the life of Henry Ford. These accounts are not generally known and have not been published in a book until now. My goal is to provide a detailed and wide-ranging look at the personal history of Henry Ford employing facts that otherwise might have been overlooked.

Here, mostly in Part I of this volume but also in appearances throughout the book, the reader will meet prominent and diverse figures of the past century, including Thomas Edison, John Burroughs, George Washington Carver, Helen Keller, and Mahatma Gandhi — all of whose lives intersected that of Henry Ford at some interesting point in his biography. Also brought to life in these pages, in Part II, are the branches of Ford's family tree, from his Irish ancestors to the descendants who carry his legacy.

It was the automobile, of course, that made Henry Ford an industrial icon, but he could boast of mechanical exploits in other arenas as well: railroads, speedboats, robotics. These are explored in Part III, and Part IV examines some of Ford's adventures in financing such endeavors as a flour mill, a rubber plantation, even a stump farm.

Ford's investments went beyond a quest for profits, however, and his humanitarian efforts are detailed in Part V, in which the reader will learn about the economic philosophy known as Fordism, the innovations of Ford Motor Company's "Sociological Department," and the founding of institutions as grand as Henry Ford Hospital and as modest as camps for boys.

Finally, Part VI of this book offers a glimpse at the luxurious lifestyle enjoyed by Henry and Clara Ford as their wealth and fame grew. Their homes included the Fair Lane residence in Dearborn, a Florida house next door to the Edisons, and a Georgia plantation. A yacht and a private railway car served as homes away from home. And they relaxed, socialized, and entertained themselves with pastimes such as dancing and antique collecting at an inn and a tavern, a country club and a mountain club.

Several of the chapters in this volume have appeared previously in the *Dearborn Historian*, a periodical sponsored by the Dearborn Historical Commission; others have been printed in the *Ford Legend*, a newsletter of the Henry Ford Heritage Association; and two were published some time ago in the *Henry Ford Museum & Greenfield Village Herald*. The majority of these accounts, however, have been written very recently from relatively obscure primary sources found in the Ford Archives at the Benson Ford Research Center of the Henry Ford Museum & Greenfield Village in Dearborn, Michigan (called HFM & GV in the end-of-chapter references), where I have worked as a volunteer for the past twenty years.

The photographs in the book are from the collections of the Henry Ford Museum & Greenfield Village, unless otherwise identified; numbers following the photo captions identify specific negatives.

F. R. B.

Acknowledgments

The compilation of these stories would not have been possible without the cooperation of the staff of the Benson Ford Research Center of Henry Ford Museum & Greenfield Village over a period of several years. Permission to examine materials in the Ford Archives has been extended by Judith Endelman and Terry Hoover. Continual assistance with locating specific artifacts in the archives and library has been cheerfully offered by Catherine Latendresse, Linda Scolarus, Romie Minor, and Patricia Orr. Selection of photographic illustrations has been assisted greatly by the support of Cynthia Read-Miller, Alene Soloway, Carol Wright, and Margaret Hoover. The high quality of photographic work is to be credited to Alan Harvey of the museum's Historical Resources Unit.

Considerable information pertaining to Dearborn history has been provided over the years by the archives and library of the Dearborn Historical Museum. Of considerable help in locating these items have been William McElhone, Helen Mamalakis, Bertha Miga, and Joan Klimchalk. Permission from Winfield Arneson, chief curator, to reprint articles previously published in the *Dearborn Historian* is hereby gratefully acknowledged. Permission to reprint articles previously published in the *Ford Legend* has been graciously provided by Linda Leggitt, editor of that periodical. Permission to reprint the two articles from the *Herald* was granted by Mark Greene of the Benson Ford Research Center.

Additional assistance was provided from time to time by Elizabeth Adkins, Darleen Flaherty, and Marcia Mason of the Ford Industrial Archives. To finalize the book, Patricia Coates provided keyboarding of the text, Wendy Warren Keebler did the editing, Mary Primeau was book compositor and designer, and Alice Nigoghosian was my publishing consultant.

To all of these people and to many others, I am deeply grateful.

F. R. B.

Part I
Friends and Acquaintances

It is not surprising that Henry Ford, the industrialist, would have such men as Thomas Edison and Harvey Firestone as friends, because they, too, operated successful businesses related to the automobile. It is very revealing, however, to find that Ford had much in common with the likes of naturalist John Burroughs, botanist George Washington Carver, and educators Martha Berry and William McGuffey.

Ford was naturally gregarious. He made friends easily, and people enjoyed his company. During his youth on the farm, he was well known for miles around but was thought to be quite "different" from the typical farm boy. At large gatherings, such as dances, although he was an excellent dancer, Henry was said to have been somewhat bashful. He was a natural leader on an individual basis but not as a public speaker; he was indeed no orator, but in a one-to-one conversation he could be very convincing. His upbringing gave him a lifelong faith in farmers and a love of children.

I

Greenfield Dancing Club of 1882

This story draws particularly on the 1950 reminiscences of Fred Gleason, a close friend of Henry Ford.

Henry Ford quit school at age sixteen in 1879, having finished the sixth grade. He immediately left the farm for Detroit in order to obtain mechanical experience. His occupations ranged from repairing watches at Magill's Jewelry Store to helping to build Great Lakes steamers at the Detroit Drydock Company. By early 1882, however, Henry was back in the Dearborn area working for Jim Gleason (Fred Gleason's father), running Gleason's Westinghouse steam engine to thresh grain and saw wood.

Henry was then nineteen years old and gaining a reputation as a "swinger" on the dance floor of the Joseph Coon Hotel and Tavern on Plymouth Road. The hotel served as a halfway overnight stop for farmers taking loads of produce such as hay or potatoes to Detroit markets from the Plymouth area. Very popular at the tavern in those days was the Phelps-Brace Orchestra, a five-piece string group including a dulcimer played by Albert Brace, a bass viol, violins, and often a cimbalom. Combinations of this sort — always including dulcimers and violins — were assembled years later by Henry Ford to preserve the spirit of those early dances. The caller for the dances was the ever-popular William Cox, proprietor of a lunch room on Grand River Avenue near 14th Street. Young people from miles around gathered at Coon's Tavern for dancing. Henry danced with many of the neighboring farm girls, including the Gleason daughters.

Quoting from Fred Gleason's memoirs:

> My first recollection of Mr. Ford was when his name was mentioned with my sister Christine. Their acquaintance became so serious, his parents objected to their seriousness and demanded that they part. However, Mr. Ford, being like General Sheridan, refused to retreat. He wrote a nice long letter to Christine asking her to reconsider her answer, that maybe his parents would reconsider their request. If so,

Published previously in the *Dearborn Historian*, Vol. 37, No. 4, 1997.

everything would be OK. As for the answer my sister Christine sent, we have no record. However, my sister Irene has the letter Mr. Ford wrote to Christine.

The reasons for Henry's family's objection is thought to have been the difference in religion. Although both families were from southern Ireland, the Gleasons were Catholic, and the Fords were Protestant. Christine apparently realized that the marriage might lead to difficulties, and, instead of marrying Henry, she chose to marry Joseph F. Shefferly, a blacksmith with a business at Livernois and Grand River Avenues.

When he was questioned later about his sister's turning down Henry Ford for a blacksmith, Fred Gleason justified her decision as follows:

> Now, to place my sister in a better light, this fellow Shefferly was the owner of a double-seat surrey, a beautiful horse, and was in business by himself. Mr. Ford did not even have a bicycle or the money to buy one. To those who knew both boys, one [was] known as Ford's fool; the other one was considered a very progressive young man. Just what would you have done? With all his faults, this Ford boy could dance and jump over board fences; perhaps it was his dancing my sister admired. If you were a good farmer boy and could dance square dances, all the girls would be looking out of the corner of their eyes at you.

Henry Ford continued to operate Gleason's steam engine, repair other Westinghouse engines, and take in the dances not only at Coon's Tavern but also at Botsford Inn and the Martindale House, dance halls on Grand River Avenue. He also attended corn-husking bees, where, if you found a red ear, you could kiss the girl with you, and box-lunch socials, where you could take a girl home by outbidding others for her lunch. It was at the Martindale House in 1885 that Henry is said to have first met his future wife, Clara Bryant.

We usually think of Henry Ford's revival of old-fashioned dancing as beginning when he met Benjamin Lovett at Wayside Inn in 1923 or when Lovett conducted the Halloween dancing party in the barn at the restored Ford Homestead in 1924. But there was an earlier event, on January 27, 1910, when Ford hosted the old-time dancing friends he remembered from his early dancing days: the Greenfield Dancing Club of 1882.

Although his home then was on Edison Avenue in Detroit, Ford was beginning to buy thousands of acres in Dearborn Township using profits from the Model T automobile. In November 1908, he purchased the eighty-acre Orrin P. Gulley farm on Michigan Avenue at Gulley Road as a gift to Clara. The old Gulley farmhouse became the setting for the 1910 reunion of the Greenfield Dancing Club of 1882. Invitations were sent to thirty-six people by Fred J. McDonald, a Detroit coal merchant, and the designated "floor manager" was William Cox, the same man who had called the Coon's Tavern dances. It was a

1882   1910

You are cordially invited to attend a
Reunion of the Greenfield Dancing Club
of 1882, at the Old Gulley Homestead,
Dearborn, given by Henry Ford on Thursday Evening, Jan. 27, 1910. Special Car
will leave Ford Bldg., cor. Griswold and
Congress Sts. at 8 o'clock p. m.

———

Old time Dancing Party consisting of
Square Dances, Virginia Reels, and old
fashioned Polkas.

Don't forget the Time, Place and the
occasion.

Wm. Cox,   F. J. McDonald,

    Floor Manager   Secretary

late-evening affair; the special streetcar bringing guests directly to the
Gulley homestead did not leave downtown Detroit until eight p.m.
About forty people were on hand for the group photograph taken that
evening in the Gulley farmhouse.

Again quoting from Fred Gleason:

About 1920 on Plymouth Road, there was a huge tavern. Mr. Ford
came to me. "Fred," he said, "I want you to buy all the land on the
north side of Plymouth Road clear to the railroad tracks (now the
C&O). I'll tell you what we'll do. We'll raise Plymouth Road up
several feet, and I'll put a big lake in there, and we'll have Coon's
Hotel remodeled. I want to keep it as a memorial to the early days

Back row: John N. Ford, Fred McDonald, Ed Vizard, Ed Henderson, Will Palmer, Mr. Snyder, Mr. Coon, Fred Martindale, George Vizard, Will Turner. *Center row:* Mrs. John H. Ford, Mrs. Nellie Scovel, Wallace Ford, Mr. Scovel, Wales Martindale, Mrs. Wallace Ford, John Ford, Nell Turner, Mrs. Snyder, Mrs. Fred Martindale, Annie Turner, Ollie Turner, Mattie McDonald, Nancy Vizard, Mrs. George Vizard, Mrs. Mary Lightbody, Mrs. Ed Henderson (Laura Martindale), Mrs. Mollie Ford, Mr. Kennedy. *Front row:* Addison Ford, Mrs. Newton, Mrs. Wales Martindale (Clara Henderson), Mrs. Bert Morton (Mattie Ruthruff), Clara Ford, Henry Ford, William Cox, Mrs. Cox, Mrs. Kennedy (MacFarlane), Laura Coon. (P.O.1492)

when we all had such a good time dancing to Phelps and Brace's Orchestra."

The water in the Rouge would be backed up clear to Redford Village. It was found that it would flood other property, and so when that came up from the engineers' report, the whole idea was abandoned, for one is not allowed to back up water on land he does not own. The engineers found there would be too much territory that would have to be acquired beyond the original estimated size of the proposed lake. While this venture was being proposed, Henry took me into the Coon Hotel. In the dancing parlor, he recalled just whom he had danced with in the early days. Before he left, he got a three-way stove pipe from the old tavern. I had never seen one like it. One part of it went into the chimney, and the other two parts went right and left into the hall to warm the hall for dancing. It became a part of the Americana at the Ford Museum.

In the mid-1930s, in preparation for Henry Ford's seventy-fifth birthday celebration in Dearborn, Larry McErlean wrote the following poem — with Fred Gleason's help, it is said:

Having inherited the privilege of knowing Mr. Henry Ford all my life, I beg your indulgence and consideration in my taking the liberty of writing some of the happy memories I still entertain and to furnish the various information compiled into, shall I say, poetry regarding the early teenage life of Mr. Ford.

'Twas July 30 in sixty-three
   That day will long remembered be,
For history will record the date
   As one important to this state.
While folks thank God, both night and morn
   That on that day a son was born
To honest humble pioneers,
   On whom we find in after years
Has climbed to honor and to fame
   Whom dual townships now would claim.

For since to manhood he has grown
   Each one proclaims him as its own,
And we can never solve for you
   Both Greenfield's claim and Dearborn's too,
For his old home, say friends of mine,
   Stood squarely on the old town line.
Then men put on their thinking caps
   And scrutinized their local maps
And since that homestead has been moved
   Their verdict never was approved.

This all agree, with judgment sane,
   That he was surely born in Wayne.
And in the midst of smiles and tears
   The old Scotch settlement appears
And memory finds us half aghast
   As we review the years that passed
For thoughts by day and dreams by night
   Transport us on our fancy's flight
To where as children oft we've played,
   And where true friends were truly made.

As we espy in youthful mode
        The old brick schoolhouse down the road,
Where in the midst of scenes like these
        We memorized our A, B, C's.
And then we see without alarm
        A young man working on a farm
Now right in here I'd like to say,
        I'm like an actor in a play
And to present the part that's mine
        I have been furnished every line.

Through stories told to me by Fred,
        With borrowed memory from the dead.
That's why my rambling rhyme may seem
        Just like some incoherent dream,
But I can understand full well
        Why those folks gather just to tell
Of other men and other years
        Producing laughter mixed with tears.
There's only one good reason why
        Fond sentiment will never die.

That's why you've gathered here tonight
        Because of love that knows no blight,
And as we're reminiscing now
        We cannot fail to see somehow
The prominence that God ordained
        One man within our time obtained.
At only eighteen years of age,
        We find this modest youthful sage
Had knowledge far beyond his years
        Of wheels and cogs and tiny gears.

An old watch furnished him a plan,
        And with a baking-powder can,
He realized his early dream,
        To see the darned thing run by steam.
He studied hard both day and night
        And with the aid of candle light
A new invention was revealed
        That in his brain had been concealed.
And though his heart was filled with joy
        He still remained that farmer boy.

For much in evidence was he
        When neighbors staged a threshing bee.
And in those good old days of yore
        He often made a perfect score
At old Coon's Tavern, Plymouth Road,
        By dancing talent that he showed,

*Greenfield Dancing
Club of 1882*

And he could swing each lady fair
        Whether shy or debonnaire,
And music led by Phelps and Brace
        Lights with a smile the dancer's face.

A joy that he was glad to show
        With heel and toe and Poke-Ke-O,
His every step was light and free
        To Souvianna's Melody.
And old Bill Cox of township lore
        Would call square dances by the score.
Full well indeed can you recall
        Those old time friends that filled the hall
Where Nancy Vizard then held sway,
        With Lorette Crane in laughter gay.

The Sheahan girls were on the scene
        With Christine Gleason, beauty's queen.
While at box socials now and then
        The ladies always pleased the men
With dainty lunches well prepared
        In which the bidder freely shared.
'Twas there two hearts beat with one thought
        As Clara Bryant's box you bought,
And you could feel within your heart
        The tickling sting of Cupid's dart.

And as so oft with youthful glee
        Her "C.B." carved in trunk of tree.
And now to other scenes than these
        Our memory moves with perfect ease,
For you can surely call to mind
        Old Davy Young so keen and kind,
Who, when he placed beneath his chin
        That aged and treasured violin,
The very songbirds seemed to know
        Against his music they'd no show.

And here Bill Hunter comes in sight
        And George Humbert's face so bright,
And as they pass in single file
        There's Mannie Griffin's Irish smile,
And as we keep watch we find
        There's William Miller close behind.
While further on among the jam
        We have the brothers Cunningham.
And then we hear those raps and knocks
        Of Henry Helner, sly old fox.

And in our line of vision now
        Comes Harry Biggetts with a bow
And in James Gleason we espy
        The Irish twinkle in his eye.
So let us all be boys once more
        Those good old days let's talk them o'er.
And all of us remember still
        Our journey to the old grist mill
And as we stood with hand on latch
        We watched the millstones grind our batch.

And when Joe Coon would take his toll
        We'd gladly start our homeward stroll,
And looking back through mists and fogs
        There's Billie Euwings scaling logs,
And that's where Henry showed his skill
        While running Gleason's old saw mill.
Sure we could ramble on and on
        And talk of Pat or Mike or John
And we could tell of feats of men
        Who've crossed the Great Divide since then.

For few there are who still survive
        Those four score years but lacking five,
So we just better concentrate
        On this the day we celebrate.
But we must mention ere we go
        George Brazeil and old Doctor Snow.
Should thoughts of those of whom we speak
        Start teardrops trickling down our cheek,
Then why should we apologize
        If deep within our souls there lies
A font of sentimental joy
        Created there when just a boy.

And our emotions now we show
        For those old friends of long ago
So let it be our daily prayer
        That that same font be always there
And nothing ever take its stead
        Until we're numbered with the dead
So now with pistons old and scored
        We're driving to you, Mister Ford,

And in our rough untutored way,
        We're wishing you on your birthday
From out our hearts without alloy,
        A load of peaceful joy,
And as the milestones come and go

Greenfield Dancing
Club of 1882

May each display a brighter glow
And each enriched by a perfect gem
To make complete your diadem.
And may you live to know and feel
The joy that no man can reveal.

And now our rambling tale we'll end
By telling you as friend to friend,
We've but one word with which to close,
A word each heart that's human knows,
And on this day with your relations
Let's all repeat — Congratulations!!

2
Thomas and Mina Edison

Thomas Alva Edison was born in Milan, Ohio, in 1847. The family moved to Port Huron, Michigan, when Tom was seven years of age. He is said to have done poorly in school and to have owed his education primarily to his mother. Like Henry Ford, Edison had great respect for his mother, saying, "My mother was the making of me. The memory of her will always be a blessing to me." Unlike Ford's mother, however, Edison's is said to have beaten young Thomas frequently with a birch switch.

The stories of young Tom Edison as a newspaper boy and as an amateur chemist on the Michigan Central Railroad between Port Huron and Detroit are already well known. And it was the first meeting between Ford and Edison in New York in 1896 that marked the beginning of Ford's worship of Edison. The two men were sixteen years apart in age, and Edison was already a national hero.

In 1871, when Edison was twenty-four and busy in his telegraphic research laboratory at Newark, New Jersey, he married Mary Stilwell of that city. In 1876, Edison moved his family, home, and laboratory to Menlo Park, New Jersey. Thomas and Mary had been married only eleven years when she died of typhoid fever on August 9, 1883, leaving him with three children: Dottie, age eleven; Thomas Alva, Jr., eight; and William, six. Mary Edison is buried in Pleasant Cemetery at Newark. Although some 420 inventions were patented while Edison was at Menlo Park — some relating to the most important, the phonograph and the incandescent lamp — Edison remembered the period at Menlo Park with sadness because of the loss of his first wife, Mary.

Edison left Menlo Park in 1885 and went back to New York. Next, he purchased a large gabled house at Orange (more precisely Llewellyn Park), New Jersey. It would be named Glenmont. It covered thirteen acres of park and garden and included an acre of greenhouses, horses, cattle, and a poultry run. Edison also acquired a more modest winter home known as Seminole Lodge on the Caloosahatchee River at Fort Myers, Florida. He hired his father to build a "portable" laboratory to be shipped to Fort Myers, where he intended to live and work during the winter months.

The restored Edison home called Seminole Lodge facing south on MacGregor Boulevard in Fort Myers, Florida, as it appeared in 1997. Attached to the Edison home on the right is the guest house. The back of the house faces the Caloosahatchee River, where the Edisons had a sizable dock. Edison's laboratory and botanical garden were across MacGregor Boulevard. (Photograph courtesy of Jim Niccum.)

In February 1885, Edison had met Mina Miller, age twenty. She was the second daughter of Lewis Miller of Akron, Ohio, the well-known cofounder of the Chatauqua and an inventor of mowing machines and grain harvesters. Mina had just returned from a journey through Europe following graduation from a Boston seminary. The two had met again at a Chatauqua assembly during the following summer, after which Edison soon proposed marriage. Their wedding was in February 1886 in Akron, amid the glamour of high society. The groom's gift to the bride was a necklace of diamonds and pearls. The couple honeymooned at Fort Myers. Although eighteen years younger than Edison, Mina was admirably suited to take care of him and his house-hold with the required discretion. Edison seems to have had intense love for Mina, and she is said to have treated him as a "big boy." She not only tolerated his deafness but made it a point to devise other means of personal communication.

When Henry Ford first met Thomas Edison in New York in July 1896, Edison was already royally ensconced at Glenmont with Mina and participating in a business arena as yet unknown to Henry and Clara. At the Paris International Exposition in 1889, Edison already had made his mark abroad with his magnificent display of electrical devices, including a mammoth generating and light distribution system for the world to admire. He had been awarded many honors by European technical soci-

Thomas A. Edison sitting on the lawn of his Glenmont home at Llewellyn Park, West Orange, New Jersey, on June 30, 1917. He holds a cigar in his right hand and a book in his left. (P.188.9755)

eties as well as by the French government. So when Ford and Edison met in New York, Edison's favorable response to a gasoline-powered engine had a very deep and lasting impact on Ford.

While Ford struggled to produce a successful automobile, Edison was considering such things as the relative merits of alternating electrical current versus direct current for power distribution and questions concerning the use of electrocution as a form of human punishment. He later began exhaustive experiments testing the practicality of long-distance electric railroads and spent considerable time and money attempting to mill iron ore by magnetic methods — losing approximately $2 million on the latter.

Another Edison venture had been the formation in 1898 of the Edison Portland Cement Company, resulting in 1908 in a patented method of pouring a complete house in six hours. By 1910, Edison was deeply involved in production of nickel-alkaline storage batteries used in city delivery trucks, which could be charged overnight and used on short trips about the city during the day.

When Ford became so successful with his Model T that he could afford to double his employees' wages, he still had not satisfied Clara, who insisted that she could not start the Model T engine using the awkward and temperamental crank. So, in 1913, Henry had bought Clara a Detroit Electric vehicle, which used Edison batteries. She liked the car so well that Henry gave an identical Detroit Electric to Thomas Edison as a Christmas present.

Ford thought Edison might be able to help with the Model T. Ford's auto needed a good battery and an electric starter. He is said to have loaned Edison $1.2 million with the presumption that he would be purchasing 100,000 batteries. There was almost daily correspondence regarding batteries, handled by Ford's secretary, Ernest Liebold, and Edison's battery chief, William G. Bee. In January 1914, Henry and Edsel Ford visited Edison at his home in Llewellyn Park, to discuss batteries. At that meeting, the Edisons invited the Fords to visit them in February at Seminole Lodge in Fort Myers.

This was perhaps the first time the Fords and the Edisons visited on a purely social basis. Along with John Burroughs and his wife, Emily, Henry and Clara arrived in Fort Myers on February 23, 1914. Two thousand townspeople turned out to welcome them. Edison liked the quiet little town of Fort Myers just as it was, and he was annoyed to find so many reporters on the scene. He complained, "There is only one Fort Myers, and now 90 million are going to find out." The Edisons had planned an extensive camping trip into the Everglades for their guests. Guides were employed to lead the way and establish the camps. Mina Edison is said to have proclaimed to her husband, "There are two kinds of automobiles, the Ford and the Cantafford." The Burroughses and the Fords left Florida on March 10. Later that month, headlines would read, "Edison's Moving Picture Plant in New York City Destroyed by Fire, Actors Flee for Their Lives, Loss Estimated at $100,000."

In October 1914, Henry and Clara Ford invited the Edisons to Dearborn. Coming back to Michigan was a treat for Edison, who enjoyed revisiting Port Huron and, with Ford observing it all, reenacting well-remembered boyhood episodes along the Grand Trunk Railroad. Some old acquaintances remembered Edison as "Al," his nickname as a boy. The Fords this time entertained the Edisons in their clapboard Bungalow on the Rouge River in Dearborn. Their Edison Avenue home in Detroit was besieged by unemployed workers begging for five-dollar-a-day jobs, and their Fair Lane residence had not yet been finished. The Bungalow registry shows the signatures of Thomas, Mina, and Charles Edison on October 25, 1914. These visits with the Edisons during 1914 established a firm relationship between the two couples.

In December 1914, a fire swept through Edison's laboratory at West Orange, with a loss estimated at $5 million. Mina reported that her husband was very depressed. Ford immediately called on Edison at his Glenmont home to give him encouragement and offer him help. The laboratories were rebuilt in record time. Bright lights allowed work to progress twenty-four hours a day.

Edison was to be honored at the Panama-Pacific Exposition on October 21, 1915. It was the thirty-sixth anniversary of the incandescent lamp. Henry Ford and Harvey Firestone, with their families, met the Edisons at San Francisco. From there, they all went up to Santa Rosa to visit Luther Burbank. Edison especially admired Burbank, and Ford also would establish an interest in Burbank's work. It was during their trip together to Santa Rosa that Edison, Ford, and Firestone planned for their famous annual "Vagabond" vacation trips.

The very next year, Edison, Firestone, and naturalist John Burroughs went camping. Ford could not go because of his son Edsel's wedding. Burroughs later wrote of Edison:

> It was a great pleasure to see Edison relax and turn vagabond so easily, sleeping in his clothes, curling up at lunch time on a blanket under a tree and dropping off to sleep like a baby, getting up to replenish the camp fire at daylight or before, making his toilet at the creek or wayside pool, and more than that, to see him practice what he preaches about our excessive eating, and at each meal taking only a little toast and a cup of hot milk.

The Fords must have believed, as the Edisons did, that Fort Myers was an ideal place to spend the winters. In June 1916, they purchased the home next door to that of the Edisons in Fort Myers. The Fords' property was known as the Mangoes.

Ford was invited to Edison's seventieth birthday party on February 10, 1917, "at the Edison Storage Battery Building, no speech making, no evening dress, only for Mr. Edison's personal friends." Liebold answered for Ford, saying, "He wishes to inform you that he will certainly be there unless he loses his legs."

During World War I, Edison's inventiveness was in demand by the Navy on projects pertaining to submarines and listening devices. Forty-one patents during this period were provided to the Navy, for which Edison won the Distinguished Service Medal. Edison's batteries were used to power submarines, and his listening devices could detect both submarines and torpedoes at great distances. In September 1917, Ford was invited by Edison to go on a submarine chaser off Long Island.

In 1916, Ford had been called an "anarchist" by the *Chicago Tribune* because of his stand regarding the use of National Guardsmen along the Mexican border. Ford sued the *Tribune* for $1 million. The case dragged on and on. On the day of World War I Armistice, Edison's assistant, W. H. Meadowcroft, wrote to Liebold, saying, "Edison hopes Ford will think the matter over carefully, and inasmuch as the war is over that Mr. Ford will call off his suit against the *Chicago Tribune* and let the matter drop." The case was finally settled in August 1919, with only six cents going to Ford.

On their annual vacation trip in 1919, Edison asked that Secretary of the Navy Josephus Daniels accompany them. Ford was not opposed; he had had dealings with Daniels in regard to building Eagle boats at the Rouge plant. The Rouge was by then already preparing for tractor production on a large scale; blast furnaces were being built requiring large amounts of cement for footings. Edison, through his Edison Portland Cement Company, was able to sell Ford 150,000 barrels of cement at $2.33 a barrel. Two twenty-five-car trains a week hauled cement to Dearborn, the limit being reached when there was a shortage of cars, not cement.

Ford was sufficiently involved in Edison's business finances to justify monthly balance sheets pertaining to "T. A. Edison, Inc., and Subsidiary Companies" to be sent to Dearborn. Assets of $15 million, with patent rights valued at nearly $8 million, appear on these records. On the other hand, monthly automobile production records were sent to Edison. On Ford's birthday, July 30, 1923, a telegraph message from Edison reads: "Congratulations to a man because he has grown older doesn't seem to be exactly right. Therefore, I will only congratulate you on your abstemiousness in the use of food, which is productive of a long and strenuous life."

In a letter from Ford's secretary to Meadowcroft, Edison's assistant, the measurements for an old-fashioned suit to fit Edison were requested. The reply:

> We are sending an old hat. Patterns are being sent from the tailor. As to Mr. Edison's collar measurement, let me say that he does not wear a separate collar. His shirts are made to order and the collars are attached. The collar is a standard one about 2¼ inches high, and open about 2 inches in front. However, the measurement of the neckband is 16⅞ inches. I would say that his shirts are not made "coat style" like modern shirts, but are closed from a point a little above the waist down to the lower end of the shirt. The bosom of his shirt is stiff and is open down to the above point, fastening with three studs. He never buttons his collar. Glove size is 8¾.

When Ford wanted to expand his business to include Muscle Shoals in Alabama, he took Edison with him to examine the project and offer advice. When Ford was tempted to run for public office, even thinking of becoming president of the United States, Edison tried to discourage him.

During 1923, the bulk of the correspondence between Ford and Edison concerned making phonograph records. In 1917, Ford had

asked Edison to record his Hawaiian Quintet; now he wanted record-ings of the Ford Motor Company Band, his Old-Time Orchestra, and individual artists such as fiddler Jep Bisbee. From Wayside Inn, Ford sent an ancient cabinet in which he wanted Edison to install a phono-graph machine. In 1912, a simple recording contract between Ford and Edison had been agreed upon. But in 1925, after the sale of thousands of records, who was to pay the income taxes on the profits was in dispute.

The Henry Fords and the Harvey Firestones were invited to the wedding of Theodore Miller Edison in Cambridge, Massachusetts, on April 25, 1925. Theodore was the second son of Thomas and Mina. Their older son, Charles, had been married on March 27, 1918.

Ford had begun to plan Greenfield Village and had arranged with Edison to move the little Fort Myers Laboratory to Dearborn. Edison's father had constructed it during the winter of 1883–84 from lumber shipped from Maine. When it was time to move the building in 1926, there were objections from the townspeople of Fort Myers and, to an extent, from Mina Edison. Edison responded with this letter on July 30, 1926:

Mr. S. O. Godman, President
Fort Myers Chamber of Commerce
Fort Myers, Florida

My Dear Mr. Godman:

    I am in receipt of your letter of July 24. Let me say by the way of explanation that a long time ago I promised Mr. Ford that he could

The Fords entertaining the Edisons and Alice Longfellow, daughter of Henry Wadsworth Longfellow, at Wayside Inn about 1924. From the left in the photograph are Mina Edison, Thomas Edison, Alice Longfellow, Henry Ford, and Clara Ford. (0-882)

remove my Fort Myers laboratory to Detroit, to be reerected in his historical collection. On his part he was to replace the laboratory at Fort Myers exactly as it stands at the present time.

You will see therefore that I am bound by an actual promise, and that I cannot now take back this promise.

Yours very truly,
Thos. A Edison

It was arranged that the laboratory would be moved after the 1927–28 winter visit of the Fords to Fort Myers. As soon as the old laboratory was moved away, Mina took charge of details concerning the replacement laboratory being financed by Ford. She saw, for example, that chauffeur's quarters were added and that trellises with flowers were included.

A wire from Mina to Liebold on November 3, 1926, reads: "Mrs. Ford sent me an old shirt of Mr. Ford's some time ago. I wish to auction it at a church fair tomorrow or Friday. Would like verifying letter or certificate with Mr. Ford's signature. Can you mail it today please. Answer immediately."

Mina was having trouble with her Lincoln limousine. At speeds over thirty miles an hour, there was a drumming sound. After dealers were unable to correct the problem, Ford ordered a new Lincoln for her, this one painted in Packard blue, with the chauffeur's compartment trimmed in black leather. The new limousine was received on July 7, 1927. Edison was later given his choice — a dark green Ford Model A touring car, serial number one — on December 15, 1927.

When Edison was visiting Luther Burbank in 1915, he was asked to fill out a visitor record answering "Name," "Address," and "Interest." Under the heading of "Interest," Edison wrote, "Everything."

When Firestone and Ford in 1923 were having problems obtaining rubber from foreign countries and needed a domestic source, Edison wrote to Liebold, saying: "Tell Ford that I have been experimenting a little with milk weed. I find the maximum amount of latex is given when the plant is half grown. When it blossoms there is scarcely any latex. Therefore we can get two crops per year." Edison readily agreed to work on the rubber problem. In early 1927, when Liebold sent Edison a sample of synthetic rubber, his response was that "all synthetic rubber is made from materials that must be grown. All the big chemists of Germany, England, and in this country are unanimous in stating that synthetic rubber cannot compete with tree rubber at forty cents." In 1927, Edison proposed that he, himself, conduct intensive and thorough research to find a plant that could be grown in the United States from which rubber could be commercially extracted. That year, Edison, Ford, and Firestone formed the equally owned Edison Botanic Research Corporation.

By early 1928, Ford was attempting to acquire the entire Edison

During Light's Golden Jubilee Celebration at Greenfield Village on October 21, 1929, the Edisons and the Fords visited the restored Menlo Park, New Jersey, laboratory building. In the photograph, Henry, Clara, and Mina Edison are standing, while Thomas A. Edison, the honored guest, is sitting. Apparatus to the left was used to evacuate experimental incandescent lamps in 1879. (P.188.1264)

Historical Collection to be displayed in his museum and village at Dearborn. Edison's assistant, Meadowcroft, explained to Liebold that it would be a complicated procedure because other parties would be involved. The Edison Collection was owned by the Association of

Edison Illuminating Companies, with the Edison Pioneers as custodians. Edison's assistant stated: "if he [Ford] can get the consent of these other parties, it will be quite satisfactory to him [Edison]." Ford was very convincing, and thousands of Edison artifacts were donated.

Mr. and Mrs. Edison were invited to Dearborn in September 1928 to lay the cornerstone of the Edison Institute Museum. At that event, before the museum was built, Edison planted a spade, which had belonged to Luther Burbank, into the fresh cement cornerstone and signed his name in the cement with a flourish. Near the entrance to the museum, Edison's signature is viewed by millions of visitors.

Also in September 1928, Edison was feted at the Hotel Astor in New York in connection with a radio industry extravaganza. The Edisons invited the Fords and the Firestones to join them for dinner before the event. The Fords accepted. Meanwhile, Meadowcroft, with the help of Charles Edison, had prepared a one-minute speech for Henry to recite that evening — presumably, Henry obliged:

> Ladies and gentlemen of my visible and invisible audience. This is Henry Ford speaking. It is my pleasant privilege this evening to introduce to you my friend Mr. Edison, and I am glad to do so for it is his fundamental discoveries and inventions that made radio possible. His discovery of etheric force in 1875 opened the way to wireless communication. His discovery and applications of the Edison Effect in 1883 is the foundation of all radio tubes, and the carbon telephone transmitter, invented by him in 1877, is substantially the microphone used in all broadcasting. He also invented and operated wireless communication between moving trains in 1888. You will see therefore how much the great radio industry owes to him, and I take pleasure in introducing my good friend Thomas A. Edison.

The next big event bringing the Fords and the Edisons together was Light's Golden Jubilee. More than five hundred notables received the following invitation:

> The Honor of your presence is requested by Mr. Henry Ford and Mr. Edsel Ford at a Celebration in honor of Mr. Thomas Alva Edison on the occasion of the Fiftieth Anniversary of his Invention of the Electric Light and the dedication of the Edison Institute of Technology by the President of the United States on Monday, October twenty-first, Nineteen hundred and twenty-nine, Dearborn, Michigan.

Edison and others arrived at Greenfield Village on an 1860s train, getting off at the same Smith Creek station at which Edison had been ejected from the train in his youth. At the reconstructed Menlo Park laboratory, he reenacted the construction of his first successful lamp and in the evening attended the huge banquet, during which 140 radio

Thomas and Mina Edison at Fort Myers about 1929, perhaps the winter following Light's Golden Jubilee. Edison was then about eighty-two years old. (0-13958)

stations were broadcasting the program; at a given signal, lights turned on all over America. Owen D. Young, chairman of General Electric Company, was toastmaster, and President Herbert Hoover was speaker of the evening.

The banquet was a little too much for Edison. Following President Hoover's lengthy address, much of which Edison could not hear, Edison responded as follows:

> This experience makes me realize as never before that Americans are sentimental and this crowning event of Light's Golden Jubilee fills me

Thomas and Mina Edison

In memory of Thomas Edison's one-hundredth birthday, this wreath was placed at the entrance of Edison's Menlo Park Laboratory in Greenfield Village in 1947. (833-83897)

with gratitude. I thank our president and you all. As to Henry Ford, words are inadequate to express my feelings. I can only say to you that, in the fullest and richest meaning of the term — he is my friend. Good night.

Edison then collapsed. Mina and the president's physician helped him to a nearby couch, where adrenaline was administered, and he slowly recovered. In a later letter to a friend, Mina reveals that she was upset at the banquet. With Young as toastmaster, she felt that General Electric basked in glory while her "Dearie" was left in the shadows.

Edison continued with intensive rubber research for the next two years — winters in Fort Myers and summers at Glenmont. In 1930, he was instrumental in the passage of a national act allowing patents to be issued to new varieties of plants or improved crops in much the same manner as they were assigned to mechanical inventions.

It was at Glenmont on October 18, 1931, that Thomas Alva Edison died. Henry and Clara Ford attended the funeral, but Henry would not view Edison in the casket. He said he wanted to remember Edison as he had known him. Edison's death ended the close relationship of the Fords with the Edison family. The Fords no longer occupied their winter home next to the Edisons'. The Ford home was instead rented, and Clara had citrus fruits shipped from the Mangoes to Dearborn until the Fort Myers home was sold in August 1945. In 1947, just two years before her death, Mina Edison donated Seminole Lodge, the Edisons' Fort Myers home, to the city of Fort Myers for use as a museum.

References

Accession 1630, Boxes 4–7, Edison Papers. Benson Ford Research Center, HFM & GV.

Israel, Paul. *Edison: A Life of Invention.* New York: John Wiley, 1998.

Pretzer, William S., ed. *Working at Invention: Thomas A. Edison and the Menlo Park Experience.* Dearborn, Mich.: Henry Ford Museum & Greenfield Village, 1989.

Simonds, William Adams. *Edison: His Life, His Work, His Genius.* New York: Bobbs-Merrill, 1934.

Upward, Geoffrey C. *A Home for Our Heritage.* Dearborn, Mich.: Henry Ford Museum Press, Edison Institute, 1950.

Wachhorst, Wyn. *Thomas Alva Edison: An American Myth.* Cambridge, Mass.: MIT Press, 1981.

3
Harvey Firestone

Henry Ford was almost thirty years old on February 10, 1893, when he bought himself a bicycle at the rather expensive price of forty dollars. His bicycle had pneumatic tires. Three years later, when he built his first automobile, the 500-pound Quadricycle, he used four bicycle wheels with 28-by-1.75-inch pneumatic tires. About that time, he met Harvey S. Firestone, a twenty-eight-year-old carriage salesman from Chicago who raced his expensive hard-rubber-tired demonstration carriage on Detroit's boulevards. Firestone was a member of the Gentlemen's Riding Club of Highland Park and won several sulky races on local tracks with his fast horses. Firestone was then selling carriages for the Columbus Buggy Company, owned by his cousin Clinton D. Firestone.

Harvey Samuel Firestone was born on December 20, 1868, on a farm in Columbiana County, Ohio. His parents were Benjamin Firestone and Catherine Flickinger Firestone. Harvey had an older brother, Elmer (born in 1864), and a younger brother, Robert (born in 1873). Harvey attended Columbiana High School, graduating in 1887, and next enrolled in a two-year course at the Spencerian Business College in Cleveland, later known as Dyke College. While selling buggies in Detroit, he had met Idabelle Smith of Jackson, Michigan, and they were married on November 20, 1895. Their first baby, Harry Firestone, died four days following birth. The Firestones would have five more sons and one daughter: Harvey S. Firestone, Jr. (born in 1898), Russell A. Firestone (1901), Leonard K. Firestone (1907), Raymond C. Firestone (1908), Roger S. Firestone (1912), and Elizabeth Idabelle Firestone (1921).

Firestone had come to Detroit in about 1890 as salesman, book-keeper, and manager for the buggy company operated by his cousin. When Henry Ford was building his third vehicle, a "Motorwagon" weighing 875 pounds, for the Detroit Automobile Company in 1899, he needed wheels and tires larger and heavier than bicycle type. Ford was able to buy the wheels and tires from Firestone's carriage and tire shop on Jefferson Avenue in Detroit.

The carriages that Firestone was trying to sell for his cousin were overpriced at $110, and the Columbus Buggy Company went out of business. By then, however, Firestone realized that the best feature of the carriages was the set of rubber-tired wheels that cost an extra forty dollars. Firestone decided to go into the business of manufacturing and selling those solid rubber tires.

The Firestone Tire & Rubber Company was incorporated in Akron, Ohio, by Harvey Firestone in August 1900. Its business concentrated on the production of solid rubber tires for carriages, heavy wagons, electric trucks, and fire engines. The Firestone "Side-Wire" tire was considered the best in the industry, and the Firestone "Internal Wire" tire was sold in any length up to 500 feet. It could be cut to fit any size wheel. By 1904, the company was the largest maker of solid rubber tires in the world.

In March 1906, when Henry Ford had become the major stockholder of Ford Motor Company and Harvey Firestone had begun to manufacture pneumatic tires for automobiles, Ford placed an order with Firestone for 2,000 tire sets for his Model N; he would later increase the order by 6,000 sets. Firestone said later, "Very little was known about pneumatic tires. It seems to me highly probable that if we had really known anything about pneumatic tires, the order would have been neither given nor taken." Firestone had priced his "straight-side" pneumatics at $55 a set, while the popular "clincher" tires sold by the United States Rubber Company were $77 per set.

Ford soon found, however, that his customers preferred the more commonplace patented clincher tire because replacements were more readily available. At that time, Ford was fighting in court against the Licensed Automobile Manufacturers and their Selden patent to avoid paying a royalty on every car he sold. He advised Firestone likewise to fight the Clincher Tire Association which was preventing Firestone from manufacturing the clincher-type tire. Ford won the Selden patent case in 1911, and Firestone's lawyers found the Clincher Tire Association's patent so weak that the case was never taken to court. Firestone just went ahead and built the clincher-type tires. Thus, Ford's tires became clinchers, and Firestone became Ford's largest supplier of tires for years to come. Ford's orders grew until, with the Model T, they amounted to $880,000 in 1911, $1.2 million in 1912, and $2 million in 1913. "No one who does business with Mr. Ford," Firestone stated, "ever gets a chance to rest."

Ford traveled to Indianapolis in 1911 to attend the first 500-mile race there. He visited his friend Barney Oldfield, who in 1909 had established several records during a 300-mile main event. The 1911 race was won by Ray Harroun in a six-cylinder Marmon averaging 74.59 miles per hour on Firestone tires. Ford sponsored a car equipped with Firestone tires in the Indianapolis 500 race in 1913 and staged a spectacular 150-car cavalcade from Detroit to Indianapolis preceding the

A formal portrait of Henry Ford, Thomas Edison, Harvey Firestone, and Luther Burbank. The birthplaces of Ford, Firestone, and Burbank are now preserved in Greenfield Village. The photograph was taken in 1915 by "Hartsook Photo, S.F.-L.A." (P.O.6432)

race. The car Ford sponsored did not win the main event, but the winner of the 500 did use Firestone tires.

Ford, Firestone, and Thomas Edison met in 1915 at the San Francisco Panama-Pacific Exposition to celebrate "The Electric Dinner," at which an all-electric kitchen was demonstrated in honor of Edison. The three men with their families traveled up to Santa Rosa, where they visited Luther Burbank. It was then that Ford, Firestone, and Edison planned their long series of summer vacation trips throughout the eastern United States.

In 1916, it was Edison's idea for the three of them to visit John Burroughs at his Woodchuck Lodge in New York State. In 1917, World

Harvey Firestone

Harvey S. Firestone
and Henry Ford in
front of the
Firestone farmhouse
in Columbiana,
Ohio, in 1918.
(34.164.18)

War I interfered with their vacation. In 1918, all four of the vacation-
ers, including Burroughs, made a long trip together through the Great
Smoky Mountains. It was back to New York State in 1919, where
Henry had obtained permission to build a power plant beside the
government's Hudson River dam at Green Island. There the four men
chiseled their names on a boulder as a memorial to their visit. In 1920,
Edison, Ford, and Firestone spent a few days at Yama Farms near
Burroughs's home. Burroughs died the next year.

Firestone led the parade of vacation travelers in 1921. Starting at
the Firestone homestead in Columbiana, the caravan of families headed
for Maryland, where they joined President Warren G. Harding.
Firestone had brought six of his prize riding horses from his farm. This
was not Henry and Clara's choice of recreation, but Harding delighted
in riding. Firestone's best horse was given to Harding, and his second
best was given to Mrs. Harding, who also liked to ride. Following
Harding's death, Mrs. Harding gave the two horses back to Firestone.
Eventually, the campers would decide that excursions such as these were
subject to far too much notoriety — "they became sort of a traveling
circus," in Firestone's words.

An entourage of this type carried the "Vagabonds" — Edison, Ford, Firestone, and Burroughs — on their annual outings. The lead cars carried the lead characters with their chauffeurs. The supply trucks, carrying the cooks, tent erectors, and wood choppers, together with their necessary paraphernalia, followed behind at a respectful distance. This caravan of about eight vehicles including sedans indicates that it is from 1921, when women decided to join the party. The men ordinarily favored open cars in order to be closer to nature. (B.34342)

Auto and tire business had been booming until early 1920, when both Ford and Firestone began to have trouble. Ford was heavily in debt because he had borrowed money to buy out his stockholders, and Wall Street bankers were ready to take over Ford Motor Company. Ford cut costs, pushed his cars and car parts onto his dealers, and sold off office furniture to collect enough cash to pay off his creditors. Firestone found he was making far more tires than he could sell. Because Henry and Edsel Ford were house guests of Firestone at his estate, a rumor spread that negotiations were in progress for the sale of the Firestone Rubber Company to Ford. The only business discussed, however, concerned the price of tires. Firestone drastically cut prices and designed a new tread for his tires. The famous "Non-Skid" design was dropped. "It was a good tread," Firestone stated, "but you know there are times when the tire business seems to have fashion. That tread is out of fashion." The new tread of "cross-and-square" design, developed for the 1921 Indianapolis race, solved Firestone's business problems.

A letter from Firestone to Ford in February 1923 called Ford's attention to the British Rubber Restriction Act, which applied to crude rubber produced in Ceylon and Malaya. The act had caused crude rubber prices to jump from fifteen to thirty-seven cents per pound. Firestone was taking the lead in fighting the restrictions which applied to the bulk of rubber being used in the United States. In a letter to Ford on March 30, 1925, Firestone stated: "Since Lord Churchill has been elected Chancellor of the Exchequer of England, they have been administering the Restriction Act very drastically and we are facing a rubber shortage and very high prices unless we can check it some way." *Harvey Firestone*

Because of the rubber price situation, both Firestone and Ford began to explore possibilities of producing rubber themselves.

Almost immediately, Ford thought of the possibility of growing rubber trees in Florida. He held a mortgage on a cattle ranch of 8,000 acres at LaBelle, Florida, in 1923. He foreclosed on that mortgage and by the summer of 1924 had planted 60 *Fiscus elastiga,* 458 *Cryptostega grandiflora,* and 100 *Cryptostegia* rubber plants to determine if they would flourish in the southern Florida climate. The climate proved to be too cool, but property values zoomed in that region with the rumor that Ford was developing a mammoth rubber plantation.

During the summer of 1923, the Fords, the Firestones, and the Edisons, together with the Edsel Fords, traveled to the Upper Peninsula of Michigan, where they took a tour of Ford lumbering operations. They saw the mammoth lumber mill at Iron Mountain, camped in the relatively luxurious lumberjack cabins at Sidnaw, visited the picturesque mill sites at L'Anse, and viewed Henry's latest acquisition, the entire lumber mill town of Pequaming.

In the summer of 1924, Clara Ford was unable to travel by motor. But while the Fords were entertaining the three couples at Wayside Inn, the men — Henry Ford, Harvey Firestone, and Thomas Edison — drove up to the home of President Calvin Coolidge in Plymouth, Vermont. On that occasion, Ford was given an old wooden sap bucket to be added to his growing collection of antiques.

Perhaps because of Edsel Ford's influence, the Model T burst forth in high style for 1924. The touring car and the roadster both sported a slanted windshield, and the touring car had a one-man top. Firestone, as early as 1922, was developing "balloon" tires, but Ford was not quick to adopt them. Balloon tires contained twice the volume of air at half the pressure of earlier tires. They had half the number of plies and a thinner tread. It was hard to believe that they could be as durable as their predecessors. But after the winning car at Indianapolis in 1925 clocked 101.13 miles per hour using Firestone's balloon tires, the Model T was equipped with balloons.

Firestone wrote the following letter to Ford on July 10, 1925:

Mr. Henry Ford
Dearborn, Michigan

Dear Mr. Ford:

I called on Mr. Edison this week and found him looking well and feeling well. I asked him if he wanted to go camping this year and he replied that he didn't believe he could this year. He put his hand to his stomach and said he was having a little trouble. He also said that he was running the sales end of his business and was very busy. He then said he would like to get out in the western mountains. His eyes brightened up with a twinkle that seemed to recall some very pleasant days, but said that he didn't think we could go this year. I told him that we must not wait too long as he was getting older and would not enjoy it as much later.

However, I do not feel we could arrange it this year for in reading of your activities in so many different things I can imagine that you would not want to take the time to make this trip, and for myself, I have a full summer if I do my duty in the rubber business, and should not take the time to make as long a trip as the western trip.

I hope, however, I will have the pleasure of seeing you some time in the summer.

With personal regards, I remain

Very very truly,
Harvey S. Firestone

In the summer of 1925, Firestone was indeed busy arranging for rubber tree plantations in Liberia, West Africa. In a long letter to Ford, Firestone suggested that Ford investigate the availability of rubber-producing land in Mexico. Acreage totaling nearly 2 million, some of it already planted to suitable rubber trees, was available in the state of Chiapas and accessible by water to New Orleans in eighty-five hours or over land to the United States by road a distance of 245 miles—the road yet to be built. These properties also produced considerable coffee, cocoa, and hardwood timber. Ford, however, turned down Firestone's suggestion because of the poor labor situation and the unstable government in Mexico.

Instead of Mexico, Ford in 1926 chose to invest in the state of Para, Brazil, where he obtained a "free" land concession of 2.5 million acres along a tributary of the Amazon River. However, to close the deal, he had to pay $125,000 in bribes to Brazilian officials. Ford's Brazilian venture was a sociological success but a commercial failure. After an estimated 3,651,500 rubber trees were planted beginning in 1928, the oldest of them were just beginning to produce well by 1942. By that time, synthetic rubber had been developed. Ford's rubber plantations were sold in 1945 at an estimated loss of $20 million.

Both Firestone and Ford had joined Thomas Edison in 1927 to form the Edison Botanic Research Corporation, which started testing 2,300 plants for rubber, finding Mexican guayule and American goldenrod probably best for producing domestic rubber.

After Ford had introduced the speedy Ford V-8 vehicles in 1932, his cars again began winning races on Firestone's tires. In fact, until the 1960s, Firestone tires were considered by most contestants the very best of racing tires. The Firestone company since the early 1920s had formally arranged to use the Indianapolis Speedway as a company testing ground. Firestone's "Gum-Dipped-Cord" tires were developed to

William Clay Ford
and Martha
Firestone Ford on
vacation in Bermuda
during the summer
of 1947. (833.84505)

decrease internal friction in tires and were tested at Indianapolis in 1933. Firestone tires dominated the lists of winners not only at Indianapolis from 1920 but also at Pikes Peak and later at Darlington and Daytona. There was little competition in racing before 1960 by other tire makers.

Harvey S. Firestone, Sr., had become chairman of the board of Firestone Tire & Rubber Company in 1932. Harvey S. Firestone, Jr., who had been vice president, then became president of the company. On February 7, 1938, Harvey Sr. died at age seventy; his wife, Idabelle, lived until 1954.

Ford died on April 7, 1947, but the Ford and Firestone families became even closer only two months later, when, on June 21, 1947, William Clay Ford and Martha Parke Firestone were married in Akron, Ohio. William was the son of Edsel Ford, and Martha was the daughter of Harvey Firestone, Jr. William was then twenty-two and Martha twenty-one years of age. Wedding festivities took place at Harbel

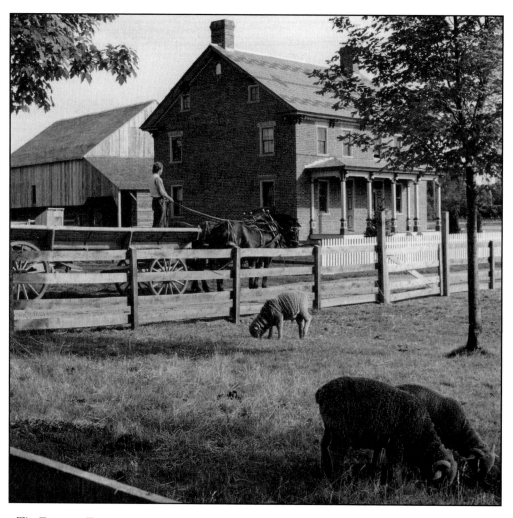

The Firestone Farm buildings as they appear today at Greenfield Village. Stocked with horses, cattle, sheep, pigs, and chickens, the farm operates year-round as it might have in 1875. (B.06459)

Manor, the home of the Firestones. Four hundred fifty guests crowded into St. Paul's Episcopal Church for the ceremony, with another 800 onlookers outside. Ford family members attending included Henry Ford II and Benson Ford, with their wives, and Clara Ford.

In 1963, the small but fast Ford-sponsored British Lotus vehicles were taking over at Indianapolis. The fifteen-inch wheel was in vogue, and Firestone intended to furnish the tire to fit that wheel only to Fords. The furor that developed resulted in Firestone releasing its tires to everyone, but the reputations of both Firestone and Ford were nonetheless damaged within racing circles. In that particular emergency, Goodyear supplied some fifteen-inch stock-car rubber which turned out to be acceptable. From that date, Goodyear was in the racing tire business, and it still is.

While the Firestone Tire & Rubber Company was flourishing in the United States, Shojiro Ishibashi was establishing a tire-manufacturing business in Japan. *Ishibashi* is Japanese for "stone bridge," and in 1931, in order to imply that the company was British or American, he named it the Bridgestone Tire Company. In the early 1960s, Bridgestone sought international prominence by adopting progressive manufacturing techniques. The first Bridgestone tires were on the American market in 1967. In 1988, Bridgestone purchased the Firestone Tire & Rubber Company and began integrating operations as Bridgestone/Firestone, Inc. Integration was completed in 1992. Headquarters are now at Nashville, Tennessee, rather than Akron, Ohio, but the Firestone name remains on the company's tires and on approximately 1,500 Firestone retail outlets throughout the United States.

Before the sale of the Firestone Tire & Rubber Company to the Bridgestone interests, Firestone family members, including Leonard K. Firestone, Raymond C. Firestone, and Martha Firestone Ford, were cooperating with Greenfield Village in Dearborn to establish an active, permanent memorial to the exceptionally close relationship between the Henry Ford and Harvey Firestone families. The memorial, now in the Village, consists of the original Firestone Homestead built in 1875, together with the large adjoining barn and other outbuildings. These were moved, brick by brick and board by board, from Columbiana to Dearborn in 1985. The Firestone Homestead buildings now have become central to a fourteen-acre Firestone Farm operating year-round in 1885 fashion in Greenfield Village.

References

Accession 89.492.1849, Firestone Family Records. Benson Ford Research Center, HFM & GV.

Accession 94.64, Firestone Family Records. Benson Ford Research Center, HFM & GV.

Accession 285, Box 372 (1924), Folder "Firestone." Benson Ford Research Center, HFM & GV.

Bridgestone Tire Company, www.bridgestone-firestone.com/public.htm.

Bryan, Ford R. *Beyond the Model T.* Detroit: Wayne State University Press, 1990.

Cousins, Peter H. "Tall Timber, Wheat, and Wrinkley Sheep: Three Generations of Ohio Farmers." *Herald,* Vol. 14, November 2, 1985. Henry Ford Museum & Greenfield Village.

Firestone, Harvey S., with Samuel Crowther. *Men and Rubber: The Story of Business.* New York: Doubleday, 1926.

Lief, Alfred. *The Firestone Story.* New York: McGraw-Hill, 1951.

—. *Harvey Firestone: Free Man of Enterprise.* New York: McGraw-Hill, 1951.

4
John Burroughs

John Burroughs, a naturalist and writer, came to Henry Ford's attention in 1912 after Ford had begun taking a serious interest in birds. That interest seems to have stemmed from his foster grandfather Patrick Ahern's nostalgic recollection of the melodious songs of birds in Ireland. Patrick had taught Henry the names of a great many birds, and Henry could cleverly imitate their calls. By early 1911, Ford already had installed hundreds of birdhouses on his Dearborn farm properties, and that year his bird sanctuary was said to have harbored more than ninety species.

Ford had never met Burroughs, but, having read some of his writings in December 1912, he informed Burroughs that he was shipping a Model T automobile to him so that he could "get around more easily to witness nature." Burroughs's son Julian taught him to drive. The very day Julian left, however, Burroughs had his first accident. He wrote:

> In driving the car in the old barn, I get rattled and let it run wild; it bursts through the side of the barn like an explosion. There is a great splintering and rattling of boards and timbers, and the car stops with its forward axle hanging out over a drop of fifteen feet. As the wheels went out, the car dropped on its flywheel, and that saved me. The wheel caught on less than a foot of the steep hill, and I should have landed on the other side of Jordan. . . . The top of the radiator is badly crumpled, otherwise the car is unhurt. I am terribly humiliated and, later, scared of my narrow escape. The thing I had feared for weeks happened. Thus does fear deliver us into the hands of the thing we fear.

About his Model T, after more than his share of mishaps, Burroughs remarked, "How ready it is to take to the ditch, or a tree, or a fence."

A year later, Burroughs was complaining:

> I saw what a fraud the car is — how much it had cheated me out of. On foot and lighthearted, you are right down amid things. How

Published previously in *The Ford Legend,* Vol. VII, No. 2, 1998.

familiar and congenial the ground, the trees, the weeds, the road, the cattle look! The car puts me in false relations to all these things. I am puffed up. I am a traveler. I am in sympathy with nothing but me; but on foot I am part of the country, and I get it into my blood. If it were not for Mrs. Burroughs I should hang up the car.

Burroughs visited Detroit in June 1913. Ford showed him around the automobile plant in Highland Park, and they were photographed together with the Quadricycle. In Detroit, Burroughs spoke to about 2,600 schoolchildren at Central High School. Henry and Clara entertained him for two days at their summer Bungalow on the west bank of the Rouge River in Dearborn. In a letter home, Burroughs stated: "I like Mr. Ford and his wife much. . . . His interest in the birds makes him forget everything else for the moment. He wants to give me more things — among them a closed car for winter use." Burroughs later received a Model T town car.

When in the autumn of 1913 Ford heard that Burroughs wished to own outright the farm on which he lived in order to keep it in the family, he was quick to respond: "Nothing in the world easier — but don't tell anyone about it." In November 1913, Henry and Clara helped Burroughs and his wife, Ursula, acquire the 319-acre farm at Roxbury,

John Burroughs in the Model T touring car that Henry Ford sent him in January 1913. The photograph was taken not far from his home in Roxbury, New York. His signature on the photograph is dated August 27, 1913.

45

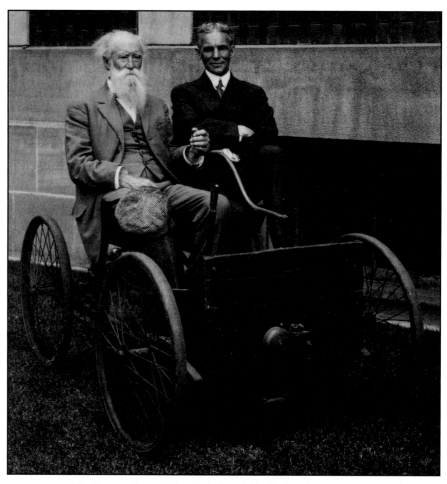

John Burroughs and Henry Ford with Ford's Quadricycle at the new Highland Park plant of Ford Motor Company in June 1913. Burroughs doesn't appear especially impressed. (188.74449)

New York. Burroughs arranged for his nephew to stay there and continue to operate it as a dairy farm, John and Ursula reserving Woodchuck Lodge for their own use.

In June 1916, after Fair Lane was built, Henry Ford and Thomas Edison dedicated an elaborate electrically heated birdbath in what is known as Burroughs Grotto at Fair Lane. Burroughs himself laid the cornerstone of the grotto, which was lined with stone from the Burroughs farm in New York State. On the site was placed a standing bronze statue of Burroughs titled *The Summit of the Years,* sculpted by C. S. Pietro of New York City. In the grotto, a small lamp was placed to glow for the remainder of Burroughs's life.

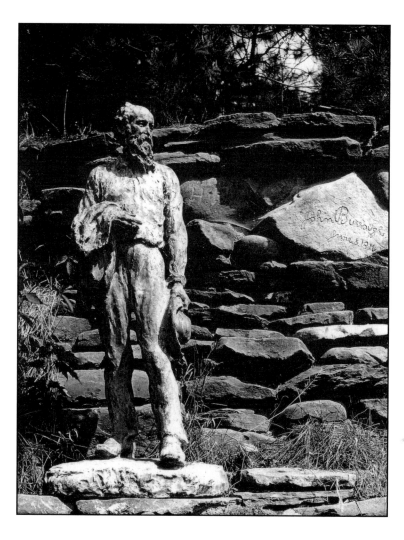

John Burroughs

Burroughs Grotto on the grounds of Fair Lane. The statue of Burroughs is 39 inches tall. The large stone at the right bears Burroughs's signature and the date June 8, 1916. Next to Burroughs's shoulder is a smaller stone with the initials "H.F." visible.

A vacation in late summer of 1916 was planned to include Ford, Edison, Firestone, and Burroughs for a trip through the Adirondacks, but Ford, because of Edsel's wedding that fall, did not go. However, in February and March 1917, Henry and Clara took Burroughs with them to Havana, Cuba, on their yacht *Sialia*. In passing the Georgia coast below Charleston, Burroughs is said to have remarked that there was "very good birding" in that region (by 1925, the Fords were buying property at Ways, Georgia). Before the Cuba trip, Burroughs's wife, Ursula, had been seriously ill for a long time, but doctors recommended that he take the trip nevertheless. Ursula died before her husband returned home. They had been married for sixty-two years.

In late August 1918, Ford, Edison, Burroughs, and Firestone toured Pennsylvania, West Virginia, Tennessee, Virginia, and Maryland

John Burroughs on the front steps of Woodchuck Lodge, carrying two of the grizzled thickset marmots after which the lodge was named.

This white plaster-of-Paris cast of John Burroughs's hands was among the objects found on his desk at the time of his death in 1921. Clara Barrus sent it to Henry Ford along with some of Burroughs's other belongings. (B.110628)

together. In December of that year, Ford sent Burroughs a Rocky Mountain donkey from Denver. Burroughs dubbed it his "Rocky Mountain Canary":

> I have been on the back of that confounded donkey but once. She used me badly. I could not get her three hundred yards from home, and when she made up her mind she wanted to go back, she went, and went down the drive on a run, with me clinging desperately to her back, expecting every minute to be hurled to the ground. But for a wonder I kept my seat until she reached the stable. I am no horseman and I guess the little big-eared beast knew it. When I came in the house, the doctor said I was very pale, and I felt pale. This donkey undoubtedly has a big streak of cussedness in her. I shall try her again, and if she does no better I shall feel like blowing her brains out. The Fords have not turned up yet. The cold has probably knocked them out. If Mr. Ford comes, I shall insist upon his mounting her.

Burroughs wrote in his journal, "Give me any horse-kind but a female donkey," and soon dispossessed the Rocky Mountain Canary.

In 1919, the camping group toured New England, and in November 1920, they visited Burroughs's home, Slabsides, and were entertained at Yama Farms Inn at Napanoch, New York. In December 1920, on his way to California, Burroughs stopped at Dearborn, where Ford had him push the button that started the machinery to grind the first wheat in the new flour mill operated in Dearborn by Ford Farms.

John Burroughs died on March 29, 1921. In his will, dated April 10, 1917, he states, "To my friend Henry Ford to whom I owe the possession of the Old Homestead Farm, I give and bequeath my rustic writing table at Woodchuck Lodge." On January 27, 1922, Henry and Clara Ford purchased the John Burroughs property at Roxbury from son Julian Burroughs and his wife, Emily, and from Dr. Clara Barrus, who had been Burroughs's nurse and companion during his later years and had been granted lifetime use of Woodchuck Lodge. The Fords paid $13,950 for the farm in order to preserve the tract intact for posterity.

On July 26, 1947, after Henry Ford had died, Clara Ford, to whom the Burroughs farm now belonged, conveyed a portion of the farm by warranty deed to the John Burroughs Memorial Association, a New York corporation. The balance of the farm was sold back to Julian and Emily Burroughs for $6,500. Certain rights were reserved, however, one of them being that Clara Ford's "heirs, executors, administrators and assigns have the right to consume the water from the spring on the premises located in the northwesterly direction from the grave of John Burroughs." So it appears that the heirs of Clara Ford, when in the proximity of Roxbury, New York, still may have permission to drink from the Roxbury springs if they should so desire.

References

Accession 1, Box 111, Fair Lane Papers. Benson Ford Research Center, HFM & GV.

Accession 23, Box 1, Henry Ford Office. Benson Ford Research Center, HFM & GV.

Accession 844, Box 1, L. J. Thompson Papers. Benson Ford Research Center, HFM & GV.

Barras, Clara. *The Life and Letters of John Burroughs*, Vol. 2. Boston: Houghton-Mifflin, 1925.

5
Martha Berry

Known as the "Sunday Lady of Possum Trot," Martha McChesney Berry (1866–1942) provided an education for hundreds of mountain boys and girls from the area surrounding Rome, Georgia. One of six daughters of wealthy plantation owner Captain Thomas Berry, Martha could have lived a life of ease and grandeur but instead renounced an aristocratic social life to undertake the teaching of illiterate children from the rolling foothills of North Georgia.

Berry herself had attended finishing school in Baltimore, but one Sunday after she'd returned to Georgia and was playing the piano in the one-room log school (Possum Trot), three small boys stopped to listen. She was so shocked by their poverty and their extreme ignorance that she decided then and there to start a Sunday Bible school, offering a warm meal as an inducement. This was the beginning of a forty-five-year effort to educate rural youth. Berry's initial objective was to offer poor farm boys a chance to attend school regardless of their means if they were willing to work for their tuition and board. Farm boys could not afford to go to high school; such schools in the state of Georgia before 1900 were few and far between.

Berry's father died in 1901, leaving the plantation house and 500 acres of land as her share, and the Berry School was formally opened in 1902. Everyone, including instructors, helped to work the farmland and take care of the livestock. The crops were to provide the cash income necessary for operating the school. Berry related this incident as representative of that period:

> One February night I heard a knock at the door. I went myself, and there stood a very small and muddy boy with a pig tied to a rope. "Please, ma'am, I'm Willie Jackson and this is my pig. We'uns has come to school. I done carried the pig here for my tuition. He's powerful lean now but he'll pick up tol'able quick."

The six-day weekly school schedule would not be easy. The sixteen-hour day, which started at five a.m. and ended at about nine p.m., included an hour for work chores in the morning, four hours of morning classes, an hour for midday chapel, four hours of afternoon classes,

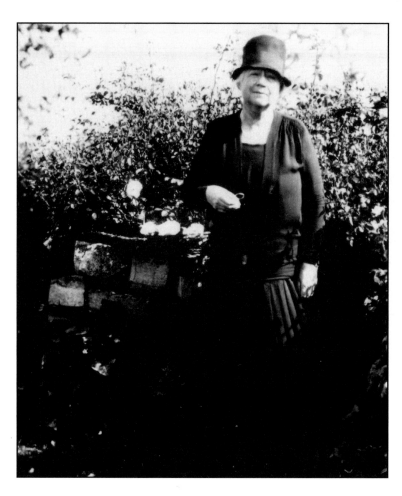

Martha Berry on the
Berry Schools campus
about 1925. (0.7109)

and an evening study hour. A thirty-minute breakfast period, a forty-five-minute lunch, and more leisurely dinner accounted for most of the remaining time.

The school shield contains four symbols: the Bible for prayer, the lamp for learning, the plow for labor, and the cabin for simplicity. It was around those symbols that Berry shaped the character of her school. But she could not do all she wanted to do without help. Thus, her lifelong occupation became mainly that of raising funds for the school. For success, her appeals needed to reach high places. Andrew Carnegie is said to have pledged $50,000 in 1909, provided that Berry could raise a matching amount within one month — which she did. President Theodore Roosevelt visited the school in 1911 and made the statement: "This is the greatest practical work for American citizenship that has been done within this decade." Adolph S. Ochs, publisher of the *New York Times*, also helped her in fund-raising efforts.

The Fords, Henry and Clara, no doubt had heard of Berry Schools, but they did not meet Berry until 1921 at the home of Thomas and Mina Edison in West Orange, New Jersey. On that occasion, Berry invited the Fords to visit her school. By that time, Berry Schools accommodated both boys and girls, in separate facilities. Clara Ford was particularly interested in the girls' accommodations. On their first visit, in 1922, the Fords were served their noon meal in the rather primitive dining room by the girls. Clara noticed the clean but austere kitchen and remarked that they deserved a better stove. That suggestion grew into plans for a whole new dining hall. That was the beginning. For the next twenty years, the Fords were major benefactors of the Berry Schools. They were quiet about their giving. They were aware that general knowledge of the generosity of the Fords would make it more difficult for Berry to raise money from other sources.

In their private railroad car, the *Fair Lane,* Henry and Clara usually went south during January and February. On the way back either from their home, the Mangoes, next to the Edisons in Fort Myers, Florida, or from their Richmond Hill winter residence at Ways, Georgia, the Fords often would stop for a day or two at Mount Berry, the location of Berry Schools. Usually, the Fords visited Berry and her school during the month of March. In all, at least a dozen such visits were made by the

Clara Hall, the million-dollar girls' dormitory built by the Fords for Berry Schools at Rome, Georgia. This was the first of several buildings that form the Ford Quadrangle on the 2,000-acre Berry campus. (P.O.9702)

Fords prior to Henry's death in 1947. To provide added privacy, Henry arranged for a railroad spur to be constructed from Rome to the Berry College campus so that the *Fair Lane* could be parked conveniently.

The first well-publicized visit by the Fords to Berry College was in 1923, when Henry and Clara, together with Mr. and Mrs. E. G. Kingsford and Ford's private secretary, Frank Campsall, stopped there in connection with Henry's campaign to harness Muscle Shoals for the good of Southern states. Henry spoke at length to the students about the benefits of waterpower to that region of the country. Clara stated:

> I have not much to say. I am very much pleased to be here. I have known Miss Berry and her splendid work for some time. I am delighted to see you all — you have such splendid faces. You should get a great deal of good out of this institution. I am interested in all of you and everything you are doing. I hope to get around and see more of the school. I am glad to be here.

Kingsford spoke to them about Ford's lumbering in the Upper Peninsula of Michigan and urged the boys to try to get the people to stop using trees for firewood.

In 1926, the Fords visited Berry on March 11, with little fanfare. Again, in mid-February 1928 and March 1929, the Fords were at Mount Berry for a day or so. In the meantime, while Martha Berry had been soliciting funds for operation of the schools, she also had been requesting help from Henry Ford. An example of the correspondence follows:

> October 28, 1928
>
> Mr. Henry Ford
> Dearborn, Mich.
>
> Dear Mr. Ford:
>
> I have spent the entire summer at Berry. I have been hoping to be able to go to Battle Creek and stop over in Detroit and have the pleasure of seeing you and Mrs. Ford.
>
> It is very difficult to raise money for running expenses. Our endowment is small, and since the beginning of this term we have not had money to pay the teachers' salaries. You were kind enough once to say that, in lieu of endowment, you would help us from time to time. I greatly appreciate this.
>
> This is a time of real need. We do not have the money to pay the past month's running expenses. I would be most grateful if you can help us now.
>
> > Faithfully yours,
> > Martha Berry

Frequent appeals such as this would result in checks for at least $25,000 each, signed by Ernest Liebold, Ford's financial secretary. In

Martha Berry, center, entertains Henry and Clara Ford at a banquet in the dining hall of Berry College about 1930. College students served the meal. (P.O.9733)

most cases, the Berry Schools comptroller communicated with Liebold on Berry's behalf concerning school affairs. In some emergencies, however, Berry herself contacted Liebold.

Over the years, besides helping with "running expenses," the Fords donated funds for several buildings on the campus of Berry Schools. Following funds for the impressive dining hall, the next major gift was for a girls' dormitory named Clara Hall to house two hundred girls. Soon a large classroom building was planned, as were a gymnasium and a recreation hall. A Henry Ford Chapel was added. The final building was another dormitory, named Mary Hall in memory of Henry's mother. A water system costing approximately $200,000 was another expense covered by Ford. In all, Clara is estimated to have given well over $1 million, Henry at least $3 million.

Ford was particularly impressed by the Berry Schools. The principles of "Earn while you learn" and "Learn by doing" were dear to his heart. His Henry Ford Trade School operated on those very same principles. He asked the Berry Schools to sell their twenty teams of mules,

Henry, with hat in hand, and Clara, in her cap and gown, are standing with college dignitaries on the Berry College campus. This was Henry Ford's very last public appearance. On this occasion, Clara received an honorary degree of Doctor of Humanities from Berry College, and Henry had been invited to help plant a magnolia tree in Martha Berry's Memorial Garden. The tree is shown at right. (0.1016)

offering to replace them with twenty Fordson tractors. He provided a brick factory, donated several new trucks, and equipped an automobile repair shop. Food, charcoal, fertilizer, and other supplies were ordered by Ford to be shipped to Mount Berry. Ford stated: "The Berry Schools stand as a demonstration of what one person with a determination can do if he keeps working." On occasion, Ford sent his old-time orchestra and dancing instructors, Mr. and Mrs. Benjamin Lovett, to Berry College to demonstrate and teach dancing to the students.

In early March 1930, the Fords were feted in grand style during a two-day stay. To greet them, a candlelit roadway led from the *Fair Lane*

Clara Ford is honored at a birthday luncheon at Berry College, probably in 1948. She is joined by college officials and served by college students. Clara sits in the ornate high-backed chair previously occupied by Martha Berry at such events. (0.9710)

station to the girls' school. Again, Henry had brought his dance master and orchestra for an all-school old-fashioned dance in the girls' gymnasium to highlight the celebration. The results of Ford gifts for buildings were now obvious. Money had been pouring in since 1922 — checks by the dozen drawn on National Shawnut Bank of Boston in amounts of $25,000 to $250,000 had been sent to Berry Schools. By this time, five new Ford buildings were much in evidence, and Berry Schools that year became Berry College, accredited as a four-year educational institution.

On at least one occasion during the 1930s, Martha Berry visited the Fords at their winter home at Richmond Hill, Georgia. She was active until the midsummer of 1940. Martha Berry died on February 27, 1942, at age seventy-five, in a Rome, Georgia, hospital. She is buried on the campus of Berry College in a plot near the school's chapel.

The last visit Henry and Clara Ford made together to Berry College was in late March 1947, when Clara received an honorary degree of Doctor of Humanities. In a speech given by John A. Sibey upon presentation of the degree, he stated that Martha Berry had three requirements for students entering her school:

1. To love God, and through knowledge, to get new insights into their lives.

2. Know the dignity of labor and that independence comes only to those who work and are not ashamed of work and the moral values that grow from the sense of work well done.

3. Know things of the mind, to lift their intellectual horizon, to join hands with the wisdom of the past and hope for the future.

Martha Berry On that same occasion, Henry Ford helped plant a magnolia tree in the Martha Berry Memorial Garden on the Berry College campus. That was Ford's last public appearance. He died on April 7 in Dearborn. At least once following Henry's death, Clara again visited Berry College.

Berry College today is recognized as one of the outstanding small comprehensive colleges in the South, an independent coeducational institution with fully accredited arts, sciences, and professional programs. Enrollment is now approximately 1,700 students, forming an interdenominational Christian congregation under the guidance of a full-time chaplain. Degrees are offered in humanities, social sciences, education, and business. Graduate degrees were offered beginning in 1972. With its 28,000 acres of land — fields, forests, lakes, and mountains — Berry College has the largest college campus in the world. Berry still offers work experience as part of every student's development. Nearly 90 percent of students are employed on campus in 120 job classifications during the academic year. By tradition, Berry alumni return each May for a week of service or work on the campus. The Ford buildings — Clara Hall, Mary Hall, Ford Hall, Ford Classroom, Ford Auditorium, and Ford Gymnasium — are still in everyday use.

References

Accession 572, Box 6. Benson Ford Research Center, HFM & GV.

Berry College. www.berry.edu/main.html.

Kane, Harnett T., with Inez Henry. *Miracle in the Mountains.* Garden City, N.Y.: Doubleday, 1956.

Roberts, David G. *The Berry School Plant.* Ypsilanti, Mich.: Eastern Michigan University, 1986.

6
George Washington Carver

Few people are surprised to find that Henry Ford came to be friends with fellow inventor Thomas Edison and fellow industrialist Harvey Firestone. Less well known are his friendships with naturalists John Burroughs and Luther Burbank and, in his later years, botanist George Washington Carver. Beginning in 1937 and continuing until Carver's death in 1943, the two men maintained a correspondence on a variety of subjects. Their letters, now in the Benson Ford Research Center, offer a fascinating glimpse of two Americans of widely differing backgrounds, each of whom made exceptional contributions to the lives of his fellow men.

Ford had a lifelong interest in agriculture, and as soon as he started to realize a significant profit from the manufacture of automobiles, around 1909, he purchased land and began to operate farms in the Dearborn area. His correspondence for the following year includes letters to the U.S. Department of Agriculture and various state departments, as well as to major universities, asking to be put on mailing lists for their publications. Always the inventor, Ford engaged in a variety of experiments, including efforts to produce dry milk powder from whole milk.

It is likely that Ford first came to know about Carver through their mutual connection with the Normal and Industrial Institute in Tuskegee, Alabama, a black educational institution directed by Booker T. Washington. In 1910, Ford contributed to a scholarship fund at the institute, where Carver was a member of the faculty.

Born a slave, kidnapped by "night riders," and traded for a horse, Carver had survived against impossible odds. His interest in agriculture went back to his childhood, when hunger drove him to sustain himself by eating wild fruits and vegetables. Curiosity, determination, and brilliance led him to pursue an education at Simpson College, Iowa, and Iowa State University while supporting himself by working at menial jobs. His bachelor's thesis at Iowa State, from which he graduated in

Reprinted with permission from the *Herald*, Vol. 12, No. 2, 1983.

1896, was entitled "Plants as Modified by Man." He was the first black person to graduate from that institution.

As head of the Tuskegee Research and Experiment Station at the Tuskegee Institute, Carver revolutionized Southern agriculture while earning a worldwide reputation. In 1906, when the boll weevil struck the cotton crop, Carver recommended peanuts as a replacement crop. The resulting glut of peanuts forced him quickly to find more uses for the lowly "goober." He soon demonstrated that foods, beverages, medicines, cosmetics, paints, plastic substances, and many other commercial items — some 300 in all — could be produced from this hardy legume, which previously had been used primarily as animal feed. He also gave a boost to the sweet potato farmer by demonstrating that more than 100 different products could be made from this common tuber. Carver was particularly interested in utilizing weeds and agricultural wastes to benefit all of humankind.

Meanwhile, Ford, having gone on to increasing success as an industrialist, became fearful that the automobile, which he had helped spread far and wide, had destroyed many of the traditional values to which he was committed. He therefore started on the course that in 1929 led to the establishment of the Edison Institute, including Henry Ford Museum and Greenfield Village. Within the village grounds, he built a chemical laboratory and a greenhouse with the objective of finding "industrial uses for farm products." Robert Boyer was put in charge of what was called the chemical plant. In his account of the plant's first year of operation in 1931, Boyer mentioned the extraction of oils from orange peels and furfural — a liquid aldehyde — from garbage, as well as experiments with wheat, soybeans, and carrots.

At about the same time, Ford was raising marijuana for possible use in the production of plastics and was sending out crews to harvest dandelion seeds with hand-operated vacuum cleaners — much to the delight of local residents. In a building near the Engineering Laboratory in Dearborn, Dr. Edsel Ruddiman, Ford's boyhood schoolmate, was experimenting with wheat, soybeans, carrots, and tomatoes in an effort to "make milk without a cow."

In early 1932, Ford issued orders to concentrate on the soybean. His tractors began to plant thousands of acres. In a twenty-five-acre field on Greenfield Village property, some 300 experimental varieties of soybeans were grown. That year, the village chemical plant extracted six tons per day of soybean oil, using it to produce soybean bread, milk, butter, ice cream, and later an experimental plastic car body.

Ford hosted the First Dearborn Conference of the National Farm Chemurgic Council in May 1935. This was the charter meeting of some 300 agricultural chemists from all over the United States who, gathered in Ford's replica of Independence Hall, signed a "Declaration of

Dependence upon the Soil." In 1937, the group met again in Dearborn, and Carver, then director of research at Tuskegee Institute, was invited to speak. Carver and an extremely competent research assistant, Austin W. Curtis, Jr., were obtaining impressive results in demonstrating the commercial and nutritive uses of weeds and crop by-products at the Tuskegee Institute. Ford visited Carver in the latter's suite at the Dearborn Inn. It appears that this was the first time the two had met in person. Ford then entertained Carver at Greenfield Village, where the Alabama agriculturist addressed students of the Edison Institute. In a letter from Tuskegee following the visit, Carver wrote: "Two of the greatest things that have ever come into my life have come this year. The first was the meeting of you, and to see the great educational project that you are carrying on in a way that I have never seen demonstrated before."

In March 1938, Ford made his first visit to Tuskegee. He wanted to talk to Carver about the problems that had arisen on his plantation, Richmond Hill in Ways, Georgia, but the men also discussed the needs of the Tuskegee Institute. Following up on the meeting, Carver wrote:

> Mr. Ford, you are right, as my observation and many years of experience have taught me that a soil cannot be worn out. It can soon be rendered non-productive, but here in the South you get results right away by just putting into these soils the things they need. If we save what we call "trash," make compost piles, and return this which we have taken from the soil, soon a non-productive soil would be a curiosity.
>
> I am thinking how these little compost piles might be of distinct value to your farms at Ways, Georgia.

In April of the following year, Ford's secretary, Frank Campsall, sent Carver "a few recent snapshots of the Colored Community School which was under construction near Ways, Georgia." He explained:

> It is planned that this will be a trade school, since it will not only give instruction in the usual grades but will have in conjunction a woodworking and machine shop — also a small sawmill — where the students will have an opportunity to learn a practical trade.
>
> Mr. Ford has expressed a desire to let this school be known as the George Washington Carver School, provided you have no objection to his doing so.

Later in 1939, Carver and Curtis visited the Fords at the Richmond Hill plantation in Ways, and on March 15, 1940, they returned for the dedication of the George Washington Carver School. Immediately following the dedication, Carver wrote to Mrs. Ford:

> Mr. Ford pointed out so many marvelously interesting possibilities in the development of Ways, I have already begun working on some of

the things. I want to help Mr. Ford prove the startling statement that he makes. "That we can live directly from products from the soil."

Enclosed you will find a little something worked out along that line which will give a pleasing variety to the diet. I believe both you and Mr. Ford will like this gravy. Modify it in any way you wish by leaving the meats out, it is yet good. I made this same gravy substituting the soy beans. I ground them up very fine and made a very rich milk, and to one pint of this milk I used a tablespoon of soy bean oil. This was cooked down until it creamed, became thick like the richest creamed chicken gravy.

I hope you and Mr. Ford will try these gravies. They are so rich in protein and other food nutrients and the meat can be greatly reduced, and with some other of Mr. Ford's fine soy bean products, can be left off altogether.

I saw some fine peanut and sweet potato land in driving around over the place.

Mrs. Ford, I am yet feasting over the way you had the flowers arranged, just great bowls, vases and streamers of natural beauty with the acme of artistic touch, emphasizing as only that could, how beautiful simple things may be when properly arranged.

Please watch the digestive tract of Mr. Ford after he has eaten the gelatinized pigs feet for a few days. Notice how his face will fill up. To clear the skin, remove wrinkles, etc., try massaging with pure refined peanut oil.

Carver and Ford were in complete agreement that plants were the solution to human problems. Students from Tuskegee were welcomed in Ford factories in the North, and around 1940, Curtis spent a summer in Dearborn working with Robert Boyer in the soybean laboratory. During these years, reports of both organic and metallurgical research being done in Dearborn by Ford Motor Company were forwarded to Carver.

The Fords traveled to Tuskegee in early March 1941 to dedicate the George Washington Carver Museum there, inscribing their names in the cement and donating soybeans and a variety of soybean plastic car parts to be placed in the cornerstone. During that visit, Ford, without Carver's knowledge, ordered an elevator installed to assist the latter to get to his second-floor apartment. Soon after the visit, Carver wrote:

How I wish you and Mrs. Ford could see the cement block. Your names are fascinatingly clear and beautiful.

After standing by the windows and watching the last car vanish from my sight, I was seized with an uncontrollable desire to do something. I went out and cut a piece of Oleander stem about a foot long and about the size of an ordinary lead pencil. I was amazed to see the little threads clinging to the knife. Under separate cover I am sending you the results although they are very, very crude.

Note the strength and fineness of the fiber. Also note the wicker possibilities of the defibrated stems, and also for paper which was

The dedication of the George Washington Carver School at Ways Station, Georgia, on March 13, 1940. From the left are Austin Curtis, Carver's assistant; presumably Dr. Patterson, president of Tuskegee Institute; Clara Ford; Henry Ford; and Carver. (P.O.4967)

pulped wholly by mechanical processes and pressed in an old wooden cheese press used in an early day for cheese making. The second fiber is from the white Mulberry. I saw both of these plants growing at Ways. I am casting about to find sources of raw material here within our borders. Sometime we must look Ways over together.

Another letter, written two days later, included the following paragraph:

I am not sure, Mr. Ford, whether I called to your attention a thing which I think will help you very much, and especially when you overindulge in sweets, fats, and things of that kind that are acid forming. I like the hydrotherapy treatment. It is an old, old custom and I find that it works wonders for me and about once every three months I keep it up for at least nine days before I stop. It adds extra fluid to the body and keeps it from drying up as it were so rapidly. Method: In the morning about fifteen minutes before breakfast take a cup of water just as hot as it is possible for you to drink, stir into it a lump of common baking soda about the size of a medium soy bean or English pea. Continue this for at least nine days which will work off any slight acidity that may form. It is most invigorating. If a person is inclined to run down in strength it is a mild invigorator, and as I stated before, it is most excellent and to be sure it is absolutely harmless.

Ford's replies were often simple letters of appreciation such as the following, written April 25, 1941:

> I wish you to know how much I enjoy your letters, and trust you will continue writing me from time to time.
> Your welcome suggestions and the scientific problems you have discussed are interesting and worthwhile discoveries, and I have taken much pleasure in looking over the various samples you forwarded.
> It is gratifying to learn that your strength is improving daily. Extending to you the best wishes of Mrs. Ford and myself —
>
> Sincerely and respectfully,
> Henry Ford

Early in the 1940s, Ford decided to have a replica of Carver's birthplace constructed in Greenfield Village. In March 1942, the Fords visited Carver once again in Tuskegee and planned a trip to Dearborn for the latter. During the following months, Curtis and Campsall exchanged letters on the subject, and Ford suggested that Carver wait until August when "flies and mosquitoes are not numerous here." At the same time, mention was made of the progress on the Carver Log Cabin and of Ford's desire to have Carver dedicate a laboratory while he was in Dearborn.

The Carver laboratory was to be installed in the abandoned Dearborn Water Works building, which required considerable renovation. When Carver decided to come in July instead of August, conversion was stepped up considerably. With help from Curtis, plans were drawn up in a day. Although wartime conditions posed some difficulties, the Ford Rouge Plant priority office cut red tape, and by the next day 300 workmen swarmed around the building. Within a week, the waterworks had been transformed into a laboratory, although the varnish was still wet on the day of occupancy.

In a letter to Ford in July 1941, Carver had referred to the *sida spinosa*, a plant of the milkweed family, as a potential source of rubber, noting, "I am very certain it contains rubber as nearly all milkweeds do." When Carver arrived in Dearborn on July 19, 1942, the local newspapers hailed him as a "chemical wizard," having come to work for Ford and to apply his secret method for making rubber. Wartime tire rationing was on the public mind, and although there is nothing in the

correspondence to suggest that Carver's visit was specifically geared to working on the production of rubber, the press drew its own conclusions, as the following items show:

Daily Morning Journal (July 20, 1942): "Negro Chemist to Work on Rubber Experiments."

Detroit Free Press (July 20, 1942): "Asked directly if he would do synthetic rubber research, Dr. Carver replied, 'I don't know.' 'How long are you going to be here?' he was asked. 'I don't know,' he replied. 'Can you tell us anything about the nature of your plans for your work here?' 'No plans have been made yet,' he replied."

Detroit News (July 22, 1942): "Ford Spikes Report Dr. Carver Will Work on Synthetic Rubber — Both Insist Negro Scientist's Visit to Industrialist Concerns Food Tests."

Pittsburgh Courier (July 23, 1942): "Dr. Carver in Detroit Can Solve Rubber Problem — Carver Tells Henry Ford. In an exclusive interview at a luncheon given by Henry Ford, Tuesday, Dr. George W.

George Washington
Carver

At the dedication of the Carver Nutritional Laboratory in Dearborn, Carver is here offering Henry Ford a sample of a weed sandwich he has prepared to demonstrate the food value of weeds. Spicy herb sandwich spreads made the sandwiches quite palatable. (188.70497-A)

Carver revealed his formula for making rubber, and for the first time confirmed the duties he will perform as a member of the great Ford organization. Dr. Carver will make rubber from the sweet potato, milk weed and dandelion."

The laboratory building dedicated by Carver on July 21 was named the Nutritional Laboratory of the Ford Motor Company. In keeping with this theme, weed sandwiches, made under Carver's supervision, were served at the dedication. And sandwich spreads were among the first developments of the laboratory. One recipe called for beets (greens and roots), carrots, cabbage, endive, Swiss chard, onions, parsley, kale, celery, rhubarb, radish seed pods, purslane, pickle, bergamot leaf, and a very small amount of ham, all finely ground. Lemon juice, salt, and mayonnaise were added. Another sandwich spread was made by grinding dandelion, plantain, chickweed, lamb's-quarters, lemon juice, and mayonnaise. Both Carver and Ford were firm believers in natural foods. Carver had stated that two full meals of nature's vegetables were the equivalent in vitamins and minerals of the average person's monthly diet of vegetables.

Carver's visit to Dearborn was ceremonial, to say the least. He was entertained royally for two weeks, with photographers on hand constantly to catch his smiling countenance and flower-decorated lapel. His residence was the Dearborn Inn. During this time, he dedicated the replica of his birthplace, spending a night in the building to add a touch of authenticity. He spoke at a chapel service at the Edison Institute and lunched at Fair Lane, the Fords' home.

During the next two weeks, Carver spent most of his time at the Nutritional Laboratory, and while he does not appear to have revealed any novel method of making rubber out of milkweed, the laboratory, under the direction of Robert Smith, soon afterward began to produce soybean milk and ice cream.

Shortly after returning to Tuskegee, Carver wrote about yet another project:

> This is just to extend to you greetings, and to very briefly call attention to the fact that I believe we have made another signal possibility with reference to helping America out in its needs.
>
> It is most interesting to note that the plant at which we were looking growing so profusely on your place can be grown in this country with but little trouble. I mean the plant known as velvet leaf, cheeses, Alutilon, and interesting to say has been familiarly known as American jute as the fiber is so much like it, and the plant is so easily grown. Of course from a child I have known it as cheese, butter print, and a general nuisance as a weed. I am going to look very much more into this side of it and see just what it promises.
>
> I want you to know that my trip there was, without question, the most remarkable trip I have ever had.

The following month, September 1942, Ford was invited to become a trustee of the George Washington Carver Foundation. He accepted.

The last letter from Carver to Dearborn was addressed to Campsall and signed for Carver by Curtis. It was received on December 28 and noted:

> The pair of black shoes that were made from my last by the shoe cobbler in Greenfield Village have arrived. I cannot tell you how much they are appreciated, and how I wish Mr. Ford would have a pair made for himself just like them. I felt all the time just as soon as I saw the old gentleman that there was a man who could make a pair of shoes I could wear, and he certainly has succeeded. If you have ever observed a little girl who had just received a bright and cheery new dress and seen her behave, you could get some sort of idea of how I am behaving in my new shoes.
>
> Please remember me most graciously to the shoe cobbler and wish for him a very happy and pleasant Christmas.
>
> I wish for you and yours, and all my friends up there a most pleasant and joyous holiday season.

The Ford Motor Company Nutritional Laboratory, better known by locals as the Carver Laboratory, located on Michigan Avenue in Dearborn. From the outside, it appears as it did when used as a water pumping station earlier days. (188.70719)

> I am looking forward to your coming down next Spring as I have missed you since my art rooms have been installed.

Carver died a few days later, on January 5, 1943. In a letter written three days after Carver's death to Dr. F. D. Patterson, chairman of the George Washington Carver Foundation, Ford spoke of both the past and the future:

> As you know, we thought very highly of him at Dearborn, where he was always an honored guest, and today we have completed what we planned some time ago — we have put his name on the laboratory which he dedicated last July. In this way we shall keep his memory green in this part of the country, and shall hope to pursue some of the lines of research he pointed out to us.

In a public statement, Ford stressed the interests the two men had shared:

> Dr. Carver had the brain of a scientist and the heart of a saint. It was always a privilege to visit him at Tuskegee or to have him visit us in Dearborn. Both of us were interested in the same thing: we believed that weeds and grasses have great possibilities as food and industrial materials, and the last time he was here we did some work together along that line. He was physically frail then, but his mind was as keenly alert as ever. His personality will be a great loss, but his work will remain and lead to greater things through the young men he inspired.

The relationship between Ford and Tuskegee did not end there, however. On October 17, 1997, Edsel Ford II, the president of Ford Motor Credit Company, visited the campus of Tuskegee University and presented to Tuskegee's president, Dr. Benjamin Payton, a gift of $1.5 million. The gift was used to enhance the library complex to be named the Ford Resource and Learning Center. Included in the gift were moneys to provide computer facilities in student residence halls. Other Ford-sponsored programs with Tuskegee University include a minority scholarship program, college recruiting efforts, and an intern/research program. A $2.5 million grant was awarded by Ford Motor Company in 1999.

George Washington Carver

References

Accession 1, Fair Lane Papers, Box 112. Benson Ford Research Center, HFM & GV.

Accession 2, Personal Records of Henry Ford, Boxes 33, 34. Benson Ford Research Center, HFM & GV.

Accession 7, Clipping Books, Vol. 125, July–August 1942. Benson Ford Research Center, HFM & GV.

Accession 285, Office of Henry Ford, Boxes 2453, 2635. Benson Ford Research Center, HFM & GV.

Accession 1202, pamphlets written by George Washington Carver, 1899–1942. Benson Ford Research Center, HFM & GV.

Accession 1600, oral interview transcript by Austin W. Curtis (assistant to Dr. Carver), July 23, 1979. Benson Ford Research Center, HFM & GV.

"Ford-Tuskegee Link Reinforced," *Ford Times*, October 1997.

Holt, Rackham. *George Washington Carver: An American Biography.* Garden City, N.Y.: Doubleday, 1943.

Kremer, Gary R. *George Washington Carver in His Own Words.* Columbia, Mo.: University of Missouri Press, 1987.

7
McGuffey Readers

Both Henry and Clara Ford studied the McGuffey Readers when they were in school. Mastering the First through Sixth Eclectic Educational Series was then an accomplishment in reading not attained until well into college in today's system of schooling. It is no wonder Henry felt he had had enough education from books after the eight years it had taken him to get through the first six grades of country school. With McGuffey's Sixth Reader finished, one would have had not only the basics of spelling and grammar but also a course in "Principles of Elocution," together with "Lessons in Prose and Poetry," followed by "Exercises in Articulation," which consisted of reading as many as four hundred pages of writings by authors such as D'Israeli, Dickens, Walpole, Irving, Goldsmith, Byron, Shakespeare, Blackstone, Addison, Webster, and Scott, as well as the Bible.

William Holmes McGuffey was a well-educated college professor and Presbyterian minister who had graduated from Washington and Jefferson College in 1826, held professorships at several universities, and was president of Ohio University. The McGuffey Readers instilled not only correct English but also lessons in morals, the desirability of temperance, and the wickedness of war — ideals Henry and Clara Ford cherished.

It is said that one afternoon, when Clara Ford heard children playing and shouting on their way home from school, she quoted from McGuffey's First Reader: "Hear the children gaily shout!" Neither she nor Henry could remember the rest of the verse: "Half past four and school is out." That began their search for a copy of McGuffey's First Reader. But the search did not end with one book. Not only did Ford want a complete set, but he had in mind reestablishing their former popularity by reprinting complete sets of McGuffey Readers by the thousands.

In his enthusiasm, Ford felt McGuffey should be immortalized. He learned that McGuffey had been born on September 28, 1800, on a rugged hillside farm in West Finley Township, fifteen miles southwest of Washington, Pennsylvania. In 1933, it belonged to Mrs. Henry Y. Blayney, a direct descendant of McGuffey. Ford lost no time in buying

The crowd of people on September 23, 1934, at the site of the William McGuffey birthplace in Washington County, Pennsylvania. At this event, sponsored by Henry and Clara Ford, a bronze marker on a granite monument was dedicated in honor of McGuffey.

the remains of the unoccupied log birthplace, including a few remaining relics such as a stove and kettles, all of which were shipped at once to Greenfield Village, where the log birthplace was restored by 1934. Along with the birthplace, logs from McGuffey barns also were moved to the Village and used to construct a schoolhouse to be known as the McGuffey School.

Not wanting to leave the site of the McGuffey birthplace unmarked, Ford arranged for a fourteen-ton granite boulder to be placed at the exact site of the fireplace and for large bronze tablets to be attached to the stone. Formal dedication of the marker was arranged for Sunday afternoon, September 23, 1934, near the 134th anniversary of McGuffey's birth. Dr. A. B. Brooks, chairman of the William Holmes McGuffey Memorial Association, organized the event, which drew an estimated fifteen thousand people, many of them from the various McGuffey Societies.

Before the program commenced, Henry's old-time orchestra, consisting of dulcimer, cimbalom, violin, bass viol, trumpet, and guitar

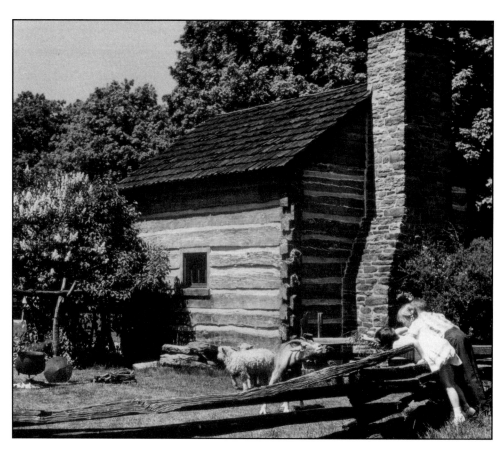

The backyard of
the McGuffey
birthplace as
reconstructed in
Greenfield Village
in 1934.
Schoolchildren
play with a goat
and sheep on this
warm day in May.

and led by Clayton Perry, shared with the Bethany College orchestra the responsibility of entertaining the crowd. When first introduced by Brooks, Clara Ford, who seldom appeared with Henry in public, was given a tremendous ovation. Henry, when asked to speak, said, "I am glad to join you today in giving honor to Dr. McGuffey. He was a great American. The McGuffey Readers taught industry and morality to America." Henry then bowed and sat down; the applauding crowd did not realize that he had omitted three paragraphs of his prepared speech.

The monument itself was formally dedicated by Andrew H. Hepburn of Indianapolis, a great-grandson of McGuffey and one of thirty-five descendants present. Prominent educators from institutions with which McGuffey had been associated were scheduled to present brief eulogies. Henry and Clara Ford were honored guests. The principal speaker representing the Fords was William J. Cameron, Henry Ford's Dearborn publicist, who delivered an address entitled "What Dr. William Holmes McGuffey Means to the Present Generation."

Cameron pointed out that McGuffey's Readers ranked third among America's best sellers, saying they were exceeded only by the Bible and the dictionary. He praised McGuffey as a teacher "before the regimentation of schools."

Portions of the two-hour program were aired by the National Broadcasting Company. Part of the broadcast was from the Blayney Farms and part from Greenfield Village. The Village program of fifteen minutes was provided by students and consisted of selections from McGuffey's Second Reader, the Ten Commandments in verse, a description of the McGuffey birthplace in the Village, and some of Henry's favorite old-time songs. To conclude, at the birthplace site in Pennsylvania, Ford unveiled the monument to McGuffey and read the inscription on the bronze tablet.

To add McGuffey reality to the Greenfield Village scene, Ford induced a nephew of McGuffey to move to Dearborn and place his son in the Edison Institute Schools of Greenfield Village. The nephew was Kingsley R. MacGuffey *(sic)*, whose wife was Sarah MacGuffey. They lived at 22621 Law Avenue in Dearborn, and their son, Henry MacGuffey, attended Greenfield Village Schools for several years.

A deed to the McGuffey farm in Pennsylvania was obtained by Henry and Clara on February 20, 1937, from Henry Y. Blayney, Arthur H. Blayney, and Henrietta V. Blayney, all of West Finley Township, Washington County, Pennsylvania, for $4,500. The property description, as presented on the old deed, not only employed the usual compass bearings but also defined distances in "perches" and boundary markers as large or small walnut trees, a sugar tree, a white oak, stones of either granite or limestone, a stake, a point in the road, and also "a point in the forks of three roads." Stated size of the entire property was 64.8275 acres.

For the two-day 1938 annual meeting of the Federation of McGuffey Societies, Henry and Clara Ford invited the entire membership to convene at Greenfield Village. Approximately 700 Society members attended from Pennsylvania, West Virginia, Ohio, and Indiana. Along with other McGuffey mementos, each was given a bronze medallion bearing a picture of McGuffey at work at his desk. Although the observance was held on a weekend in July, Edison Institute schoolchildren were out in force to entertain the visitors. Students ushered the guests into the restored McGuffey birthplace and the schoolhouse named for McGuffey, demonstrated children's old-fashioned games on the Village Green, and conducted an old-time spelling bee.

As a special event on Saturday afternoon, the Ackley covered bridge, which had stood for more than a century just seven miles from McGuffey's birthplace, was dedicated as part of the McGuffey program. Beams and planks from the bridge had been dismantled in Pennsylvania

Henry and Clara
greeting members of
McGuffey Societies
at an annual meeting
in Greenfield Village
on July 2, 1938.
(188.23542)

by Ford crews during the previous winter and reassembled in Greenfield Village during the spring of 1938. Cameron gave the dedicatory address. At the conclusion of the dedication, Henry and Clara rode with some of the guests over the historic bridge in an ancient stagecoach drawn by a four-horse team. On Saturday evening, the guests were entertained in the school auditorium by students who provided an elaborate dramatization of events in the life of William Holmes McGuffey. The Saturday evening program ended with old-fashioned dancing in the Lovett Hall ballroom.

The Sunday schedule started with a service on the Village Green in front of Martha-Mary Chapel. As was customary in the Village, an Edison Institute student presided over the services. After prayer, hymns, and the reading of the Ten Commandments in verse from McGuffey's Second Reader, Dr. Charles Frederick Wishart, president of the College of Wooster in Ohio, spoke of the religious influence of the McGuffey Readers. During an afternoon buffet luncheon on the lawn below the Stephen Foster House, students on the nearby steamer *Suwanee* sang old familiar songs, including some of the most popular melodies of Stephen Foster.

The McGuffey birthplace was open to tourists visiting Greenfield Village from the time it was reconstructed in the Village in 1934 until very recently; it now requires re-restoration. The McGuffey Schoolhouse has been in use as a classroom since 1934 and is still being used

by students of modern schools to learn what a school day was like in the 1840s. Students and teachers come to the Village in period clothing, bring lunches typical of the period, and are taught from McGuffey Readers. In the gift shops of the Museum and Village, McGuffey Readers are sold by the set of six.

The bronze marker that was attached to the granite monument at the site of William McGuffey's birthplace. In the center is an image of the birthplace with the woodshed to the right, and to the left is the image of the McGuffey School as built in Greenfield Village. (188.66552)

References

Accession 23, Box 16, Henry Ford Office Papers. Benson Ford Research Center, HFM & GV.

Accession 587, Office of Henry & Clara Ford Estate, Property Records. Benson Ford Research Center, HFM & GV.

"Fifteen Thousand Hear Ford Dedicate McGuffey Memorial." *Wheeling Register*, September 24, 1934.

"Stone to Be Dedicated at McGuffey Birthplace." *Pittsburgh Sun Times*, September 20, 1934.

"Thousands Attend McGuffey Ceremony." *Washington Observer*, September 22, 1934.

"Traditions of William Holmes McGuffey Observed in Two-day Meeting." *Herald*, July 22, 1938.

"William Holmes McGuffey." *Herald*, October 4, 1935.

8

Mahatma Gandhi

Mohandas Karamchand Gandhi (1869–1948), a frail, ascetic Hindu, spent most of his life in a nonviolent struggle to free India from British domination. At age eighteen, he had gone to London, where he studied law at the University of London and was admitted to the bar. In South Africa, he spent nearly two decades championing the Hindu cause. In 1915, back in India during World War I, Gandhi, while strongly advocating pacifism, organized an ambulance corps for the British Army and won two medals for bravery.

In 1920, in a general campaign of nonviolent noncooperation against Great Britain, Gandhi, with millions of followers, started a passive-resistance crusade advocating the boycott of foreign goods and the adoption of the spinning wheel as an emblem of economic independence. As a result, Gandhi was thrown into jail for two years. In 1929, the National Congress Party put him in charge of a campaign to win complete independence for India from Great Britain. His first tactic was to advocate avoidance of the government's salt tax, suggesting that everyone draw salt illegally from seawater. Again, he was jailed.

In and out of jail, Gandhi fasted "unto death" in protest of British rule and the Hindu caste system. He tried to renounce the title *Mahatma* ("Great Soul") without success. In 1939, he continued his hunger strike, insisting that India's independence be granted as a price of India's participation in World War II. Britain offered only an arrangement of equal partnership.

It was on July 25, 1941, before the United States had entered the war, that Henry Ford wrote to Gandhi:

Dear Mr. Gandhi:

I want to take this opportunity of sending you a message through Mr. T. A. Raman, to tell you how deeply I admire your life and message. You are one of the greatest men the world has ever known. May God help and guide your lofty work.

Published previously in *The Ford Legend*, Vol. VII, No. 1, 1998.

The presentation of the Gandhi spinning wheel on December 28, 1942, in the foyer of Henry Ford Museum. The handle of Luther Burbank's spade embedded in cement appears in the foreground. From left are Mrs. T. A. Raman, T. A. Raman, Henry Ford, and Clara Ford. The photographer who has Clara's attention was George Ebling, the Fords' personal photographer. (P.O.19769)

From the tiny village of Sevagram near Warda in central India, Ford received the following handwritten reply, dated April 16, 1942:

Dear Friend:

I am much obliged for your kind letter.

Yours truly,
M. K. Gandhi

The relationship did not end there. T. A. Raman, London editor of the United Press of India, reveals the following details:

Mahatma Gandhi was delighted — and somewhat surprised — to receive greetings and good wishes from Mr. Henry Ford. It was the day after Pearl Harbor too, and Gandhi in his hermitage at Sevagram, was visibly grieved by the extension of the conflict to the whole world. The message from Mr. Ford came as a relief.

I told him of Mr. Ford's admiration for his selfless life and the ideals which inspired them. Gandhi said he was deeply touched by the message and asked me to convey his regards to Mr. Ford.

I asked him whether I may take back his message in the shape of the simple machine with which Gandhi's name is associated, the spinning wheel. He agreed instantly and sent a secretary and his disciple Madeloine Slade to fetch an old spinning wheel he had used.

He autographed it in Hindu and English twice over. While he was writing I said jokingly, "Ford seems to think that you are the one sensible man in the world!" Gandhi laughed and as he handed it over said with a smile, "So, this goes from one sensible man to another!"

He then asked me about Mr. Ford's health, his many activities and his views on a variety of international problems. He was particularly interested in Dearborn village and the educational work being done there. He told me in parting to make sure to convey to Mr. Ford his best wishes for his health and the success of his many great undertakings.

The spinning wheel however had to travel 12,000 miles through perilous submarine infested waters before it reached the U.S. All the way, the blacked-out ship zigzagged and changed course making the journey from Bombay to New York through Cape Town and Trinidad, even longer.

I got the Captain's special permission to carry the spinning wheel with me into the lifeboat in the event of an emergency. But we got through without mishap though missing disaster several times only by a few minutes or miles.

And so, safe now, this token of sympathy between two of the most remarkable men of our century rests in this fascinating museum. They are very different, these two men, but they are alike in simplicity, selflessness and all-conquering faith.

Raman made the presentation of the spinning wheel on Gandhi's behalf on December 28, 1942, in the Edison Institute entrance foyer with Mr. and Mrs. Ford attending.

Immediately following the war, Britain offered India full dominion status, which still did not satisfy Gandhi. It was not until July 18, 1947, that India became independent of Britain. Gandhi died only a few months later on January 30, 1948, at age seventy-nine, of a gunshot wound inflicted by a member of the Hindu Mahasabha.

References

Accession 292, Box 47, Henry Ford Office, Miscellany. Benson Ford Research Center, HFM & GV.

9
Henry Clausen

Back in 1872, along with thousands of others, a twenty-six-year-old man named Henry Clausen came to America from Germany. During the period following the Civil War, many Germans came to Dearborn Township, as they did to other sections of America where land was flat and rich. In 1873, the capital of the plains state of North Dakota was named Bismarck by the German immigrants in honor of their German emperor. Clausen, born in Holstein, Germany, arrived seemingly all by himself and was soon to have the nickname "Bismarck" because of his Prussian origin — a nickname he detested in time.

Clausen is listed in the 1900 Dearborn Township census as age fifty-three, single, a day laborer living in a house on the property of Dudley Coon, located on Ann Arbor Trail between the present Warren Avenue and Ford Road. In 1920, he is listed as a ditcher, age seventy-four, single head of household, occupying a house on Ford Road east of Telegraph Road between Military Avenue and Telegraph Road. This was in the area of the sizable Maxwell Ditch on which he may have worked.

When the land in Dearborn Township had been cleared of trees, it next needed to be drained to obtain a good crop yield — whatever kind of crop was to be planted. These drainage systems, well below plowing depth, were dug by hand, placing one-foot-long clay tiles end to end, leading to some creek or gulley. Clausen is said to have dug these drains for a large number of settlers in the Dearborn area. In fact, he is said to have drained the farm of William Ford, Henry's father, and Henry knew him as a boy.

Clausen is presumed to have carried on primarily as a ditch digger until old age, when he was literally worn out. His health also had become very poor as a result of his having been intoxicated much of the time. It must have been about 1915 when Henry Ford took notice of the condition of his old friend and decided to help him. One source of information states that Ford gave Clausen a Model T, but Clausen needed much more basic help than an automobile.

Sources agree that Clausen was allowed to live in a house at Nankin Mills near the Rouge River through the courtesy of Ford. That situation has been well described by Ford employee Fred Gleason:

A copy of Henry Clausen's death certificate.

I am going to mention a story of which I was a part. Many years ago there was a man named Henry Clausen. He was also known by many as Old Bismarck, a name he inherited from some nobility in Germany — a name he did not like. Now for the story. This man underdrained nearly all the farms in and around Detroit including that of Mr. Ford's father, William. He, as well as many of us, year by year grew older to such rapidity, Father Time overcame his youth to such an extent he no longer was able to care for himself. I had the task of cutting his hair. I also had the privilege of dining with him at the same table as the mice used, but they, believe me or not, had gone home. [Catered meals often were delivered by George Burns, one of Henry Ford's chauffeurs.]

Mr. Ford delegated two men to visit Bismarck twice a week and see that he had plenty to eat and clean clothing, bedding, etc. This

NUMBER OF FUNERAL 479	NUMBER FOR THE CURRENT YEAR 6	ITEMS OF BILL (Cross out printed items not furnished).		
Name of deceased *Henry Clausen*		(Full description of Casket or Coffin and Trimmings.)	225	00
Late Residence *Dearborn, Mich.*				
Cause of Death *Apoplexy*		No. Handles		
Date of Death *July 13, 1927*		No. Plate		
Date of Burial *July 14, 1927*		Outside Box, Pine, Chestnut, Oak, Cedar	15	00
Certifying Physician *H. E. Foley*		No. Shroud	5	00
Place of Burial *Dearborn* Cemetery		Personal Attendance — Porters and Help.		
Funeral at house or *Chapel* Church		prs. Gloves for		
Grave or Lot No.		Use of Chairs		
Section No.		Cemetery Charges, opening grave		
Bill rendered to *Mr. Dipple of Ford Mtr.*		Washing and Laying out Remains—Shaving.		
Date when rendered *July 15, 1927* Amount 300.00		Keeping in Ice, in Freezer, or Embalming.	35	00
Payments		Carriages to Cemetery.		
		Flowers		
		Advertising		
		Crape for Door		
		Hearse	15	00
		Chapel	5	00
		Amount of Bill	300	00

A copy of a receipt found in Henry Ford's archival papers.

kind act of disturbing his bed twice a week did not please Clausen. He always lay down in a half circle when he went to bed. He told me it would take him two nights to make that half circle, then they would come and mess it all up.

This man also had been a great horse trainer. A family named Zink lived on Military Road at that time. They asked Bismarck if he would loan them his horse, which he did. As time went on, Bismarck asked for his horse and they would not return it. About five o'clock one morning, Bismarck somehow got through and into Mr. Ford's estate. He wanted to see Mr. Ford. The watchman tried to hold him back lest he might try to shoot Mr. Ford if he could get near him. Mr. Ford heard the two men wrestling in the middle of the dam which is near the house. After a time, Mr. Ford recognized Bismarck's voice and told the watchman to let his visitor come across the dam. When Mr. Ford heard Bismarck's story, he said, "You go home, and if your horse is not in your barn by twelve o'clock let me know." Needless for me to tell you, the horse was back in due time. This old man, through the remainder of his life, was cared for through the kindness of Mr. Ford.

Another glimpse of Clausen is provided by Earl Ford, who lived on Joy Road near Southfield Road. Earl Ford remembered Clausen as he passed by the Ford farm from time to time in a spring wagon pulled by an old white horse. One day, the horse and wagon were seen coming along the road heading westward toward Nankin Mills with no driver

Henry Clausen   in sight. Earl and his brother, Ralph, climbed onto the milk platform alongside the road, and as the wagon passed, they saw Clausen lying on the bottom of the wagon being taken home by his trusty old horse.

Earl Ford, incidentally, became trustee of the Ford Cemetery on Joy Road near Greenfield Road. Both he and his sister, Myrtle, relate that when Clausen died, Henry Ford ordered Ray Dahlinger, his farm manager, to bury him under a pine tree in the southwest corner of the Ford Cemetery. The fresh grave was almost immediately noticed by other members of the Ford family, whereupon Anna Ford, a Scotch Settlement schoolteacher and Earl's sister, was delegated spokesperson for the family in demanding of Henry Ford that Clausen be removed immediately from their hallowed ground. Henry was not available, so his secretary, Frank Campsall, became Anna's target. Old Bismarck was removed, it is said, within twenty-four hours.

According to Robert Smith, an agricultural chemist living and working for Henry Ford in the Square House near Ford and Southfield Roads, Ford came into the house early one rainy morning all covered with mud and reported that he had been "gravedigging." Smith estimated the date to be about 1930. Whether this related to Clausen is not known.

The death certificate prepared for Henry Clausen and filed July 30, 1927, indicates that he died on July 13, 1927, at age eighty-two, and was attended by Dr. H. S. Foley of Dearborn. Foley diagnosed the cause of death as apoplexy. The party who provided personal information regarding Clausen was M. H. Sipple, an employee of Ford Motor Company. Funeral services were conducted by Daly Brothers of Dearborn. Their bill, rendered July 15, amounted to $300, including casket, outside box, shroud, embalming, hearse, and chapel. Date of burial is recorded as July 14, 1927, but nowhere is there the name of the cemetery. Daly Brothers indicate "Place of Burial — Dearborn Cemetery," and Earl Ford has stated that Clausen was reburied "in a Dearborn cemetery."

This writer, after considerable searching of local cemetery records, including the Ford Cemetery, has been unable to find Clausen's grave. So this story ends with an appeal to readers to offer any reasonable clues pertaining to the whereabouts of Clausen's physical remains.

Part II
Relatives

*H*enry Ford's grandfather, John Ford, held a life lease on a twenty-eight-acre farm near Clonakilty, Ireland, until 1847, when the family emigrated to Michigan to escape the terrible potato famine in Ireland. With the John Ford family was son William Ford, who would become Henry Ford's father. Other families of Fords, brothers of John and also from Clonakilty, had arrived previously in Dearborn Township beginning in 1832, paving the way for John Ford and his family. The early Fords are thought to have come to Michigan because the brothers Samuel and John Ford had married sisters named Smith who had relatives living in Detroit's Corktown. Within another generation in the Dearborn area, there were at least fifty Ford family members living within a mile or so of one another.

Henry Ford's mother, Mary Litogot, was born in Michigan about 1840 and was orphaned at age three. The European origin of the Litogot family has not been determined, but they are thought to have emigrated from the Netherlands, Belgium, or northern France. Henry Ford tried at length to determine the ancestral background of his mother but with little success. Michigan census records indicate that Mary's brother, Saphara, was living on a farm in Taylor Township, Wayne County, Michigan, in 1860. Litogot descendants are still working to trace their genealogy further.

10
Ford Family Tree

The Ford family tree, in whatever form it is found, is based on the work of Raymond H. Laird, a Ford Motor Company engine engineer and husband of Emma Ford, a cousin of Henry Ford. The tree is depicted in botanical form in a drawing by Laird, in four looseleaf genealogical books assembled by Laird, and in charts prepared by this author. Impetus and support for the years of work done by Laird were provided by Henry Ford.

When Henry, Clara, and Edsel Ford traveled to England and Ireland in the summer of 1912, Clara found the home of her mother in Warwick, England; Henry inquired in Cork, Ireland, regarding his foster grandfather, Patrick Ahern; and Edsel reported in his diary that they found the house in Clonakilty, Ireland, where his great-aunt Nancy had lived. Serious work on Ford genealogy did not start, however, until twelve years later. Laird tells of this beginning in a letter dated November 8, 1965, to some friends:

> As I recall, your main question was regarding the origin of the Ford family tree of which you have a print. Here's how it started. In 1924 Mr. Ford called me into his office and showed me a sketch of the Ford family tree that Mabel Ford had drawn from what data she had been able to gather. This had kindled Mr. Ford's interest and he designated me to obtain all information that I could, and draw as complete a tree as possible.
>
> During the next few years I drove tens of thousands of miles to interview people; gather data from family Bibles, photographs, letters, gravestones and cemetery records; arrange these data in order to draw the family tree of which you have a copy. We also checked all available records in Ireland. This investigation was suggested by Mr. Grace as he managed the Ford Plant there, and he was aided greatly by Charles A. Webster, D.D., rector of Blackrock, Cork. Only fragmented data was available, however. During World War I, all records of the area from which Mr. Ford's ancestors came were sent to the Four Courts Building in Dublin for safekeeping. This building was bombed and most of the records were destroyed.
>
> From the time I completed the data until I retired from the Ford Motor Co. in 1949, all correspondence claiming relationship to Mr. Ford was referred to me for my comments before being answered.

In a letter to Henry Ford's secretaries E. G. Liebold and Frank Campsall, Laird had occasion in 1939 to summarize the results of the 1925 Irish research:

The Ford family tree as drawn by Raymond Laird between 1924 and 1927, with a few later additions to the William Ford branches. The original drawing, 31 by 20 inches, allows individual names to be read.

In 1585 Queen Elizabeth selected a number of English gentlemen who were to people Munster (one of four Irish provinces) with settlers from England. Among those gentlemen was Sir John Starvell who was to bring to Ireland and settle on the estate granted to him "such of the gentlemen of the country of Somerset as he found able and willing to come." It is also an historical fact that about the year 1601 a large number of the gentry of Somerset and Devon, mostly younger sons, went over to Ireland. From time to time in the succeeding years others came over to settle the nearly 600,000 acres granted in Munster. Queen Elizabeth was bound on her part to maintain certain forces for security of the settlers.

Early in the seventeenth century an Anthony Starvell had property in the neighborhood of Clonakilty, as had also a member of the Honner family. These two families were united by marriage in 1694 and by terms of the marriage settlement the Madame estate came into the possession of the Starvell family. Early records show that the Fords were tenants of Starvell at Madame and of Honner at Croghane, and indicate that these Fords were descendants of the Fords of Somerset and Devon who came to Ireland to help people the confiscated lands. It is also an interesting fact that the connection

Genealogy and History of the Family and Descendants
————OF————

WILLIAM FORD

REBECCA JENNINGS

Please fill the blanks below, and add on the other side of this sheet any information you can, not embraced in the blanks. Kindly give your ancestry as far back as possible, the history of each person, their residence, occupation, what they have accomplished of note, when and where graduated, whether in the army and what company and regiment or in the navy, what boat, what church if any, what offices, either church, military or civil, public or private. Write full name and middle name, if any, and underline the name by which usually called. Be careful to give correct dates, name and facts, and write PLAIN.

Yours respectfully,

FAMILY RECORD

Of.... Henry Ford .... of.. Bath, Placer Co. Cal. ....

Occupation.... Miner .... Church, if any,.. Cathlic, Forest Hill

Society, if any,...

Military Record ....

Offices held ....

	When	Where		When	Where buried
Born....	1830	Ireland	Died..	May 4, 1901	Forest Hill, Cal.

Married.. Aug. 25, 1857 San Francisco, Cal.   *Whom* Katherine O'Leary

Born.... Nov. 1829 Ireland   Died.. August 15, 1912 Forest Hill, Cal.

Church and Society...

Offices held ....

REMARKS: ....

CHILDREN

NAME	BORN When and Where		DIED WHEN	Where Buried
1. Mary Jane Ford (Bayles)	July 24, 1858	Bath	July 14, 1910	Forest Hill
2. Rebecca Ford (Henning)	Sept. 4, 1859	Bath	July 1, 1914	Forest Hill
3. Henrietta Ford (DeBons)	June 19, 1861	Bath	Sept 20, 1910	Forest Hill
4. William Henry Ford	Feb. 5, 1864	Bath	Dec. 13, 1931	Forest Hill
5. Anna Agusta Ford	Dec. 1, 1965	Bath	1870	Forest Hill
6. George Samuel Ford	Oct. 19, 1867	Bath		
7. Francis Albert Ford	Nov. 29, 1869	Bath	Feb. 11, 1928	
8. Alice Ford (Bequette)	Sept. 27, 1871	Bath		
9.				
10.				
11.				
12.				

FATHER OF FIRST PERSON NAMED IN THIS RECORD

Full Name.... John Ford .... Residence.. Dearborn, Mich.

Born.... 1799 Ireland .... Died.. Mar. 22, 1864 Ford Cemetery

Married.. Feb. 14, 1824 Ireland (Parish of Desertserges) Thomasine Smith

Born.......... Klonekilty, Ireland Died.. 1847-On ship enroute to America

GRANDFATHER ON FATHER'S SIDE

Name.... William Ford .... Residence.. Klonekilty, Ireland

Born.... 1775 Ireland .... Died.. 1818 Ireland

Married.. Ireland   *Whom* Rebecca Jennings

Born.... 1776 Ireland .... Died.. May 1, 1851 Grand Lawn, Detroit

GRANDFATHER ON MOTHER'S SIDE

Name... Residence..................................

Born.. Died.....................................

Married..

Born.. Died.....................................

REMARKS: ....

NAME.... Alice Ford Bequette

Person making out the above

ADDRESS.... Auburn, Placer Co. Cal.

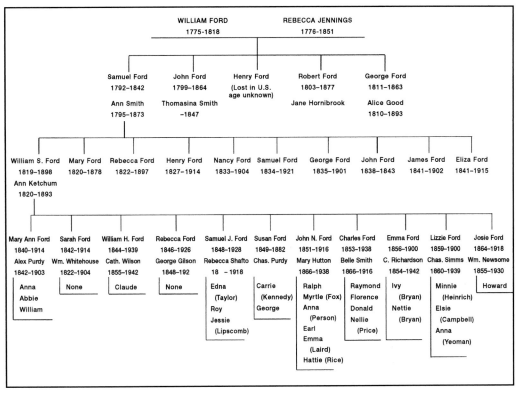

Family of
Samuel Ford
(above)

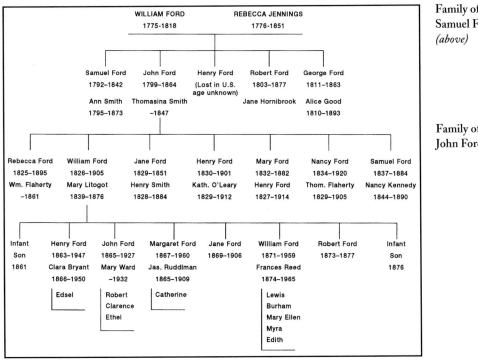

Family of
John Ford *(left)*

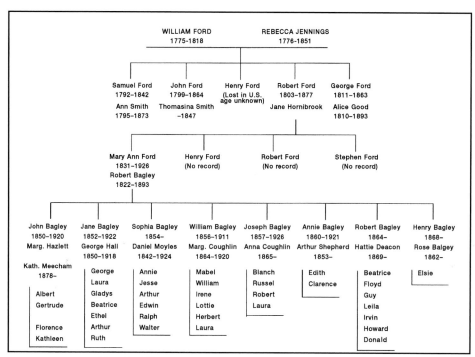

Family of Robert Ford

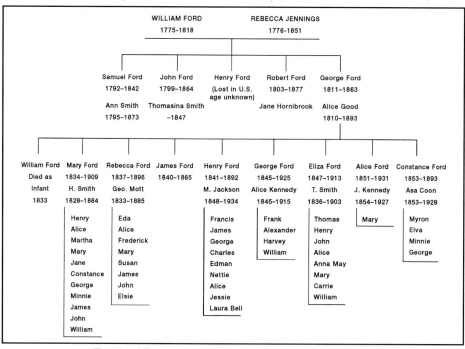

Family of George Ford

between the Ford and Starvell families existed in Somersetshire as early as the first part of the thirteenth century before either family came to Ireland.

I have a fairly complete record of the descendants of Mr. Ford's grandparents, William Ford and Rebecca Jennings, who were born in 1775 and 1776. William Ford died in Ireland, but his wife Rebecca, and their sons Samuel (1791), John (1799) and George (1811) came to America and all settled in the vicinity of Dearborn. John was Mr. Ford's grandfather. They came to America in 1847. This was the year of the great potato famine when times in Ireland were exceedingly hard.

In the early records the name Ford is variously spelled; Ford, Forde, Foord, De Ford and De La Ford, two or more spellings sometimes being used in the same article. The two latter spellings indicate Norman origin.

So the Ford family tree is well established following the names of William Ford and Rebecca Jennings. Laird assembled genealogical material quite steadily until he was needed by Henry Ford to work full-time on the Model A engine in 1927. Only a few items were added after that. Copies of the Laird genealogy papers were kept by Ford in his office files at the Engineering Laboratory in Dearborn. A story that Ford ignored the tree because he learned of a horse thief among his forebears has no credence.

The family tree drawn by Laird as a botanical tree twenty by thirty-one inches in size was incomplete as of 1927 because he had not yet had time to include the limb representing the Robert Ford family. The tree thus gives the impression of having been struck by lightning. Names of individuals are legible on the tree only when reproduced at full size. Laird's most complete data, by far, are in the form of hundreds of genealogical sheets sent to heads of families who supplied needed information. These sheets are in separate books representing the four main branches of the Ford family. From data in those books, four individual tables representing the four family branches have been prepared.

The illustrations in this chapter include a much-reduced copy of the Ford family tree drawn by Laird, a one-page sample of the large number of genealogical sheets collected by Laird, and four charts prepared from genealogy sheet data and each representing one branch of the family.

References

Accession 28, Box 27, Henry Ford Office. Benson Ford Research Center, HFM & GV.

Accession 1635, Box 1, Ralph Laird Papers. Benson Ford Research Center, HFM & GV.

Laird, Raymond H. "I Worked for Henry Ford." *Dearborn Historian,* Vol. 10, No. 1, 1970.

II

Ford Cemetery

In 1832, Samuel Ford and Ann (Nancy) Smith Ford, both of Ireland, settled on eighty acres at what is now the southwest corner of Joy and Greenfield Roads in Detroit. There were no roads at that time, and the property was in the northeast corner of what was to be Dearborn Township, on the town line between Dearborn and Redford Townships. After only ten years in this country, Samuel Ford died in 1842 and was buried on his own property. This was the first burial in what became the Ford Cemetery. George Ford, a brother of Samuel, also had purchased eighty acres east of Samuel in 1832, and another brother, John, arrived from Ireland and settled on the same town line a mile west of Samuel in 1847. Members of these other Ford families also began to be buried in the same lot with Samuel.

Following the death of Samuel's wife, Nancy Ford, in 1870, his eighty acres were left to her sons, James and George, each receiving forty acres. George received the forty that contained the Ford Cemetery. In 1893, a deed of trust was formulated. George Ford and Mary Jones Ford, his wife, conveyed the cemetery property to a board of trustees to be operated "as a place of burial for the heirs and descendants and the families of heirs and descendants" of Samuel Ford, George Ford, and John Ford — the three brothers from Ireland. Each of the three trustees was to represent his or her respective branch of the family.

When George Ford, the owner of the farm surrounding the cemetery, died in 1901, his wife, Mary, deeded the farm to Addison Ford, their only son. In 1919, Mary died, and Addison died in 1920. Addison's son, Clyde M. Ford, inherited the farm. By then, Henry Ford was buying up Dearborn land and acquired from Clyde Ford the forty acres in which the Ford Cemetery was located. Henry neglected to inquire about the cemetery trust deed, assumed he had bought the cemetery, and took over its maintenance, about which none of the relatives complained.

About this time, Raymond Laird was assigned by Henry Ford to compile a record of all persons buried in Ford Cemetery and to draw a

Previously published in the *Dearborn Historian,* Vol. 39, No. 3, 1999.

St. Martha's Episcopal Church and the Ford Cemetery on Joy Road near Greenfield Road, where Henry and Clara Ford are buried. The tall 1876 obelisk to the left in the cemetery marks the grave of Henry's mother, Mary. The long flat stones near the obelisk mark the graves of Henry and Clara. The photograph was taken in May 1954, only a few months after the dedication of the church. Henry's sister Margaret and brother William are buried in this cemetery, but his brother John is not. Clara is the only Bryant in the cemetery. (Photograph courtesy of Dearborn Historical Museum.)

plat showing the location of all graves therein. Arrangements for additional burials were made at first through M. H. Sipple of Henry Ford's staff. Following Sipple's death, permission for burials was obtained through Henry's secretary, Frank Campsall, who granted permission for people to make their own arrangements for burial. No death certificates or reports were filed.

When Henry Ford died on April 7, 1947, he had that very same day commented to his chauffeur, Robert Rankin, that he was to be buried in the Ford Cemetery. He was buried there, but it immediately became a problem for his wife, Clara. The grave had to be guarded day

Edison Institute people attending a ceremony at the gravesite of Henry and Clara Ford in the Ford Cemetery. The date is April 11, 1966, the hundredth anniversary of Clara Ford's birth. (B.61683-2)

and night. Whether the little cemetery was the proper place for such a prominent figure was much debated. There were suggestions that Ford's grave should be moved to Greenfield Village, and it was suggested that perhaps the whole cemetery should be moved there. It was rumored that Ford's body already had been moved to St. Paul's Episcopal Church in Detroit, and there are people to this day who question whether Henry Ford is really buried in the Ford Cemetery.

It was not until Clara Ford suggested that an Episcopal church be built next to the cemetery on adjoining land that Ford Motor Company lawyers discovered the existence of the 1893 trust deed of ownership of the cemetery. The assumption had been that Henry Ford had owned the cemetery since 1920. This posed a very serious problem. There were two options: contest the trust deed, or activate the board of trustees and gain its permission for control of the cemetery. The latter choice was adopted. It was found that two of the original trustees of the cemetery had died and that Earl Ford, representing Samuel's branch of the family, was the only one living. Earl Ford had been a trustee since 1921, having replaced his father, John N. Ford, who died in 1916.

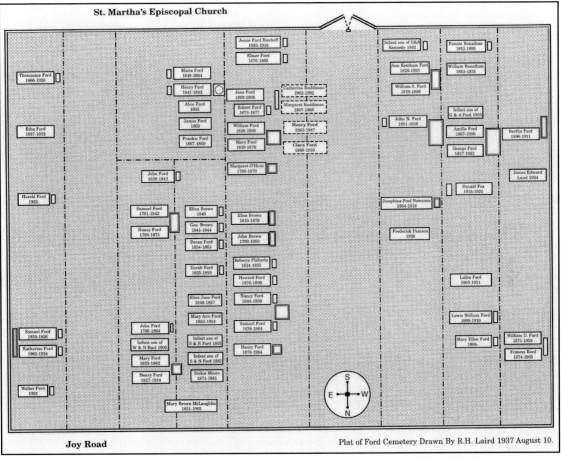

Plat of Ford Cemetery, drawn by R. H. Laird, August 10, 1937.

Then living in Ypsilanti, Michigan, Earl Ford was asked to call a meeting of all living descendants of the original three brothers for whose families the cemetery was established in 1893. To prepare this list of descendants, the genealogical data previously collected by Laird were of tremendous value. The meeting was held at the Edison Institute on November 23, 1948. A relatively small number of people — perhaps seventy-five — attended. Notice of the meeting had briefly explained the history of the cemetery, referring primarily to the need to elect two new trustees. The following statements were included in the meeting notice:

> This letter is meant to notify you as an heir that we will meet on the day mentioned at which time you will be asked to name, vote on, and elect two successor trustees to act with me in the carrying out of the purposes and uses for which the Ford Cemetery was created.
>
> At the meeting you will also be requested to pass on the matter of

certain improvements in the Ford Cemetery and the care thereof, and such other business as appropriately may come before the meeting.

Earl Ford chaired the meeting with the object of voting for two additional trustees. Elected were Mabel Nancy Ford and Laurence Ford. Clara Ford was there, and her attorney, Clifford B. Longley, used drawings to explain her generous offer to fence and care for the cemetery. The meeting, as this writer remembers, was similar to a Ford family reunion, with relatives who hadn't seen one another for months, or even years, anxious to chat.

Clara Ford devoted the next year and a half to planning how to protect the little Ford Cemetery for posterity. Her final decision was to purchase land enough adjacent to the cemetery to build an Episcopal church, including a parish hall, a rectory, and a sexton's house, to be called St. Martha's in honor of her mother. In June 1950, Clara Ford offered to the Episcopal Diocese of Michigan a gift of eight acres of land surrounding the cemetery, sufficient property in trust to raise $700,000 to be used in building a church and its future maintenance, and a perpetual trust valued at $300,000 derived from Ford Motor Company stock for maintenance of the cemetery and St. Martha's Church.

During 1949 and 1950, Clara Ford had given her architect, Arthur Hyde, and her personal secretary, H. Rex Waddell, detailed descriptions of the type of church she wanted. But she died on September 29, 1950, and did not live to witness the construction of St. Martha's Church. Groundbreaking ceremonies were held on June 22, 1952, and the church was dedicated in 1954. The Ford Cemetery, together with St. Martha's Church, is now under the jurisdiction of the Episcopal Diocese of Michigan. The cemetery is open to the public, and both church and cemetery can be seen readily on the south side of Joy Road a short distance west of Greenfield Road in Detroit.

References

Accession 1, Box 27, Fair Lane Papers. Benson Ford Research Center, HFM & GV.

Accession 23, Box 28, Henry Ford Office. Benson Ford Research Center, HFM & GV.

Accession 587, Box 15, Office of Henry and Clara Ford Estate. Benson Ford Research Center, HFM & GV.

Accession 1635, Ralph Laird Papers. Benson Ford Research Center, HFM & GV.

12

Great-grandmother Rebecca

Rebecca Jennings Ford (1776–1851) and William Ford (1775–1818) were ancestors of all the Fords of Dearborn — that is, all the many Fords related to the famous automotive Henry Ford. In Ireland between 1792 and 1811, Rebecca bore five sons: Samuel, John, Henry, Robert, and George — no daughters to our knowledge. William Ford died in Ireland in 1818 and was buried in the Kilnagross churchyard a few miles inland from Clonakilty. Following William Ford's death, Rebecca and her second son, John, in 1819 took over the land lease covering twenty-three acres for which 29 pounds, 2 shillings, 10 pence were payable each year. This property, with its small dry-stone cottage, had been leased by the Ford family for several generations. Their landlord's family, who had been granted thousands of acres of land by Queen Elizabeth in the 1600s, lived in a castle at Kilbrittain nearly ten miles away.

The first of Rebecca's sons came to America in 1832 from Crohane and Ballinascarthy in County Cork, Ireland. The group included her

This monument marks the burial sites of the George Ford family in Detroit's Grand Lawn Cemetery.

Among the many
individual
gravestones of the
George Ford family
is this one on the
grave of Rebecca
Jennings Ford.

eldest son, Samuel, age forty-two, with his wife, Nancy, and their four children: two sons and two daughters ranging in age from five to thirteen years. Also with them was Samuel's twenty-one-year-old brother, George, who was unmarried. Samuel is said to have been given some money by Rebecca to help finance the trip to America. This was not a famine year in Ireland, but Nancy, Samuel's wife, had heard from her relatives, the Smiths in Detroit's Corktown, that a common person could own land in Michigan at small expense. That was not possible in Ireland.

Upon arriving at Detroit, both sons purchased forest land on what is now Joy Road — Samuel in Dearborn Township, George across the township line in adjacent Greenfield Township. (This township line later became Division Road and still later Greenfield Road.) Samuel bought eighty acres, and George purchased forty acres that year. George acquired another forty acres the following year. The Samuel Ford family quickly established itself in the remote woods of Dearborn, while George is said to have worked awhile in 1832 as a hod carrier in Detroit before building a log cabin on his wooded land. Before the cabin was finished, George married Alice Good, a recently arrived Irish girl of about his own age.

After George had built the crude log cabin on his property, he sent to Detroit for Alice. He asked a local Indian chief, Tebow, who owned riding ponies, to bring his bride to the nearby Indian village (a service that in its time was equivalent to stretch-limousine service today). When Tebow and Alice arrived, all of the Indians chanted, "Tebow's new wife! Tebow's new wife!" This reception greatly frightened Alice

Kilnagross church in Ireland is where William Ford (1775–1818) is buried, near the church wall by the center window. Shown on this misty May 1992 day is Hazel Ford Buttimer (facing camera) in conversation with Roxanne LaChance of Dearborn, a descendant of William Ford.

until she saw George smiling in the crowd. And the ride with Tebow had been the first she had ever had on horseback.

Mabel N. Ford, a great-granddaughter of Samuel Ford, wrote a short history of these George Fords, which includes the following:

> George Ford had to cut down trees from which he built his house. After it had been erected his young wife had to gather moss to chink in the spaces between the logs to make it weatherproof. Not far from their home was a large village of Indians. They were no longer on the warpath, but the settlers were not too sure of that, and it was several years before they felt comfortable with these neighbors. One time Alice Ford saw the Indians; they had been skinning deer which they had slain in the nearby forest and their hands were red with blood. Mrs. Ford took one look at them and fainted. She told her children years later that she thought they were on a scalping party and had come to kill all the whites in the vicinity. However, if Mrs. Ford fainted at the sight of the Indians, that is the only occasion on record when she showed any weakness. She lived to the age of eighty-two and was never sick a day in her life until her final illness.
>
> If the house was crude and the woods were full of Indians, pioneer life had its compensations. The fields abounded with wild turkeys which provided plenty of game for the bill-of-fare, and if the Indians could kill deer, so could the whites. The wolves, however, were a nuisance, and in order to save their pigs and cattle from these roam-

ing marauders the Fords had to nail shut the doors of their barns at night — and for a long time had to take turns standing guard at night, gun in hand, so bold were the wolves.

George and Alice had their first child, William, in 1833, but he died as an infant. A daughter, Mary, was born in 1834, another daughter, Rebecca, in 1837. James was born in 1840. The 1840 Greenfield Township census lists the three children plus George, age twenty-nine, and Alice, age thirty.

This background about the George Ford family is pertinent because seven years later, in 1847, the next contingent of Fords came to Michigan from Ireland. These Fords came because of the terrible famine conditions in Ireland. The lease, upon which the family had depended for generations and under which Rebecca and John had labored for twenty-eight years, was finally given up. The leader of this group coming to America was John Ford, brother of Samuel and George, and Henry's grandfather. John Ford's wife, Tomasina Smith, sister of Samuel Ford's wife, Nancy Smith, died before reaching Québec on the passage to this country. John's children were Rebecca, William, Jane, Henry, Mary, Nancy, and Samuel. This William, age twenty-one, was Henry's father. Also coming with John and his family was Rebecca, the mother of Samuel, George, and John. She no longer had sons in Ireland and was now seventy-one. Although her name was Rebecca, it seems that in America she was always known as Mrs. Jennings.

John Ford, with his large family, had no home upon his arrival in 1847 but promptly bought land and began to build one of logs, with his son William (Henry's father) providing considerable help. But where was Rebecca to stay? Her son Samuel had died in 1842, and Samuel's wife, Nancy, was running that farm with her six children. So Rebecca elected to stay with her youngest son, George, and his wife, Alice, who were by this time well situated.

By the time Rebecca arrived, Michigan was a state, roads were beginning to be built, and the Indians were no longer a problem. She must have felt welcome because there were at least twenty-five of her grandchildren within a mile of the George Ford home, three of them named Rebecca, and also a one-year-old great-granddaughter named Rebecca. But wherever she stayed, it would have been crowded. Just as in Ireland, Rebecca now lived with a large family in a very small cabin. But these were of logs on land owned by her own family, whereas the Irish stone cottage would always belong to someone else.

The families of both Samuel and George worshipped at Mariner's Church in Detroit, and Rebecca attended with the George Fords. There is very little recorded about Rebecca other than her name on the 1850 Greenfield Township census and Mariner's Church records because she only lived in America for four years.

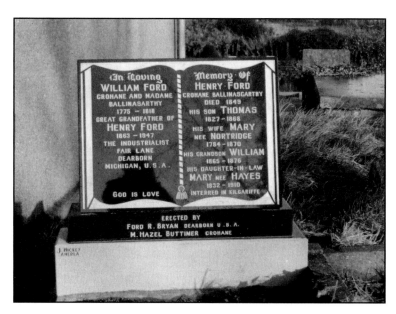

On the Ford plot in Kilnagross churchyard is this black granite stone, which has now been placed to mark the graves of early Fords. On the left half of the booklike marker is the inscription pertaining to William Ford, great-grandfather of Henry Ford of Dearborn. The marker faces the pathway leading into the church.

When Rebecca died in 1851, she was buried in the small cemetery on Samuel Ford's property along with Samuel and, over time, other Fords including George and Alice. But in the early twentieth century, there was much concern regarding the permanency and desirability of small private and parochial cemeteries such as the little Ford Cemetery on Joy Road near Greenfield. On July 3, 1919, Rebecca's grandson George (1845–1925) purchased Lots 82 and 83, Section 4, of Grand Lawn Cemetery for $1,102.80; and on October 16, 1919, ten reburials were recorded. These included "Grandma" Rebecca Jennings, "Father" George Ford, and "Mother" Alice Ford, all of whom had been removed from the Ford Cemetery on Joy Road by Northrup Funeral Home of Detroit.

A large upright marble stone bearing the name Ford now dominates these lots in Grand Lawn Cemetery. Arranged in an arc facing the stone are flat ground-level markers for twelve graves including those marked "Grandma/1776–1851," "Mother/1810–1893," and "Father/ 1811–1863." The names of Rebecca, Alice, and George do not appear on the markers. The grandson's own marker is "George/1845–1925," and his wife's marker is "Alice/1846–1916."

Great-grandmother
Rebecca

Only recently has the burial location of William Ford, Rebecca's husband, of whom we know essentially nothing but who is nonetheless father of all the Dearborn Fords, been verified in Kilnagross churchyard in Ireland, and in January 1995, his grave was marked with an appropriate stone. The inscription reads: "In Loving Memory of William Ford, Crohane and Madame, Ballinascarthy, 1775–1818, Great Grandfather of Henry Ford, 1863–1947, The Industrialist, Fair Lane, Dearborn, Michigan, U.S.A."

References

Accession 1, Box 1, Fair Lane Papers, Henry Ford Genealogy. Benson Ford Research Center, HFM & GV.

Accession 23, Box 28, Henry Ford Office—General, Folder 4. Benson Ford Research Center, HFM & GV.

Burial records of Grand Lawn Cemetery, 23501 Grand River Avenue, Detroit, Michigan.

Conversations with Hazel Ford Buttimer. Crohane, Ballinascarthy, Clonakilty, County Cork, Ireland.

Nevins, Allan. *Ford: The Times, the Man, the Company*. New York: Scribner's, 1954, pp. 32, 34, 592.

13
Great-uncle Robert

The Ford family tree as drawn by Raymond H. Laird in 1925–26 has a main branch missing: the family of Robert Ford. There were four Ford brothers who came to America from Ireland in the mid-nineteenth century. They were Samuel, George, John, and Robert. John was Henry's grandfather. The families of Samuel, George, and John are well documented. The family of Robert, however, has incomplete documentation in the Ford Archives in Dearborn. There are but thirty unbound sheets pertaining to Robert Ford's family. None of Robert's family came to Dearborn, to our knowledge, although some were as close as Owosso, Michigan, between 1880 and 1910.

Although we know relatively little about the Robert Ford family, what information we have is quite interesting. Robert was born in Ireland in 1803, the son of William Ford and Rebecca Jennings. He is said to have worked as an "interior decorator" in Ireland. He married Jane Elisha Hornibrook in Cork, Ireland, on December 15, 1827. In Ireland, Robert and Jane had four children: Mary Ann, Henry, Robert, and Stephen. Mary Ann was born in 1831, and her brothers also were born in Ireland.

The entire Robert Ford family came to America with John Ford's family in 1847. The two families landed in Québec, Canada, but whereas John and his family moved on to Michigan and Dearborn, the Robert Fords settled near Québec. There, Robert and Jane's eldest daughter, Mary Ann, married an Irishman, Robert Bagley, in 1849 and, between 1850 and 1864, had seven children in Standon, Canada, near Québec. These children later moved to upper Michigan and out west to Montana, Washington, and Oregon. Mary Ann died on November 29, 1909, and is buried at Owosso, Michigan.

But none of the three brothers of Mary Ann has been traced. So we are missing perhaps three-quarters of the Robert Ford branch of the family tree. And if it was difficult for Laird to locate these missing Fords in 1925, it is next to impossible now. So what follows here is a glimpse of some of the records of the Mary Ann Ford Bagley branch of the

Previously published in the *Dearborn Historian,* Vol. 38, No. 1, 1998.

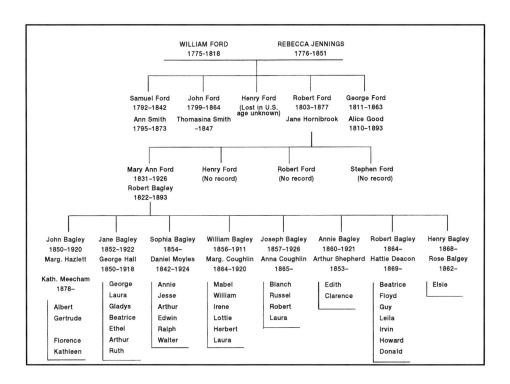

Robert Ford family. The prominent names are not Ford at all but include Bagley, Hall, Shepherd, and Moyles.

John Bagley, Mary Ann's eldest son, married Margaret Hazlett at Tacoma, Washington, in 1876. The couple had two children, Albert and Gertrude. John Bagley became vice president and general manager of the Tacoma Eastern Railroad, president of the Cascade & Mineral Lake Lumber Company, president of the Bagley Grader Company, and director of the National Bank of Tacoma. This same John Bagley married Katherine Meecham in 1904 at fifty-four years of age. Another two children, Florence and Kathleen, were born of this second marriage. John Bagley died in 1920 and is buried in Tacoma.

Mary Ann's daughter, Jane Bagley, married George Hall in 1881 at Calumet, Michigan. Hall became a contractor, road and railroad builder, and councilman of the village of Laurium, Michigan. The Halls had seven children. In 1891, the family seems to have been struck by a devastating plague. Four of the seven children, between the ages of one and eight, died in less than a year. George Hall died in 1918, Jane in 1922.

George Hall, Jr., who survived the tragedy of 1891, grew up to marry Bertha Palmer of Exeter, Michigan, in November 1917 at Detroit. Young George took up his father's business of road building and contracting, with jobs in Bessemer and Negaunee, Michigan, before becoming an insurance agent in Calumet. There were three children in the family: William, Robert, and Alfred.

Gladys Hall, the second surviving child of the Calumet tragedy, graduated from the University of Michigan School of Music in 1907 and married John D. Kerr in 1911 at Laurium. Kerr was a successful lawyer. The Kerrs had no children, according to Dearborn records.

The youngest of the Hall children of Calumet was Ruth, born in 1894. She graduated from the Oberlin Kindergarten Training School in 1915 and from the Laurium Commercial School in 1918. Ruth stayed at home until shortly after her widowed mother, Jane, died in June 1922. In September of that same year, she married Peter Sandstrom, who is noted as having been a corporal of the 310th Ammunition Train, 151st Infantry. The couple was living in Mankato, Minnesota, when their daughter, Elizabeth Jane, was born in 1924.

Among prominent descendants of the Robert Bagley line are people by the name of Moyles. Sophia Bagley, born in 1854 in Québec, daughter of Mary Ann Ford and Robert Bagley, married Daniel H. Moyles, also of Québec, in 1877. This couple had six children born between 1883 and 1894 in Owosso, Michigan. These were Emma, Jessie, Arthur, Edwin, Ralph, and Walter. In 1925, when Laird requested information, Jesse, Arthur, and Walter lived in Tacoma, Washington; Edwin in Portland, Oregon; and Ralph in Cedar Falls, Washington. These children, in turn, listed seven of their own children in those locations.

The above notes are representative of the information contained on the thirty genealogical sheets collected from seventeen separate sources by Laird. There are a total of about 135 names listed. Most have dates of birth as of 1925 but not dates of death. Now, however, even the youngest listed would be nearly one hundred years of age and without a known address.

References

Accession 1, Box 1, Fair Lane Papers, Henry Ford Genealogy. Benson Ford Research Center, HFM & GV.

Accession 23, Box 27, Henry Ford Office—General, Bagley Folder. Benson Ford Research Center, HFM & GV.

Accession 23, Box 28, Henry Ford Office—General, Bagley Correspondence. Benson Ford Research Center, HFM & GV.

14
Brother John

John Ford, born February 4, 1865, in the Ford homestead in Springwells Township at the southeast corner of Ford Road and Greenfield, was the son of William Ford (1826–1905) and Mary Litogot Ford (1839–1875). John was named after his grandfather John Ford (1799–1864), who came to America from Ireland in 1847 during the Irish potato famine. John never knew his grandfather or his grandmother, Tomasina Smith Ford, who died at sea on her way to America.

Although two years younger than his brother Henry, John led a considerably different style of life. Of the two, Henry, because of his age, was the leader. From the beginning, John was subject to the will of Henry, just as a generation later Benson Ford would be subject to the will of Henry Ford II. Henry and John attended the same elementary schools and played with the same group of children, but there is little recorded about John, whereas every trivial move of Henry during that period is immortalized.

John attended the Scotch Settlement and Miller grade schools with his siblings Henry, Margaret, Jane, and William Jr. John was only eleven years old when his mother died. This was a severe shock to the whole family because Mary Litogot Ford was only thirty-nine years old. John's sister Margaret, who was only nine years old, was forced to carry a great deal more responsibility in their home. After elementary school, John attended a business school in Detroit, probably the popular Goldsmith, Bryant & Stratton Business University that Henry briefly attended. When John was about twenty-five years old and William Jr. about nineteen, the two of them together operated a milk and egg route in Detroit. The newly married Henry and Clara Ford were among their Detroit customers.

John's father, William Sr., owned about 230 acres by the time the children were grown. Henry had been promised the use of the eighty-acre Moir farm by William Sr. in 1887, hoping to induce Henry to become a farmer rather than a mechanic. In 1896, William Sr. prepared his will. In it, he willed the forty acres with the homestead to William Jr., the youngest, who was still living there and working the farm. John Ford was to have the forty acres directly east of the homestead. John paid the 1896 taxes on this property.

John Ford, brother
of Henry Ford, in a
formal portrait taken
in 1895, two years
before his marriage
to Mary Ward.
(188.25665)

In 1897, at age thirty-two, John Ford married Mary J. Ward, daughter of William M. Ward, a well-known Dearborn Township resident. Mary Ward was then only twenty years old, and yet she is said to have been born in a log cabin. John and Mary built a new frame house on the Chase Road about one-quarter mile east of the Ford homestead. This address later became 5265 Chase Road in the city of Fordson. A son, Robert W. Ford, was born in 1897; another son, Clarence W. Ford, in 1899; and later a daughter, Ethel M. Ford.

John had immediately become a dairy farmer, working the forty acres in typical farming fashion. And as late as 1917, he was paying taxes on the entire forty acres.

With the construction of the River Rouge plant of Ford Motor Company, the city of Fordson was created, and land for housing was at a premium. Starting in 1917, John Ford subdivided his forty-acre farm, with the exception of his three-acre residence, and began to sell it off as

Mary Ward and John Ford, Henry's brother, about the time of their marriage, which took place in 1897. Henry probably took this photograph. The John Fords lived on the Dearborn land inherited from William throughout their married lives but were not particularly intimate with Henry and Clara. John operated a real estate business and was a Dearborn city councilman at the time of his death in 1927. John and Mary Ford are buried in Grand Lawn Cemetery in Detroit. (0.1122)

lots. He then became a partner in the firm of Castle and Ford, Inc. In the business of real estate, he is said to have become a millionaire in his own right. As a gentleman farmer, John had become active in Springwells politics; later, as a businessman, he was active in Fordson politics. Besides being president and a longtime member of the Fordson City Council, he also met with the Wayne County Board of Supervisors. He was a member of the board of directors of the Wayne County and Home Bank of Fordson. In 1927, he was appointed by Governor Fred W. Green as a member of the board of managers of the Michigan State Fair.

In 1927, John's oldest son, Robert, obtained a Ford car dealership in Fordson. According to the Fordson City Directory for 1927, Robert's dealership was located at 13469 Michigan Avenue, and working with him were his younger brother, Clarence, and his sister, Ethel. John and

John Ford (left) with his brother Henry. This photograph was taken shortly before John's untimely death in September 1927 at age sixty-two. (P.O.18206)

Mary Ford were still living in their original home at 5265 Chase Road at that time.

Also in 1927, at age sixty-two, John Ford was stricken by a heart attack on September 27. He had attended a city council meeting that evening and was overcome on his way home from the meeting. He had managed to reach an unoccupied house that he owned, and there he was found dead on a bed. Funeral services were held at his home on Chase Road, and burial was in Grand Lawn Cemetery in Detroit. John is the only one of William Ford, Sr.'s children who is not buried in the Ford Cemetery.

John Ford's attendance record at council meetings indicates that he had probably gone south during the winters of 1926 and 1927. He was absent from meetings from January until May. During the summer of 1927, he was present on most occasions, and in September, the month he died, he was present at each of the four weekly sessions. On the day he died, the council handled problems concerning water mains, gas mains, street lighting, fire and police pensions, and city bonds.

Mary Ward in the chair and John Ford, Henry's brother, standing beside her, pose for this formal photograph taken at the time of their marriage in 1895. (P.O.8391)

On September 29, 1927, John W. Smith, mayor of Detroit, sent the following letter:

To the Honorable the Common Council
Fordson, Michigan

Gentlemen:

As the Mayor of the neighboring City of Detroit, I wish to express to you my grief at the sudden death of John Ford, a member of your Honorable Body and a leading citizen of Fordson.

Mr. Ford was my friend and in knowing him I can appreciate the loss that Fordson has suffered. Your City has been deprived by death of one who was a great force for good, a man whose place will never be filled.

Sincerely,
John W. Smith
Mayor

After a respectable period, on October 11, 1927, John's son Clarence was appointed by the Fordson City Council to fill his father's vacancy.

John and Mary's son Robert became more widely known than his father. The Bob Ford dealership at 14585 Michigan Avenue in Dearborn was said to be the largest Ford dealership in the world in the 1930s and 1940s. It handled Ford cars, Fordson tractors, and Ford trucks. The Ford buses used by the city of Detroit are said to have been purchased through Robert Ford's agency. This dealership is still in business at the same location and is known as Fairlane Ford, but it is no longer the property of the Robert Ford family.

After the death of John Ford, Mary Ward Ford resided at 5261 Orchard Street, only a stone's throw away from their original home and the home of her daughter, Ethel. On February 27, 1932, after an illness of only one week, Mary died at her daughter's residence. She was fifty-six years old.

There is very little information concerning the John Ford family in the archives of Henry Ford Museum & Greenfield Village. The survey of Ford family members sponsored by Henry Ford in 1925–26 contains an insignificant amount about the families of either John or William Ford, Jr. John's family, in particular, was not close to Henry and Clara. There is no record of Henry's ever needing to help John directly. Clara is quoted as having once stated that she did not want any other Ford than Henry to be prominent in the community. The families of John and William Jr. are not known to have visited the Henry Fords at Fair Lane; Henry managed to see his Ford relatives elsewhere.

References

Accession 1, Box 33, copy of will of William Ford, Sr., June 10, 1896. Benson Ford Research Center, HFM & GV.

Accession 23, Box 3, John Ford Obituary, *Detroit Times*, September 28, 1927. Benson Ford Research Center, HFM & GV.

Accession 23, Box 27, John Ford Genealogical Records. Benson Ford Research Center, HFM & GV.

Bryan, Ford R. *The Fords of Dearborn*. Detroit: Harlo Press, 1987.

Detroit City Directory, 1896–1905.

Fordson City Directory, 1927–1932.

Mary J. Ford obituary. *Dearborn Press*, March 3, 1932. Dearborn Historical Museum.

15
Sisters Margaret and Jane

Margaret Ford was born on August 14, 1867, in the Ford homestead on the southeast corner of what are now Greenfield and Ford Roads in Springwells Township, Michigan. Her father, William, was then forty-two years of age, and her mother, Mary, was twenty-eight. Margaret had two older brothers: John, who was two, and Henry, who was four. Two years later, Margaret would have a sister, Jane; four years later a brother, William; and six years later a brother, Robert. A baby boy, stillborn in 1861, had not been named.

Also living in the Ford household were Mary Ford's foster parents, Patrick and Margaret Ahern, who had earlier built the house and owned the land. It is very likely that Margaret Ford was named after her foster grandmother, Margaret Ahern, who would die in 1870 when Margaret was three years old. Her grandfather Patrick lived with the William Ford family until 1881, when Margaret would have been fourteen. All of the five Ford children knew Patrick well, and Henry especially idolized him.

Margaret was nicknamed Maggie by the time she entered the one-room Scotch Settlement School, walking there with her two older brothers a distance of a mile north and a half mile west from their home. Although Henry has had a lot to say about his schooling and tried his own hand at establishing more progressive educational institutions, Margaret and her other two brothers have had little to say about their education.

Margaret was only nine years old and Jane was seven when tragedy struck the family on March 29, 1876. Mary Litogot Ford, their beloved mother, died of complications resulting from the birth of a seventh child, a son. To manage the household temporarily, William arranged for his sister Rebecca Flaherty's twenty-year-old daughter, Jane, to stay with them and do the housework. Margaret and Jane Flaherty worked together well; Margaret stated afterward that Jane had become like a sister to them. But it wasn't long before Jane Flaherty left and Margaret was in charge of the house with her younger sister helping.

Then, as if losing their mother wasn't enough, tragedy struck the family again in 1877 when four-year-old Robert died. The specific reason for Robert's death is obscure.

Taken by Henry Ford with his new camera in 1896, this photograph shows the family standing in the middle of Ford Road and in front of the homestead. At the far left is Henry's jovial sister Jane, who has the dog in front of her doing a trick that is very amusing to three-year-old Edsel. Henry's sister Margaret stands next to Jane. Neither of Henry's sisters was married at this time, and they were staying at the farm. Clara is keeping Edsel in place with her gloved hands on his shoulders, and William, at the right, appears to be questioning the photographic procedure. Henry, Clara, and Edsel may have driven out to the farm from Detroit on the Quadricycle. (P.O.972)

Margaret remembers that their father, William,

was a strict disciplinarian, but not harsh. He had a sense of humor and enjoyed a prank now and then. He allowed cards to be played in the evening on the dining room table, but if the games became too noisy and there was bickering, William, lying on the couch in the sitting

Henry's sister Margaret (Maggie) was four years younger than Henry. When their mother died in 1876, Margaret was nine years old and pressed into housekeeping work, helping her cousin Jane Flaherty, a hired girl. She lived with her father until she was thirty-two, when she married James Ruddiman, a brother of Henry's classmate Edsel Ruddiman. They had a daughter named Catherine in 1903. James died in 1909 at age forty-four. From that time on, Henry and Clara Ford made certain that Margaret and her daughter lived comfortably. Margaret died in Dearborn in 1960. (P.O.3184)

room, would say, "Time for bed." They all knew that meant no more cards for that evening.

The Ford children attended the Scotch Settlement School in Dearborn Township most of the time but for a year or so switched to the Miller School in Springwells Township to follow one of their favorite teachers, John Chapman. This their father allowed them to do because their house straddled the township line, and they were therefore residents of both Springwells and Dearborn school districts.

James Ernest Ruddiman (1860-1909) about the time of his marriage to Margaret Ford on November 7, 1900. James had a younger brother, Edsel A. Ruddiman (1866–1947), who had been a schoolmate and lifelong friend of Margaret's brother, Henry Ford. (0.7192)

In 1896, William Ford prepared a will leaving the homestead with forty acres to William Jr., the forty acres across the road to Margaret, and twenty acres next to Margaret's to Jane. About that time, Margaret was attending the Liggett School for Girls, a boarding school on Cass Avenue in Detroit. She returned home to the farm on weekends. Margaret was always tall, slender, and somewhat dignified. Jane was also tall, not so slender, and rather jovial. Jane liked to cook and liked to eat.

In late 1897, William Sr. retired from the farm and moved with Margaret and Jane into Detroit, renting a house at 582 West Grand Boulevard. Margaret began to take lessons in embroidery, a fashionable occupation in that day. Jane, who was not too well, helped with the housework and shopping. Henry, Clara, and seven-year-old Edsel moved in with them in January 1901 to save expenses. Henry was then struggling desperately to gain a foothold in the automobile business.

On November 7, 1900, Margaret had married James Ernest Ruddiman, a former schoolmate of the Ford children and son of William and Catherine Ruddiman, Dearborn Township pioneers.

James was an older brother of Henry Ford's classmate Edsel A. Ruddiman, after whom Edsel B. Ford, Henry's son, was named. James Ruddiman was seven years older than Margaret Ford. Following their marriage, sixty acres of land and the Ruddiman farmhouse became theirs. On November 23, 1902, their only child, Mary Catherine Ruddiman, was born. Their daughter went by the name of Catherine, the name of her grandmother.

Jane continued to stay with her father, William, and together they moved to 338 Hendrie Avenue in December 1901 to be close to Henry and Clara, who had moved into their own flat at 332 Hendrie Avenue in November. Henry had won his very first auto race in October of that year and was feeling quite important. He is said to have been noticeably annoyed at William's habit of coming over to see him and expecting to sit and talk as in earlier days.

While at the Hendrie address, William died on March 8, 1905. What became of Jane following the death of her father is not clear. In September 1906, records show a large medical bill from a Christopher Campbell, M.D., of 318 West Grand Boulevard. The bill had been sent to "Miss Jane Ford, 177 Joseph Campau Ave." and was paid on October 10. The Joseph Campau address is listed in the Detroit City Directory for 1906 as a boarding house operated by Ernest G. and Ida Gearhart. Jane died on November 26, 1906, at age thirty-seven. She is recorded as having died from hemiplegia. She is buried in the Ford Cemetery, but her grave is unmarked.

Margaret's husband, James, was not well and was having difficulty doing his farm work. His brother Edsel, a college professor, was spending summers on the Ruddiman farm helping James. About 1908, James Ruddiman became too ill to work the farm. He and his family spent the winter in San Diego, California, returning to Michigan in early 1909. They lived in the "Square House," built in 1890 by Henry and Clara Ford, until James's death from heart failure on August 5, 1909, at age fifty. Undertakers V. Geist & Son of Detroit handled the funeral, and Henry Ford paid the bill of $263.20. James Ernest Ruddiman was buried in Evergreen Cemetery on Warren Avenue between Greenfield and Southfield Roads. The farm was rented out by Margaret, and she and Catherine were invited to live with Henry and Clara at 66 Edison Avenue in Detroit until a new home for them was built nearby at 120 Glynn Court.

Margaret and Catherine stayed at their Glynn Court address in Detroit until 1920. The farm by then had been subdivided and sold as lots. Catherine graduated from Detroit Northern High School and then Connecticut College in New London in 1924. Both she and Margaret moved to Boston, Massachusetts, and spent some time at Wayside Inn, which had been acquired in 1923 by Henry and Clara. The Ruddimans

On the right is Margaret Ford Ruddiman, and on the left is Nancy Turner Ford. Nancy is the wife of Wallace Ford, a first cousin of Margaret and the mother of Grace, Mabel, and Olive Ford. They are attending the 1951 wedding of Ann Elizabeth Davis, a descendant of Margaret's aunt Nancy Ford, in Northville, Michigan. (0.7193)

Mary Catherine Ruddiman (1902–1992), daughter of James and Margaret Ford Ruddiman. This photograph was taken in 1986 when she was living in Florida. Although her name was Mary Catherine, she preferred Catherine, the name of her grandmother, Catherine Ruddiman. (0.7195)

returned to Detroit in 1928 and resided on Longacre Street in the subdivision formed from their former farm.

During the summer of 1940, Henry became interested in restoring the old Ruddiman farmhouse. He didn't plan to put it in Greenfield Village but instead assigned his Village architect, Edward Cutler, to build a solid brick home for Margaret, making use of the original bricks, fireplace mantel, solid walnut banister, and other valuable items from the original home. Margaret and Catherine moved into this new home at 154 River Lane, Dearborn, in 1941. The property was deeded by Henry and Clara Ford to Margaret and Catherine Ruddiman on November 9, 1944, "for and in consideration of the sum of one dollar and other valuable considerations."

Henry Ford had supported Margaret and Catherine to a conservative degree ever since the death of James Ruddiman in 1909. And after

Henry died in April 1947, Clara, in October of the same year, provided *Sisters Margaret* Margaret and Catherine with an annuity that paid them $150 a month *and Jane* as long as either of them survived. Margaret and Catherine lived at 154 River Lane in Dearborn until Margaret's death on March 1, 1960, at age ninety-two. Margaret Ford Ruddiman is buried next to Henry Ford in the Ford Cemetery.

Catherine lived at 154 River Lane until 1981, when she sold the home and moved to an apartment in Boca Raton, Florida. She returned to Dearborn in 1990 to reside at Oakbrook Common, a retirement village. She died there on December 30, 1992, at age ninety. She is buried next to her mother in the Ford Cemetery.

References

Accession 1, Box 33, copy of will of William Ford, Sr., dated June 10, 1896. Benson Ford Research Center, HFM & GV.

Bryan, Ford R. *The Fords of Dearborn*. Detroit: Harlo Press, 1987.

Margaret Ford Ruddiman obituary. *Dearborn Press*, March 2, 1960.

"Mary Ruddiman Dies." *Dearborn Times-Herald,* December 30, 1992.

Ruddiman, Catherine. *Henry Ford: Boy with Ideas*. New York: Bobbs-Merrill, 1960.

———. "The William Ruddiman Family and the Ruddiman Farmhouse." May 1, 1984. (Copy at the Dearborn Historical Museum.)

Ruddiman, Margaret Ford. "Memories of My Brother Henry Ford." *Michigan History,* Michigan Historical Commission, September 1953.

16
Brother Will

Will Ford has been described as having lived in the shadow of Henry. But Will Ford was anything but a shadowy figure. He was considered to be an upright, straightforward gentleman, less glorified but perhaps better liked by many locals than Henry.

William Ford, Jr., was born on July 14, 1871, in the Ford homestead at the corner of Ford Road and Greenfield, in the house Henry Ford would move to Greenfield Village in 1941. Very little has been written about the boyhood of William Jr., the youngest of the five children of William Ford, Sr., and Mary Litogot Ford.

William Jr., called Will, lived at the homestead fully twice as long as did his brother Henry. Will stayed on the farm, working the land with his father, until after he married Frances Ann Reed of Redford Township on October 27, 1897. That same year, William Sr. retired and moved into a Detroit apartment, taking his two unmarried daughters, Margaret and Jane, with him. Henry at this time was married and working for the Edison Illuminating Company in Detroit.

While farming at the homestead, Will and Frances had two sons, Lewis W. on February 25, 1899, and Burnham T. on February 19, 1902. Also while at the homestead, W. D. Ford was operating a business. His stationery in 1899 read: "Dealer in All Kinds of Farm Machinery." Will Ford stayed at the homestead until 1903, when the house had to be moved several hundred feet to the east to allow Greenfield Road to be extended southward to Michigan Avenue. At that time, Henry Ford took possession of the house and farm while Will and Frances moved into Detroit to the corner of what is now Tireman and Scotten Avenues.

The Detroit City Directory in 1904 lists William D. Ford as an "engineer" living at the Holden-Scotten address. He is said to have been working at the Detroit Lubricator Company, first as a machinist and later in sales. Will seems to have continued in the farm implement business to an extent during this period.

Previously published in the *Dearborn Historian*, Vol. 32, No. 4, 1992.

Henry took this photograph at the Ford Homestead in 1896. From left to right are Margaret, Henry's sister; Jane, his other sister, holding Edsel; Will Ford, Henry's brother, who was working the farm; and Clara, who appears to be eating some grapes. This is definitely a candid shot; the photographer does not have their attention at all. Will's playful dog in front of Clara may have been the attraction. (0.1112)

On January 15, 1906, twin girls, Mary Ellen and Myra Frances, were born to the Will Fords. Mary Ellen died only three months later. In 1907, a William D. Ford is listed as living on the south side of Larchmont Avenue west of Grand River Avenue. On July 10, 1910, Edith Margaret Ford was born.

In 1912, William D. Ford is listed as a "farmer" living on Grand River Avenue. He was operating farm threshing machinery in the Dearborn area. He had two or three threshing crews with steam traction engines, separators, and water wagons making the rounds each summer. As Henry Ford began farming in this area, Will did threshing for him and by 1914 sold his equipment to Henry and became superintendent of Ford Farms, a position he held until 1921.

From about 1907, Henry Ford had been experimenting with gasoline farm tractors. Both Will and Lewis became especially interested in the development of the Fordson tractor in 1915. Along with his job as farm superintendent, Will was put in charge of the service department at the tractor plant on Elm Street in Dearborn, and Lewis Ford became a tractor test driver. The family moved into the village of Dearborn in 1916. Charles Sorensen, superintendent of the tractor plant, judged Will as being too generous with his services; his department was spending too much. Will was then made employment manager at the tractor plant, a position he kept for about two years. When World War I was over and Fordson tractors were in great demand, Will and Lewis obtained the Fordson tractor distributorship for sections of Michigan, Ohio, and Indiana. Their business was the William Ford Tractor Sales Company with headquarters on Monroe Avenue in Dearborn.

But on February 16, 1919, Lewis died at age nineteen, presumably from an attack of influenza. Burnham, age sixteen, was graduating from high school that year and joined his father, Will, in the tractor distribution business.

Because Ford Motor Company sold tractors without implements, Will acted as wholesale distributor of implements as well as tractors. Some of these plows, cultivators, seeders, and binders he kept in storage, but most were ordered from manufacturers to be delivered to Fordson dealers (Ford car dealers), who sold the tractor-implement combinations to the farmers.

In 1922, Will was quite a man-about-town. He was both president of Dearborn and its chief of police. He was described in a local newspaper as being "the biggest man in town and the best liked. . . . He knows every one of the 2000 people in Dearborn and calls everybody by his first name and never gets puffed up over his brother's riches."

Will Ford founded the Oddfellows Dearborn Lodge in 1918, later served as president of the board of the Jackson Oddfellows Home for twenty-five years, and was also active in the Dearborn Masonic Lodge. In addition to his tractor and implement dealership, Will operated an artificial ice plant near the railroad depot. Burnham often worked the night shift at the ice plant. The Will Fords then lived at 146 Garrison Avenue.

In 1924, Burnham Ford, in partnership with a close friend, Thad Moon, and with the help of his father, purchased the Ford dealership in Flat Rock, Michigan. Burnham operated this dealership until 1933, when he could not meet the combined interest and principal payments due on a mortgage held by Dearborn State Bank, owned by Henry Ford. Neither Ernest Liebold, president of the bank, nor Henry Ford would accept any less than the full amount due. The dealership was lost, and Burnham took a position as sales manager for the Wayne, Michigan, Ford dealer.

Will Ford, in 1926, with assurances from Henry Ford that tractor production would be steady for years, organized an expanded operation

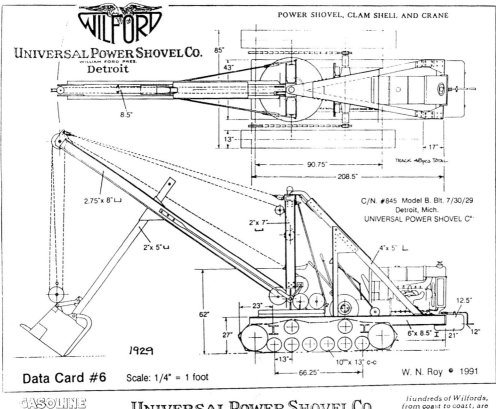

A page from a brochure advertising William Ford's "Universal Power Shovel" powered by a Fordson tractor engine.

at 15841 Second Boulevard in Highland Park, Michigan, very close to the Ford Motor Company plant. This new business was the Universal Power Shovel Company with William Ford as president, D. Harrison Miller as vice president, and Frank Temple as secretary-treasurer. The business was not incorporated, and Will had invested heavily with his own money. It consisted of manufacturing and selling power shovels, clam shells, and cranes with the trade name Wilford. These machines employed Fordson tractor power plants for operation.

The daughters, Myra and Edith, were now grown, and in 1928, Myra is listed as an accountant and Edith as a teacher. Frances Ford, fondly known as Frankie, managed a wholesome domestic establishment. She was not particularly prominent socially but was well known and very well liked. The Will Fords seldom saw Henry to talk to him, but when he was trying to restore the homestead to its early condition, they were visited often by Henry in his anxiety to obtain from them

Henry Ford's younger brother William, on the left, with Henry at a tractor convention in Dearborn in 1940, promoting the Ford tractor with "Wheel-Less Implements." Will was then sixty-nine and Henry seventy-seven years old. Will was in the farm implement business in 1903, several years before Henry had developed his tractor. (188.27022)

pieces of original homestead furniture. Otherwise, their contacts were said to have been sightings at weddings or funerals.

Also in 1928, with little warning, Fordson tractor production was transferred to Cork, Ireland. Without Fordson power for his products, Will was in big trouble, and by 1929, the Universal Power Shovel Company was bankrupt. Will's relatives were amazed that the brother of Henry Ford could be bankrupt, but such was the case. Very much out of character, Will was forced to default on debts to some of his very good friends.

It was not Henry but Edsel Ford who, in 1930, came to Will's rescue. Edsel asked Will if he wanted to get back into the tractor implement business, arranged a drawing account at Manufacturers National Bank, and suggested a group of financial experts, employees of Ford Motor Company, as consultants to the business. This new William Ford Tractor Sales Company was located at 6405 Schaefer Road in Dearborn. Officers were William Ford, president; B. J. Craig, vice president; H. L. Moekle, secretary-treasurer; and Marshall T. Allen, assistant secretary-treasurer. It is not known whether Edsel helped Will independently of Henry or whether Henry instructed Edsel to assist Will.

The Edsel Ford bank loan is said to have been paid back in two years, but the tractor business could not have been very brisk during these depression times because the 1934 Dearborn directory lists William Ford as crew manager at Robert W. Ford Sales and Burnham Ford as a salesman at that same dealership owned by Will's brother John's boy, Robert.

Headquarters of the William Ford Sales Company had moved to 14401 Ford Road by 1936, with Marshall T. Allen as manager. By 1940,

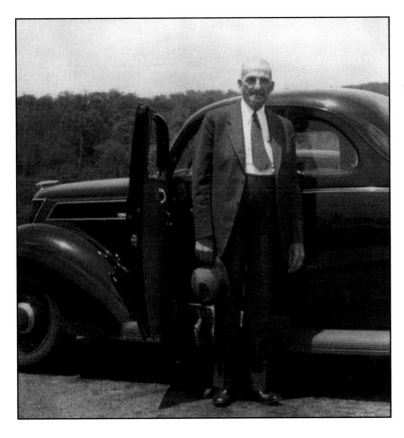

William Ford, Jr., vacationed with his wife, Frances, in the Eastern Mountains during the summer of 1937. (P.O.7196)

Brother Will	the company had become the Ford-Allen Company, Tractor and Implement Distributors. Will and Frances Ford themselves had moved from their Garrison Avenue home in Dearborn to their 500-acre farm on Pleasant Valley Road near Brighton, Michigan, in 1937. They were on their farm when Henry Ford died in 1947. The Ford-Allen Company was still operating in 1948, with William H. Breech as president. He was the son of Ford Motor Company's president Ernest R. Breech.

Will Ford died at the Whitehall Convalescent Home in Brighton on May 6, 1959, at age eighty-seven. Surviving him were Frances, Burnham, and the two daughters, Myra Hendry and Edith Roth. At that date, the Will Fords had four grandchildren and three great-grandchildren.

Frances Reed Ford died in 1965, followed by Burnham in 1978, Edith in 1986, and Myra in 1995. All are buried in the northwest corner of the Ford Cemetery.

References

Accession 1, Box 173, Fair Lane Papers. Benson Ford Research Center, HFM & GV.

Accession 65, Reminiscences, Burnham Ford (son of William). Benson Ford Research Center, HFM & GV.

Accession 65, Reminiscences, E. G. Liebold. Benson Ford Research Center, HFM & GV.

Accession 285, Box 439, Henry Ford Office, Folder N-S 588. Benson Ford Research Center, HFM & GV.

Accession 351, Box 1, William Ford Tractor Sales Company, Corporate Papers. Benson Ford Research Center, HFM & GV.

Bryan, Ford R. *The Fords of Dearborn.* Detroit: Harlo Press, 1987.

Dearborn City Directories, 1916-1937.

Detroit City Directories, 1904-1916.

17
The Litogots

The Litogot name, as influential in Henry Ford's bloodline as the Ford name, has been difficult to trace. It is known that Henry's grandfather William Litogot had settled in the vicinity of Taylor Township, Michigan, considerably before the Civil War. From whence he came, however, is not at all clear. Henry went to great lengths to find Litogots in Europe but could not locate individuals with that exact name. The consensus, however, is that the name is associated with either Holland or Belgium.

Henry Ford's mother was born Mary Litogot, probably in the year 1840. We know her father's name was William Litogot, but we do not know her mother's name, birthdate, or date of death. William and his wife had four children: Saphara (1832), John (1835), Barney (1838), and Mary (1840). The death of their mother is thought to have taken place soon after Mary's birth. In 1842, William was killed in an accident while hauling logs with oxen from their farm into Detroit. He drowned when the ice broke while getting the load across the Rouge River. At that time, without either parent, the three orphaned boys were apparently taken care of by relatives or friends, and Mary was put into the care of Patrick and Margaret Ahern, who lived on a farm in Dearborn Township. The Aherns are said to have been looking for a child, and with the help of Hanna Flowers, who was acquainted with both the Litogots and the Aherns, Mary was adopted in 1843.

The life of Mary Ahern, her attendance at the Scotch Settlement School, her marriage to William Ford, and their five children who grew to adulthood (Henry, John, Margaret, Jane, and William) are well documented. Mary died following another childbirth in 1876, a serious blow to Henry, then age thirteen. His reverence for his mother rather than his father and his insistence that the homestead farm belonged to his mother, not his father, show his attachment to the Litogot side of the family. In Henry's mind, the Litogot family did not at all fade from the scene with the death of his mother, Mary Litogot Ahern.

Saphara, Mary's eldest brother, was a farmer and also followed the trade of carpenter. He married Lethera Brown in the early 1850s, and they had at least six children: Charles, Inez, Abner, Mina, Rachel, and

This is said to be the only picture of Henry Ford's mother, Mary; Henry apparently searched in vain for others. Mary Litogot was left as an orphan with her three brothers in 1842 when she was almost three years old. She was adopted by Margaret and Patrick Ahern, a childless couple living in a log cabin on a 91-acre Dearborn Township farm. Mary attended the Scotch Settlement School one mile north of the farm. William Ford, a carpenter, worked for Patrick Ahern in 1860, building a frame house for the Aherns. During that time, William became well acquainted with Mary. On April 21, 1861, when Mary was twenty-two and William was thirty-four, they were married. After the death of an earlier, unnamed infant, the second of a total of eight children born to William and Mary was Henry Ford, born in 1863. Mary Litogot Ford died as a result of complications from childbirth on March 29, 1876. Henry, age thirteen, was devastated by her death. (188.2907)

Barney. Saphara owned and farmed a piece of land in the vicinity of Telegraph Road and the Taylor-Brownstown Townline Road (now Pennsylvania Road) in Wayne County.

The 1860 Michigan Agricultural Census describes "Saphara Ledigot" as having 109 acres of land in Taylor Township, Wayne

This rather proper and solemn photograph taken in the 1890s shows Henry's father, William Ford. He was born in a small dry-stone cottage on 28 acres of leased land in Ireland near the town of Clonakilty in County Cork. His father was John Ford, his grandfather William Ford. He was trained as a carpenter before coming to America with his family in 1847. William eventually obtained half of his father's 80-acre farm in Redford Township, Michigan, purchased another 80 acres in Dearborn Township, and, by marriage to Mary Litogot Ahern, acquired another 91 acres. Having prospered as a Dearborn farmer, he became a staunch and respected citizen of the community. (P.O.360)

County. Of the 109 acres, 49 acres were classified as unimproved. The cash value of the farm was $2,000, and his farm equipment was valued at $50. He had one horse, one milk cow, and four other cattle. He had no oxen and no sheep but had six swine. His livestock was valued at $150. His crops consisted of 300 bushels of Indian corn, 300 bushels of Irish potatoes, 30 bushels of oats, and 25 tons of hay. One hundred pounds of butter had been produced, and orchard products were valued at $100. His post office is listed as Wyandotte.

In 1867, Saphara lost his wife, Lethera, to a neighbor, Andrew Threadgold, who operated a nearby sawmill. From 1868 to 1872, it appears that Saphara was living on his farm and doing carpenter work. One of the houses he built during that period was on Taylor Townline Road at Taylor Center, between the villages of Flat Rock and Brownstown. This had been built in 1868 for J. P. Clark. When Henry Ford was assembling Greenfield Village in 1930, he decided to include this house built by his uncle Saphara. At least thirty-five photographs

The marriage certificate of William Ford and Mary Ahern, dated April 25, 1861.

of the house from every angle, inside and out, were taken in order to reconstruct it exactly in the Village. Reconstruction was nearly finished when Ford unaccountably changed his mind and had his men dismantle it, using the lumber for other Village structures.

John Litogot, Mary's second eldest brother, was living with his brother Saphara in 1860. On July 14, 1862, age twenty-seven and unmarried, John volunteered for service in the Civil War. He was five feet, eight inches tall, with gray eyes, brown hair, and fair complexion. He joined the 24th Michigan Volunteers, Company K. John's brother Barney, two years younger and already married to Caroline Amelia Taylor in May 1861, joined the same Company K, on August 14. The two brothers left Detroit together the last week of August. By October, the 24th Michigan Volunteers had been selected to join the famous Iron Brigade. On December 13, 1862, during the second day of the battle of

The house built by Henry Ford's uncle Saphara Litogot in 1868, as it appeared being rebuilt in Greenfield Village on June 23, 1930. Before it was completely rebuilt, however, Ford changed his mind and erected in its place a "Swiss chalet." Ford was particularly whimsical in his choice of buildings for the Village. (P.A.5464)

Fredericksburg, John is said to have been beheaded by a cannonball. He is presumed buried where he fell, near the banks of the Rappahannock. This news was terribly upsetting to Mary, and she no doubt impressed the horrors of war upon her son Henry as he was growing up.

For two more years, Barney Litogot continued to serve his country at Fredericksburg, Chancellorsville, Gettysburg, Wilderness, Spotsylvania, Cold Harbor, Bethesda Church, and more. In these battles, the 24th Michigan is said to have been reduced from 1,040 men to fewer than 100 men. Barney was wounded twice in battle. On April 15, 1865, the 24th Michigan was assigned to escort President Abraham Lincoln, their dead commander-in-chief, to his final resting place. Barney Litogot was mustered out in June 1865 as a sergeant.

Following the Civil War, Barney Litogot, with his wife and sons, lived for a short time on Grosse Ile and in Wyandotte until 1873, when Barney was appointed keeper of the lighthouse on Mamajuda Island in the Detroit River at the upper end of Grosse Ile. In December of that year, however, Barney died of tuberculosis at age thirty-five. His wife, Caroline, now with two small sons, was appointed acting lighthouse keeper while a permanent successor was chosen. Caroline received many recommendations for the position from other lighthouse keepers and in

William Litogot's sons, John (1835–1862) and Barney (1838–1873), in their Union Army uniforms in 1862. John was killed at Fredericksburg in December 1862, a severe blow to Mary, and her feelings were very likely reflected in Henry Ford's strong aversion to war. (0.1256)

June 1876 was made official keeper of the lights at Mamajuda. In 1882, she married Adolph Antaya, owner of a large fishery at Lakeport near Port Huron, Michigan. She kept her lighthouse position, however, until 1885, when she retired and the family moved to Lakeport. In 1887, they moved to Detroit, where Caroline died in 1903.

In order to have better records of the entire Litogot family, Henry Ford in the summer of 1930 invited to Greenfield Village as many of his mother's family as he could locate. Some of them were toddlers; some were in their eighties. Nearly a hundred photographs of Litogot relatives were collected that day. A good share were taken at the Village, some individually and some of groups. Group photographs include Litogots together with Henry, Henry II, and Benson Ford. Also at that time,

Some of the descendants of Barney Litogot are shown here as guests of Henry Ford at Greenfield Village on May 10, 1930. Standing from the left are Benson Ford, Henry Ford, Arthur (Artemus) Litogot, Henry Ford II, and Henry Sandusky. Seated from left are Ruth Sandusky, Loine Litogot, Lena Litogot, Ida Litogot Sandusky, and Margaret Sandusky. (188.2356)

many early Litogot photographs were presented to Henry by family members from their personal albums. Essentially, all of the photographs are well identified and are now kept in the archives of the Benson Ford Research Center of Henry Ford Museum & Greenfield Village.

Several of the Litogot descendants are working on their own genealogies. Their most difficult problem is learning more about William Litogot and his wife, whose name is not known. How and when the Litogots arrived in America, the question upon which Henry Ford spent considerable effort without success, never has been determined for certain. It is still thought that the Litogot name may have been of Flemish origin. It is not a common name anywhere. Mary's mother may have been British, inasmuch as her four children all married into British-American families and Mary adopted the Episcopal religion.

References

Accession 34, Photographs of the Litogot Family. Benson Ford Research Center, HFM & GV.

Barr, Jeff. "Readers Unearth a Grave Mystery." *Wyandotte News,* July 1995.

David Litogot Papers. Benson Ford Research Center, HFM & GV. (David Litogot is a descendant of Saphara Litogot.)

George, William, Jr. "The Litogot Family." Unpublished history of the Litogot family by the great-grandson of Artemus Litogot. Vertical file. Benson Ford Research Center, HFM & GV.

Nevins, Allan. *Ford: The Times, the Man, the Company.* New York: Scribner's, 1954.

Notes from Barbara Gaskell, great-granddaughter of Artemus Litogot.

Notes from Margaret Sandusky Hair, granddaughter of Artemus Litogot.

Part III
Mechanical Exploits

Although Henry Ford was certainly a mechanical genius who produced a wide array of ingenious mechanical devices for a multitude of purposes, he was not successful in every case. The most successful, as everyone knows, was his gasoline-driven automobile, of which he sold millions. Next most successful was perhaps the Fordson tractor, of which he sold several hundred thousand.

The following stories describe how Ford, with help from his wife, Clara, for years tried to get into the automobile business. Following success with the Model T, by far his greatest triumph, he ventured into several lesser mechanical projects. Some of these efforts were successful, and some were not. All were associated with problems of one sort or another.

18
Getting Started

Henry Ford grew up on a prosperous farm in Springwells Township about seven miles due west of Detroit. He attended school through the sixth grade and in 1879, at age sixteen, despite his father's wishes, walked into Detroit and obtained work at the Michigan Car Company Works, where streetcars were built. But Henry was fired from the job after only six days. Henry's father then arranged for him to become an apprentice machinist at the James Flower & Brothers Machine Shop. Henry was then much more interested in machinery than in farming. In 1880, his apprentice wages of $2.50 per week were a dollar less than his room and board, inducing him to seek evening work in a jewelry store to provide the difference.

In 1881, Henry was working for the Detroit Drydock Company, where he learned a great deal about heavy industry, but by the summer of 1882, he was back on the farm operating a small steam traction engine for a neighboring farmer, Jim Gleason, and soon after was repairing such engines manufactured by the Westinghouse Company. While home on the farm, he met Clara Bryant; the two married in April 1888 and set up housekeeping on an eighty-acre farm given to Henry by his father in 1886.

Henry had no intention of farming the land as his father would have expected. Instead, he spent the next two years using a steam engine to cut wood off his land and that of his neighbors. After they had built their honeymoon cottage, the "Square House," it was rather shocking to Clara, who liked living in the country, to find Henry in September 1891 wanting to move into Detroit to accept a position as night operating engineer at a substation of the Edison Illuminating Company for forty dollars a month. They moved into a rented flat at 618 John R Street on September 25, 1891. The position at Edison Illuminating appealed to Henry because he would be learning electrical engineering as well as steam engineering.

Previously published in the *Dearborn Historian*, Vol. 36, No. 4, 1996.

Henry Ford, at left with mustache, in the generator room of the main powerhouse of the Edison Illuminating Company. With him are William F. Bartels and George W. Cato. This was 1893, the year Henry bought a bicycle and the year Edsel was born. The balcony above the stairs is filled with switches, meters, and gauges. The new generating engine at right, built by the Edison Electric Light Company of New York, reveals a patent date of September 14, 1882, and displays number A-14. Ford's diary of this period records repairs he made on engines numbered 11, 12, and 13. (0.491)

By October 1892, Henry and Clara Ford were living in a flat at 162 Cass Avenue, where they were paying fifteen dollars a month rent. That same year, Henry was called upon to take charge of maintenance of steam engines in the main downtown Edison power plant on Washington Boulevard and State Street, with a salary of seventy-five dollars per month. He was on twenty-four-hour call. He did not have an engineer's license and perhaps could not have passed the test for one, for he had had no formal training. It is said that he was "free lance and got by with it; that he never liked to stay around the big engines at the powerhouse but needed to be nearby in case something went wrong."

This was a bonanza for Ford, for he then had plenty of free time to experiment with gasoline engines. He utilized not only the Edison boiler room as a workshop but also the basement of a storage building across the alley, where, with his mechanically inclined cronies, he spent

Inside this brick woodshed behind the residence at 58 Bagley Avenue is where Henry Ford assembled his first vehicle, the Quadricycle, in 1896. The shed was meant for the use of two families, but Ford had permission to use the entire interior. The door on the right is larger than the one on the left because the Quadricycle was too large to get out of either of the doors until Ford, in a great hurry to get the contraption out and give it a test, widened the one door by knocking out some of the bricks. The landlord was fit to be tied, but Ford calmed him by explaining how nicely the little vehicle worked. The photograph was taken in 1919. (833.27218)

many hours discussing and experimenting with gasoline engines. For use of this space, Ford is said to have paid seventy-five cents a month. He was spending most of his time directing his experimental gasoline engine work in these two shops. Ford had the ideas and had the knack to get others to do the work. He was spending very little time at home.

Frederick Strauss, a machinist, relates that in 1893, while Ford was

Henry Ford on the contraption he called a Quadricycle on a quiet street in Detroit in 1896. By this time, he had boxed in the engine and installed a doorbell on the front. He sold it to his friend Chappie Ainsley for two hundred dollars. (833.89114)

working for Edison, he and Ford built Ford's first gasoline engine in that basement shop mostly out of scrap. When the one-cylinder engine was finished, it was taken over to his friend Albert Peck's bicycle shop at 81 Park Place, where it was sold to Peck's friend Charles Ainsley and successfully installed in a rowboat. (It is questionable whether Ford produced that engine as early as 1893.)

Henry and Clara stayed at the 162 Cass Avenue location only eight months before moving to 570 Forest Avenue in September 1893. Henry was paying about forty dollars a year in taxes on his farm property in Dearborn Township and twenty-nine cents in annual taxes on a subdivision lot on which he and Clara intended to build a house for themselves. It was at 570 Forest that their only child, Edsel, was born on

November 6, 1893. At that Forest Avenue location in mid-1893, Henry was purchasing gasoline in fifty-two-gallon barrels at 7.5 cents a gallon.

To be closer to the Edison plant during that very cold winter, the Fords moved to 58 Bagley Avenue in December 1893 and paid rent of twenty-five dollars per month. Edsel was then only six weeks old. In a small brick shed behind this rented apartment, Henry set up a third shop for his auto experiments and is said to have operated his midget one-cylinder pipe engine (the one tried out on the kitchen sink) that Christmas Eve.

By 1894, Ford was making one hundred dollars per month as chief engineer at Edison. He made friends easily. On November 29, 1894, he joined the Palestine Masonic Lodge with his Edison coworkers George W. Cato and James W. Bishop. Alexander Dow, Ford's new boss in 1896, would rather Henry had dropped his experiments with the gasoline car and paid full attention to his Edison responsibilities. Dow was a strong advocate of electricity for motive power and wanted no hazardous gasoline on his property. He introduced Ford to Thomas Edison in New York in the summer of 1896, hoping that Edison would talk Ford out of gasoline as a motive power, but Edison surprisingly encouraged Ford.

Ford's many experimental automotive parts had been fabricated at or next door to the Edison shops, but final assembly of his first vehicle, the Quadricycle, completed on June 4, 1896, was in the brick shed at the back of the house at 58 Bagley. During 1894, 1895, and 1896, the cost of Henry's numerous experimental auto parts was taxing Clara's family budget. Henry's credit had been limited to fifteen dollars by Strelinger, one of his major hardware suppliers. Clara recognized that materials for the car ate up all the family's surplus above necessary home expenses. It is said that her only concern then was the immediate one that Henry needed parts for his work. She wanted to be sure that there was sufficient money in the bank to pay for them and wondered more than once if she would ever live to see the bank balance restored.

Ford and his friends were developing a second car in the little basement shop next to the Edison plant while he was still employed by Edison but thinking more and more about automobile manufacturing in quantity. In January 1897, he was seeking financial help to manufacture automobiles. With moral backing from William C. Maybury, his Irish friend who was then mayor of Detroit, and some of his Edison cohorts, he was ready to move ahead. Ford's little shops at the Edison location were not complete enough to supply all of the machined parts necessary for his engine experiments. During 1897, he found a storefront at 151 Shelby Street for his machinist friend Frederick Strauss. At that address, Ford paid a rent of thirty dollars per month and furnished Strauss with at least one hundred dollars' worth of tools for machining experimental engine parts.

William Cotter Maybury, Henry Ford's earliest and most valuable backer in Detroit. The Maybury family came from Cork County, Ireland, on the same boat as Ford's father, who married Mary Litogot at the home of William Maybury's father, Thomas C. Maybury. William Maybury graduated in law from the University of Michigan. He was a born politician and was mayor of Detroit while Ford was trying to develop an automobile. Besides furnishing Ford with small amounts of money of his own, he introduced him to prominent and wealthy investors such as William H. Murphy and the McMillan group. (P.O.3092)

In June 1897, Henry moved his family to 72 East Alexandrine Street, a mile and a half north of the main Edison plant, with a lower rent of fifteen dollars a month. Bills for hardware and plumbing supplies for experimental engine parts were very conspicuous during this period. Henry continued work during 1898 at the Edison plant using the basement quarters next door for both automotive work and garnering financial support. After trying this and trying that and discarding many trial parts, his second car, considerably better than the Quadricycle, was finished in early 1898. He also obtained his first patent on a carburetor during 1898. It wasn't until July 1899, however, when Ford drove wealthy lumber merchant William H. Murphy on a three-and-a-half-hour, sixty-mile demonstration ride to Farmington, Pontiac, and back to Detroit, that Ford gained a strong financial backer.

In early August 1899, Alexander Dow demanded a decision from Ford: it was to be either Edison or automobiles, not both. On August 5, the Detroit Automobile Company, under Murphy's leadership, was formed, with eleven stockholders including Ford and with Ford as

William H. Murphy, after a sixty-mile demonstration ride in Henry Ford's experimental car in July 1899, offered Ford $150 a month to be "mechanical superintendent" of the Detroit Automobile Company being formed to manufacture cars of Ford's design. This offer caused Ford to leave the Edison Illuminating Company in favor of the automobile business. Murphy was born in Bangor, Maine, on the Penobscot River, and his family was in the lumber business. They came to Michigan in 1866 to harvest pine and became prominent citizens of Detroit. Murphy's association with Ford led to Ford's introduction to Detroit's financial circles. In addition to fostering a variety of Detroit businesses, Murphy built in downtown Detroit the forty-seven-story Penobscot building, named after the river on which he lived in Maine. (P.O.3136)

superintendent. Beginning in September, Ford's salary was $150 a month. The manufacturing plant was to be at 1343 Cass Avenue at Amsterdam. On August 15, 1899, Ford resigned from the Edison Illuminating Company, turning down a promised salary of $1,900 a year. In October 1899, the Fords moved to 1292 Second Boulevard, not far from the location of the shops of the Detroit Automobile Company.

Stockholders of the Detroit Automobile Company included several of the most influential names in Detroit: in addition to William Murphy, among them were James and Hugh McMillan, owners of railroads, steamship lines, iron smelters, the Detroit Drydock Company, and Michigan Car Works; William McMillan, vice president, Union Trust Company; Dexter M. Ferry of the Ferry Seed Company; Thomas Palmer, lumber baron and U.S. senator; and George Peck, president of Michigan Savings Bank and the Edison Illuminating Company. Henry's mayoral friend William C. Maybury had introduced him to the members of this financially interlaced McMillan crowd.

The first product of the Detroit Automobile Company, a delivery wagon, was completed in January 1900 and demonstrated with some success. Major stockholders, however, were pushing for a variety of vehicles and were in a hurry to make profits while Ford was beset by a number of engineering problems. His experience had not included making more than one car at a time. Several cars were produced but not of the quality Henry would have liked and priced too expensively to sell. Henry received

Henry Ford at the wheel of the racer in which he beat Alexander Winton on October 10, 1901. Oliver Barthel, who worked with Ford in designing the vehicle, is riding with him. Described by Ford as "a two-cylinder enclosed engine . . . fitted into a skeleton chassis," it had a wheelbase of 96 inches and developed 26 horsepower. The driver sits on the right with a steering wheel replacing the tiller. This vehicle was a great improvement over the Quadricycle of only five years earlier. (B.90951)

what appears to have been his final check for seventy-five dollars on October 29, 1900. By November, the Detroit Automobile Company had ground to a halt, and it was officially dissolved in January 1901.

The Fords must have moved from 1292 Second Boulevard by then, because Clara paid eleven dollars for room and board to a Mrs. Hewitt for one week ending October 29, 1900. That fall, Henry's father, William, had retired and with Henry's sister Jane was living in Detroit at 582 West Grand Boulevard. On January 8, 1901, Henry, Clara, and Edsel moved into the same building, William apparently paying the rent. Records show that on January 8, 1901, a load of furniture was moved from the Moir House (Henry's farm in Dearborn) to 582 West Grand Boulevard at a cost of $3.50. These must have been trying times for Clara as well as for Henry.

Henry Ford still had friends in Detroit. Some of the former stockholders of the Detroit Automobile Company retained a portion of the Cass Avenue plant so that Ford could build a car his way. He had been thinking about a racer. His specialty was engines, and he was convinced that racing would attract the attention necessary to establish himself in the automotive field. He announced to his family that he would be spending many nights on a cot at the Cass Avenue plant. With part-time help from his friends Ed Huff, Oliver Barthel, and Harold Wills, he worked around the clock. A lightweight two-cylinder racer of 26 horsepower was finished in mid-1901. This car is said to have cost about $5,000 to build, with much of the cost again covered by Murphy. It was raced at the Grosse Pointe equestrian track on October 10, 1901, where Ford beat Alexander Winton's 40-horsepower racer in a ten-mile race going nearly a mile a minute, with Huff hanging on a running board balancing the car on turns. Bicyclists Tom Cooper and Barney Oldfield also raced that day. Ford received a $1,000 award, as well as a cut-glass punchbowl and much favorable publicity for his victory.

The second of Ford's racers, his 999. This monstrous vehicle, of four 7-by-7-inch cylinders producing nearly 100 horsepower and emitting a corresponding amount of noise and smoke, literally scared the men who produced it. But after the race, Ford was hailed as the top engine engineer in the country. (A.2583)

The 1903 Model A Ford, the first automobile built by Ford Motor Company. It was a two-cylinder, 8-horsepower vehicle weighing 1,250 pounds and capable of a speed of 30 miles per hour. It sold for $850 cash. (188.10193)

There must have been considerable financial gain, because the Henry Fords, much to Clara's satisfaction, moved out of his father's residence into a rented flat of their own at 332 Hendrie Street. To celebrate, Henry bought a new Winchester rifle and organized a duck-hunting expedition to the Lake St. Clair Flats.

With Ford's much enhanced reputation, Murphy and other members of the former Detroit Automobile Company formed the Henry Ford Company on November 30, 1901. Ford was named chief engineer, with one-sixth of the company stock valued at $10,000, but there is no record of wages. The goal was to build a lightweight runabout to sell for about $1,000. But Henry is said to have had "racing fever" and to have had in mind a giant four-cylinder racing car. He was spending most of his time on the design of this new racing car engine. Although Murphy had financed the two-cylinder racer, he did not want Ford working on a larger racer. And to Ford's annoyance, Murphy was dealing with Henry M. Leland, a well-respected mechanical engineer, as a consultant.

On March 3, 1902, Tom Cooper, the wealthy bicyclist, was in touch with Ford, wanting him to build a racer. On March 10, Ford left the Henry Ford Company with an agreement that they were no longer to use his name and were to give him $900 and the drawings for the big

Henry Ford's crowning achievement — the Model T automobile introduced in October 1908. Fifteen million of the Model Ts would be sold over the next twenty years. Ford's basic chassis design remained essentially the same during the whole period, whereas some cosmetic and body styling changes were later developed due considerably to Edsel's influence. In 1908, this Model T Touring Car with lights and horn sold for $850. It had a speed of 40 miles per hour, carried 10 gallons of gas or enough for 225 miles, had tires of 30 x 3½ inches, had a 100-inch wheelbase, and weighed 1,200 pounds. A Roadster, Coupe, and Town Car were introduced the same year. (B.4449)

race car. Oliver Barthel maintains that he prepared the layout drawings for the racer, with Harold Wills making the detailed drawings. At that point, Leland took charge at Henry Ford Company, changing the name to Cadillac Automobile Company.

Ford and Cooper arranged for shop space at 81 Park Place in downtown Detroit in May 1902. Albert Peck may still have been operating his bicycle shop at 81 Park Place, because Ford, strapped for money, is also reported to have been a "mender of bicycles" at that location at that time. But the major projects were the building of the two racers, the 999 for Ford and the Arrow for Cooper. These were named after two fast railroad express trains. According to John Wandersee, there were about ten employees in that shop, each working ten hours a day for ten cents an hour. Wandersee states that Ford was around most of the time, always in neatly laundered blue overalls. Clara's brother Milton, then a drug salesman in Louisville, Kentucky, was anxious to become Ford's racing manager, and he had Clara's support. But in a June 14, 1902, letter from Ford and Cooper (signed by Cooper), Milton was told "it was not our intention to engage a manager but simply thought it would be a good chance to make some money by getting together and running a few meets."

The first race they had in mind was the Manufacturers' Challenge Cup at Grosse Pointe on October 25, 1902. Working on the cars were Ford and his chief helpers, Wills, Huff, and Gus Degener. When Ford's 999, developing somewhere between 80 and 100 horsepower, was ready for tests, Ford, Cooper, and Huff tried it, but none was willing to drive it in a race. So Cooper got his friend Barney Oldfield to learn to drive it, which he did in one week. Oldfield won the race, and Ford's name was bigger than ever. Cooper, with his Arrow, a near duplicate of the 999, left Detroit, and to Clara it was good riddance. She did not like Cooper's racing crowd at all.

Even before the race on August 20, 1902, Henry had been in touch with Alexander Malcomson, the Detroit coal dealer, in regard to marketing a motor car of simple design. Wills had made the drawings, and a partnership of Ford and Malcomson was arranged to continue work at 81 Park Place. Under this arrangement, Wills was to receive a wage of $125 a month to be split fifty-fifty with Ford. So Ford was then working as an employee of Malcomson, who was paying the bills. In December 1902, the partnership took on the name of Ford & Malcomson, Ltd., and a car was assembled before Christmas. Plans to move operations to a larger Mack Avenue building, leased by Malcomson for seventy-five dollars a month, were made in January 1903, and they moved to the new plant on May 1, 1903. However, Ford & Malcomson could not raise sufficient funds to capitalize adequately. It was John S. Gray, Malcomson's wealthy uncle, who came to the rescue with $10,000 in cash and the proviso that he become president of this new organization, to be called the Ford Motor Company. Incorporation was on June 16, 1903. Ford at last had solid backing for the car of his dreams.

References

Accession 1, Boxes 31–32, Fair Lane Papers. Benson Ford Research Center, HFM & GV.

Accession 65, David M. Bell Reminiscences. Benson Ford Research Center, HFM & GV.

Accession 65, Frederick Strauss Reminiscences. Benson Ford Research Center, HFM & GV.

Accession 65, John Wandersee Reminiscences. Benson Ford Research Center, HFM & GV.

Accession 65, Oliver E. Barthel Reminiscences. Benson Ford Research Center, HFM & GV.

Accession 65, William Pring Reminiscences. Benson Ford Research Center, HFM & GV.

Accession 102, Boxes 1, 2, Milton Bryant Correspondence. Benson Ford Research Center, HFM & GV.

Ford, Henry, with Samuel Crowther. *My Life and Works*. New York: Doubleday, 1922.

"Ford Was a Mender of Bicycles." *Boston Post*, January 12, 1914.

Nevins, Allan. *Ford: The Times, the Man, the Company*. New York: Scribner's, 1954.

Olson, Sidney. *Young Henry Ford*. Detroit: Wayne State University Press, 1963.

Ruddiman, Margaret Ford. "Memories of My Brother Henry Ford." *Michigan History*, Michigan Historical Commission, September 1953.

19
Gasoline Rail Car

Detroit truly could be described as having rapid transit when the electric streetcar replaced the horse car on Jefferson Avenue beginning on August 23, 1892. Twenty years earlier, the pokey horse-car system had left commuters completely stranded for several days when an epidemic of epizootic, the dreaded horse disease, struck Detroit and no horse cars were in service. Now, with the electrics, the daily ride was more sanitary, faster, and much more thrilling.

A multitude of small horse-car lines were converted to electricity during the period from 1892 to 1900. Although most of them thrived financially, riders constantly complained about service and exorbitant fares of as much as five cents. Public transportation had become a sizzling political issue with the election of Hazen S. Pingree as mayor in 1889. Pingree was a shoe manufacturer who campaigned on a three-cent maximum fare platform. There was persistent pressure on car line management to extend lines, upgrade equipment, improve service, and lower fares or else lose their franchises.

In 1901, the ambitious Cleveland-based Everett-Moore syndicate, of which Detroit Citizens Railway was a part, formed the Detroit United Railway and took over five of the independent lines running into the city. (This same company took over the Detroit, Ann Arbor & Jackson Railway from the Hawks-Angus syndicate in 1907.) This mammoth DUR network, centered in Detroit, reached from Port Huron and Flint to Toledo, Cleveland, and Kalamazoo. H. Everett believed that there would be practically one solid city from Port Huron to Buffalo within a decade. But the syndicate had overextended itself, and the entire property was soon in the hands of Canadian investors, "the Gray Nuns of Montreal."

The DUR, operating essentially all of the car lines in the city of Detroit, could not satisfy the people. Each city administration tried to analyze the problems, propose changes, and threaten operators of the lines. In 1909, the city established a "Committee of Fifty" to study tran-

Previously published in the *Dearborn Historian*, Vol. 26, No. 2, 1986.

sit needs. The committee reported, among other things, the need for a nucleus of a subway. In 1913, the voters approved a charter amendment providing for municipal ownership, and the Detroit Street Railway Commission was appointed. This three-man commission included two men, John Dodge and James Couzens, who were engaged in the manufacture of automobiles. Over the years, automotive interests continued to be exceptionally well represented. Again, in 1914, a report to the commissioners recommended a subway and rerouting of several lines in the downtown area. In early 1915, the city tried to buy the DUR holdings for $23,285,000; the DUR refused the offer.

Couzens, while general manager of Ford Motor Company, was a strong proponent of municipal operation of the city streetcar system. He became involved in city affairs to the extent that Henry Ford took issue with the way he was spending his time. Differences on political matters resulted in Couzens's resigning from Ford Motor Company on October 13, 1915. He ran for mayor of Detroit in 1918 on a platform of municipal operation of the streetcar lines. His campaign was successful, but a proposal on April 7, 1919, to purchase the DUR for $31,500,000 was rejected by the voters. His railway commissioners, favoring a subway plan that Couzens had vetoed, resigned en masse on November 19, 1919.

Henry Ford had now entered the city's political picture. He placed his chief engineer, William B. Mayo, on the three-man board of railway commissioners. He was no longer an ally of Couzens. Perhaps he was somewhat jealous of Couzens's political success. (Henry Ford had lost the U.S. Senate race to Truman H. Newberry the same year Couzens became mayor of Detroit.) Ford had decided to torpedo Couzens's plan to purchase the DUR by announcing that electric streetcars were obsolete. The torpedo was launched by means of a widely publicized speech given by Charles Sorensen, Ford's production manager, on April 1, 1919, just one week before the vote rejecting municipal ownership.

Electric streetcar obsolescence was based on an idea of Ford's that a gasoline-powered car could be operated more economically than an electrically powered car. This premise he immediately set out to prove. Colonel Hall of the Hall-Scott Motor Car Company of California — builder of gasoline-powered rail cars — was hired as a consultant. Design work, which was started in March 1919, was done at the Fair Lane laboratory (powerhouse building) by Allan Horton and Harold Hicks under Hall's direction. Hicks, a graduate mechanical engineer, had prepared a cost study of gasoline versus electric operation giving a 31.04- versus 33.08-cents-per-mile advantage to gasoline. Experimental engines were built at the nearby tractor plant on Elm Street, where Sorensen was boss. The all-steel car body was built by Kuhlman Car Company of Cleveland, Ohio.

Work on the car progressed throughout 1919, Couzens insisting

that a gasoline car was not practical and Sorensen, speaking for Ford, insisting that it was. Ford remained somewhat aloof of the fray, and Edsel, the new president of Ford Motor Company, was a mere onlooker, it seems. (The project was that of Henry Ford & Son, not Ford Motor Company.) Newspapers were giving Ford a definite edge in the publicity battle. The gasoline car, it was said, would race the *Wolverine*, the Michigan Central flyer to Chicago, when the car was completed. This same year, Ford obtained a twenty-year franchise to operate a car line out Detroit's Fort Street and up South Dearborn Road to his shipbuilding plant on the Rouge River and to his tractor plant in Dearborn using gasoline rail cars. Hicks relates that Ford told him, "You know, down at the Rouge, someday we're going to build a factory two miles long to build these streetcars."

March 1920 saw the completion of the gasoline rail car and its inspection by Couzens and the Detroit City Council. The car was about half the weight of a corresponding electric car, had a 75-horsepower engine, and could seat forty-two. The engine was a four-cylinder horizontally opposed configuration with five-inch bore and seven-inch stroke (the same individual cylinder displacement as the wartime "Liberty" engine). Quoting Sorensen:

The gasoline-powered street railway car, *Dearborn*, promoted as an economical substitute for electric trolley cars in Detroit. This photograph was taken on July 12, 1920. (189.1128)

The luxuriously appointed and more powerful *Dearborn* ready for fast service on the DT&I Railroad. This photograph was taken on July 20, 1922. (189.1139)

It is an engine, an air compressor, an electrical generator, and a heating and lighting plant all in one. The power that moves the car also compresses air for the brakes and generates electric current for the lighting and signal system, while a sirocco fan draws air in through the housing of the engine where it is heated, then exhausted through heating pipes to warm the car.

Couzens's opinion of the car was that it was designed more for interurban use than as a city streetcar, and he was skeptical of its alleged low operational costs.

In July 1920, Ford purchased the Detroit, Toledo & Ironton Railroad, a steam railroad system extending from Dearborn to the Ohio

River. He now had 456 miles of his own track on which to test his car.
He no longer needed to borrow the Michigan Central tracks and race
the *Wolverine* to Chicago. Of course, he had other good reasons for
buying the DT&I besides testing his gasoline rail car. But it was now
announced that Ford intended to use his gasoline rail cars to provide
passenger service on the DT&I through Ohio.

For trials on the DT&I, Ford ordered a double engine of eight
cylinders supplying 150 horsepower to provide a speed of 80 miles per
hour. This first and only Ford gasoline rail car, aptly christened the
Dearborn, was then equipped with about fourteen comfortable wicker
chairs, a kitchen, and a lavatory; it was admirably suited for use as a
private car for inspecting his railroad. There must have been at least two
inspection trips. One is described as being of very short duration, with
Jimmy Smith as motorman, when, after only a very few miles down the
line, a minor mechanical problem developed, aborting the trip. The car
returned slowly on one engine while Henry returned to Dearborn by
automobile. Another excursion with the gasoline rail car is described in
the *Ford Times* as being a round trip of 216 miles on the DT&I to

Charles E. Sorensen, who
favorably publicized the gasoline
rail car on behalf of Henry Ford
in order to counteract James
Couzens's attempt to promote
municipal ownership of electric
streetcars. (P.O.14986)

Springfield, Ohio, at speeds up to 72 miles per hour and with Edsel Ford sometimes at the controls. Any further use of the car seems to be undocumented. Presumably, the car was soon scrapped, its demise unpublicized.

But the project cannot be considered a complete failure — perhaps not a failure at all. Indeed, in at least two aspects it was a definite success. First, the gasoline rail car was a sufficient threat to DUR interests to force it to lower the price of its city system to $19,850,000, thereby saving Detroit many millions of dollars when the system was finally purchased by the city in 1922. Second, when one examines the months and months of favorable publicity given Ford for his ingenuity and his effort to serve the public, one finds the advertising value priceless — no doubt far exceeding the actual expense of building the car. And, in addition, the project must have served Ford's original purpose of thwarting Couzens's early attempt toward municipal ownership of the Detroit streetcar system. Ford in this case seems to have had no leanings toward socialism.

References

Accession 7, Newspaper Clipping Books, Microfilm, 1919–1920. Benson Ford Research Center, HFM &GV.

Accession 65, Harold Hicks Reminiscences. Benson Ford Research Center, HFM & GV.

Accession 78, Box 46, Sorensen Papers. Benson Ford Research Center, HFM & GV.

Barnard, H. *Independent Man.* New York: Scribner's, 1958.

Baut, Donald V. "Track 'N' Trolley." *Dearborn Historian,* Vol. 11, No. 1, 1971, pp. 3–22.

"Ford's Street Car Pronounced Success." *Motor World,* October 22, 1919, p. 40.

Schramm, J. E., and W. H. Henning. *Detroit's Street Railways, 1863–1922.* Chicago: Central Electric Railways Association, 1978.

20

Ford-Edison Electric Car

While working for the Edison Illuminating Company in Detroit, Henry Ford had put together his first automobile, the Quadricycle, which he drove on the streets of Detroit in the early morning of June 4, 1896. In August of that year, young Ford was sent as a delegate to the annual convention of the Association of Edison Illuminating Companies, which took place in the Oriental Hotel on Manhattan Beach, Long Island, New York. At the convention, Ford's boss, Alex Dow, introduced him to Thomas Edison. When Ford described his gasoline car to Edison, he was both surprised and elated that Edison did not deride the gasoline car as inferior to an electric vehicle but instead praised the idea of a gasoline-fueled vehicle as being very practical. Ford was never to forget Edison's encouragement at that crucial time of his life. He proceeded to go ahead with the gasoline car, gathering a respect for Edison that approached adoration. Although Edison had encouraged Ford regarding the gasoline car, the shortcomings of gasoline vehicles (dirty, smelly, complicated, and hard to start) were fully recognized by Edison. He was really a believer in electricity for motive power.

One of Edison's major experimental endeavors was electrochemistry. A self-educated chemist, Edison filled his laboratory at Menlo Park with bottles of nearly every substance available on earth. His experiments with telegraphy had necessitated chemical cells to provide electricity. As early as 1895, Edison had built a three-wheel electric automobile and was attempting to develop batteries suitable for propelling vehicles of various descriptions — streetcars, delivery trucks, and submarines. He realized that conventional lead-acid batteries were too heavy and short-lived to be entirely satisfactory.

Edison was looking for metallic substances, lighter than lead, to be used with weak alkaline electrolytes rather than the corrosive sulfuric acid. He organized the Edison Storage Battery Company in 1902. By 1903, the year Ford Motor Company was founded, Edison had begun a long series of experiments to find a desirable electrical cell combination.

Previously published in the *Dearborn Historian*, Vol. 36, No. 1, 1996

Said to be the first battery-powered electric automobile, this vehicle was built by Thomas Edison in 1895. Two electric motors producing 5 horsepower drive the front wheels. At the right of the seat, a tiller steers the vehicle by means of the rear wheel, and an electrical switch controls the speed of the car. The rear compartment contains the batteries. (B.14441)

By 1908, he had chosen a combination of nickel and iron plates in a solution of potassium hydroxide as being far superior to the lead-acid cells then in common use. Ford, on the other hand, annoyed with the problems of batteries for the Model T, was devising a flywheel magneto to supply electricity for gasoline engine ignition. Ford, however, depended on the hand crank for starting the motor.

Charles F. Kettering had devised an electric starting system which he had sold to the Cadillac company in 1912. Ford and Edison decided they would develop their own electric starter using the new Edison nickel-iron battery. Edison had been quite successful with this new battery, and he should have been, because he is said to have spent

$1,750,000 in developing the battery and building a large manufacturing plant solely for battery production. This plant at Orange, New Jersey, was a four-story structure with 200,000 square feet of floor space.

Ford-Edison Electric Car

A trade catalog issued by the Edison Storage Battery Company in 1910 describes the battery in detail. Edison's nickel-iron batteries became especially popular in powering trucks for city delivery use. They were also found useful in lighting railroad cars, in battery-operated streetcars, and especially in submarines because they did not emit toxic fumes as did lead-acid batteries. Not depending on gasoline, electric trucks could be operated inside buildings and on docks and terminals where gasoline was prohibited because of the fire hazard.

Edison cells were of three types with ampere-hour output of 150, 225, and 300 and corresponding weights of 13, 20, and 25 pounds each. (A modern automotive lead-acid battery provides about 60 ampere-hours output.) The cells sold for almost exactly one dollar per pound —not inexpensive. These could be assembled in a variety of battery sizes, ranging from two cells to ten cells and fitted into trays 6.5 inches wide and from 8 to 36 inches long. They were said to have the advantages of being more durable and requiring less maintenance than lead-acid batteries. The June 1, 1911, *Detroit Free Press* echoed other newspapers: "Edison Perfects Storage Battery; New Battery Will Revolutionize Car Systems."

All motive power at the turn of the century was competing with the horse. As late as 1913, Edison is quoted as saying: "The horse is a mighty poor motor. A horse eats ten pounds of food for every hour he works. He eats 12,000 pounds of food every year. A motor truck consumes no fuel when it is not working. The minute the motor truck stops the feeding cost stops." The choice between gasoline and electric vehicles in place of the horse was resolved as being a choice between the needs of city transportation and suburban needs. For the short haul, electrics were considered best; for longer trips, the gasoline vehicle was superior.

The more stops per mile, the better the electrics. Electrics had excellent acceleration but low top speed. Gasoline vehicles had high top speed but could not use that speed in heavy traffic areas. The average mileage operated by the American Railway Express delivery service using three types of vehicles was reported as follows:

8,200 horse wagons operating 12 miles per day
1,400 electric trucks operating 20 miles per day
2,500 gas trucks operating 28 miles per day
Average horse life in service — 5 years
Gasoline truck depreciation — 30% per year
Electric truck depreciation — 0% per year

Very similar rules applied to gasoline and electric passenger vehicles as well. In Detroit, electrics were seen in the streets downtown but not in the suburbs. The most popular was the Detroit Electric built by the Anderson Carriage Company of Detroit and owned by automotive families including Henry Ford, James Couzens, and H. H. Rackham of Ford Motor Company. Other owners were Wilfred C. Leland of Cadillac, Henry B. Joy of Packard, J. Walter Drake of Hupmobile, William E. Scripps of Scripps Motor Company, and George W. Dunham of Chalmers. The electrics were used primarily by the wives of these executives for running errands and attending social events. Ford bought a 1913 Detroit Electric for Clara, who used hers to travel from Detroit to their farm in Dearborn, sometimes running down the battery before she reached home. Henry installed a battery charger for her at the Dearborn location.

The Detroit Electric was one of the few electric passenger cars employing Edison's batteries. Anderson was a friend of both Ford and Edison. During the summer of 1913, Ford and Edison had been motoring through the White Mountains in an open car when Edison caught a severe cold. Ford's advice to Edison was to use a closed car. Remembering what he had said and appreciating the quality of the Detroit Electric he himself owned, Ford purchased a second Detroit Electric as a 1913 Christmas gift to Edison. By March 1914, the Anderson Electric Car Company was advertising in the *Saturday Evening Post* the fact that both Ford and Edison had chosen the Detroit Electric as their personal cars.

January 2, 1914, was the beginning of the five-dollar day at Ford Motor Company and the distribution of $10 million in profits to its workers. Newspapers across the country heralded the announcement. Despite all the commotion in progress, Henry, Clara, and Edsel Ford took off for New York on January 9 to attend the auto show and visit Edison at West Orange, New Jersey. They stayed at the Belmont in Manhattan and were swamped by reporters concerned with the newspaper headlines from Detroit and asking for the reason for his great generosity. Instead, Ford was eager to tell reporters about his business with Edison, which was to discuss batteries for the new, small, and economical electric car which would be built in Detroit in a new factory managed by Edsel Ford.

Edsel Ford was now barely twenty-one years old, just two years out of high school, and the electric car project was to be his chance to go it alone. Henry, Edsel, and Edison spent more than three hours in Edison's library at Glenmont in Llewellyn Park on January 9, 1914. Henry reported that evening that cars with the Edison battery were then undergoing road tests and that he expected to put a machine on the market in about a year. He predicted the car batteries would weigh 405 pounds, the entire car would weigh about 1,100 pounds, it would run for 100 miles without recharging, and it would cost about $600 to

Interior of the frame barn at the Snell Farm on Woodward Avenue between Manchester and Ferris Avenues at Highland Park, Michigan, in 1909. To the right of the stove, Henry Ford can be seen sitting with chin in hand, watching workers experimenting with an electric vehicle. A steam traction engine in the far corner furnishes belt power for the machinery beyond the stove. At this same time, the Model T was being built at the Piquette plant, and the mammoth Highland Park plant was under construction immediately to the south on Woodward Avenue. (188.72077)

the public. He expected it to run at speeds up to 25 miles an hour. Edsel is not quoted by the New York newspapers as having said a thing about the experimental car.

Ernest Liebold, Henry Ford's secretary, credits himself with being in charge of the entire project and indeed was the one who handled Ford's correspondence concerning the experimental work with Edison's representative William G. Bee, head of the Edison Storage Battery Company of West Orange.

The electric car was meant to be equipped with a brougham body but never seems to have been. The first experimental car, finished in late 1913, had an underslung frame unlike the Model T. It was equipped

Ford-Edison
Electric Car

with a single reduction worm drive as designed by Eugene Farkas, who reports that he had trouble selecting materials light enough to please Ford. The large Edison battery, weighing perhaps as much as 400 pounds, occupied all of the space under the single seat, and the vehicle was steered by means of a tiller.

The electric motor for the vehicle was designed by Fred Allison, an electrical engineer. The electrical system and overall design were the

Fred Allison with the first Ford-Edison electric car in front of the Highland Park plant of Ford Motor Company in early 1914. This car is equipped with a set of Edison nickel-iron batteries located under the driver's seat. The electric car, according to Henry Ford's announcement to the press in New York in January 1914, was to be manufactured by a new company organized for Edsel Ford and to be managed by Edsel, now age twenty-one. (0.1923)

The second Ford-Edison electric car, again with Fred Allison aboard, is here shown outside the Snell barn in Highland Park during midsummer 1914. This car has essentially a Model T chassis and two sets of Edison batteries; one set is under the seat as before, and another set is in the Model T engine position. A steering wheel takes the place of the tiller on the earlier car. It seems that this model ended Ford's experimental work on the electric car. (188.72082)

responsibility of Alexander Churchward, vice president of Gray & Davis, Inc., of Boston and technical consultant to the project. Samuel F. Wilson, a former employee of Cadillac who had worked with the Kettering electric starter system, was hired as mechanic. Nowhere in the reminiscences is Edsel Ford mentioned as participating. Liebold reported that "the internal resistance of the batteries was very high and increasingly so during the extremely cold weather. It offered a problem in what we were going to do in wintertime with this difficulty in not being able to get sufficient voltage, how we were going to operate the starting motors."

Again, according to Liebold:

I remember one time about the time we were ready to complete the assembly of the car, Mr. Ford was in Florida or absent from the city on vacation. The boys, knowing that the Edison batteries, due to their high internal resistance, wouldn't successfully operate the car, put some lead batteries in there. When Mr. Ford came back and saw the lead batteries in there, he became very disturbed over the matter and raised the devil all over the place. He made them get rid of them and told them they weren't building a car for lead batteries; they were building it to use Edison's batteries.

The second experimental electric car was completed on June 10, 1914. A communication to Edison the next day stated that Ford had ridden in it that morning and said it ran very smoothly and was almost noiseless. This second vehicle had a standard Model T frame, springs, and front axle, as well as a Model T steering column and wheel. The batteries in this case were divided between the under-the-seat location and in front of the cowl, where the gasoline motor normally would be. Test results were reported as follows:

Weight of vehicle with batteries — 1,350 pounds
Weight with two passengers — 1,760 pounds
Battery G7, 30 cells
Speed — 7 miles per hour
Climbed 19 percent grade 90 feet long
Total watt consumption .92 per pound

The same communication stated: "It is interesting to note what has been accomplished in building this car over the first one but we have already gathered enough bugs to start right in with building another which should be a vast improvement over this one." But no third electric vehicle seems to have been completed, and the project slowly withered into oblivion. Liebold, in answering dozens of inquiries throughout 1914 and 1915 concerning the Ford-Edison electric car, pointed out that it was not planned to be a Ford Motor Company product, but he never admitted the project was entirely dead.

It is obvious that Ford wanted to help his friend Edison furnish nickel-iron batteries for Ford products just as his friend Harvey Firestone furnished tires. Ford is said to have loaned Edison $1.2 million to help him with his battery business. Bee, in charge of Edison battery production, is said to have ordered 100,000 batteries to be manufactured for Ford Motor Company based on an assumed future order. Neither the Ford-Edison electric car nor the Ford-Edison electric starter system was to utilize the Edison battery. Ford did not have a starter system for the Model T until 1919. He did not introduce a gasoline truck until 1916. These delays were quite likely because of Ford's tremendous faith in the Edison battery.

Ford had other things on his mind. He was experimenting with tractors and organizing Henry Ford & Son. He was contemplating the Rouge plant and concerned about the war in Europe. Edison was invited to lay the cornerstone of the powerhouse for Fair Lane on August 26, 1914. Together, they were trying to stamp out cigarette smoking in the United States. The Fords visited the Edisons in Fort

Myers, Florida, in 1914 and purchased a winter home, the Mangoes, next to the Edisons in 1916. Ford, Edison, Firestone, and Burbank all met in California in the summer of 1915 and instituted the well-known summer excursions of the "Vagabonds." The failure of the Ford-Edison electric car seems not at all to have diminished the friendly relationship between the two families. The Edison Institute in 1929 became a monument to that relationship. The Fords and the Edisons were close friends until Edison's death in 1931.

Ford-Edison Electric Car

References

Accession 7, 1911–1915, Clipping Books. Benson Ford Research Center, HFM & GV.

Accession 38.372.2, Automobile — Detroit Electric — 1913. Benson Ford Research Center, HFM & GV.

Accession 62, Box 45, Henry Ford Office. Benson Ford Research Center, HFM & GV.

Accession 65, E. G. Liebold Reminiscences. Benson Ford Research Center, HFM & GV.

Accession 65, Eugene Farkas Reminiscences. Benson Ford Research Center, HFM & GV.

"Advantages of the Electric Vehicle." *Electrical World,* March 28, 1925.

"The Commercial Truck vs. the Horse." *Scientific American,* January 16, 1909.

"Data on the Recent Storage Battery Development." *Electrical World and Electrical Engineer,* March 25, 1899.

Edison, Thomas A. "The Storage Battery and the Motor Car." *North American Review,* July 1902.

"The Edison Storage Battery, Its Pre-eminent Fitness for Vehicle Service." *Electrical World,* April 28, 1910.

"Electrical Vehicle Progress during 1913." *Electrical World,* January 3, 1914.

"Ford's Son Will Also Run Profit Sharing Shop." *New York American,* January 10, 1914.

"Henry Ford Seeks Mr. Edison's Aid, Inventor May Construct Battery for Motor to Be Built by Manufacturer's Son." *New York Herald,* January 10, 1914.

"Henry Ford and Thomas A. Edison Buy the Detroit Electric." *Saturday Evening Post,* March 28, 1914.

"The New Edison Storage Battery Is Now Ready." Trade Catalog, Edison Storage Battery Company, Orange, New Jersey, 1910.

Schiffer, Michael. *Taking Charge.* Washington, D.C.: Smithsonian Institution Press, 1994.

21

Excursion into Railroading

In 1920, Henry Ford acquired 456 miles of deteriorated roadbed, forty-one railroad stations, seventy-five steam locomotives, 2,800 mortgaged freight cars, and twenty-seven vintage passenger cars from a line disparaged as "a streak of rust." Did he know what he was doing?

Ford was a man who was easily annoyed. His Model T automobile manufacturing plant at Highland Park, Michigan, was a model of efficiency, innovative beyond compare, and the envy of other manufacturers. Yet Ford detected weaknesses. His own tremendous success on that fifty-six-acre site had put him into a landlocked situation from which expansion was next to impossible. Another annoyance was his dependence on unreliable transportation to move materials to and from his factory. As early as 1917, six years before the Highland Park facility had reached its peak output, Ford told relatives that what he had at Highland Park was merely "a drop in the bucket" compared with his plans for "the Rouge." He already had purchased thousands of acres out in the Dearborn area and had decided that his major plants would henceforth be on navigable water. In 1918, he began coi'struction of the Rouge plant.

Building the Rouge proved difficult. Ford's stockholders, including the Dodge brothers, were dead set against it and had to be bought out at tremendous expense. The land bordering the Rouge River was swampy, and the river itself had to be straightened and dredged to allow sizable ships to navigate. Use of the waterway also required the rebuilding of several bridges across the river downstream of the plant.

One of these bridges belonged to the Detroit, Toledo & Ironton Railroad (the DT&I), a nearly defunct enterprise that was fully mortgaged and unable to raise the $350,000 necessary to rebuild its bridge. The company asked Ford to guarantee the bonds that would have to be issued to raise the necessary money. Ford not only advanced $521,000 toward reconstruction costs and bond interest payments for the DT&I, but by July 9, 1920, he had purchased controlling interest in the entire

Reprinted with permission from the *Herald*, Vol. 15, No. 1, 1986.

The Detroit, Toledo & Ironton bridge spanning the Short-Cut Canal that connects the River Rouge Ship Canal with the Detroit River. The bridge has unique underslung counterweights. (833.34942)

system. The following January, a $15 million improvement program was announced, and on March 4, 1921, Ford became president of the railroad. He had paid approximately $5 million for nearly all of the outstanding stock except that held by two bothersome New Yorkers, and he was now responsible for a complete but totally decrepit railroad system.

The Detroit, Toledo & Ironton Railroad had started out as the old Iron Railway in 1849, a small but ambitious line. It extended only six miles from Ironton, Ohio, on the Ohio River, to Vesuvius, Ohio. But this short stretch of road into the hills included a 958-foot tunnel and a wrought-iron bridge 97 feet long. Gradually, the Iron Railway was refashioned through purchases, consolidations, and leases of dubious value, until in 1903 it became the Detroit, Toledo & Ironton with its northern terminal in Detroit. By the time Ford became its owner, the railroad had been through twenty-six unsuccessful reorganizations but had remained chiefly a coal-hauling line with miles of branches and sidings leading from small southern Ohio mines to its main north-south system. But a long period of deferred maintenance had earned the DT&I the nickname "Dirty, Twisted, and Inconvenient." Wags insisted that there was enough scrap iron throughout the system to be worth the price Ford had paid for it.

But Ford had not acquired the DT&I blindly. He had clearly visualized the benefits it might provide for his own automotive operations.

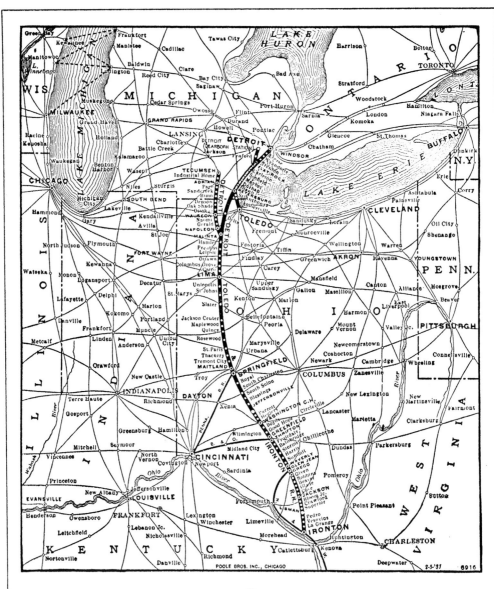

DETROIT, TOLEDO AND IRONTON RAILROAD COMPANY

Simultaneously with his purchase of the railroad, Ford had acquired two coal mines at Wallins Creek and Tinsdale, Kentucky. Later that year, he bought a coal mine at Nuttalburg, West Virginia. These were forerunners of the Fordson Coal Company, a $15 million operation that would more than supply the coal needs of the Ford Motor Company. The DT&I would help bring this coal directly to his Rouge plant.

Of course, Ford could not bear to be associated for long with such a disreputable piece of property. Immediately upon becoming president of the railroad, he embarked upon renovations. Incumbent DT&I officers were replaced by Ford men, all with executive offices in Dearborn. High efficiency and good wages were the keynotes. Some 400 illegal encroachments were found to exist on DT&I property. Businesses as well as individual squatters had usurped portions of DT&I territory, erecting eyesore shacks along the right-of-way. Strict enforcement of property rights reduced these encroachments to fewer than a dozen. Railroad accounting procedures were centralized and paperwork cut in half. The legal department was abolished, with the claims department absorbing the work. The backlog of freight damage claims was reduced from 1,209 to 68.

The total work force was cut from 2,760 to 1,650, and the pay of the remaining employees was raised from around $3.75 for eight hours to the $6.00 minimum wage current in Ford plants. Soon the average office worker was receiving $8.11, and others were getting $7.26 per day. With these increased wages, Ford was able to abrogate all union contracts and assign workers to any job they were capable of handling. The wages were above those prescribed by the Railway Labor Board and high enough to receive acclaim from the Railroad Brotherhood. Before long, the sixteen-hour maximum workday was reduced to twelve hours, with management forecasting an eight-hour maximum for the future.

An employee investment program was inaugurated; it yielded 10 to 16 percent annual interest over the next several years. Coal was offered to employees at wholesale prices: "run of mine" for $3.00 per ton, "egg" for $3.25, "lump" for $3.50. An employee newsletter, the *DT&I Railroad News,* was initiated in January 1923 and continued as a semimonthly publication until December 1927. This eight-page publication described DT&I construction projects and delivered general advice to workmen. It devoted at least two pages in each issue to railroad safety and included a practical medical column written by a staff doctor of Henry Ford Hospital.

But work requirements were strict. Ford expected hard work, cleanliness, punctuality, sobriety, and thrift. Train crews were to be clean-shaven and were to wear clean overalls, white caps, and goggles. There was to be no smoking of tobacco or idleness. Of the crew of a waiting train, all but the flagman were to be either polishing the locomotive or cleaning the caboose rather than just standing around. At the end of a run, a dirty engine was immediately cleaned and polished by the engine crew before being dispatched on another run. An "impact recorder" hidden on the train recorded the degree to which the cars had been bumped or jostled in transit, thus monitoring the performance of the engineer and reducing damage claims. Crossing guards were expected to care for a small vegetable garden or flower bed in their spare time.

This revitalized work force soon put the long-neglected railroad properties in order. Miles of roadbed were reballasted with rock, gravel, and by-product slag from the Rouge factories. Old lightweight, 60-pound rail was replaced with new 80-pound rail purchased from Belgium. Old rails were employed as grade crossing reinforcement. Old ties were converted to charcoal for commercial use. The Rouge concrete casting plant supplied concrete replacement fence posts for use along the rights-of-way. Bridges were rebuilt with cement shipped from Fordson. Stations and tool houses were repaired and repainted. Major shops and roundhouses were reequipped, and a large locomotive repair facility that would employ 475 men was constructed at the Rouge. Ten new steam locomotives and 800 freight cars were purchased in this initial phase of renovation.

About 350 new Hamilton watches, which were checked periodically for accuracy, were loaned to employees. An electrically controlled clock system, regulated from Dearborn, automatically adjusted clocks in stations the entire length of the system. New copper telegraph and telephone wires replaced the badly rusted iron wire, to provide clear message and dispatch signals throughout the system. Dispatching was done at Fordson and Springfield, Ohio. For a time, a radio system, with stations in Dearborn; Jackson, Ohio; and Springfield, Ohio, handled traffic messages at the rate of 10,000 per month.

Of the seventy-five steam locomotives Ford had acquired, only fifty were usable. The others had been stored along the line in various states of disrepair. At least ten, originally built for Russia, had been designed for a wide (60-inch) tread and were somewhat top-heavy for the narrower American tracks. (Hundreds of locomotives were built for the Russian government before World War I. After the fall of the tsarist government, many were assigned to various U.S. railroads, including the DT&I.) To correct this deficiency, the Fordson shops initiated a program to rebuild four locomotives a month. In all, seventy-three locomotives were completely overhauled and fitted out with the characteristic nickel-plated fixtures, polished boiler sheet, and white-painted wheels insisted on by Ford.

Upkeep of passenger and freight cars was handled at Jackson, Ohio, where elaborate erecting and machine shops could repair or rebuild all common types of cars. New dining cars, compartment cars, work cars, and cabooses were fitted out at this facility. In addition to the earlier purchase, new freight cars were added in 1927 with the acquisition of 1,000 box cars, 400 gondolas, 50 flat cars, and 40 cabooses.

By July 1922, the railroad was approaching profitability, and a request by DT&I for a 20-percent reduction in freight rates was granted by the Interstate Commerce Commission despite the protests of other railroads. At that same time, a major project was in the planning stage. This included the construction of a new 13.5-mile double track directly connecting the Rouge plant with the DT&I tracks at Flat Rock and electrification of the new lines between the Rouge (Fordson) and Flat Rock. This direct link to Flat Rock would eliminate switching charges and costly delays. The electrified system was separately incorporated as the Detroit & Ironton Railroad and leased to the DT&I. Henry and Clara Ford and their son, Edsel, were the sole owners.

One of Henry Ford's DT&I locomotives, fully restored and highly polished, at the machine shop in the Rouge plant at Dearborn in August 1924. Ford insisted that any machinery he owned be in excellent operating condition. (833.38376)

The Fordson-Flat Rock lines were major investments. In addition to the new heavy-service double tracks, there were large electrified classification yards just north of Flat Rock (South Yards) and at Fordson (North Yards). Some 365 reinforced concrete arches spanned the tracks at 300-foot intervals and supported the trolley wires. Power for the electrified system was generated at the Rouge powerhouse by 62,500-horsepower steam turbines supplying 60-cycle alternating current.

Normally, four freight trains ran between Fordson and Ironton. From 1921 to 1923, car-miles and ton-miles doubled as locomotives traveled farther and hauled larger loads. By 1926, the DT&I handled 4,100 cars per day, compared with only 600 cars per day when it had passed into Ford's hands six years earlier. At one point, 70 percent of DT&I traffic was Ford freight. The trip from Fordson to Ironton took twenty-four to twenty-six hours. On the way, several connections were made throughout central Ohio with main east-west carriers such as the New York Central, Pennsylvania, and Baltimore & Ohio. Farther south, connections were made with the Chesapeake & Ohio and the Norfolk & Western, large coal carriers from Kentucky and West Virginia. At the end of the DT&I line at Ironton, there was a rail/river transfer point on the river's edge where a specially designed old "cradle" rolled freight cars onto and off Ohio River barges.

Passenger traffic on the DT&I was essentially nil. However, the Interstate Commerce Commission forced the railroad to maintain passenger and mail service between Detroit and Springfield, Ohio, with a daily round trip. An effort to abandon the passenger trains proved of no avail. In 1926, two gasoline-electric, Pullman-built cars replaced the passenger trains on the 280-mile run between Detroit and Bainbridge, Ohio. These benzol-burning coaches were fast and economical. And instead of a special steam train, flanged-wheel Model T sedans were used to carry track inspectors over the lines in comfort.

Although electrification for the DT&I was completed as far as Flat Rock, with trolley supports to Carlton, there were plans to electrify the lines as far as Springfield, Ohio. Surveys also were made for a line from Bainbridge to Portsmouth on the Ohio River. Serious consideration was given to purchasing the Virginian Railroad, an electrified system that would have provided an outlet from Portsmouth to the Atlantic coast and ocean shipping. But these plans did not materialize for several reasons.

From the outset, Ford was nettled by the government regulations limiting the independence of the railroads. The very year he purchased the DT&I, the Transportation Act of 1920 instructed the Interstate Commerce Commission to "prepare and adopt a plan for the consolidation of the railway properties of the continental United States into a limited number of systems." Under this plan, the DT&I was to be merged with the Pere Marquette Railroad. Although the merger was

This powerful electric locomotive is pulling freight cars from Fordson to Flat Rock, Michigan, in April 1926. Ford's intention was to electrify the DT&I down through Ohio and beyond. (833.43350)

never pressed during Ford's ownership, the mere threat served to dampen his enthusiasm for railroading.

Another restrictive government regulation concerned profits. Of any profits above 6 percent of the value of the road, half was to be turned over to the Interstate Commerce Commission for distribution to other railroads. This penalized efficient management and made it difficult to modernize a railroad from its own profits. The Fords were taking no dividends; all of the earnings were used for improvements to the system.

The federal government had never quite surrendered its wartime control over freight rates, wages, hours, accounting procedures, and many other aspects of the railroad business, and this left very little flexibility or room for initiative. Ford's interest in the use of lightweight rolling stock, for example, had been completely blocked by the Interstate Commerce Commission. By 1927, Ford had lost interest in the railroad and relinquished the presidency to Stanley Ruddiman and overall responsibility to Edsel Ford. The final blow may well have been a $20,000 fine imposed in 1928 for violation of the Elkins Act, passed in 1903 to prevent rate discrimination by railroads. Apparently, DT&I was not charging Ford Motor Company standard demurrage for freight cars parked at the Rouge plant.

In the year of the fine, Edsel Ford is said to have approached the Detroit agent of the Pennsylvania Railroad with the opening comment, "My father and I have had our fun with the DT&I." As a result, the Pennsylvania Railroad formed the Pennroad Corporation to purchase the Ford railroad properties. After much negotiation and the waiving of an illegal gentlemen's agreement to continue to favor DT&I with Ford Motor Company shipments, the $33.5 million sale was concluded on June 27, 1929.

It turned out to have been the right time to sell. In spite of huge investments in roadbed, shops, and rolling stock, Ford's railroad had been especially profitable between 1923 and 1926. His profits had totaled about $9 million, and he sold the line just before the onset of the Great Depression. He had had his fling at railroading and had demonstrated how a railroad could be run despite contentious stockholders and government regulators. Now he would be content with his private railway car, the *Fair Lane,* riding on someone else's rails.

When Ford sold his railroad properties, Ruddiman became vice president under the new Pennsylvania management. Later, Ruddiman again assumed the presidency, serving in that capacity from 1933 until his retirement in 1952. The DT&I had maintained its corporate identity but was controlled by the Pennsylvania Railroad from 1929 until 1968. At that time, the Pennsylvania merged with the New York Central to form the Penn-Central Corporation, which declared bankruptcy two years later.

Although the DT&I was considered choice property, the massive 1973-1976 reorganization resulting in Conrail delayed its sale for several years. In December 1979, the Interstate Commerce Commission approved a bid from the Grand Trunk Western, and the sale was concluded on June 24, 1980, for $25,600,000. Grand Trunk operated the DT&I profitably as its Ohio division, using diesel locomotives. Ford's giant electric locomotives had been scrapped in 1937, and steam operation ended on Christmas Eve, 1954.

In April 1984, the Grand Trunk Corporation announced completion of a consolidation creating a 1,514-mile system in Michigan, Ohio, Indiana, Illinois, Kentucky, and Ontario. For several years, the DT&I logo remained painted on its bridges, viaducts, and overpasses. Now, other than a few of the 27-ton concrete arches still firmly implanted over the rails between Dearborn and Flat Rock, the chief physical reminders of the DT&I are a locomotive, a caboose, and a freight car or two at Henry Ford Museum & Greenfield Village in Dearborn.

References

Accession 6, Box 281, DT&I, Edsel Ford Papers. Benson Ford Research Center, HFM & GV.

DT&I Railroad News, Vols. 1–5 (January 1923–December 1927). Benson Ford Research Center, HFM & GV.

Lewis, David L. *The Public Image of Henry Ford.* Detroit: Wayne State University Press, 1976, pp. 165–67.

Middleton, W. V. "Henry Ford and His Electric Locomotive." *Train Magazine,* September 1976, pp. 22–26.

"Mr. Ford's Ten Years as a Railroad Owner: A Decade of Progress," S. J. Ruddiman (no date), Vertical File. Benson Ford Research Center, HFM & GV.

Nevins, Allan, and Frank Ernest Hill. *Ford: Expansion and Challenge, 1915–1932.* New York: Scribner's, 1957, pp. 220–25.

"A Railroad Link between the Ohio and Detroit Rivers." *Grand Trunk Reporter,* July–August 1980.

Trostel, Scott D. *The Detroit, Toledo and Ironton Railroad: Henry Ford's Railroad.* Fletcher, Ohio: Cam-Tech Publishing, 1988.

22

Fordson Truck

The well-known Fordson tractor, designed by Eugene Farkas and first built by Henry Ford & Son — not by Ford Motor Company — was produced in Henry, Edsel, and Clara Ford's brickyard factory on Elm Street in old Dearborn. The Fordson tractor was as important to American farmers as was the Ford Model T automobile. Work on experimental tractors was begun by Ford as early as 1904, four years before the Model T was introduced. After the Model T was well developed, Ford put it to work as a farm tractor on his farm in Dearborn, but it was not strong enough to pull as much as a strong team of horses. So work began on a more powerful tractor, resulting in the famous Fordson, which was built in large numbers beginning in 1917. Some 552,799 Fordson tractors were built in Dearborn factories before manufacturing was transferred to Cork, Ireland, in 1928.

By 1915, Ford Motor Company was selling the Model T chassis for $360, upon which body builders fitted various types of commercial bodies. The following year, Ford Motor Company began selling its own one-ton Model T truck. These lightweight trucks with stake bodies became very popular with farmers. The trucks were first produced in Highland Park, Michigan, and 1,283,975 were sold between 1916 and 1928, when Ford Model AA trucks took their place.

Ford had realized back in 1916 that the Model T, with its 25-horsepower motor, provided a good lightweight truck that served farmers well, but for some trucking purposes a stronger vehicle was necessary. While he was manufacturing thousands of Fordson tractors on Elm Street during 1917–18, he was also contemplating a truck using the stronger tractor motor. This was to be the two-ton Fordson truck. There were several practical obstacles to be overcome, however, before he could go ahead and build the Fordson truck. His plans for the fledgling Rouge plant (a Ford Motor Company facility) at that time were being hindered not only by World War I but also by his minority stockholders. In fact, Ford was so disgusted with his "greedy" stockholders that in December 1918, he

Previously published in the *Dearborn Historian*, Vol. 32, No. 1, 1992.

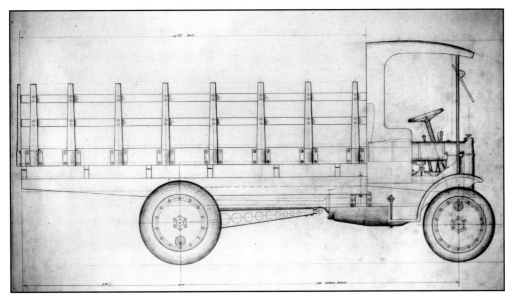

turned the presidency of Ford Motor Company over to his son, Edsel, and left for California, where he announced that he would form a new company, market an automobile at $250, and drive his "parasitic" stockholders out of business. So it was well after the war and after his complete buyout of Ford Motor Company minor stockholders in July 1919 that engineering drawings and photographs of a Fordson truck appeared.

Eugene Farkas, who had designed the very successful Fordson tractor, was assigned by Ford to design the Fordson truck chassis. Joseph Galamb was to design the bodies, and they were to be built by Budd Wheel Company of Detroit. During this same period, Fordson tractors were beginning to be built at the Rouge plant, but photographs indicate the new Fordson truck experimental work was being carried out on Elm Street at the old brickyard tractor plant, the birthplace of the Fordson tractor. Creating a truck from a tractor required considerable reengineering of the driveline; the Fordson tractor's top speed of only 6.75 miles per hour would hardly be fast enough for a truck.

Farkas, in his reminiscences, relates that his very first sketches for the Fordson truck were made in the powerhouse drafting room at the Fair Lane residence. Ford had told him that he wanted to have a chassis for both trucks and buses to carry schoolchildren. He also wanted Farkas to employ a worm gear rear axle in the truck as was used in the Fordson tractor. The tractor transmission gearbox was to be used, with three-speed sliding gears similar to the tractor but, of course, having appropriate gear ratios. The standard Fordson tractor engine of 30 horsepower would be used. There was much discussion concerning spring suspension. The front axle and spring were to be similar to the

This drawing of the proposed Fordson truck is dated September 9, 1920. Wheelbase is 136 inches; overall length with stake body is 213 inches. The open cab is over the engine, with the driver sitting above the engine and next to the gasoline tank. (0.1190)

An overhead view of the chassis of the two-ton Fordson truck as photographed on December 3, 1924, in Dearborn. The differential cover is removed to show ring and pinion gears. (189.2423)

Side view of the two-ton Fordson truck chassis taken on December 3, 1924. The building beyond is the original Fordson tractor plant in Dearborn, where Fordson tractors were built from 1917 to 1920; it is the building in which the Fordson truck was being developed. (189.2424)

Model T. Ford was convinced, however, that for rear suspension, two long cantilever springs with a feather edge on the axle and the thick portion fastened to the frame would be best. A similar type was apparently then used on Rolls-Royce automobiles.

The appearance of the truck was indeed strange inasmuch as the cab was over the engine, the hood was in the cab, and the driver sat alongside the engine. The radiator, bearing the name *Fordson*, projected only about four inches beyond the dash. After Ford had purchased the Lincoln plant in 1922, he wanted the Fordson truck's rear axle to be interchangeable with the Lincoln axle. Preferring the worm drive, he tried such an axle in a Lincoln but without much success.

Drawings made by Farkas are dated between 1920 and 1924. At that time, Farkas relates, he was busy with too many things. Besides working on the Fordson truck, he also was struggling with Ford's X engines and developing a method of manufacturing welded wire wheels for both the truck and the Lincoln. He found he could not use his wire wheels as the truck's dual rear wheels and had to resort to disc dual wheels. According

to Farkas, a total of at least twelve Fordson trucks were made. Few, if any, still exist. In 1926, Ford sent the latest prototype Fordson truck to his longtime friend Arthur Brisbane, editor of Hearst newspapers, for testing. Farkas knew by then that the Fordson truck was very definitely underpowered. Its 30-horsepower tractor engine did not compete at all favorably with REO's 50-horsepower, two-ton Speed Wagon, for example. To provide power for possibly eighteen-hour-per-day service, a truck needed considerably more power than an automobile.

Another factor influencing production of the Fordson truck may have been Edsel Ford's relative disinterest in tractors and trucks. From childhood, Edsel had been a connoisseur of automotive design. His intense interest in the elegant custom coachwork featured on his Lincolns would not likely have encompassed Galamb's cab-over-engine body design on the Fordson truck. Although there is no record of Edsel's having openly criticized the Fordson truck, he was also not promoting it. Edsel, with his Lincoln responsibilities, was at that very time establishing the details of automotive design that would enhance the success of all upcoming Ford Motor Company vehicles, both cars and trucks: the 1928 "Baby Lincolns."

Ford had been under pressure for years to produce a replacement for the Model T. It was Farkas, the engineer, who finally convinced him that it was really necessary. Along with the new Model A would be a Model AA truck. Farkas was then asked to drop his X engine and

The Fordson truck with a steel paywagon body used to deliver cash to workers at the Rouge plant about 1930. (833.57599.1)

Fordson truck projects and devote himself to Model A and AA chassis and suspension design. The Farkas welded wire wheels had first been installed on the Lincoln, then on the Model Ts just before their demise, and now were to become standard on the new Ford, the Model A.

References

Accession 65, Eugene Farkas Reminiscences. Benson Ford Research Center, HFM & GV.

Accession 1660, Box 152 J, Experimental Trucks (Photographs). Benson Ford Research Center, HFM & GV.

23
Ford's Amazing X-8 Vehicle

We have quite universally recognized the Ford Model T as an outstanding automobile for its time. Henry Ford is given major credit for it, although men such as C. Harold Wills, Joseph Galamb, Charles Sorensen, Eugene J. Farkas, and Edward S. (Spyder) Huff also deserve credit for significant contributions. Wills was an outstanding automotive designer and an accomplished metallurgist, Galamb was an expert at sheetmetal fabrication and body design, Sorensen was noted for his ability to produce intricate iron castings, Farkas was a chassis engineering genius, and Huff was an electrical wizard.

Farkas was the man Ford picked to help develop the Ford-Edison electric car in 1914. He was again chosen by Ford and Sorensen to be chief engineer of Henry Ford & Son and to design the very successful Fordson tractor. When Fordson tractor production matured and was shifted to the Rouge plant in 1920, Ford turned his attention to the replacement of the Model T with an automobile of revolutionary design — an automobile as innovative as the Model T was in 1908.

Ford began with the concept of an engine distinctly different from the standard automotive design. In 1920, he put to work an ingenious self-made engineer named Allan Horton in his very private powerhouse drafting room and shop at the Fair Lane residence in Dearborn. In about 1922, Ford was sufficiently encouraged to proceed with further development and testing of this engine, placing the project under Farkas, working in the "Fireplace Room" of the old tractor plant in Dearborn. There it was to be tested in comparison with other engines such as an in-line six and a V-6.

Ford's experimental engine being further developed by Farkas was a very compact eight-cylinder configuration with four cylinders facing upward and another four cylinders facing downward. One could think of it as a very compact double bank of four-cylinder radial engines. In any case, it was a very radical configuration for an automobile. At least twenty experimental X engines were built by the Farkas group — one of

---

Published previously in *The Ford Legend,* Vol. V, No. 1, 1996.

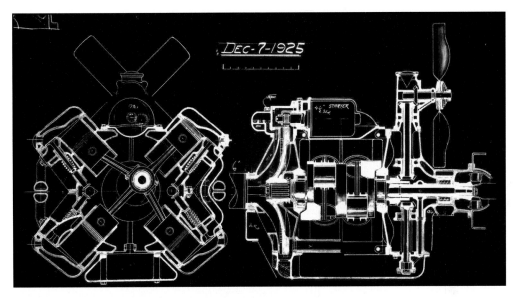

A December 1925 blackboard drawing by Eugene Farkas of one of the experimental X-8 engines which was to replace the four-cylinder Model T engine. It is very compact, occupying approximately one cubic foot in size. Both water- and air-cooled versions were built and tested. (189.3169)

them a twenty-four-cylinder monster designed for speedboat racing. By April 1925, several reasonably workable X-8s were ready for testing — some air-cooled, some water-cooled.

Incorporated into the X-8 was a battery-powered dual ignition, a single-unit starter generator, roller main bearings, a supercharger built into the flywheel, and a three-speed planetary transmission (the Model T had a two-speed). Any one of these changes from the Model T would have been considered a major development. The X-8 was first tested in a Model T and found too heavy for the chassis. By September 1925, a new chassis and body had been designed to accommodate the X-8 engine.

Further testing of the engine, however, began to reveal its ultimate weaknesses. Two major defects proved especially difficult to overcome. The flywheel speed was not sufficient to provide adequate supercharger performance, and a most annoying inconvenience was the constant fouling of spark plugs on the bottom of the engine by the accumulation of oil, water, and dirt.

By 1926, Edsel Ford, and to a great extent the general public, had hinted to Henry Ford that perhaps the Model T had become obsolete and he needed a more attractive Ford car. Henry, of course, had been

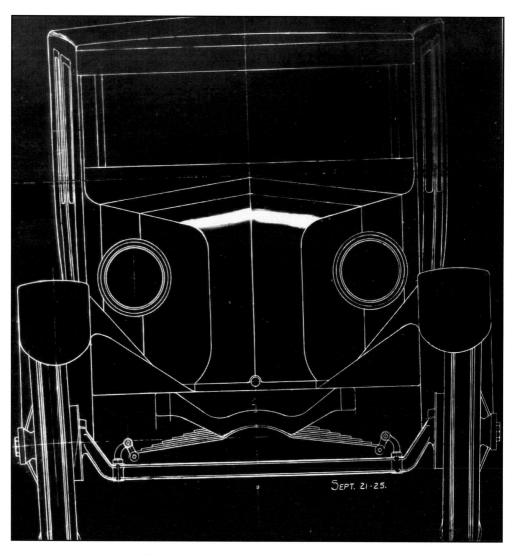

Sept. 21·25.

A Farkas blackboard drawing of the front view of the X-engined four-door sedan, also dated September 21, 1925. There is no attached crank as there was on the Model T. The front axle provides no more than ten inches of ground clearance. There is the appearance of four-wheel brakes and perhaps wire wheels. Fender surfaces are relatively wide and flat. The general frontal appearance is far different from and, for its time, more stylish than the Model T. (189.3018)

Blackboard drawing by Eugene Farkas of an X-engined four-door sedan, dated September 21, 1925. Note the 120-inch wheelbase, the longitudinal rear springs, the low road clearance of the front axle, and the cowl locations of water and gas openings calling for a long cowl and a short "Franklin"-type hood. The side-mounted spare wheel, "drum" headlights, and slanting windshield indicate that body styling was given considerable attention, although it is doubtful that Edsel Ford was much involved. (189.3024)

Ford's Amazing X-8 Vehicle

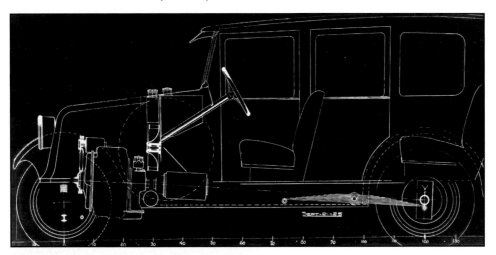

Allan A. Horton, the chief engineer of the air-cooled X-8 engine. Horton shared working space with Henry Ford on the top floor of the Fair Lane powerhouse. This portrait was taken about 1915, shortly before he started working for Henry Ford. (Photo courtesy of Fair Lane Archives.)

planning on a new car with the X-8 engine. Farkas was under extreme pressure to perfect the X-8. Ernest Kanzler, a brother-in-law of Edsel and a Ford executive, became so convinced about the falling popularity of the Model T that he wrote a letter to Henry Ford in January 1926, stating the seriousness of the situation. Ford executives, in general, did not dare criticize Henry's plans to his face. As for Kanzler's letter, Henry not only did not answer it, but he became so openly discourteous that Kanzler was forced to resign from the company. Farkas continued to explain the difficulties with the X-8 engine to Ford, who had more patience with Farkas, an engineer, than with Kanzler, an office man.

Later in 1926, Ford said to Farkas, "Now, we don't want to abandon the X-8 engine. That's something for the future. But now we've got to design a car for the market, a four-cylinder one" (the Model A). Ford did not care for six-cylinder engines at all. And he never openly admitted that his six years of experimenting with the X-type engine had been a failure, although it had delayed introduction of the Model A for several years. So Farkas and others went to work on the new Model A Ford, and the X-8 engine has become merely a very interesting museum piece. In fact, a good example of Ford's X-8 engine is now on display in the powerhouse of the Fair Lane estate, where Allan Horton began the X engine project in 1920.

References

Accession 65, Eugene Farkas Reminiscences. Benson Ford Research Center, HFM & GV.

Accession 65, Harold Hicks Reminiscences. Benson Ford Research Center, HFM & GV.

Accession 65, L. S. Sheldrick Reminiscences. Benson Ford Reasearch Center, HFM & GV.

Accession 65, Howard Simpson Reminiscences. Benson Ford Reasearch Center, HFM & GV.

Accession 901, Box 5, Bombard Engineering File. Benson Ford Research Center, HFM & GV.

Accession 1660, Box 45, Photographs. Benson Ford Research Center, HFM & GV.

24
The Speedboat *Miss Dearborn*

From 1920 until 1925, Edsel Ford, then in his late twenties, was playing with speedboats as well as with foreign sports cars. He did not race them himself because it was too dangerous. Although he would often drive the boats on practice runs, for serious racing he employed such daredevils as Ray Dahlinger, Jimmy Smith, Paul Strasburg, and Johnnie Stroh — but always cautioning them to be careful. Edsel's fleet of speedboats during that period included *Goldfish, Woodfish, Comanche, 999, Greyhound, Jr.,* and probably others. Edsel competed in regattas such as the Niagara River Races at Buffalo in June 1921 and the Mississippi Valley Power Boat Association races at Peoria, Illinois, in July 1921. In these races, he was not the winner.

It was in 1920 that Edsel had decided to compete in the International Sweepstakes on the Detroit River, also scheduled for the summer of 1921. Prominent contenders were Horace Dodge, Garfield (Gar) Wood, a Mr. Greening of Canada, and a Colonel Vincent of Packard Motor Car Company. Wood, chairman of the race committee and frequent winner of such races, was to set the specification limits for boats entering this race. Both Edsel and Henry Ford eyed the very favorable publicity to come from winning such a race in Detroit. They would build a boat that would surely win.

Edsel had in mind a sleek monoplane hull with lines borrowed from some of the fastest boats in racing. Both Edsel and Henry wanted to experiment with aluminum hull fabrication — Henry was thinking of producing large amounts of aluminum at Muscle Shoals, Alabama, and building Model T bodies of aluminum. When it came to the engine for the speedboat, a souped-up World War I twelve-cylinder Liberty engine likely would have been Edsel's choice, but Henry had a different idea. He was experimenting with a small X engine. Eugene Farkas was directing the work. The X engine was to replace the Model T engine in a revolutionary new Ford automobile.

Previously published in the *Dearborn Historian*, Vol. 38, No. 1, 1998.

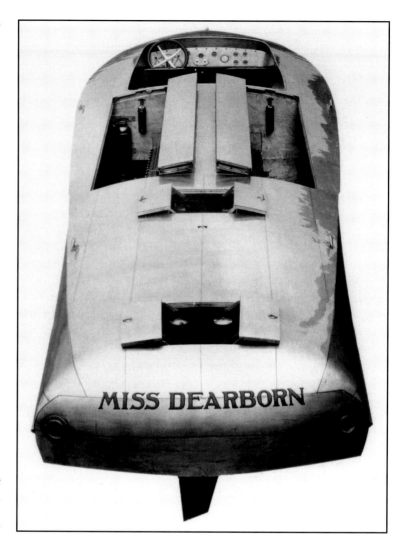

Both the engine and the hull were built in Dearborn in secret. Work on the engine design was started by Allan Horton in the power-house building at Fair Lane. Later, Harold Hicks, Farkas, and Howard Simpson took part in the development. The boat was laid out full-size on the second floor of the tractor plant office building, the hull just large enough to house the engine adequately. Carl Schultz did the layout detail work, and a Swiss draftsman, Carl Marti, helped. The hull was about 33 feet long and 9 feet wide at its maximum width. There were to be no nonessential protuberances such as windshield or running lights. Everything was flush except the cleats with which the boat was tied to the dock. The headlights popped up with the touch of a button; side running lights worked similarly.

There were seats for four in the boat. Two-seated speedboats were not yet in vogue. The cockpit was forward, and the engine was in a large compartment in back of the passenger seat. Gas tanks were in the rear.

The primary feature of the speedboat, however, was Henry Ford's monster engine. This X engine turned out to be a twenty-four-cylinder of 4400-cubic-inch piston displacement. It consisted of four L-head, six-cylinder engines placed at right angles to one another driving a single ball-bearing crankshaft. It was equipped with dual ignition and magnesium pistons. The engine was designed to produce 1,000 horse-power and drive the boat at 60 miles per hour. Every part of the entire speedboat, including carburetors, distributors, reduction gears, and oil pumps, was built in Dearborn, it is said, with the exception of the forty-eight spark plugs. The boat was very aptly named *Miss Dearborn*.

As building of the *Miss Dearborn* progressed, Wood heard of it and lowered the maximum cylinder displacement allowable in the race to 3,000 cubic inches and finally, on March 3, 1921, to 2,150 cubic inches. This was only half the displacement of the *Miss Dearborn*. So, for the Detroit River race, the *Miss Dearborn* was much too large to qualify. When completed, the *Miss Dearborn* was taken to Edsel's Grosse Pointe estate boathouse, where maintenance and testing were under the management of a Captain Anderson and Johnnie Johnson. Eight or ten men were at work on speedboats at that location much of the time.

The X engine was so evenly balanced that it "ran like a sewing machine," said Hicks. It had sufficient acceleration from 1,200 rpm to promptly seat a person who was trying to stand in the boat. The engine satisfied Ford's belief that multiples of four cylinders were better balanced than any other combination. Thus, with time, came Ford's four-cylinder Model A, the V-8 Ford, the V-12 Lincoln Zephyr, and the sixteen-cylinder big Lincoln.

Although the *Miss Dearborn*, with its X-24 engine, had cost the Fords at least $125,000, it had its mechanical shortcomings. The twelve cylinders, with their twenty-four spark plugs on the lower side, were almost constantly fouled by oil. Servicing these lower cylinders without removing the engine from the boat was very difficult. Lubrication furnished by a splash-type system suggested by Ford was not sufficient to prevent frequent burning out of connecting rods, but a crankshaft was never lost on the X engine.

Being too large for racing, the *Miss Dearborn* was used as a test craft for a variety of engine combinations following the abandonment of the X design. Carl Arndt installed a pair of Liberties, and later the larger Packard marine engines were tried. But the *Miss Dearborn* never entered competition. Dahlinger continued to drive the various racing boats with Jimmy Smith or Frank McCormick as mechanics.

Edsel seldom beat the cunning Wood in a race. But in 1922, with his *Woodfish*, he set a new world's record in the Gold Cup International Sweepstakes. Then, in Miami, Florida, during the winter of 1924, Dahlinger, with Smith in Edsel's *999* with a Ford-built Liberty engine, beat Wood. Edsel soon dropped the sport of boat racing and became an energetic sponsor of aviation.

References

Accession 65, A. L. Esper Reminiscences. Benson Ford Research Center, HFM & GV.

Accession 65, Harold Hicks Reminiscences. Benson Ford Research Center, HFM & GV.

Accession 65, Howard Simpson Reminiscences. Benson Ford Research Center, HFM & GV.

Accession 65, C. J. (Jimmy) Smith Reminiscences. Benson Ford Research Center, HFM & GV.

25
Ford's Robot Engines

The Bug

In utmost secrecy during 1917, aircraft and engine specialists gathered at a farmhouse in an isolated section of Ohio to develop an odd vehicle to win the war in Europe. Involved were Henry Ford; his chief engineer, C. H. Wills; Charles F. Kettering, head of research at Dayton Metal Products Company; Harold Morehouse, draftsman with Dayton-Wright Aircraft Company; Wilbur Wright; and Elmer Sperry. Kettering led the project under Colonel H. H. Arnold of the U.S. Signal Corps. Details of the project were not publicly revealed until about fifteen years following World War II.

The vehicle was to be a pilotless guided missile requiring the talents of the best aeronautical, propulsion, and guidance system minds available in this country. Wright provided aeronautical advice, Ford took responsibility for the engine, and Sperry led guidance systems. Kettering was overall administrator reporting to Arnold.

The robot was to deliver a warhead of 200 pounds for any distance from 50 to 200 miles to reach its target. It was to be a low-cost, long-range, self-guided, self-propelled aerial torpedo. In principle, it was simple; in practice, it was complex. A gasoline engine was simply to be supplied with only enough fuel to carry a plane and bomb a selected distance in the right direction.

The engine, developed by Wills, was an air-cooled V-4 generating 40 horsepower — well advanced for the period. It had no carburetor, the air-fuel mixture being set before takeoff. Ford said the engine could be mass-produced for about $40. (The entire vehicle was to cost no more than $200.) The engine developed no troubles whatsoever.

Aiming of the "Bug" was more of a problem. Sperry, with Kettering, worked on the complications of head winds, cross winds, updrafts, and downdrafts. An ultrasensitive aneroid barometer was designed to correct for updrafts and downdrafts. A subtracting anemometer provided a means of stopping the motor after an exact

Published previously in the *Dearborn Historian*, Vol. 31, No. 1, 1991.

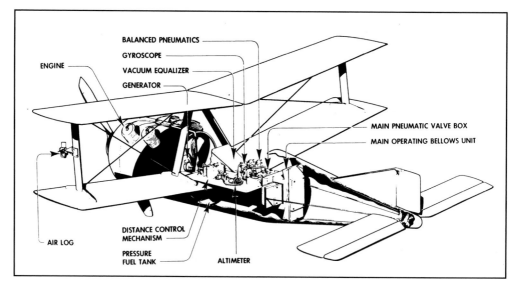

Schematic drawing of the "Bug," which was produced during World War I. Henry Ford and C. Harold Wills of Ford Motor Company designed and built a lightweight, air-cooled, four-cylinder engine for it.

WWI propeller-driven guided missile Bugs being assembled in a secret factory in 1918. The factory was likely near Dayton, Ohio. (189.63701)

number of engine revolutions for more perfect distance control. The plane had a wingspan of 17 feet, a length of 12.5 feet, and a weight of 350 pounds without payload. Its speed was 55 miles per hour, and it was designed to release its wings to let the fuselage fall to earth as a bomb.

When the device was ready and had passed its tests, Arnold went to Europe to prepare launching sites. But by the time Arnold's preparations had begun, a serious defect in the plan had developed: they had run out of war; peace had broken out.

In 1941 the Bug, still a secret weapon, was proposed again to fight the Germans, but its range was not long enough to fly from England to Germany. It would have dropped its bomb on friendly soil. The B-17 bomber was chosen in place of the Bug but not without much added expense and loss of life.

The Buzz Bomb

During World War II, England had been bombed mercilessly by German V-1 robots. From the debris of the first hundred or so of these exploded robots in England, the Allied War Council arranged for the collection of pieces of wreckage and, from visual examination of these parts, prepared a short (five-page) memorandum concerning those lethal vehicles. A bomber load of mutilated V-1 parts, together with the short written report, was urgently flown to the Army Air Force Materiel Command at Wright Field. On July 15, 1944, while Ford Motor Company was already deeply involved in aircraft work at the Rouge and Willow Run plants, Colonel J. D. Keirn of Wright Field contacted Ford officials regarding manufacture of a robot equal or superior to the V-1 used by the Germans.

Six experimental WWI guided missile Bugs ready for launch at a secret takeoff site in Ohio in 1918. Because the robot has no landing gear, a four-wheel carriage on a long track provides for easy takeoff. (189.63700)

A PJ-31-1 engine as installed on a JB-2 robomb.

One of the reasons Ford Motor Company was selected for this assignment was Arnold's recollection of Ford's pioneering work with the robot engines during World War I. At that time, in 1918, Ford Motor Company had built a successful engine for the Bug. Arnold had been in charge of the project, and he was proud of its success.

Ford personnel negotiated a contract with Keirn at Wright Field resulting in an arrangement whereby Ford Motor Company would design and build the intermittent-jet-type engine, with the airplane portion of the robot — warhead, fuselage, and so on — assigned to other manufacturers. The first contract for these engines, calling for twenty-five experimental prototypes, was signed on July 19, 1944. The Ford people, by piecing together parts, preparing detailed drawings, and chemically analyzing the metals involved, were able to duplicate the German engine closely. The project, classified as secret, was known to top brass as MX-544.

Three handmade engines, the type designated PJ-31-1, were sent to Dayton on October 9, 1944. These were immediately approved by the Air Materiel Command, and the balance of twenty-two experimental engines was not considered necessary. A larger production order would be forthcoming. Assembly work on these first engines was done in the southeast corner of the cinderblock and wood aluminum foundry building at the Rouge plant. To other workers in the same building during 1944, including this writer, the project was indeed mysterious.

On August 2, 1944, the Army Air Force had prepared a contract for Ford's production and delivery of 1,500 engines to be used with the Army Air Force Type JB-2 Airframe. An Army appropriation of $1,442,307 was approved, with $450,000 immediately available for supplies — tools, fixtures, and so on. The engines were to be built according to prints prepared by Ford Motor Company inasmuch as the Army Air Force had none of its own, and Ford was to be the sole producer of the PJ-31-1. An additional $100,000 was provided for research in collaboration with Wright Field. Ford personnel employed in the MX-544 project were mostly men who had recently completed the Ford turbo-supercharger contract.

In the aluminum foundry building, where aluminum cylinder heads for the Pratt-Whitney aircraft engines had been produced, production facilities for the intermittent-jet-type engine were installed. Because of safety requirements, the engine test stand was erected outside the south doors of the building. Four 500-horsepower electric blowers forced 300-mile-per-hour air toward the engine. The engine, mounted on a carriage, was supplied with fuel and compressed air to provide a forward thrust sufficient to buck the wind from the blowers. The aluminum foundry area provided more than 100,000 square feet of inside space for high-volume production and assembly, while outside the south end of the building was another 40,000 square feet suitable for expanded test facilities.

The fuel metering system and the metallurgical properties of the flapper blades became major technical problems facing Ford engineers. To be successful, the engine had to perform flawlessly for approximately two hours at power that would drive the engine with its attached bomb load through the air at 400 miles per hour. When the engines were undergoing tests, the noise was terrific, attracting much attention. To the casual listener who had never heard that strange noise before, the pulse-jet engine project remained a complete mystery. When there was a gentle breeze from the southeast, people in West Dearborn, five miles away, could hear that peculiar roar coming from the direction of the Rouge plant.

On January 1, 1945, Ford was requested to submit plans to Wright Field regarding facilities that would be necessary to produce engines at the rates of 100, 500, and 1,000 per day. By January 11, the previous order for 1,500 engines was increased to 2,500 engines at an estimated coast of $4,510,000. Ford was advised on January 17 to plan a long-range development program including adaptations to make the engine useful for an extended number of purposes. In May 1945, Ford had quoted on a request from Wright Field for 7,000 engines. And Ford had been authorized to erect a large wind tunnel to adjoin the aluminum foundry building.

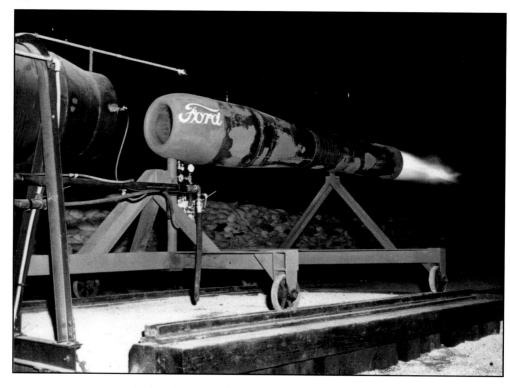

A nighttime view of an intermittent-jet-type engine operating under its own power with a 350-mile-per-hour wind blast feeding the necessary air into the engine. The carriage upon which the engine was mounted was attached to a thrust output measuring device which reacted to the forward push of the engine to indicate power output. (833.80765.9)

But on July 2, 1945, Wright Field notified Ford that the order for 7,000 engines was not forthcoming and that a previous order for 3,000 would be cut to 1,600. Wind tunnel construction was to be continued, however.

The war in Europe had gone favorably. The balance of Ford's engine orders were to be completed at the rate of only ten a day. These would be used in tests against Japan. If these tests had shown promise, unlimited numbers might have been needed, so the Ford facilities were to remain operational. As we know, however, other tactics were used with Japan. It was not until May 1946 that wind tunnel construction was terminated at Dearborn, and the 75-percent-finished structure was disassembled and shipped to Wright Field.

More than 2,400 pulse-jet engines were delivered during the approximately one year of Ford production. The Air Force Logistics

Command at Wright-Patterson Air Force Base reports that the PJ-31-1 was used to power three types of missiles. These were the Army Air Force's JB-2 and JB-10 and the Navy's Loon. The JB-2 and the Loon were copies of the German V-1 buzz bomb. The JB-10 was a Northrup Aircraft flying-wing missile of which only eleven were built. The last of the JB-10 missiles was withheld from tests and retained by the Air Force at Freeman Field in Seymour, Indiana, as a museum piece.

References

Accession 65, Eugene Farkas Reminiscences. Benson Ford Research Center, HFM & GV.

Accession 65, J. L. McCloud Reminiscences. Benson Ford Research Center, HFM & GV.

Accession 435, "History of the Ford War Effort," E. O. LaCroix. Benson Ford Research Center, HFM & GV.

"Reveal U.S. Perfected Guided Missile in 1917." *Detroit News,* November 24, 1961.

Vertical Files, "Ford, Henry, Aircraft." Benson Ford Research Center, HFM & GV.

26
Ford and the Metric Dilemma

In August 1922, the editor of Ford's *Dearborn Independent* received a letter from Aubrey Drury, executive secretary of the World Metric Standardization Council. It reads as follows:

Dear Sir:

Some weeks ago we sent you, for review, the new book, *World Metric Standardization: An Urgent Issue.* We trust that this volume reached you safely. If not we should be glad to send another volume for your review, as we desire very much that the *Dearborn Independent* should notice this book, and especially the subject of world standardization.

The book has been accorded scores of favorable reviews, indicating that the importance of this topic is widely recognized. The *Boston Transcript* declares this book "Fires a shot that will be heard round the world."

We trust that the *Dearborn Independent* will likewise print a review of this vital world issue.

Respectfully yours

A postscript at the end of the letter reads: "The Ford Motor Co. has purchased a book — Henry Ford has strongly urged the metric advance." Although the advisory committee of the World Metric Standardization Council included prominent scientists such as Luther Burbank, A. F. DuPont, Charles W. Eliot, William Noyes, and the presidents of both the American and the British Metric Association, the editor of the *Dearborn Independent* at the time seems not to have responded favorably to the request.

In March 1924, Henry Ford's secretary, Ernest Liebold, sent the following communication to Edsel Ford's secretary, A. J. Lepine:

Our files do not show that Mr. Ford ever made any definite statement with regard to the adoption of the Metric System. However, the writer recalls that about six or seven years ago while the matter was under discussion and of much interest, a census was taken among the Department heads of the Ford Motor Company and expressions obtained from them concerning the Metric System, and

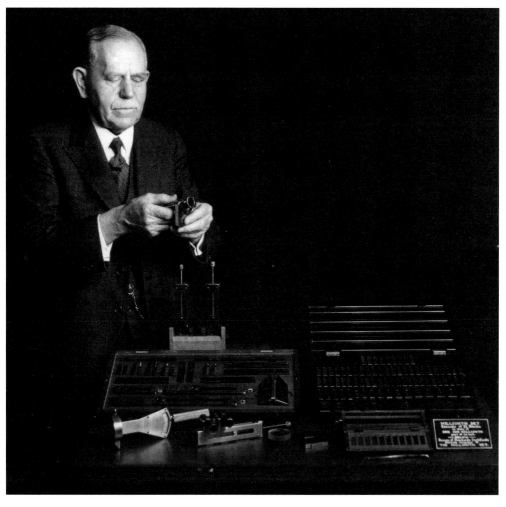

Carl Edward Johansson with an exhibit of his gauge blocks and fixtures at Dearborn in March 1935. (189.11091)

if I remember correctly ten were in favor of it as compared with one against it.

Prior to construction of the Fordson Tractor the writer discussed with Mr. Ford on various occasions the matter of adopting the metric system. However, since then interest seems to have lagged and in view of the fact that much of our industrial development has been made without its adoption, the matter of its adoption as a standard seems farther off than ever.

Henry Ford, however, had not let the matter of standardization lag. He had been using the gauge blocks standardized by Carl Johansson, the Swedish craftsman. These blocks had been calibrated to link British and metric systems by matching the length of one inch with exactly 25.4 millimeters. This relationship was recognized by the National Bureau of

Standards in Washington, the National Physical Laboratory in London, and corresponding establishments in Paris and Berlin. In fact, Ford was so dependent on these "Jo-Blocks" that when Johansson's business faltered in 1923, Ford rescued it by bringing Johansson to Dearborn, making his business the Johansson Division of Ford Motor Company.

At Dearborn, Johansson manufactured and sold individual blocks and sets of blocks, both English and metric, in three grades of quality. English blocks, at that time more popular than metric blocks, sold in sets of 81 blocks which would provide 120,000 different sizes in steps of 0.0001 inch from a minimum of 0.2 inch to more than 12 inches. A set of 103 metric blocks would cover a range from 2 millimeters to 250 millimeters in steps of 0.005 millimeter.

So Ford seemed well equipped to standardize in either English or metric system and to help others do the same. But there must have been some reluctance on his part to promote the metric system in preference to the English system. In the *Dearborn Independent* beginning in February 1925, a series of articles pertained to weights and measures. The first began, "Do you know what full measure is? What is a pound? A yard? A gallon? What is it fundamentally? No use saying a pound is sixteen ounces — what is an ounce? No use saying an ounce is 437½ grains — what is a grain?" The article, written by S. R. Winters, provides a general history of weights and measures over the centuries with special emphasis on the roles of Presidents Washington, Jefferson, and John Quincy Adams in the United States and the various acts of the U.S. Congress. Mention is made of the metric system having been legalized by Congress in 1866.

The title of another article in the *Dearborn Independent,* in July 1925, was "Pounds or Kilograms: Story of an Attempt to Abolish American System of Weights." The three-page article begins with:

> If you ordered a quart of milk and were told that you could have a liter — which measures less.
>
> If your yard of dress goods became a meter, at a higher price.
>
> If your No. 16 collar became a No. 40½ collar, centimeter.
>
> If your grocer said he could not sell you a pound of butter at 45 cents, but would gladly sell you .454 kilogram at 99 cents a kilogram.
>
> If the lady's No. 4 shoe became overnight a No. 25½ shoe.
>
> Then we should have what Bills in Congress, Committee Reports and other forms of propaganda are determined that we shall have. For there has been for years a movement on foot to change American weights and measures to the European system. It is an aggressive movement. It has won influence in the government itself. It has worked itself into a position of importance, and the American people are still ignorant of its existence.

This article includes six sections, from which the following excerpts are taken:

Origin of the Metric System

The new system known as the metric system was based on decimals, or a system of ten. The basis was earth measurement, a meter being the measure of length equal to one ten-millionth part of a terrestrial meridian contained between the north pole and the equator. It was an attempt to discover a scientific measurement based on an unchangeable fact. But there is something stronger than the ideals of academic scientists, and that is popular custom.

The "Human" System of Twelve

The difference between the French (metric) system and the English is that one is artificial and the other is human. It is not a system of tens but of twelves. There are twelve hours on our clocks, twelve months in our year, twelve men on our juries, twelve units in a dozen, twelve inches in a foot, twelve twelves in a gross, Twelfth Night—and so on back to the twelve disciples of the Lord and twelve political tribes of Israel. Twelve is a number ingrained in the history, experience and customs of the Anglo-Saxons.

Metric System Unnecessary in Foreign Trade

One of the countries impressed . . . in favor of the metric system was Germany. She made great strides among the South American countries. Germany succeeded in securing official sanction for the metric system in most countries in South and Central America. Government and customhouse run by the metric system, but the people carry on their business on the "systeme usuelle," that is, the usual system which approximates that of pints, pounds and inches. In the meantime Britain and America were flooding the world with all sorts of goods, made without reference to the metric system.

Confusion Caused by Metric System

The introduction of the metric system into South America did not unify or standardize the system of weights or measures, but created two systems, made confusion worse confounded, because the people would not accept the new order. And the United States is asked to add to the confusion by creating the same conditions here. When we go to South America, in all the Latin-Spanish countries, we find a system point for point like the English and Americans. Officially, the government may on a metric basis, but actually the people are on the English basis.

The "Foot" Is a Unit the World Over

If the interested reader would consult the Century Dictionary, under the article "foot," he will see at a glance how in ancient and modern times the "foot" of the great peoples has always approximated the foot which we use. The metric system came too late; it has missed all the human rootage; it has not captured any people that has maintained its place in the world; and the demand that the world should surrender to it is somewhat premature.

Profiteering Dangers of Metric System

In 1911 there was considerable discussion about the variety of sizes of berry boxes used in this country. So, assisted by experts and the produce men, Congress framed a bill which included this passage: "Provided that nothing in this Act shall prevent the sale of such small fruits and berries by weight or by liter, half liter, or multiples of the liter." But an investigation revealed that the produce men were behind the experts in providing for the liter because the liter is 10 percent smaller than the quart. The Bill permitted them to sell liters for quarts. And when finally the law was passed in 1916, the metric provision was omitted in the interest of the people.

A most fascinating study awaits the inquirer into the human origin of our system of weights and measures. And if the insistent propaganda to overthrow it continues in the future as it has in the past, we may expect to see a rather widespread interest created in feet, pints and pounds, their origin and their meaning, and the consequences that might ensue if they were changed.

In August 1925, the *Dearborn Independent* published an article entitled "Metric System Means Muddle." It states:

A previous article gave a general view of the matter. This present article presents a view of the changes in domestic and industrial life which would be caused by the introduction of the metric system, to which is added something of the tremendous cost that would be involved. . . . These are matters for the people themselves to consider, not for specialists alone, since the popular effects would be most far-reaching. The proposal to substitute the metric system for our present weights and measures is not merely a change in names, confusing as that would be, and impossible of accomplishment by compulsion in this country. . . . The immediate effect of the compulsory imposition of the metric system on industry would be destructive confusion which would unsettle trade and commerce and leave the country more helpless than under a foreign military invasion. The United States, in mechanical confusion, would be a pitiable spectacle and an invitation to wholesale violation of world peace.

It is assumed that Henry Ford was at least aware of the anti-metric system statements made in his *Dearborn Independent,* and he may have even authorized them. The possibility of the metric system being mandated by the government was likely very bothersome to Ford. Although, with his metric Jo-Blocks at hand, he was ready and able to apply the metric system if need be in his manufacturing business, he no doubt greatly preferred to decide the issue himself rather than be subject to a decision by Congress.

The Ford Motor Company, on June 4, 1948, little more than a year following Ford's death, released the following announcement:

Sale of the Johansson Gage Division of the Ford Motor Company to Brown and Sharpe Mfg. Co., precision tool makers of Providence, R.I., was announced today by Henry Ford II, president.

Careful consideration was given to the selection of a buyer for the Johansson blocks, Mr. Ford stated. Our main objective was to select a firm with the necessary skill and background essential in producing the gages and carrying on the Johansson tradition of quality.

We felt that their 115 years of experience in the building of precision tools and their excellent standing in American industry made Brown and Sharpe an ideal choice.

Britain and Canada gradually have replaced much of their historic English system of measurements with metric units. In America, by the early 1970s, the metric system had progressed in the automotive industry to a point where mechanics and customers were accepting metric dimensions for automotive components without complaint. At present — by agreement, not mandate — automotive manufacturers have universally adopted the metric system, a procedure of which Henry Ford would have approved.

References

Accession 285, Box 234, Henry Ford Office. Benson Ford Research Center, HFM & GV.

Bryan, Ford R. *Henry's Lieutenants*. Detroit: Wayne State University Press, 1993.

Dearborn Independent, February, July, and August 1925. Benson Ford Research Center, HFM & GV.

Vertical File, "Johansson." Benson Ford Research Center, HFM & GV.

Part IV
Financial Investments

*O*ther than those dealing directly with the automobile business, Henry Ford's financial investments seldom produced a monetary profit. His investments in farming resulted in dollar losses of tens of millions, as did his investments in education. Ford, however, considered such losses beneficial to the communities in which his money was being spent, and he enjoyed spending in that fashion. Some of his investments, however, must have been distinctly disappointing even to Ford himself.

One disappointing investment that has been well publicized was his $20 million loss in an attempt to grow rubber trees in Brazil. And his ten-year publication of the Dearborn Independent *quite likely caused him more trouble than it was worth. Several other Ford investments, both large and small, that have had little public attention are described briefly in the stories that follow.*

27
Kansas City, Mexico &
Orient Railway

The Detroit, Toledo & Ironton Railroad was not the first railroad in which Henry Ford invested. Eleven years earlier, he began investing heavily in the now-defunct Kansas City, Mexico & Orient Railway Company.

On January 1, 1901, the Kansas City, Mexico & Orient Railway Company was formed for the purpose of constructing a railroad line from Kansas City, Missouri, to Topolobampo, Mexico, on the Gulf of California, a distance of approximately 1,600 miles. It was organized by Arthur E. Stilwell, a railroad builder who with Dutch money had built the Kansas City, Pittsburgh & Gulf Railroad and after whom Port Arthur, Texas, is named. Stilwell's Kansas City, Mexico & Orient Railway was to be financed with both English and American capital.

Several predictions prompted the line's construction. Within five years of its completion, it was expected to earn $12 million to $15 million per year, which would be more than 10 percent on a capitalization of $100 million. Upon completion, it would form the shortest line from Kansas City to the Pacific coast and also a large portion of the shortest line between Chicago and Mexico City. The majority of the railroads in this area of the United States and Mexico ran north and south; the Kansas City, Mexico & Orient would cross them at right angles and pick up additional business.

Kansas City was the second-largest railway center in the United States, ahead of New York and second only to Chicago. It was fifth in bank clearings. Its annual sales of Pullman tickets led all American cities. It was near the geographical center of the United States and the country's center of population. Business interests in livestock, grain, lumber, oil, and farming implements were increasing rapidly. More long-distance railway freight was reshipped at Kansas City than at any other city except Chicago. Several northern and eastern railroads terminating at Kansas City needed such a southern and western transcontinental connection.

The southern terminal was to be Topolobampo in Mexico, which is halfway between Liverpool and Hong Kong. There were very extensive

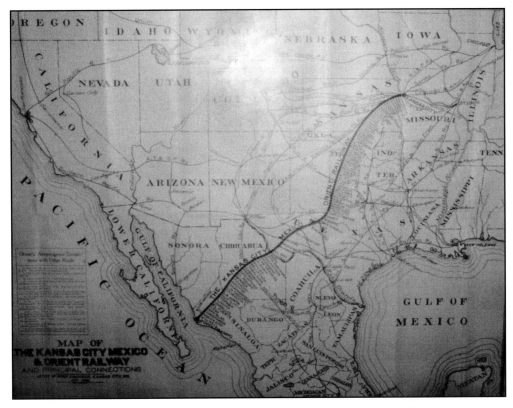

Map of the
Kansas City, Mexico
& Orient Railway.
(Courtesy of Spencer
J. Pattison.)

coal fields along the railroad close to this port, and the coal could be delivered to the ships without a long rail haul. The proposed route of this railroad was also the shortest distance between the Hawaiian Islands and Chicago; being a Mexican port, foreign vessels could be loaded for coastal trade on the Islands, while from San Francisco and Portland, only American vessels could be used.

This railroad would reduce the rail distance by half on Texas cotton, which was then shipped to China and Japan via San Francisco and Seattle. Australian mails and passengers for Europe could be landed at Topolobampo, carried by rail to New York, and embarked on the Atlantic by the time the Australian steamer would reach Vancouver. Some rail hauls to the east would be shortened by 600 miles. It also would serve in the event that the Panama Canal were damaged by an act of war. Hamburg-American once considered a line of ships across the Pacific to the Orient on completion of a railroad to Topolobampo.

Besides coal and timber, oil, gas, iron ore, silver, mercury, gypsum, marble, lignite, lead, zinc, copper, and vanadium were found along the right-of-way. At that time, the trend of tourist travel, the movement of population, and the development of agriculture, commerce, and industry were south and west toward the Pacific and milder climates, with plant-growing weather all year.

There was also an opinion that the Mexican people had learned at last that evolution was far better than revolution and that the assistance this railroad would give industry, mining, and agriculture would aid General Alvaro Obregon, his ministers, and the people to bring the country back to the ways and methods of peace. Approximately 500 miles of this railroad and the southern terminal would be in Mexico. Both the Venustiano Carranza and Obregon governments seriously considered either financing or completing the Mexican portion of this road.

The construction of this railroad would appeal to Henry Ford for at least three reasons: (1) it would promote profitable agriculture, commerce, and industry; (2) it would demonstrate Ford's international motto of "Business, Not Bullets"; (3) it would save time and expense in automotive transportation.

By 1909, Ford had found that it was much more economical to ship Model T parts that could be assembled close to where the cars were being sold than to ship assembled cars. That same year, Ford invested $30,000 in a Model T assembly plant in Kansas City. This was the first of a long series of assembly plants built throughout the United States. He was already exporting assembled Model Ts to Australia, India, and Japan, with his agents selling the Model T taxicab in particular in order to acquaint the people with Ford automobiles.

On October 23, 1909, Ford wrote his first check, for $25,216.67, to the Old Detroit National Bank for twenty-five-year First Mortgage 4 percent bonds of the Kansas City, Mexico & Orient Railway Company. Between July and December 1911, he wrote six more checks totaling $50,000.

By March 7, 1912, 659 miles of mainline railroad and 102 miles of yard and terminal tracks had been completed, and fifty-year First Mortgage 4 percent gold bonds totaling $24,538,000 had been issued. However, a receiver was appointed, and a committee undertook to organize a new company. Approximately $22 million worth of these new gold bonds were deposited with financial institutions subject to the control of this committee. In a letter dated June 18, 1912, to Lord Monson, chairman of the bondholders' committee in London, it was recommended that a Kansas City Belt Railway be financed at a cost of $999,000 to furnish necessary connections with the Santa Fe Railway. Ford received from this reorganization committee four certificates of deposit dated December 17 and 27, 1912, totaling $305,000.

On July 6, 1914, the railroad was sold under the mortgage securing these fifty-year 4 percent bonds for $6,001,000 to a new company again known as the Kansas City, Mexico & Orient Railway Company and

Trackside view of the Kansas City, Mexico & Orient Railway depot at San Angelo, Texas. The depot was built in 1909. San Angelo is about 130 miles from the Mexican border city of Presidio, Texas. (Photograph courtesy of Spencer J. Pattison.)

composed of the holders of approximately $22 million of the 4 percent bonds of the predecessor company. The new company issued $5,640,200 in two-year 6 percent gold notes. The U.S. government loaned the receiver of this company $2 million to mature on December 1, 1923. The business faltered, however, and W. T. Kemper of Kansas City, himself an owner of considerable stock and representing British interests as well, was appointed receiver in 1917.

In 1922, Kemper was pleading for aid from the U.S. Commerce Commission, decrying the impending $300 million loss, the eighty-five towns and 26,000 people left without rail service, and 2,000 men left without work. Kemper declared:

> The Orient is dead broke. If a barefoot man went into a shoe store to buy shoes, his condition might excite the pity of the clerk, but he will not get the shoes unless he can pay for them. The Orient is barefooted — it cannot pay for its shoes.

The railroad never did extend into Mexico or connect directly to Kansas City. It was sold for $3 million on March 27, 1924, at a foreclosure sale by the U.S. District Court. Purchasers were Kemper, Clifford Histed of Kansas City, and the English investors. Nothing was realized from this sale by the holders of the two issues of earlier bonds, including Henry Ford. For the next four years, the Kemper-Histed-English syndicate operated the railroad and invested another $2 million to keep it going. During this period, oil gushers were discovered along the road's tracks, greatly raising the value of the road. The English investors who owned 40 percent then wanted out, and the obvious solution was to sell to one of the major trunk lines. In 1928, the 750-mile line was sold to the Santa Fe for $14.5 million. Arthur Stilwell and his original investors, including Ford, had lost $20 million. Kemper had become the major beneficiary.

Although Ford lost his money on the Kansas City, Mexico & Orient Railway, he had now learned by experience that he should fully own and manage his businesses for himself. Thus, he purchased the Detroit, Toledo & Ironton Railroad outright in 1920.

The American portion of the Kansas City, Mexico & Orient was next operated by the Santa Fe. Quite recently, the segment from San Angelo, Texas, to the Mexican border at Presidio was operated by the South Orient Railway. The segment north from San Angelo to Altus, Oklahoma, north of the Oklahoma-Texas border, was abandoned. The segment north from Altus to the Kansas state line is used in small segments by the Farm/GrainBelt Corporation. The segments in Kansas are used by the Central Kansas based in Wichita. The old shops and yard trackage in Wichita are still used by the Central Kansas. The segment from Wichita to Kansas City was never built because the

Atchison, Topeka & Santa Fe provided that connection and in 1928 had purchased the Kansas City, Mexico & Orient to preclude its further development as a competitor.

At San Angelo, a city about the size of Dearborn, the Kansas City, Mexico & Orient Railway station built in 1909 now has been restored by the Historic Orient-Santa Fe Depot, Inc., and has been rededicated as a museum. The current operator of the railroad through San Angelo being the South Orient Railroad, several examples of historic locomotives and cars representing both the South Orient and the Santa Fe railroads are now displayed near the station.

References

Accession 844, Box 1, L. J. Thompson Records. Benson Ford Research Center, HFM & GV.

Correspondence with Spencer J. Pattison, Carrollton, Texas.

Kansas City Public Library. Publications concerning Arthur Stilwell, William Kemper, and the Kansas City & Orient Railway.

Kansas City Southern Historical Society, Shreveport, Louisiana.

"Orient Depot Restored." *Trains*, August 1997, p. 78.

"Report on the Kansas City, Mexico & Orient Railway Company and the Kansas City Outer Belt & Electric Railroad Company." Santa Fe Railway Historical & Modeling Society, June 18, 1912.

28
Michigan Stump Farm

The great white pine forests of Clare County in Michigan's Lower Peninsula had been completely ravaged by greedy lumber barons by the end of the nineteenth century. In the aftermath, however, much of what was known as Pine Barrens became popular as a region where wealthy farming entrepreneurs were buying up the denuded land at tax sales and developing beautiful showplace ranches producing prize-winning stock, grains, vegetables, and fruits. Prosperous businessmen from Indiana, Illinois, Kentucky, and Michigan were participating in these exciting ventures. The Pine Barrens of Clare County were by 1905–06 being advertised by promoters as the "Garden of Eden."

In 1911, Henry Ford must have been bitten by the bug. Besides investing in Dearborn land at that time, he reached out and purchased 1,600 acres of this cutover land known as Tax Homestead Land. This acreage was in Sections 16, 17, and 18 of Greenwood Township, six miles west of the town of Harrison. He paid $45,950, or $30 an acre. Ford had missed by several years the earlier bargain prices, when much of the same land had sold for $5 an acre for taxes. Section 16 was purchased from D. P. Lapham, Section 17 from the S. A. Wilson Estate and J. J. Graves, and 80 acres in Section 18 from F. H. Loose.

On Ford's 1,600 acres there remained, firmly rooted in the soil, every last stump left years earlier by the lumber merchants. The stumps were estimated to number at least 5,000. There seems to have been little activity on the Ford farm until about 1917, when Henry was testing and promoting his Fordson tractor. At that time, E. C. Bruce of Harrison, Michigan, had become manager of the farm, and the main concern was understandably the problem of getting all of the old stumps pulled. Ford's assistant secretary, Frank Campsall, after a train trip to Harrison in April 1918, reported this assessment of the Harrison Farm to Ernest Liebold, Ford's general secretary:

Published previously in *The Ford Legend,* Vol. VIII, No. 2, 1999.

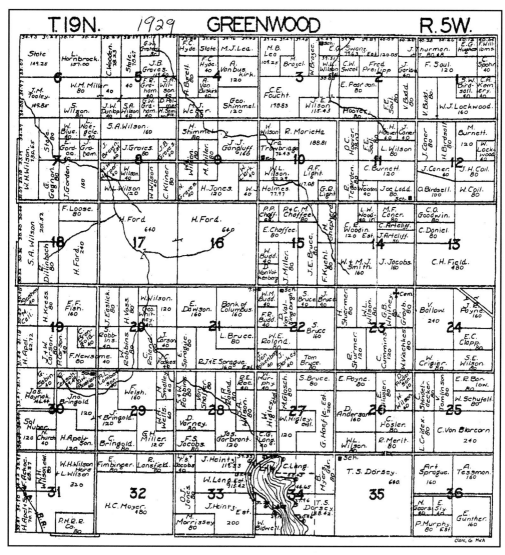

Greenwood
Township in Clare
County, Michigan,
in 1929.

Relative to the farm

I walked over a good portion of the farm and would estimate the condition as follows: About 200 acres of bush, 25 acres clear without stumps, and about 75 acres partly cleared which can be cleared within two weeks after the stumping men commence work.

At the present time 8 men are working at clearing with two more to start Monday. I went over to where they were working without their knowledge and found them all digging in in good shape. The men he employs come from a radius of practically five miles and it is necessary that practically all of them be furnished board and lodging.

Relative to stumping

I drove over to Marion, Michigan, and saw Mr. G. A. Rupert *[sic]* who is the gentleman that made the former quotation of 65¢. I also saw Mr. Budd of Harrison whose price was $1.25. Both of them have raised considerably since quotations were furnished, which they state were made last fall, on account of the high cost of labor. Mr. Rupert *[sic]* now quotes: $1.25 per stump to pull and dispose of it. Mr. Budd quotes $1.50 per stump to pull and pile. In my opinion Mr. Rupert's *[sic]* price would be the better provided you do not care to utilize the stumps for fire wood after pulling, although I believe Mr. Budd is the more reliable of the two and judging from his conversation, believe he would be the biggest hustler.

The piling of the stumps also includes the cleaning which I am informed is practically as hard work as pulling. These piles usually include about 12 to 15 stumps where they could be either burned or later cut into fire wood. I also asked Mr. Budd the cost of one of the stumping machines and he offered to sell his machine for $200. I should judge that a new machine would cost $250 to $275. Both stumping men have informed me that they can pull a minimum of 7 stumps per day, the quantity depending of course on the size of the stump. A tractor or team could be utilized with block and chain for pulling grubs, this effecting a great savings as otherwise it would be necessary to have these pulled by stumping men.

I took up the matter of plowing with Mr. Bruce and it was his opinion that the ground should be worked even if no planting was done particularly to prepare the ground and also to level it off. A plow, harrow and disc are the attachments that would be necessary.

Relative to the house

We got in touch with a man named Dan Varney who is a carpenter and all around man, at a price of 40¢ per hour. We had him look over the house and barn and he estimated the cost would be about $200 to fix up the extra house suitable for living purposes.

The following work is necessary: Tar paper outside, beaver board inside; 7 new windows; 2 doors; new lumber on floor; also a new tile chimney and he has promised to complete this within a week or ten days.

Relative to barn

New concrete floor will be necessary in the basement for which about 40 barrels of cement will be required at $2.50 per barrel. The sand and gravel can be secured merely for the price of hauling. Will also need 3000 feet of lumber for siding on which we secured a price of $40 per thousand. In connection with the hauling of cement and gravel etc. believe a price of $3.00 per day allowance for Mr. Bruce's team and wagon, if same should be used, would be a fair price. He has the following equipment which he will sell to Mr. Ford at the following prices: Team and harness $400; Heavy wagon complete $65; Mowing machine $40; Rake $25; Team plow $15. I will say also, in compliance with our talk will change Mr. Bruce's rate from $3.00 to $3.50 per day starting Monday April 15th.

An undated memorandum from Harrison lists these buildings on the Harrison Farm:

Section 16	Section 17
House 22 x 22	House 16 x 24 with wing 16 x 20
House 20 x 20	Chicken House 12 x 16
Garage 12 x 16	Corn Crib 20 x 24
Well House 12 x 18	Barn 40 x 100 with wing 24 x 40
Chicken House 10 x 16	
Basement Barn 40 x 60	*Section 18*
Grain House 24 x 30	None
Tool House & Shop 24 x 102	
Building remodeled for Ice House 12 x 12	

The following agreement was prepared for the signature of G. A. Ruppert in May 1918:

> This agreement made and entered into by and between G. A. Rupert *[sic]* of the Village of Harrison, Michigan, party of the first part and E. G. Liebold of the City of Highland Park, Wayne County, Michigan, (authorized to act in behalf of Henry Ford, of the Township of Dearborn, Wayne County, Michigan), party of the second part.
>
> WITNESSETH, that the said party of the first part hereby agrees to pull out and burn on the property any and all tree stumps of a circumference of _____ inches or more on the following described premises:

The entire section of 16 in Town 19
North Range 5 West Township of Greenwood,
Clare County, Michigan

For which the party of the second part hereby agrees to pay the said first party at the rate of $1.50 for each tree stump pulled and burned on the above described premises.

Payment to be made on the 10th and 25th day of each month according to certified statements which said first party will mail to the party of the second part each Saturday, which statement shall show the number of stumps pulled and burned each day for the current week.

This agreement to take effect May 10th, 1918 and shall remain in force until November 1st, 1918, unless the work herein described shall be sooner completed or written permission to continue beyond this date is given by the party of the second part.

At Dearborn on July 20, 1918, Ernest Kanzler, working for Henry Ford & Son, sent the following letter to Ernest Liebold, who was overseeing the Harrison Farm for Henry:

In accordance with your recent communication we shipped out yesterday two FORDSON Tractors, serial number 13322 and 13300, consigned to Mr. E. C. Bruce, Harrison, Clare County, Michigan. Included with the above tractors were the following implements:

2 plows
4 extra plow points
2 discs
2 grain drills
2 sets of drags
2 sets of spring teeth
1 box of parts

and also 12090 lbs. of Fall Wheat, making approximately two hundred bushels. All this material has been invoiced memorandum charged, as it is our understanding that all the above farm implements we are sending Mr. Bruce will be returned about August 20.

With reference to our sending a man down to help Mr. Bruce unload. This will be done upon our receiving notice as to when the tractors will arrive at Harrison, and we will endeavor to have a man arrive simultaneously with the arrival of the tractors to help with the unloading and the farm work.

We are sending Mr. Bruce a copy of this letter.

Liebold had set up a checking account at the State Savings Bank at Harrison, "The Oldest Bank in Clare County," whereby Bruce could pay his employees and for other expenses. Each month or so, a check for $250 was deposited in the bank by Liebold for farm operations under Bruce. Ruppert, however, was paid directly by Liebold from Henry Ford's account.

A pair of Fordson tractors struggle on the Ford ranch at Harrison, Michigan, to pull a double-bottom plow through this land never tilled before. Although the stumps with their giant roots had been pulled, smaller roots still permeated the soil, and Henry Ford insisted that the plowing be deep. The Harrison farm was used to test these early Fordson tractors. (Photograph courtesy of Kenneth Brown.)

Following one of his trips to Harrison, Campsall wrote this memo to Liebold:

My personal opinion of Mr. Bruce is as follows:

I don't believe that he is a "born leader" but do believe that he is conscientious as far as Mr. Ford's interests are concerned, and while possibly some one more of the type of Ray [Dahlinger] would get more work out of a gang, do not believe that the class of help available in Clare County would stand for a driver of his type especially at the rate of wages which we are paying.

I rather believe I mentioned the foregoing to you before, and I would also call your attention to another one of his faults which I called him for on my present visit. A box of repair parts which we brought up from the express office was opened by Bruce and consisted of numerous small parts. Instead of having his men carry these to the repair shop, he was assisting in doing this himself thus holding up both the writer and himself from some more important work until I called the same to his attention and criticized him rather severely.

On October 1, 1918, a telegram from Liebold at Dearborn to Bruce at Harrison reads: "Return all tractors and machinery as instructed by

Milton Bryant, with head in hand, the brother of Clara Ford, sits with his crew of men at the Ford Farm at Harrison, Michigan, during the summer of 1919. Wet weather disrupted their plans to harvest wheat that day. (B113398)

Mr. Dahlinger." (Dahlinger was in charge of the Ford Farms at Dearborn.)

Beginning in October, a series of letters between Campsall and Bruce pertained to the 1918 potato crop at Harrison:

October 15, 1918
Mr. E. C. Bruce

Dear Sir:

We are in receipt of your favor of the 14th instant, advising us that you had gathered 110 bushels of Potatoes and also that you will need 50 bushels for yourself.

In connection with the above, we would call your attention to our letter of May 11th wherein you were instructed to plant enough Potatoes so that 100 bushels might be realized. The writer was advised and in turn instructed you that Mr. Liebold desired 100 bushels of Potatoes. You will, therefore see that this quantity is placed where they will not be frozen, until after his return from the South which we expect will be about November 15th, when shipping instructions will be given you.

Kindly acknowledge receipt of this letter and advise that these instructions are being followed.

Very truly yours
Frank Campsall

November 14, 1918
Mr. Frank Campsall

Dear Sir:

I have shipped via express to E. G. Liebold 5 bu of potatoes 11-15-1918 and expect to ship via freight 95 bu 11-15-1918. Freight rate is 31½¢ per 100, and there will be about 3800 lbs, and will have to buy about 40 sacks at 25¢ each. Freight and sacks will be about $28.25

Very truly
E. C. Bruce

November 18, 1918
Mr. E. C. Bruce

Dear Sir:

We are in receipt of your favors of the 11th and 14th inst.

We do not wish to put too much expense in the fixing up of the house in which you are living as it is not improbable that same will be torn down in the spring.

Relative to the potatoes, I notice you expected to ship 95 bushels by freight on the 15th inst. If this has been done, you have acted contrary to instructions as you were previously advised to hold these until shipping instructions were given.

Very truly yours
Frank Campsall

More than 350 bushels of potatoes were requested from Dearborn that fall. Various Ford Motor Company departments wanted 125 bushels; Henry Ford Hospital received 200 bushels; Liebold and his friends took 30 bushels.

From May through October, Ruppert had been pulling and burning stumps. Each week, he sent a postcard indicating how many he had pulled and how many he had burned. On October 22, 1918, he received a check from Ford for $602.63, which was 75 percent of the amount due for pulling and cleaning 6,343 stumps and burning 4,015 stumps up to and including October 15.

On December 7, 1918, Campsall wrote the following to Ruppert:

We are enclosing herewith Mr. Ford's check No 9915 for $427.31, this being in payment of 75% of amount due you for pulling and cleaning, also burning Stumps, up to and including November 30th, less the amount previously paid.

The writer would appreciate estimate from you as to the amount of Stumps still left on Section 16, and also as to whether or not you can complete the work this Fall.

Kindly acknowledge receipt of the attached check.

Very truly yours
Frank Campsall

Ruppert replied December 30, 1918:

In reply to yours of Dec 7 in regards of estimate would be very safe to say their is more than four thousand left on No 16 if the writer would be here I could easily convince him in a few minutes walk. I expect to come down to Detroit soon and would be glad to meet you and Mr. Ford. I also acknowledge chech No 9975 Dec 23 1918 of $275.50 as part payment on stumps pult. Thanking you very kindly

> Very truly yours
> Geo A. Ruppert

Henry and Clara Ford had staked Clara's brother Milton Bryant to a Ford car and tractor dealership in Traverse City in 1917. In a letter on Grand Traverse Auto Company stationery on July 24, 1919, Milton wrote to Clara:

We have been expecting you for the last three weeks, but we presume the reason you have not come is because Henry has been very busy, as we noticed by the bulletins. We have been on his farm in Clare county and finished cutting his wheat, and we expect to go back there next week Monday, and finish the thrashing. The reason we did not finish up at that time was because the wheat was too green, and I was afraid it would spoil in shipping. I am enclosing a few pictures of the crew.

You can tell Henry that four of us went from Traverse City and cut sixty-five acres in exactly twenty-four hours. It was a beautiful field as you will notice by the pictures.

The reason we have not sent you more cherries was because we expected you up each weekend.

> Very truly,
> M. D. Bryant

A July 28, 1919, letter from Bruce to Campsall reveals a visit to Harrison by Henry Ford himself:

Mr. Ford paid us a very welcome visit Sat 25th and said that he was very well pleased with our progress with the farm.

While here he mentioned putting in a flour mill at the Harrison Elevator and I should take the matter up with Mr. Liebold.

We got together yesterday and they informed me that they had incorporated for $15,000 and had $10,000 paid up stocks and the remaining $5,000 is yet for sale.

And they figure that it would cost somewhere near $3,000 to install same and would be glad to have Mr. Ford connected with it.

I am enclosing herein a report of the auditing committee of the company which was handed me.

> Very Truly Yours,
> E. C. Bruce

A crew of men with a wagonload of wheat and a grain separator in a wheat field on the Ford Farm at Harrison, Michigan, during the summer of 1919. A Fordson tractor takes the place of the conventional steam engine in furnishing power to the separator. (Photograph courtesy of Milton Bryant.)

Ford no doubt had stopped that day on his way to or from Traverse City, where he and Clara often visited Milton. Both wheat and potatoes had been planted at Harrison that year, and it was apparent from Henry's remarks that he was planning how his grain would be marketed in the future.

A letter August 6, 1919, from Bruce to Campsall describes some of the problems in harvesting grain:

Well the reason that you have had no word from me lately is this. When wheat was cut Mr. Bryant expected to thresh direct from the field, but it was unfit so he went home and in the meantime it rained and when Mr. Ford came he advised me to put it in the barn when dry enough. So we have been drying and handling wheat nights and Sundays and all.

I have it all in the barn but twenty acres and expect to put that in this afternoon.

And for threshing we have no power, you know Bryant took his tractors away. I have been looking for some tractors from you. That is what Mr. Ford talked about when here. These I wish you would send as soon as possible and when you send tractors and plows and other machinery be sure and send belt pulley and 75 ft. belt.

And will you send me some more time cards and large envelopes as I haven't cards enough for another payday.

Very truly yours,
E. C. Bruce

How Bruce made out with the wheat crop that year is not clear, but Campsall's December 3, 1919, memo to George Brubaker of the Rouge Traffic Department speaks of the manner of disposing of potatoes:

Within the next few days we will have approximately 800 bushels of potatoes put up 2½ bushels to the sack for which we will accept orders delivery to be made by purchaser from Henry Ford & Son, minimum order of
2½ bushels, at the rate of $4.38 per sack, which is $1.75 per bushel.

Kindly advise not later than Friday whether you or anyone in
your department desire them at the above price.

During 1920 and 1921, Bruce was sending his expense bills to L. J.
Thompson in Dearborn for payment, but Campsall was still involved
with management supervision at Harrison. In a letter dated May 27,
1922, Campsall sent a report to Liebold including the following:

In accordance with your request, visited Harrison yesterday, the 26th,
and found Bruce still living in the house, his wife and one child sick
in bed. He understands fully, however, that he is through. Talked with
two parties yesterday with reference to taking charge of the farm. I
was recommended to J. E. Ladd by several people with whom I
talked, and called at his home, but found that he had gone trout fishing and would not be back until next week. Understand he is a man
about 45 years old who has had considerable experience in clearing
and farming but knows nothing relative to the tractor. Sent word to
Ford agent to make up a list of people that could be recommended.

At the present time Ruppert has two crews pulling and another
piling and burning and seems to be making satisfactory progress. He
wishes his original proposition to stand: that is, based on the rate
of $5.00 per acre on about 200 acres in Section 16, $30.00 per acre
on about 450 acres in Section 17. In Section 18 there appears to
be in the neighborhood of 100 acres to be cleared and 40 acres of
maple grove which he might want to save. This section to be at the
rate of $10.00.

At the present time there is 180 acres in spring wheat and 20
acres in fall wheat, the seed for which we recently forwarded to him.
There is considerable drainage to be done, although I believe that if
proper ditches were built around the property by the County Drain
Commission should be responsible for, it would offset considerable of
this as in certain sections of the property it is very mucky.

I believe it a good idea to send up 4 or 5 tractors and plow up all
available cleared lands.

In June 1922, Bruce resigned as manager of the Ford Farm at
Harrison, and C. E. Pratt, an auctioneer, became the new manager.

On July 22, 1922, an agreement appears to have been made
between Henry Ford and Trueman Huntwork of the village of Marion
in Osceola County, Michigan, for clearing most of Section 17 of
Greenwood Township:

Said party of the first part is desirous of having said land plowed and
dragged, and cleared of all logs, grubs, brush and stumps . . . for the

consideration of the sum of Twenty Dollars ($20.00) per acre to be paid to second party by said first party . . . Twelve Dollars ($12.00) per acre for the clearing and burning of all logs, grubs, brush and stumps, and the balance of Eight Dollars ($8.00) per acre when the second party has completed the work in a manner satisfactory to the first part. Payments to be made on the 10th and 25th of each month.

In early spring of 1923, Ruppert was having trouble communicating with Campsall and wrote thus to Thompson:

I have wroat to Mr. Campsell twice in regards of my back remittance to me. From last fall i have bin to big expense. since i received my last check my book shows 385 stumps pulled which i have had no check for. also got about 6000 stumps field redie to burn want to start burning as soon as the sno is goan. got no money on hand to pay my help pleas advise me wh i shoud hear from you Foaks in regards of this Matter

Very truly yours
Geo A. Ruppert

Ruppert's troubles continued all year until he made a trip to Dearborn for help from Thompson, the accountant. As a result, on November 23, 1923, Thompson wrote as follows to Campsall:

Mr. George Rupert *[sic]* of Harrison was in this morning and advises that he is held up in his work and can hardly do any more on account of the ground not having been put in condition by Pratt. He claims that this condition has been more or less aggravating all summer but has just now reached a climax.

He also claims that our men under Pratt's direction pull all the small stumps which can be handled by teams without a machine and owing to the fact that a great many of the larger ones which he is required to pull cost him from $5.00 to $8.00 apiece, he claims that he cannot go on with the work at this price unless he pulls all of the stumps.

He also advises that Pratt is not doing as he should by us—that his own teams which are hired by us are fed from our crops and that he also feeds cattle and hogs from his own farm which is some twenty miles away. He also states that he uses the company's truck for his own personal use, besides numerous other little things of a like nature.

I advised Rupert that you had been away longer than you had expected to be and that it was your intention to come up to Harrison at the earliest possible moment when you were free from your other duties. I also advised him I would write you as above and he would no doubt hear from either you or I shortly. Under these circumstances your advice is requested.

Very truly yours
L. J. Thompson

A 1923 report of crops and revenues shows a larger variety of crops than in earlier years:

Wheat	$1532.88
Corn	740.20
Hay	608.13
Oats	410.00
Beans	123.20
Potatoes	365.06
Straw	128.54
Buckwheat	6.33
Screenings	109.88
Land and Pasture Rent	121.75
Misc. Grain	11.41
	$4157.38

Pratt was in touch with Campsall on March 17, 1925:

This will advise you that i have three hundred & fifty acres faul plowed that I plan to put to spring crops. I also have one hundred acres more that should be plowed for spring crops.

I now have three tractors in runing order and owing to the fact that two of these should be put on the breaker that would leave me but one tractor for fitting.

If you would send me two more tractors it would inable me to accomplish what i maped out to accomplish the coming season. I also nead three sets of rims for the old tractors as the ones I have are worn out.

I am pleased to advise you that i broke two hundred & fifty acres new ground last year, also that i reploud the same amount which was broken the year before. Hoping that this will meat your aprovil and that you will visit me soon

> Yours Very Truly
> C. E. Pratt

On April 28, Pratt wrote again to Campsall:

This is to advise you that Mr. Rupert *[sic]* is making but little progress burning stumps, he is working one team and two men, he is putting in some crops and I would amagine from the looks that he is not figuring on getting away this year. if there is any possible way for you to get up hear I would be pleased to have you. I will have to have some more grain room this season as our granary rooms was much too small last year. If I could have those buildings on Sec 17 that he is using it would help as considerable of my work is on that side of the farm this year, if we had those buildings we could get to our work in shorter time. Please advise me if you could handle car of oats for me about 40¢ per bushel is the market her. Try to make me a visit.

> Yours Verry Truly
> C. E. Pratt

Pratt received this answer dated May 4:

Your letter of April 28th received.
     Mr. Campsall is now in Massachusetts but will be home in a day
or so and he is arranging a trip to Harrison.
     Mr. Ford would like you to send the car of oats to Dearborn.

Very truly yours
H. M. Cordell
Office of Henry Ford

As the Harrison acreage was cleared, it became evident that Ford
had in mind operating it as a general farm much like neighboring farms
in the area, other than its being unusually large, perhaps somewhat
better maintained, and well supplied with Ford tractors. Two or three
horses were used to cultivate row crops, but five or six tractors often
were seen at work. Wheat, oats, corn, hay, and potatoes were major
crops. Soybeans were tried only once and unsuccessfully, the climate
being too cold.

While raising crops, most of the workers on the farm were
employed only part of the year. Apparently, Ford once offered to build a
manufacturing plant at Harrison, but the community was not in favor
of it. The factory would have employed farm workers during the winter,
in accordance with Ford's village industries philosophy.

Although the Harrison Farm had its own manager, its relationship
with the Ford Farms in the Dearborn area increased with time. By 1928,
Newton Kress had become manager at Harrison and was sending some
of his expense bills to Raymond Dahlinger, as well as to L. J. Thompson.
While Kress was manager, the Harrison Farm turned considerably into
a stock farm. In August 1935, the following items were purchased:

Saddles & Supplies
4 #32 Saddles
6 Salt Sacks
6 #2 sponges
1 doz Mate Brushes
1 doz #174 Brushes
1/6 doz pts Blue Ribbon Polish
1 doz Properts Saddle Soap
2 3/8 Bridles
4 5/8 Bridles
4 #3615 Non Rust Chains
1 Saddle
2 Saddles repaired
Cost: $346.12

Records show that these costs were paid by the Ford Farms
managed by Dahlinger. By this time, the Ford Farms were not only in

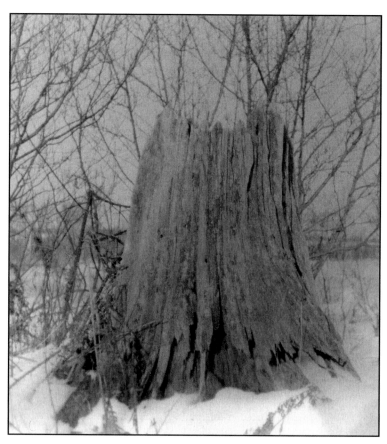

This is the last of the thousands of stumps that once covered Henry Ford's Harrison Farm. The stump stands next to a small stream which may have prevented a stump-pulling rig from straddling it. The photograph was taken by Kenneth W. Brown of Harrison during the early winter of 1997–98. (Photograph courtesy of Kenneth Brown.)

Dearborn but now extended to Washtenaw, Monroe, and Lenawee Counties in Michigan, all with excellent soybean land.

John Chaffee took over the management of the Harrison Farm about 1940. At that time, beef and sheep were being raised together with feed for the same. In 1940, Chaffee hired Howard Davis, who recalls that at age twenty-three, he was paid $.40 per hour working ten-hour days bulldogging steer on a cutting horse. Approximately 200 head of sheep and 350 to 400 head of grass cattle were being raised at that time. Many of the "feeders" were brought from Texas and Montana. In

April 1940, an order of 100 steers costing $4,600 for the Harrison Farm is recorded among Dahlinger's farm expenses. The check for the steers was made out to Robert Shull, who raised stock on Ford pasture land rented by Chaffee.

Cash crops had not been forgotten, however, and in December 1941, the Harrison Farm shipped 1,144 bags of potatoes to Dearborn, where Dahlinger paid $.75 per bag. And according to Davis, the nine farm workers for Ford were also then growing 200 acres of corn and 200 acres of oats. Davis remembers Ford visiting the Harrison Farm at least once during the early 1940s. John Cook, who began working on the farm in 1927, remembers that Ford visited twice while he was there. Cook worked as a painter and also built wire fences, of which there must have been miles.

Dahlinger, on the other hand, was now selling hay to Robert Shull in 100-ton lots at $27 a ton to feed Shull's steers grazing on Ford land at Harrison. Dahlinger was managing farms of tremendous size at Belleville and Cherry Hill in southeastern Michigan, where a single field of 374 acres, called the Big Field, produced an abundance of hay for sale.

On July 3, 1944, department heads of Ford Motor Company were notified of the "Transfer and Operation of Henry Ford Farms as a department of Ford Motor Company." This mandate referred to "the properties in southern Michigan" and did not expressly apply to the Harrison Farm. But by December 1944, the Johnson Real Estate Company of Dearborn was asked to provide an appraisal of the Harrison property. That appraisal was as follows:

> I have appraised the Harrison property in Clare County. I discussed land values in that vicinity, and after thorough investigation and examination, I believe the following to be the true value of this property.

Section 16

640 acres (D. P. Lapham) @ 75.00 per acre	$48,000.00
Buildings:	
House	750.00
Garage	50.00
Poultry house	50.00
Well and oil storage building	250.00
Granary	550.00
Workshop and storage shed	1,500.00
2 Corn cribs	200.00
Barn	3,750.00
Fence (Board)	267.50
Tiling	550.00
Fence (Wire)	2,640.00
	$58,557.50

Michigan	Section 17 (and part of Section 18)	
Stump Farm	160 acres (Wilson Estate) @ 50.00 per acre	8,000.00
	Fence	360.00
		8,360.00
	200 Acres (J. J. Graves) @ 50.00 per acre	10,000.00
	Fence	480.00
		10,480.00
	520 acres (S. L. Wilson) @ 50.00 per acre	26,000.00
	Buildings:	
	Large barn	7,200.00
	Well and pump house	175.00
	Shed (cattle shelter)	648.00
	Fence (board)	490.00
	Fence (wire)	2,040.00
		36,553.00
	Section 18	
	80 Acres (F. H. Loose) @ 50.00 per acre	4,000.00
	Old house (beyond repair)	100.00
	Fence	480.00
		4,580.00
	Grand Total	$118,530.50

Respectfully submitted,
Jamie L. Johnson

Henry Ford's Harrison Farm was sold for $118,500 in 1944 to Shull, the Clare cattleman who had been renting land from Ford. Even after the sale of the Harrison Farm, there was considerable business between Shull and the farms at Belleville and Cherry Hill now owned by Ford Motor Company. In particular, transactions with both Shull and the Harrison Elevator Company involved hay, beef, and wool. Shull died in an airplane crash in 1950. The farm sat idle until 1959, when it was purchased by Curtis M. Brown. The farm is now owned by the Brown family and operated by Kenneth W. Brown, a grandson of Curtis Brown. The farm is now known as Kitty Kurtis Ranch, and it is said that only one large pine stump remains.

References

Accession 1, Box 53, Milton Bryant Papers (correspondence, photos). Benson Ford Research Center, HFM & GV.

Accession 62, Box 94, Henry Ford Office Correspondence, 1911–1919. Benson Ford Research Center, HFM & GV.

Accession 285, Boxes 10, 11, 66, 83, 112, 144, 162, 193, 266, 416, 1612, 2665, Henry Ford Office, 1920–1947. Benson Ford Research Center, HFM & GV.

Accession 380, Box 22, Correspondence, 1917–1924. Benson Ford Research Center, HFM & GV.

Accession 445, Box 2, Henry Ford Farms (cost books), 1937–1947. Benson Ford Research Center, HFM & GV.

Accession 587, Box 103, Employee Record Cards (including Harrison Farm workers). Benson Ford Research Center, HFM & GV.

29
Experiences at Cape May

Henry Ford, in January 1904 at age forty, had broken the world's automotive speed record by bouncing and skidding across the bumpy ice of Lake St. Clair in 39.4 seconds per mile. Winning races such as these was to prove the speed and durability of Ford automobiles. At that particular time, the large and expensive four-cylinder, 24-horsepower Ford Model B, with a selling price of $2,000, was especially difficult to market. Ford's Lake St. Clair glory lasted only a few days, however, because William K. Vanderbilt, racing on the smooth sands of Ormond Beach, Florida, bettered Henry's speed by driving the mile in an even 39 seconds (92.30769 miles per hour vs. Henry's 91.370556).

By 1905, Ford Motor Company business was booming. The little two-cylinder, 8-horsepower Model A was being phased out, and the two-cylinder Model C of 10 horsepower and the two-cylinder Model F of 15 horsepower were taking its place. The large and expensive Model B was selling fairly well, and a still larger six-cylinder Model K of 40 horsepower was being developed.

Despite this prosperity, Ford was itching to enter the race for the Dewar Trophy, a one-mile straightaway race. Although he missed competing for the Dewar, in late August 1905, with a new racing car based on the big 405-cubic-inch Model K engine, he tried his luck competing on the beach at Cape May, New Jersey. The race course was from Sewell's Point to the Cape May Hotel. In one of the races, he is said to have been winning against Louis Chevrolet, Alexander Winton, and Walter Christie when an ocean wave hit his racer and knocked him out of the race. The best time he recorded during these Cape May trials was a slow 41 seconds per mile (87.80487 miles per hour).

A story is told that Ford sought a loan to pay his hotel bill after he lost in the Cape May trials. He finally sold the Model F touring car he had used to tow his racer to Cape May for $400 to Daniel Focer, an engineer for the West Jersey Railroad. Focer had refused an offer to buy Ford Motor Company stock, saying it was too risky. Ford is said to have pledged to make Focer the first dealer for his new car when it came to market. Focer did, indeed, begin selling Ford cars, and at age seventy-five in 1922, he was still co-owner of Focer & Mecray, Cape May Ford deal-

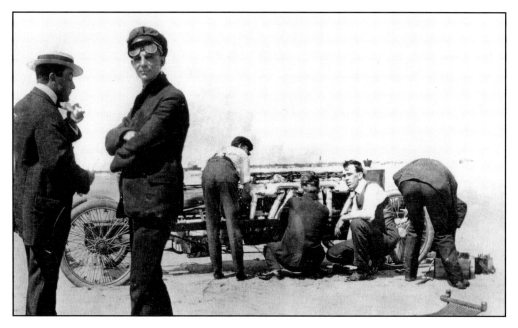

Henry Ford appears confident as his mechanics work on his racing machine at Cape May in August 1905. The vehicle was a racing version of Ford Motor Company's new Model K equipped with a six-cylinder engine producing 40 horsepower. Standing with him is Gaston Plantiff, head of Ford Motor Company's New York office. (0.430)

ers. There he was proud to display the Model F he had purchased directly from Henry Ford and was claiming that he was Ford's oldest dealer.

Ford's further connection with Cape May was of longer duration but with no greater success. In 1908, Ford and James Couzens were interested in Cape May as a site for a transatlantic shipping port for Ford automobiles. On October 28, 1908, Ford and Couzens together purchased seven tracts of land at Cape May from Emlen Physick for $40,000, each paying $20,000. One half was in the names of Henry and Clara Ford, the other in the names of James and Margaret Couzens. Ten years later, on June 6, 1918, Mr. and Mrs. Couzens deeded their land to Henry S. Morgan (Couzens's secretary) for the consideration of one dollar. On June 11, 1918, Morgan and his wife, Marian, deeded the same land to Henry Ford, also for the consideration of one dollar. A check for $33,600 was then given by Ford to Couzens for his half of the Cape May property on June 24, 1918. It seems nothing had been done in the meantime to develop these properties commercially.

Experience at
Cape May

Although it was rumored that Ford had assembled a 1,200-acre farm tract, records show the property consisted of 357 acres of farm land and marsh on Cape May Harbor west of the inland waterway. It thus would have provided a seawater loading and unloading port in the event that the Delaware River was blockaded with ice during winter. It was said in a proposal to build a canal from Cape May Harbor to Delaware Bay: "Cape May is no different than hundreds of other capes or mountains. It is seldom one can find good weather on both sides. Ninety percent of the bad weather on Cape May is from ocean waves, fogs, and easterly winds."

According to Ford's financial records, income from the Cape May property consisted of rental receipts of only $8,505.39, while taxes during the same period had been $18,414.21. When the property was finally sold to Philip Stinger and his wife, Fannie, on July 22, 1938, the land was assessed at $23,200, the buildings at $3,600. The sales price is listed, however, at an unbelievably low $4,500. The cost of the property had been the initial $20,000 plus $33,600 for Couzens's half, totaling $53,600. With consideration given to depreciation allowances and expense of improvements, the resulting overall loss to Ford in 1938 is reported as $44,871.30. Based on the records found, Ford's experiences at Cape May were decidedly unprofitable.

References

Accession 285, Boxes 57, 96, Henry Ford Office Correspondence. Benson Ford Research Center, HFM & GV.

Accession 384, Box 1, L. J. Thompson Research Papers. Benson Ford Research Center, HFM & GV.

Beitel, Herbert M., and Vance C. Enck. *Cape May County: A Pictorial History.* Norfolk: Donning, 1988.

Lewis, David L. *The Public Image of Henry Ford.* Detroit: Wayne State University Press, 1975.

Nevins, Allan. *Ford: The Times, the Man, the Company.* New York: Scribner's, 1954.

30
Dearborn's Deep Test Well

Henry Ford was not only a very inquisitive person, but he also had the financial means to satisfy his curiosity in a number of unorthodox ways. Beginning in 1912, when Ford had perhaps more money than he knew how to spend, he began to explore the earth beneath him with a number of deep wells on his various properties. One well was drilled in 1912 at Ford's Highland Park manufacturing plant to a depth of 2,500 feet. In 1924, he drilled a well on his Detroit, Toledo & Ironton Railroad property at Jackson, Ohio, where he struck gas at 1,925 feet. In 1937, at his assembly plant in Long Beach, California, both gas and petroleum oil were being pumped from wells at depths of about 2,000 feet.

On June 19, 1915, the *Detroit News* ran the following:

Henry Ford Digging a Hole a Mile Deep on His Farm at Dearborn
It is just like this [quoting Ford]: Last fall when Mr. Edison was visiting me, he and I went over the country here a good deal together and one day he said to me: "Why don't you dig a hole around here some place?" And I said, "Well it never occurred to me but maybe I will some day." And Mr. Edison said, "You might as well." I got to thinking it over during the winter and as soon as the frost left the ground I got the contractors busy. They're down about 300 feet and acted kind of discouraged. They said they hadn't found anything. And I said, "Well just keep going. That's the only way you're ever going to find anything. You go down at least 5,000 feet, and every five feet you take a sample of the earth and see what is in it. You never can tell, they might find gas, they might find oil, they might find potash. You never can tell."

A little later that year, on October 22, 1915, the *Dearborn Independent* described drilling at the Ford tractor plant in Dearborn:

Work at the experimental well was suspended Monday because of water struck below the Trenton rock which rose to within less than 200 feet of the top. This caused a breaking down of the walls above

Published previously in the *Dearborn Historian*, Vol. 36, No. 2, 1996.

DEEP TEST WELL AT DEARBORN? MICH.
Location
100 ft. South of the FORD Machine Shops
Drilled--1915 to 1916

Section	Feet	Series	Formation	Lithologic description
	100	Pleistocene	Wisconsin Drift	Clay with thin gravel beds
	200	Middle Devonian	Dundee (Onondaga) limestone	Light to dark gray and cherty lime stones.
	300	Discon-formity	Upper Monroe or Detroit River Series	Dark brown & light gray to buff dolo-mite;argillaceous and with black bituminous streaks Streaks of pure white anhydrite.
	400	Upper Silurian		
	500	or		
	600	Monroan	Sylvania or Middle Monroe	Grayish to pure white sandstone. A GLASS SAND.
	700	and Salinan	Raisin River dolomite Put-in-Bay dolomite	Light to dark buff and gray dolo-mite--Argillaceous in places.
	800		Tymochtee shale Greenfield dolomite	Light buff gray anhydrite, and dolomite
	900			Chiefly dark gray shale and shaley dolomite
	1000	Discon-formity		WHITE SALT
	1100			Streaks of gray shale& buff dolomite Gray shale with white and red salt
	1200			Whitesalt with streaks of dolmite and anhydrite. White salt.
	1300			
	1400		SALINA	Light to dark gray shale and dolomite
	1500			White salt
	1600	Upper Silurian		Gray shale and buff dolmite. White salt with buff dolomite at the bottom, and in the middle
	1700			Buff to brown dol.
	1800			White salt with shale at the top.
	1900		Lower Salina	Dark gray shaly dolomite and dark gray shale with some white streaks near the bottom.
	2000			

870'

550' salt.

Depth (ft)	System/Series	Formation	Lithology
			White salt with shale at the top.
1900		Lower Salina	Dark gray shaly dolomite and dark gray shale with some white streaks near the bottom.
2000			
2100			Light to very dark gray buff & and brown bituminous dolomite.
2200			
2300	Middle Silurian or Niagaran	Guelph limestone	Pure white to bluish white crystalline dolomite
2400	Lower Silurian or Oswegan	Cabot Head shale Manitoulin limestone	Gray to green shale very fissile in places.
2500			
	disconformity	Queenston shale	Greenish gray shale.
2600			
2700		Richton shales	Dark gray and greenish gray pyritic shale.
2800	Upper Ordovician or Cincinnatian	Lorraine (Eden?- Ulrich) shale	Grayish blue shale fossiliferous in places but much less than above.
2900			
3000		Utica shale	Dark brownish gray shale & dark brown bituminous shale.
3100			White to dark gray buff limestone
3200			Very dark buff & brown bituminous limestone and some gray shale
3300			
3400	Middle Ordovician or Champlainian	"Trenton" limestone (Mainly Black River with probably some Stones River in the lower part—Ulrich)	Grayish to black bituminous and argillaceous limestone- fossiliferous.
3500			
3600			Light to dark buff limestone, darker toward the bottom.
3700			
3800			Grayish buff and some light buff limestone.
3900			
4000	Lower Ordovician	St. Peter Calciferous sandstones	White to light gray & buff dolomitic sandstone.

4035

the Trenton formation, necessitating the extension of the casing about 1,100 feet. The depth reached is 4,036 feet so far, Trenton rock being pierced at about 4,000 feet. The water is strongly impregnated with salt. The present casing is about 2,300 feet deep and must be taken out to permit the introduction of the new pipe.

On November 26, 1915, there is this report:

At the experimental well Monday the drillers had almost reached the bottom of the 4,036 foot hole, which they have been cleaning out, and expected to begin drilling at once.

Another account of the activities at the Ford tractor plant appears in the *Dearborn Independent* on March 31, 1916, where well drilling is mentioned and a photograph of the plant is shown identifying, among other things, the approximately 50-foot-high drilling rig.

The personal reminiscences of William Mielke of Dearborn add considerably to our knowledge of Ford's Dearborn well operations:

About 400 feet south of the railway, Elm Street made a turn to the right and then became an east and west street lining up with the present Beech Street. Just south of Elm Street, after it had made its turn, there stood a drilling rig very substantially built of oak. Of course almost everyone in Dearborn was curious to know what Ford had in mind. Some of us were eager to know what formations were below us. As with most drill crews, the information given to the public was vague and misleading. However, I kept on asking them questions but never found out what was below us until years later. Finally I was able to procure a log or chart of findings which disclosed formations similar to other wells in the state. However, the thickness of the salt area was enormous starting at 985 feet down.

The drillers worked two shifts and made good progress, as they started in June 1915 and by October were down 4,035 feet. Some Dearborn people protested about the noise made at night, so orders were given to be more quiet. Over the weekends the crew used to mount a stuffed pair of overalls on top of the rig, which gave the impression that there was always someone there.

Mr. Ford was there a lot as he then lived at Fair Lane. The objective of the depth was 5,000 feet, then unheard of in Michigan, but at 4,035 feet the drill hit a cavity and became wedged and the cable snapped. As Mr. Ford was quite insistent that nothing was impossible, he urged them to continue. Although at this time they were 350 feet deeper than the deepest Michigan well at Mt. Pleasant, the crew used all the tricks of the trade trying to fish for the drill. They became very discouraged at their failure, and finally, in June 1916, the well was abandoned and the rig dismantled.

Geological data obtained from this 4,036-foot Dearborn well drilled in 1915 and 1916 are still valid today. There is proof that

The site of the deep test well that had been dug behind the old Ford tractor plant in 1915 and 1916, as found behind the Ford EEE Building in 1987. (B.101884)

Dearborn is supported by common sedimentary rock and salt, offering little prospect of an abundant flow of easy mineral riches, although salt has been commercially mined in the Dearborn area for years.

The exact location of Ford's 1915 deep test well was never marked. At the approximate location of the well, the Ford tractor plant was torn down and Ford Engineering Laboratories were constructed in 1923–24. The building nearest the well location is the Engine and Electrical Engineering Building, referred to as the EEE Building of the Ford Engineering and Research Center. During the summer of 1987, a new fire line was installed around the EEE Building. During that installation, a study was made of the 1915 newspaper articles and of Mielke's reminiscences to determine the most likely location of the well. During installation of the fire line, the head of the well was unearthed a few feet below several layers of Elm Street paving. A valve with an eight-inch wheel tops the well casing which is bricked in for several feet below the valve. A four-inch pipe leads from the valve to beneath the EEE Building. The well is on the west edge of Elm Street, 28 feet out from the east wall of the EEE Building and 112 feet north of the building's south end.

The top of the deep test well as uncovered in 1987 during construction of a fire line around the Engineering Building. A large valve, within a brick-enclosed well head, controls the water line into the basement of the building. (B.101883)

References

Accession 23, Box 2, Deep Test Well at Dearborn, Michigan. Benson Ford Research Center, HFM & GV.

Accession 23, Box 2, Deep Test Well at Highland Park. Benson Ford Research Center, HFM & GV.

Accession 65, William Mielke Reminiscences. Benson Ford Research Center, HFM & GV.

Dearborn Independent, October 22, 1915; November 26, 1915; March 31, 1916.

Detroit News, June 19, 1915.

31
Dearborn Flour Mill

When Henry Ford was growing up on the farm, he was fascinated with mills operated by waterpower. Streams throughout the countryside were spotted with small sawmills sawing logs into lumber and gristmills grinding grain into flour. In those horse-and-wagon days, there was need especially for a gristmill within a very few miles of the farm in order to have wheat flour and corn meal for daily bread. Ford's admiration for the waterpowered gristmill led him eventually to restore several such picturesque mills, one at Wayside Inn in Massachusetts, one at Berry College in Georgia, and others in southeastern Michigan.

After becoming wealthy from the automobile business, fully satisfied with the Model T automobile, and well along with development of the Fordson tractor, Ford became a gentleman farmer himself. By 1915, he was building his elaborate Dearborn home, Fair Lane, and had already accumulated 2,843 acres of farm land in the Dearborn area. These were known as Henry Ford Farms, managed by Raymond Dahlinger, with specific, almost daily, directions provided by Ford. Although he had a dairy farm, his major crops were grains, particularly wheat. This was fifteen years before he discovered the phenomenal value of soybeans.

With scores of Fordson tractors working the land, pulling the binders, and threshing the wheat in the fields with machines powered by Fordsons, Ford was proving he did not need horses. But where was he going to put the wheat from his growing number of acres until it was sold? As part of Ford Farms operations, he decided he should have his own grain elevator in Dearborn to store the wheat produced. On October 13, 1917, Ford made an agreement with S. J. McQueen & Co. of Fort William, Ontario, for the construction of a concrete grain elevator on the Michigan Central Railroad at Oakwood Boulevard. The elevator, costing $74,448, was to have fifteen circular bins, each 65 feet high, and a conveyor to handle 2,000 bushels per hour. Capacity of the elevator was estimated to be 99,800 bushels.

In order to carry grain processing further, on March 2, 1920, Ford made an agreement with his own Dearborn Realty & Construction Company for the erection of a four-story, fireproof, reinforced concrete

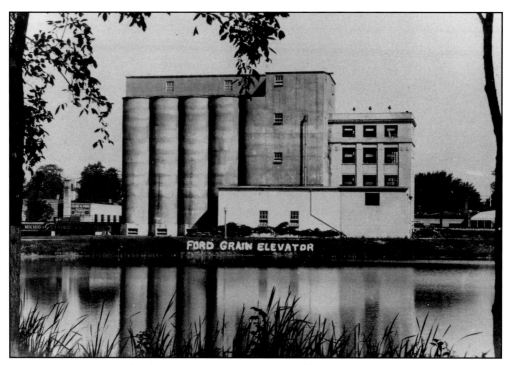

Ford Farms elevator and grain mill. The mill is the four-story building to the right of the elevator. The long, low building in the foreground is the barn housing the *Fair Lane,* the private railroad car used by the Fords. (Photograph courtesy of Dearborn Historical Museum.)

flour mill adjacent to the grain elevator. Dearborn Realty & Construction had been organized by Ford in the spring of 1919 to construct housing in Dearborn for Ford employees. Ernest Liebold, general secretary to Ford and holding power of attorney, was also president of Dearborn Realty & Construction. So only Liebold's signatures appear on the agreement. The cost of the flour mill without the milling machinery was about $48,000. Machinery was purchased from the Nordyke & Harmon Company of Indianapolis, bringing the total cost of the flour mill to $120,117. In December 1920, the milling machinery was first started. On that date, Ford's old friend John Burroughs happened to be in Dearborn, and Ford had him push the button to start the machinery. At the beginning of operations, the Ford Flour Mill obtained its electricity from the Rouge power plant of Ford Motor Company at no charge.

Ralph Shackleton was in charge of the mill, with Mrs. Raymond Dahlinger as treasurer and Liebold representing Ford. A dozen or so white-smocked employees kept the place running and the building clean. Dust collectors and vacuum cleaners were in constant use, the fear of explosion being always in mind. In operation, the wheat was never allowed to stand long in one bin but was kept almost constantly moving from one bin to another. A cleaning separator removed straws, husks, dirt, and weed seed; next came a scouring machine and an application of heat and moisture. Instead of the old-fashioned grinding stones, the process used several sets of rollers, which produced a series of diminishing particle sizes, or "breaks," leading to the finest flour.

Ford had a means of selling his flour directly to his employees. In 1920, he had begun operating commissaries that provided groceries, meats, clothing, shoes, coal, coke, and plant fertilizer to employee families at prices very little above cost. Ford flour, for example, sold in 25-pound bags for three cents a pound. By means of the Ford Motor Company publication *Ford Times*, Ford Flour was touted as far superior to other flours. Homemade bread was said to account for most of the bread eaten during that period and to be superior to baker's bread. To encourage baking bread at home, *Ford Times* printed a recipe for making three loaves of bread from Ford Flour, with these ingredients:

> 1 medium-sized white potato
> 1 pint potato water
> 1 pint scalded milk
> 2 tablespoons lard
> 2 tablespoons butter
> 4 tablespoons salt
> 1 cake compressed yeast
> Ford bread flour (about 12 cups)

Ford employees were unquestionably obtaining bargain prices, but how was the Ford Flour Mill doing financially? Wheat to supply the mill was purchased from Ford Farms at the market price per bushel at the time of purchase. Combinations of "soft" (summer) wheat and "hard" (winter) wheat were blended to produce bread flour and pastry flour. Hard wheat was slightly more expensive than soft wheat. A small amount of whole wheat flour was also produced. By-products of the milling process included bran, middlings, and screenings which were resold to Ford Farms. Bread flour, pastry flour, and whole wheat flour were sold not only through the Ford Motor Company commissaries in Michigan but also in Kentucky and Georgia. Bakeries supplying Ford cafeterias were using Ford Flour, and Henry Ford Hospital in Detroit was also a customer.

Accurate financial records were difficult to keep because of the wheat being purchased by the bushel, the flour being sold by the barrel or pound, and grain moisture being modified during the milling process. Because production reported by the mill superintendent did not match that of the treasurer who reported sales, the sales figures were finally considered more valid in calculating profit and loss. The following is an early and encouraging report:

July 1922 to June 1923 both inclusive
REVENUES (as per Flour Mill Reports)

1,163,250#	Flour	$35,988.20
50,690#	(Low Grade)	912.42
162,600#	Middlings	2,396.78
313,600#	Bran	4,212.90
		$43,510.27

EXPENSES (as per ledger account)

Labor	$10,267.80
Bags & Twine	1,048.24
Wheat (purchased)	18,732.16
Fgt. & Express	2,229.00
Misc. Supplies	619.81
Repairs	4,341.02
Depreciation	5,235.19
	$42,473.22

The following report, however, indicates that the year 1924 was quite unfavorable financially:

January 1, 1924 to October 31, 1924
REVENUES

Sales of Flour, Bran, Middlings	$79,832.37
Sales of Bran, Middlings, etc.	
used on the Farm	3,397.89
Total Revenue	$83,230.26

COSTS
Wheat Used

Inventory Dec. 31, 1923	$2,372.00
Purchases, 10 months	92,572.78
Total	94,944.78
Less Inventory Oct. 31, 1924	28,845.46
	$66,099.32

EXPENSES

Labor	$9,992.30
Freight and Express	6,462.10
Bags	5,688.46
Repairs	1,793.53
Taxes	2,610.70

FOR RENT

Concrete Grain Elevator

at

Dearborn, Mich.

Capacity 100,000 Bushels

Individual Drives Throughout—2-Way Power
Shovel for Unloading—Car Puller—400-
Bushel Receiving Separator—M. C. R. R. Siding

Henry Ford

Engineering Laboratory
Dearborn   -   Michigan

Electricity	2,267.50
Miscellaneous	249.90
Total Expenses	33,441.99
Total Cost of Production	99,541.31
Deduct Increase in Finished Stock Inventory	940.48
Net Costs of Sales	98,600.83
Net Loss for Ten Months	15,370.57
10,925 Bbls. Flour Produced Net Loss per Bbl. Flour	1.406

A memo from J. T. Russell of the purchasing department to Ernest
Liebold on August 27, 1925, reveals the status of operations at that date:
I have been advised by Mr. Shackleton that the wheat capacity at the

Flour Mill is 110,000 bushels. We have approximately 8,000 bushels on order. It is estimated that the crop on the Ford Farms will amount to about 20,000 bushels.

There are also about 10,000 bushels of oats at the Flour Mill and 2,000 bushels screenings and buckwheat combined.

The above figures will total 46,000 bushels. If we were to fill the elevator to capacity we could purchase 64,000 bushels at the present time; or, if delivery were to be stretched over a period of possibly sixty days, we could undoubtedly get 70,000 or 75,000 bushels.

Mr. Shackleton estimates that 60,000 bushels, running the mill one shift as they are now doing, will last approximately one year.

A 1928 financial report indicates a loss of $.007 per barrel of flour produced. Since the grain elevator was not able to show the least bit of profit, a form was prepared in March 1929 to advertise it for rent. Liebold, however, advised postponing rental of the elevator. Soybean production was now in the offing, and by 1932, soybeans began to be produced in considerable quantity on Ford Farms. Ford Flour Mill products then offered for sale included the following:

	Size	Price/barrel
Pastry flour	100#	$4.25
Pastry flour	5#	6.00
Bread flour	25# and 100#	6.00
Soybean flour	100#	6.00
Soybean flour	5#	7.00
Low grade	Ton	30.00
Middlings	Ton	28.00
Bran	Ton	28.00

Ford's soybean production by 1936 utilized 12,000 acres of his own land, providing about 190,000 bushels. This was enough soybean meal for use in his automobile plastic applications but not enough oil for his soybean automotive paints. Additional soybean oil had to be purchased from other soybean processors.

In 1941, prices on all Ford Flour Mill products were raised about 20 percent. Ford Motor Company was then processing its own soybeans into meal and oil and using the grain elevator primarily for storage. Shackleton then advised Dahlinger:

In order to reimburse Mr. Henry Ford for expense incurred in handling, hauling, drying and storing the Ford Motor Company's soy beans, we should charge a nominal flat rate of 7¢ per bushel to cover same, Ford Motor Company to absorb the actual loss in weight due to evaporation of excessive moisture.

During World War II, Ford Farms were required to meet grain storage quotas under the emergency provisions of the Agricultural Adjustment Act, quotas that ensured adequate food and feed supplies for the nation's war effort. Young men working on farms were deferred by the nation's draft boards. Wheat marketing quotas were suspended in 1943.

Records indicate that the Ford Flour Mill in 1942 and 1943 supplied flour to Ford Motor Company Foundry, Highland Park Commissary, Rouge Plant Cafeteria, Willow Run Plant Cafeteria, and Berry College in Georgia. In September 1944, however, personal property of Henry Ford, including all of Ford Farms, was appraised for purchase by Ford Motor Company. The elevator and flour mill land was appraised at $1,000, the building at $133,068. The mill continued to operate under Ford Motor Company as part of Ford Farms. A 1950 report shows losses for Ford Farms from 1947 to 1949 averaging well over half a million dollars each year. During these years, nearly all of the Ford Farms acreage was sold by Ford Motor Company to the public. The elevator and flour mill were torn down in 1957.

References

Accession 47, Box 1, Dearborn Realty and Construction Company. Benson Ford Research Center, HFM & GV.

Accession 272, Box 7, Payroll Records. Benson Ford Research Center, HFM & GV.

Accession 284, Box 8, Office of Henry Ford (1920). Benson Ford Research Center, HFM & GV.

Accession 285, Boxes 26, 374, 629, 788, 965, 1576, 2665, Office of Henry Ford (1921–1949). Benson Ford Research Center, HFM & GV.

"Ford Flour, Producing Loaf of Superior Quality, Finds Favor." *Ford News,* April 1, 1923.

"Modern Milling Methods Exemplified in Ford Flour Mill; Superior Product." *Ford News,* March 15, 1923.

Taylor, Robert L. "How Soybeans Help Build Fords." *Chemical & Metallurgical Engineering,* April 1936.

32
Florida Rubber Plantation

In February 1923, Harvey Firestone warned Henry Ford of an impending crisis in the supply of rubber for automobile tires. The British Rubber Restriction Act had become effective on November 1, 1922. This situation came about because a British-Dutch cartel then controlled world production of the high-yielding *Hevea* rubber in the Far Eastern countries of Malaya, Ceylon, and Java. Firestone, Goodyear, and now Ford realized that the United States would need an independent and preferably domestic supply of rubber.

In 1915, Ford, Thomas Edison, John Burroughs, and others are said to have visited Old Fort Thompson at LaBelle and the Goodno Ranch in the seasonally flooded Caloosahatchee River valley of Florida. Ford was impressed with the extensive lush green pastures, the beautiful cattle, and especially the thousands of white herons flying about.

On May 15, 1922, Ford accepted a mortgage note for $166,986.46 from his friend Edgar E. Goodno of LaBelle, receiving as collateral Goodno's property consisting of Old Fort Thompson in the town of LaBelle, Goodno's 7,290-acre ranch, and other businesses Goodno had owned and operated for the past twenty years. Goodno was not only supervising the ranch, where he raised chiefly Poll Angus cattle with some Brahma (the sacred cattle of India) and some Angora goats, but also operating the Everett Hotel, an electric system, an ice plant, and the Red Front Garage.

Two years after accepting the mortgage, accrued interest and taxes had increased Goodno's debt to $178,429.50. On May 15, 1924, Ford accepted the Goodno property as full payment and hired his friend and former owner Edgar Goodno as superintendent at a wage of $250 a month. On May 27, 1924, identical announcements in the *Detroit News* and the *Detroit Times* flashed the news: "Ford is reported to have paid $500,000 for 8,000 acres — to presage the early development of a large rubber growing industry in Florida."

In a speech prepared for a barbecue at LaBelle in the summer of 1924, Goodno described his former property as "the most beautiful and valuable estate in the South." He went on to say:

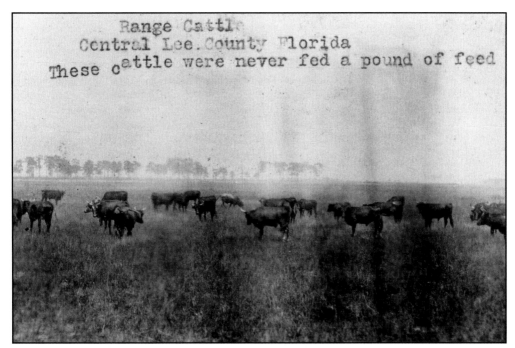

The letterhead of the stationery used by Edgar E. Goodno during his early correspondence with Henry Ford and Ernest Liebold during 1922–1924.

The news of Henry Ford's coming to Hendry County marks the era for a great rejoicing in this section of Florida, for Mr. Ford will bring into this new project his vast capital and the same energy and good business sense which he has used in his wonder game. If so, then why should not we feast and rejoice?

The property was described in a June 25, 1924, memo by W. L. R. Blakeley, associated with the Ford Dearborn office, as follows:

The Goodno Plantation consists of 8,200 acres mostly along the Caloosahatchee River, 5,500 acres of which are cleared and runs from a mucky loam in low sections to a sandy loam. Improvements consist of hotel and one 4-room house in LaBelle; hotel containing 22 rooms, and three store houses now rented to the city. In the yard is a concrete swimming pool about 18 x 35 feet fed by a 5-inch artesian well which forces water through the hotel as high as the second floor; the well flows 15,000 gallons per minute it is claimed.

At the Home Place is the residence of 9 rooms, a hotel of about 15 rooms, a barn and electric light plant and an ice plant of 160 cakes capacity. At Goodno there are two tenant houses. On the 20 acre orange grove site is a 5-room house. Crops consist of pineapples, potatoes, tomatoes, grapes, coconuts, mangoes, avocados, oranges and grapefruit.

Natives tell me that vegetables grow well although I saw no truck gardens. It seems we might ship certain crops to Ford Commissary for disposal. Nearly all of past grapefruit crop was allowed to rot on the ground, prices received did not pay picking and packing expense.

We planted 60 Ficus Elastiga plants, 458 Cryptostegia grandiflora, and 100 Cryptostegia managascariensis, ranging in height from six inches to two feet, 10 of the Ficus being about five inches tall. I feel someone should collect shoots from Grandiflora and grow shoots under shade, by which method we could have 12,000 to 15,000 plants beyond danger of frost by sixty days. We all concur that for the present Cryptostegia grandiflora offers best possibilities for rubber, but all are dubious as to its growing well at LaBelle on account of temperature. Mr. Roche of Miami, says he would recommend the grafting of grandiflora to the trunk of Ficus elastica in order to change growth of grandiflora.

Mr. A. C. Steger of Jacksonville Branch assisted in transporting and setting out the plants on the Plantation, and was of considerable help in gathering data. Mr. Goodno is still on the property. He will see the plants every few days and in case they need care will get Barry Scott to do the work and send the bill to the Dearborn Plant.

Summaries of laboratory data providing percentage values for moisture, rubber, resin, and insoluble matter for seven varieties of rubber plants from various parts of the world appeared on the last page of the Blakeley report.

The activities at LaBelle had not gone unnoticed by local newspapers or aggressive Florida land speculators. On August 15, 1924, the *Caloosahatchee Current* carried the headline "Hendry County Valuation Increases 20 Percent 1st Year."

On August 8, Dr. N. Lyncker of Jacksonville had sent the following letter to Dearborn:

> Would you be kindly enough and give me a confidential information. An agent with the name of Watts offered me 10 lots in LaBelle, Florida. He informed that Mr. Ford will start there a big rubber tree farm.
>
> Before I buy the ten lots I would like to know if this information is right. I have eight children from 15 months to 14 years and I cannot lose money. I would like to go to LaBelle as a physician but before I do it I would like to have your advice.
>
> I have saved $10,000 and could invest this money.
> Very truly your's,
> N. Lyncker

Ernest Liebold, general secretary to Henry Ford, answered Lyncker's letter on August 20, 1924:

In answer to your letter of August 8th we beg to advise that we have no present intention of starting a rubber tree farm.

We have experimented some with rubber producing plants, but merely for the purpose of ascertaining what percentage of rubber could be obtained from them.

Very truly yours,
E. G. Liebold

A letter from the Fordson tractor dealer in Moore Haven, Florida, reported the following to Henry Ford on November 3, 1924:

In reply to your letter regarding taking a tractor to LaBelle to demonstrate on grove, I drove to within a mile of LaBelle yesterday and went the rest of the way by boat. All the south side of the Caloosahatchee River, including your property, has been under water an average of five feet of water for the last ten days. At present, they average from 24 to 36 inches of water.

I talked with Mr. Goodno and he said that it would be five weeks before the water would be off the grove and a little longer before we could plow there. I will keep in touch with Mr. Goodno and the moment we can do anything will take a tractor and plow down and demonstrate, as per your instructions.

An undated memo from a Colonel Elliott to a Captain Menge at LaBelle pertains to "Flood Control, Caloosahatchee River." Following are excerpts from the memo:

The floods which occasionally occur in the Caloosahatchee Valley are recurrent in character. The causes of the floods rest in heavy periodic rainfall, and may therefore be expected from time to time. The complete control of these periodic floods within channels below banks may not be possible within a cost which would be warranted. The reduction of these floods to a level and to a time limit which will greatly reduce flood damage can probably be accomplished within an expense which would be justified.

The damage from floods lies largely in the time which water stands upon the ground. The passing of surplus water, therefore, within a time limit which will prevent serious damage appears to be the problem which should be considered. Correction of conditions must lie in improving the river from Fort Thompson toward Fort Myers.

The *Detroit Times*, on February 22, 1925, reported that Henry Ford himself had conducted "inspections of holdings where he is to develop rubber plantations." In April, land speculators were again active, and Liebold found it necessary to send a warning to the editor of the *Miami Herald*, Frank B. Shutts:

My attention has just been called to an advertisement which appeared in the *Herald* on Sunday, April 12th on pages 11-D advertising lands of the Florida and Cape Cod Realty Company located in Hendrie County, Florida.

In connection with this it mentions the property "adjoining the Ford and Edison Tracts where Henry Ford and Thomas A. Edison are developing cotton and rubber plantations." The facts in connection with this matter are that Mr. Edison is not interested with Mr. Ford in such experiments. A few rubber plants have been set out, nothing being contemplated with reference to cotton. Such statements misrepresent the facts to those who are misled. I do not feel that you would want the *Herald* to publish such unreliable advertisements.

Very truly yours
E. G. Liebold

From Mr. Shutts's reply:

We have no way of knowing that property advertised in some other county does not adjoin tracts mentioned as being owned by Mr. Ford and Mr. Edison. . . . We have called upon the officials of the Florida and Cape Cod Realty Company and have asked them to refrain from making any statements in the future such as this of which you complain. These gentlemen have promised to govern themselves accordingly, and I think so far as the *Herald is* concerned, it will not occur again.

Trusting this is satisfactory, I am

Very truly yours,
Frank B. Shutts

A letter from the Michigan Securities Commission reached Liebold on May 9, 1925:

This office has been informed that real estate dealers are about to offer lots in the vicinity of LaBelle, Florida, for sale to Ford employees for $25 per lot and their excuse for selling said lots is that Mr. Ford has supposedly acquired 7,500 acres of land in the vicinity, upon which to experiment on the raising of rubber trees.

Will you kindly inform us as to whether or not it is Mr. Ford's intention to experiment in rubber in Florida, for if he does not intend to do so this Department will stop misrepresentation made in the sale of such lots.

No doubt a good many Ford employees will be buncoed, as they will undoubtedly buy lots on the strength of Mr. Ford's supposed rubber experiment. An early reply from you would be greatly appreciated.

Very truly yours,
Albert A. Town
Chief Investigator

Liebold replied:

Mr. Ford came into possession of 7,600 acres of land in the vicinity of LaBelle, Florida about one year ago. It has been advertised that Mr. Ford and Mr. Edison bought this property and it is to be used for a large rubber plantation. The fact is that Mr. Edison is in no way interested in this property and about fifty or sixty rubber plants of various species have been planted for the purpose of trying out the soil. We have no plans of establishing a rubber plantation as we are not satisfied that the plants that have been planted will successfully produce rubber.

 The land in the vicinity is worth perhaps forty to fifty dollars per acre, although in some instances, it is bringing a much higher price. We assure you of our cooperation in this connection as we are receiving quite a number of letters from prospective purchasers who are requesting information, and from the advertising being distributed, the matter is being quite extensively misrepresented.

 Very truly yours,
 E. G. Liebold

In October 1925, Liebold received the following letter from the editor of the magazine *The Rubber Age:*

We recently read in "The Manufacturers Record" that you would like to tell the truth about Mr. Ford's "rubber plantation in Florida."

 We would like very much to have you write an article for The *Rubber Age* setting forth the truth of this matter, and putting the rumors to rest. This article could be as long or as short as you desire.

 Very truly yours,
 G. H. Trimingham

Liebold's "article" was indeed short:

Gentlemen: Attention Mr. G. H. Trimingham
 There is not much of a story in connection with Mr. Ford's "rubber plantation."

 A few experimental plants were set out merely for the purpose of ascertaining whether or not the various rubber plants could be grown in Florida. A small tract of about one acre in area is still being cultivated for this purpose. The idea of a rubber plantation is largely mythical.

 Very truly yours,
 E. G. Liebold

The outlandish publicity concerning Ford's rubber plantation in Florida was fast fading, however, as Ford was now concentrating on Brazil as the location of his rubber activities. In 1926, Ford sponsored James Weir and Carl LaRue in an exploratory survey of rubber development in the Amazon; that same year, transactions were begun with the Brazilian government for a land concession amounting to 2.5 million acres for rubber development. Firestone was likewise developing a large plantation in Liberia, and Goodyear was investing in Costa Rica and Panama.

So what became of the LaBelle property in Florida? There are stacks of correspondence between Goodno and Liebold concerning the details of operating the Florida properties — about Fort Thompson, the hotel, the electric lighting system, the grapefruit crops, and so on. Goodno had been accustomed to making his own decisions concerning operations, but now he found Liebold insisted on micromanaging the plantation. Such questions as whether to meter the electricity sold to customers and what wages the hotel staff was to be paid were decided by Liebold. There was considerable difficulty obtaining labor for menial work. In 1932, the hotel was closed, and Goodno's pay was cut to $225 per month.

Financial records listing revenues and expenses from 1924 to 1942 reveal the hotel profiting by $786 in 1925 and after that showing about $3,000 average in losses until it closed in 1932. Other operations, presumably farming and ranching, seem to have been fairly consistent losers by about $500 per year. Ford sold the entire property in 1942 to J. B. Hendry, a resident rancher, for only $50,000; the ten-room house Hendry had occupied had burned in February 1941. Property losses of $128,429.50 and operating losses of $101,781.12 combine for a total cost of about $230,000 for Ford's "rubber plantation" in Florida.

References

Accession 285, Boxes 243, 389, 502, 642, 643, Henry Ford Office. Benson Ford Research Center, HFM & GV.

Accession 844, Box 1, L. J. Thompson Papers. Benson Ford Research Center, HFM & GV.

33
Edison Botanic Research Corporation

At Fort Myers, Florida, in March 1924, Harvey Firestone and rubber experts from Liberia and Singapore were conferring with Thomas Edison concerning the possibility of rubber production in the United States. Tire manufacturers could no longer depend on supplies from foreign countries at reasonable prices. Edison was questioned about possibilities of growing rubber domestically. Firestone was making a move to establish his own plantation in Liberia. Henry Ford was planning to buy 70,000 acres of land at Ways Station, Georgia, possibly for rubber experiments, and was also negotiating in Brazil for plantation acreage. Edison, thinking of his friend Luther Burbank's work with plants, looked forward to the challenge of such a project.

Before Charles Goodyear discovered and patented vulcanization in 1844, rubber had been a useless curiosity. Brazil's jungle rubber trees, the *Hevea brasilensis*, provided the world's major supply. However, with the extensive use of rubber tires for automotive vehicles, rubber became a major commercial product. The British and the Dutch, by stealing seeds from the wild trees in Brazil, were able to establish in Ceylon, India, and Malaya huge plantations devoted to rubber culture. The British, in particular, aimed to control production and prices. By 1922, the British were supplying two-thirds of the world's rubber, and Brazil's wild rubber amounted to less than 5 percent of the total.

Firestone took the lead in an attempt to fight the British monopoly, which by 1923 had tripled the price of rubber. Firestone's March 1924 meeting with Edison and rubber experts from the Far East was part of that effort. Although Ford did not attend that particular meeting, he and Edison had been considering the possibilities of a domestic rubber source. At the same time, Edison was developing a battery and an electric starter for the Model T car. Edison included these paragraphs in a letter to Ford:

> I am experimenting on the giant milk weed you found in Michigan. I will send results when finished. It grows all along the road on which I came back to Orange, except I saw none in limestone soils. There I found another variety resembling the giant but also saw two other kinds of milk weed. Am making rapid progress on the Ford starter.

I enclose a piece of rubber I extracted from the Guayule. It can be further purified.

A letter from Edison to Ford's secretary, Ernest Liebold, dated July 19, 1923, reads as follows:

Tell Ford that I have been experimenting a little with milk weed. I find the maximum amount of latex is given when the plant is half grown. When it blossoms there is scarcely any latex. Therefore, we can get two crops per year.

It is going to be a difficult matter to get a commercial process to get the latex out. The percentage of rubber is small but there is considerable resin; far more than I thought.

Yours very truly,
Thos. A. Edison

In May 1925, Florida newspapers announced:

Rubber Crisis Threatens America: Firestone Seeking New Sources of Supply

Two years ago Harvey Firestone predicted a rubber shortage and said British crude rubber restrictions would cost the American people millions of dollars. The British colonial possessions in the Far East produce about 80% of the world's supply of rubber while America consumes 75% of the world's supply.

December 1925 brought further pronouncements:

Emancipate America from Rubber Extortion

America will use 400,000 tons of rubber in 1925. At the price of rubber prevailing a year ago, which was 35¢, our rubber bill was $313,360,000. The same amount of rubber consumed during 1926, at the prevailing rate of $1.05 per pound, will cost America $940,000,000, an increase of over 200%.

A January 1926 headline read: "Firestone May Use Florida Rubber to Break Rubber Monopoly. American Millions Enter Rubber War." And in March 1926: "Growing of Rubber under U.S. Flag Urged in Congress."

Edison was eighty years old on February 11, 1927. Asked when he was going to retire, he answered, "Just a few days before my funeral." That same month, Ford received through Ford Motor Company of Canada 70 pounds of *Cryptostigia madagascariensis* seed from Edwin Mayer & Company, Ltd., of Tananarive, Madagascar, for Edison to use in his experiments. Ford also invited Edison to try these seeds on the 8,000-acre plantation Ford owned at LaBelle, Florida, about fifty miles east of Fort Myers. A letter dated June 8, 1927, from Edison's assistant, W. H. Meadowcroft, to Liebold, Ford's secretary, reads as follows:

Referring to your letter of May 31, in regard to the utilization of some of Mr. Ford's land in Georgia, Mr. Edison has been busy the last few days, and therefore the answer to your letter has been delayed.

He says that as a preliminary he wanted to get to the location of Mr. Ford's property down in Georgia. As soon as his nine acres at Fort Myers, Florida are full and three or four acres that he is planting at Oneco, Florida, are filled up, he will have gotten a pretty good idea of what he wants to plant at Mr. Ford's place.

The experiments he will want to conduct on the land in Georgia will be with plants that can stand a very considerable frost. Mr. Edison says that when he is ready, he will have a man go down to Georgia and pick out seven to ten acres that will answer for the experiment.

Yours very truly,
W. H. Meadowcroft

*Edison Botanic
Research Corporation*

Edison was already spending most of his time and energy on rubber experiments. Firestone previously had suggested a formal company to support Edison financially. A July 26, 1927, a letter from Edison to Firestone mentions the subject:

I have been working at the Botanical Gardens in New York all week, but got back to the office this morning and found your letter of July 11th.

I am sorry to say that I cannot go joy riding this year as I am too busily engaged on the rubber investigation. I have out at this time twelve field men collecting specimens, and on Monday I will have another one who will go to Cuba.

I will attend the organization of the Company.

I am enjoying the rubber investigation very much and thus far have been well this summer. Hoping to see you before long, I remain

Sincerely,
Thos. A. Edison

On July 29, there was another letter from Firestone to Edison:

When I was in Detroit last week I had a talk with Mr. Ford and Mr. Liebold in regard to the organization of a company for research and development work in rubber and the suggestion was made that the company be organized for $75,000.

Mr. Ford would put in $25,000, I $25,000, and you would put in your services for the other $25,000, which I trust will be agreeable to you, and I enclose check for $25,000 for my stock in the company. As you wrote me, you would look after the organization of the company. If I can be of any assistance or help at any time in organizing or after the company becomes organized, I hope that you will call upon me as I have a very sincere interest in your work and am looking forward to great developments.

I will come to see you the first time I am in the East.

With personal regards,
Harvey S. Firestone

Edison sent a summary of the arrangement to Ford on August 5, 1927:

The organization of the new company to take over the rubber exper-
imental work is practically completed. We have settled on the name
Edison Botanic Research Corporation, with head office here in
Orange. The stockholders will be yourself, Mr. Firestone and myself,
with two qualifying directors, my son Charles Edison, and John V.
Miller.

The Company is organized on an authorized capital stock of
$75,000.00, of which each of us will hold 1/3. As soon as the forms
are received, stock certificates will be issued.

In order to complete the papers in connection with the organization, I am sending you, attached, a form which we would request
you to sign on the middle line, as indicated by your initials. Upon
return of this paper from you, we will forward to Mr. Firestone for his
signature.

In connection with the work, I would say that I have now in the
field about fourteen men who are sending in, almost daily, numerous
samples of plants which I am having planted, some here in Orange,
others in Fort Myers, and the third lot at Oneco, Florida. Many of
them look good. I am also carrying on considerable research work in
the chemical end of the proposition and whenever you come to
Orange you will be interested, I am sure, in seeing what progress has
been made so far.

Thos. A. Edison

Liebold replied to Meadowcroft:

I have received yours of August 5th relative to the organization of the
new company, the Edison Botanic Research Corporation.

We shall be interested in hearing from you from time to time
regarding the progress being made by the men in the field.

As requested, I am returning herewith Mr. Ford's subscription
bearing his signature.

Thanking you for your kind attention,

Very truly yours,
E. G. Liebold

From Orange, New Jersey, on August 11, 1927, Edison wrote to Ford:

Enclosed herewith I am sending you certificate of stock No. 5 for 250
shares of the capital stock of the Edison Botanic Research
Corporation. Will you kindly acknowledge receipt of same?

Specimen plants are coming from all parts of the country and I

Thomas Edison in a Florida experimental plot of goldenrod planted in rows.
The photograph was taken on May 26, 1929. (0.14155)

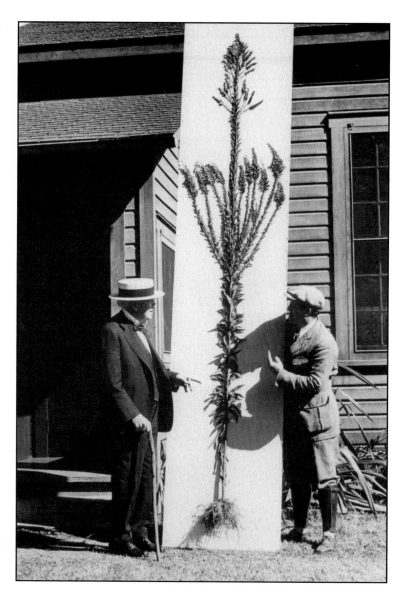

Thomas Edison
(left) and assistant
Mr. Archer, with a
single plant of
Solidaco edisoniana
goldenrod. The
photograph was
taken in Fort Myers,
Florida, on January
28, 1931, the year
Edison died.
(0.14160)

have quite a garden of them now at my place in Llewellyn Park.
Experiments in the chemical end are progressing fairly well.

I want to thank you again for joining me in this undertaking, and I
certainly trust that we will soon have some good results to report to you.

Yours very truly,
Thos. A. Edison

Firestone and Ford were not depending on Edison primarily. They
were investing much more heavily in Liberia and Brazil. Edison contin-

ued, however, and of the hundreds and hundreds of plants tested, he found that a giant goldenrod offered the best possibilities. The seeds of *Solidaco leavenworthii Edisoniana* produced plants ten feet in height.

When the Fords arrived at their winter home in Ways, Georgia, on February 20, 1930, the *New York Times* reported from Savannah:

> Henry Ford came to his Bryan County farm today supposedly to inspect operations for the raising of goldenrod from which Thomas A. Edison will produce rubber. The flower grows wild in this section, and there has been marked wonder among the natives that Mr. Ford is preparing a large acreage on his antebellum plantation to grow it as he would any other crop. The farm is a scene of great activity as the ground is being broken, apparently in preparation for the planting of the goldenrod. All of the work is being done behind a well-constructed fence and gate, which keeps trespassers from venturing too near the scene of operations.

Edison's work with plants led him in 1930 to promote a bill in Congress that would provide for new varieties of plants or improved crops to be patented in much the same manner as mechanical inventions. The new patent bill was passed at Edison's suggestion in order to encourage the development of new and better varieties of plants and crops.

Edison's experiments with goldenrod had been his chief occupation in the winter of 1930-31 at Fort Myers. By the time he returned to his home at Glenmont in mid-June 1931, he was not only tired but seriously ill. Edison died on October 21, 1931, at age eighty-four. Both the Ford and the Firestone families attended the funeral.

The goldenrod project continued, however, for a few more years at Fort Myers under the direction of Edison's employee, H. G. Ukkelberg. Firestone withdrew from the Edison Botanic Research Corporation in 1936 because of synthetic rubber developments in Germany. Ford then hired Ukkelberg to work for him on his plantation at Ways. But when Ukkelberg asked Ford whether he was to raise a crop of goldenrod, Ford's answer was, "Just a small patch in memory of Mr. Edison."

References

Accession 572, Box 6, Selected Research Papers. Benson Ford Research Center, HFM & GV.

Accession 1630, Boxes 4–7, Edison Papers. Benson Ford Research Center, HFM & GV.

Nevins, Allan, and Frank Ernest Hill. *Ford: Expansion and Challenge, 1915–1932.* New York: Scribner's, 1957.

34

Frischkorn Investment Company

During the mid-1920s, business was booming in Detroit. Real estate, in particular, was growing in value by leaps and bounds. In the New Center area out Woodward Avenue, a little more than four miles north of Detroit City Hall, the magnificent Fisher Building and General Motors Building were built by the GM crowd. Henry Ford must have taken notice. According to Ernest Liebold, Ford's general secretary, Ford said, "I want to buy a big tract of land downtown. It's right down on the corner of Fort Street." The owner, however, wanted $1 million for it. To that, Ford responded, "I don't think I want to buy it there anyway. I think I have a better place on Michigan Avenue, right opposite the Michigan Central Depot. You get two solid blocks of land down there." Liebold said: "I think he thought he was going to do something to either equal or outdo the General Motors Corporation. That may have been in the back of his mind."

The land was to be acquired without the public knowing it was being purchased by Henry Ford. Perhaps the largest Detroit real estate firm at that time was Frischkorn Associated Companies, with their main offices at the corner of West Fort and Wayne Streets in downtown Detroit. The president was E. S. Frischkorn, and the vice president was George M. Frischkorn. Ford was acquainted with George Frischkorn and trusted him. Frischkorn Associated Companies consisted of the Frischkorn Land Company, the Frischkorn Real Estate Company, the Frischkorn Development Company, and the Frischkorn Construction Company. Advertisements described their operations as "Owners of Improved Subdivisions, Developers of Home Communities, Brokers in Improved Properties, Agents in Real Estate Purchase, Managers of Income Properties, Councillors in Realty Investments." Exclusively to purchase the Michigan Avenue property for Ford, the Frischkorn Investment Company was organized. As the Frischkorns were operating their businesses throughout the Detroit area, the land being purchased for Ford was not an especially conspicuous operation.

Published previously in the *Dearborn Historian*, Vol.39, No. 1,1999.

Detroit's new and magnificent railroad passenger terminal facing Roosevelt Park on Michigan Avenue. Offices of New York and Michigan Central, Detroit's major railroads, were also housed in this seventeen-story building. In the 1920s, both business and vacation travelers depended on railroads for transportation from city to city. The interstate highway system as we know it did not exist, and airline passenger service was not yet practical. What better location for Ford's company headquarters than one directly facing the transportation heart of Detroit? (B.113845)

Just why the land was being purchased was never certain. Some thought Frischkorn was buying for the Pennsylvania Railroad to build a giant railroad station opposite the Michigan Central Station. It was also rumored that there was to be a National League baseball park there. Liebold himself had the impression that Ford intended to build a fairly tall building, the first floor to be used for vehicle displays, the next five or six floors to be Ford Motor Company offices, and a multistoried hotel above the offices. Liebold indicated that Ford was willing to spend about $25 million on the project.

Beginning in 1927, Ford bought the stock of Frischkorn Investment Company. His first payment amounted to $1,695,516.05. As proof of proper investment of Ford's money, Frischkorn Investment

Company furnished Liebold with unsigned deeds covering each piece of Michigan Avenue property purchased. Between 1927 and 1935, Ford advanced a total of $2,497,860.69. The more than fifty pieces of property purchased by Frischkorn Investment Company for Ford were on Michigan Avenue from Vermont to the intersection of Vernor and bounded by Michigan Avenue, 14th Street, Pine Street, and 17th Street. Average cost of Michigan Avenue business frontage at that time was $9.004 per square foot.

Liebold was in constant touch with George Frischkorn regarding prices paid for property, sometimes suggesting that a purchase price was too high. Property already purchased was rented. Rental operations were handled by Frischkorn Real Estate Company. In 1931, at 2300 Michigan Avenue, for example, the Abram Cement Tool Company paid $500 per month, while the *Detroit Times* at 2066 Michigan Avenue was paying only $10 per month, and the Kroger Company at 2108 Michigan Avenue paid $80 per month. Private residences on 15th, 16th, and 17th Streets between 1928 and 1935 were renting for $10 to $150 per month. As the Great Depression advanced, rents were reduced by about one-third. Some of these residences were occupied by as many as eight tenants between 1927 and 1931. Frischkorn's yearly statement for 1931 lists revenues of $496,642.09 and disbursements of $481,344.34, leaving a gain for the year of $15,297.75.

Progress in buying was eventually blocked by owners of one piece of property central to the area required. This was occupied by a building belonging to the Conductors Protective Association. It had cost $300,000 to build, and they were asking $900,000 for it. Ford would offer no more than $600,000. The property was never bought by Ford, but serious consideration was given to building all the way around it on property Ford already owned.

By 1937, Ford apparently had given up his plans for developing the Michigan Avenue property in Detroit and agreed to have the property sold at a loss of 25 percent of cost. As late as 1941, however, Frischkorn was advocating the purchase of a 25-foot piece of Michigan Avenue

Opposite page: A 1944 map of Detroit's Michigan Avenue area across from the Michigan Central Passenger Station, showing the properties (darkened plots) that had been purchased by Frischkorn Investment Company for Henry Ford. These properties were that same year transferred from Frischkorn Investment Company to Oakwood Realty Company, a subsidiary of Ford Motor Company. (Map courtesy of Ford Industrial Archives.)

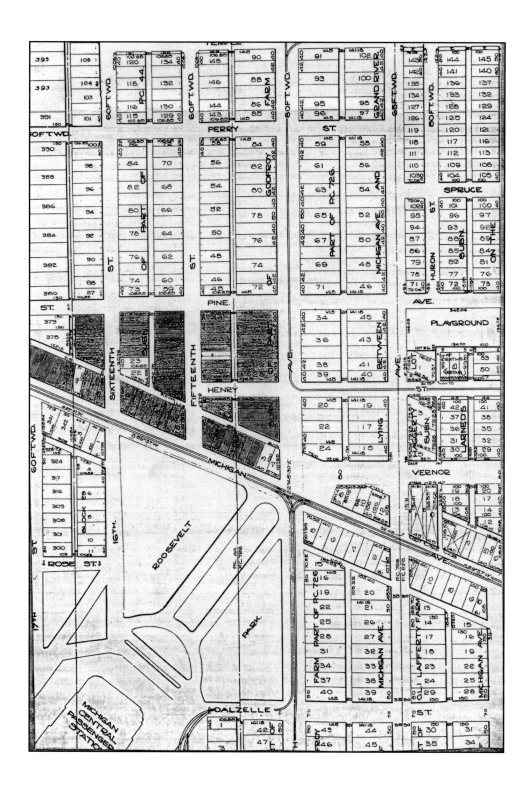

259

frontage previously priced at $30,000 and then for sale for $5,000, saying: "As we own all remaining frontage in this block it is desirable that this frontage be acquired." Frischkorn was instructed by Liebold to offer $3,500 in cash for a good title.

On June 16, 1944, the following memo was sent by B. J. Craig (treasurer of Ford Motor Company) to Frank Campsall (secretary to Henry Ford):

> I discussed the matter of the Frischkorn Investment Company with Mr. Capizzi [Ford lawyer] yesterday afternoon, and in his opinion you should get in touch with the Frischkorn Bros. and advise them that one of our subsidiary companies would like to take over the Frischkorn Investment Company and manage the property. If the Frischkorn Bros. assented to this, the procedure would be as follows:
>
> A letter should be sent to the Frischkorn Bros. asking that their stock in the Frischkorn Investment Company be delivered to F. A. Thomson [Ford Motor Company accountant], this stock to be endorsed in blank. They should also be asked to deliver their stock book and their corporate minute book. The stock would then be transferred to the Seaboard Properties Company [subsidiary of Ford Motor Company].
>
> After receipt of these records, the Seaboard Properties Company would have to hold a stockholders' meeting and elect new directors of the Frischkorn Investment Company. The directors would, in turn, elect officers.
>
> Suggest the following officers and directors of the Frischkorn Investment Company:
>
> Frank Campsall — President
> B. J. Craig — Vice President & Treasurer
> H. L. Moekle — Secretary & Asst. Treasurer
> F. A. Thomson — Asst. Sec'y & Asst. Treasurer
>
> In connection with the management and sale of the various properties, the writer suggests that we negotiate with the Real Estate Department of the Detroit Trust Company, who are equipped to handle this type of property. They would pay the taxes, insurance and repairs, and also make such sales as authorized, collect rents, and, in every way, take the position of the owner.
>
> If you are agreeable to the above program, the writer will have a letter prepared by Fred Thomson and will also consult with the Detroit Trust Company for the management and sale of the properties.

A phone call to George Frischkorn that same day resulted in his stating that they would agree to anything Ford wished and upon receipt of a letter of authority would turn over any documents requested. On June 30, 1944, forty-nine deeds were received from Frischkorn Investment Company. An agreement with the Detroit Trust Company to handle the property already had been made on June 27.

Ernest G. Liebold, with power of attorney for both Henry and Clara Ford, handled practically all Ford business other than that of Ford Motor Company — and it was a tremendous amount. Without bothering Henry Ford, Liebold settled the bills, answered business inquiries, and micromanaged personal projects both large and small. Liebold's name or initials are on hundreds and hundreds of documents pertaining to the multitude of personal enterprises in which the Fords were engaged. (189.2540)

On August 17, 1944, Thomson sent the following memo to Craig and Campsall:

Please be advised that by Certificate of Amendment filed in Lansing on August 15, 1944, the name of Frischkorn Investment Company was changed to — OAKWOOD REALTY COMPANY.

The registered office has been changed to 3000 Schaefer Road, Dearborn, Michigan, and F. A. Thomson has been appointed the Statutory Agent.

Oakwood Realty Company transferred the same properties to Ford Motor Company on November 30, 1946, for $344,865.14, estimating Henry Ford's loss since 1927 to be $2,152,995.55. Ford Motor Company then made an agreement with S. O. August and J. O. Hearn, Realtors, giving exclusive rights for six months to sell the Michigan Avenue properties. Proposed asking prices for the fifty-six parcels totaled $682,500, with Ford Motor Company to be assured of at least $475,000, offering extra commission if sales exceeded $500,000. It was not until December 1951 that Ford Motor Company finally disposed of the properties that Frischkorn had purchased for Henry Ford. A letter from H. D. Newberry of the property management department to A. L. Gornick, tax counsel, dated January 4, 1952, reads as follows:

> SUBJECT: Final Liquidation of Properties Acquired from Oakwood Realty Company
>
> All properties acquired from the subject company November 30, 1946, being in the vicinity of Michigan Avenue and 14th Street, Detroit, have been sold for cash or on land contracts dated prior to December 15, 1951. Of the original 57 parcels so acquired, one parcel was sold in 1947 for $3,700 cash [sold by Detroit Trust Company].
>
> The remaining 56 parcels were sold pursuant to an agreement dated June 2, 1949, with two realtors, J. O. Hearn and S. O. August and produced aggregate sales of $650,150.00, as detailed on map and schedules attached.
>
> Previous management trust with Detroit Trust Company, covering management of these properties since June 27, 1944, was terminated by a final cash settlement of $1,105.49 received December 26, 1951.
>
> The Office of Tax Counsel will note this liquidation as completed in 1951 for any tax adjustments caused thereby.

Thus, Henry Ford's plans, however grandiose they may have been, did not materialize. Before he could acquire every bit of property he needed for his anticipated project, the Great Depression had reared its ugly head. Very few people knew who was really buying the Michigan Avenue property or that Henry Ford was at all associated with Frischkorn Investment Company. Whatever Ford might have done for Detroit, barring the Depression, is at this date merely conjecture.

References

Accession 65, Ernest G. Liebold Reminiscences. Benson Ford Research Center, HFM & GV.

Accession 384, Box 1, L. J. Thompson Papers. Benson Ford Research Center, HFM & GV.

Accessions AR-70-26:13 and AR-83-26246:1. Ford Industrial Archives, Dearborn, Mich.

35
The Ford Foundation

At least two factors persuaded the Ford family in 1936 to consider the future of Ford Motor Company. One of these was Henry's health, which in January 1936 had suffered a setback caused by "a cerebral vascular accident and consequent brain injury," according to Dr. Frank Sladen of Henry Ford Hospital. The other factor was the federal government's "wealth tax" of 70 percent applied in 1935 to estates of more than $50 million.

If Ford's estate, consisting of the majority of stock in Ford Motor Company, had been sold upon his death to satisfy the government, the family would have lost control of the company. To prevent this from happening, Edsel Ford and the Ford family lawyer, Clifford B. Longley, devised a method by which Ford family members could retain management control of the company even though losing most of the cash value of the Henry Ford stock.

The solution proposed by Longley was to declare 95 percent of Ford Motor Company stock nonvoting stock, with the remaining 5 percent as voting stock. The monetary value of each type of stock would be equal. A nonprofit organization would be formed to accept blocks of nonvoting stock as charitable gifts from Ford family members. Thus, the bulk of Ford wealth ultimately would go to this charitable institution without diminishing Ford family control of the company.

The resulting plan provided for the Ford Foundation, a nonprofit Michigan corporation with three trustees: Edsel B. Ford, president of Ford Motor Company; Burt J. Craig, treasurer of Ford Motor Company; and Clifford B. Longley. Articles of incorporation were filed in the County of Wayne, Michigan, on January 17, 1936, and read as follows:

ARTICLES OF INCORPORATION
of
THE FORD FOUNDATION.

Articles of Incorporation.
Dated January 13, 1936.
Acknowledged January 13, 1936.
Filed January 17, 1936.

File No. 39491 Associations, Partnerships
And Corporations in the Office of the Clerk
For the County of Wayne, Michigan.

These Articles of Incorporation are signed and acknowledged by the incorporators for the purpose of forming a non-profit corporation known as a Foundation under the provisions of Act. No. 327 of the Public Acts of 1931, known as the Michigan General Corporation Act, as follows:

Article I.

The name of this corporation is The Ford Foundation.

Article II.

The purpose or purposes of this corporation are as follows:

To receive and administer funds for scientific, educational and charitable purposes, all for the public welfare and for no other purposes and to that end to take and hold by bequest, devise, gift, purchase or lease, either absolutely or in trust for such objects and purposes or any of them, any property, real, personal, or mixed, without limitation as to amount or value, except such limitations, if any, as may be imposed by law; to sell, convey and dispose of any such property and to invest and re-invest the principal thereof, and to deal with and expend the income therefrom for any of the before mentioned purposes, without limitation, except such limitations, if any, as may be contained in the instrument under which such property is received; to receive any property, real, personal or mixed, in trust, under the terms of any will, deed of trust, or other trust instrument for the foregoing purposes or any of them (but for no other purposes) and in administering the same to carry out the directions and exercise the powers contained in the trust instrument under which the property is received, including the expenditure of the principal, as well as the income, for one or more of such purposes, if authorized or directed in the trust instrument under which it is received; to receive, take title to, hold and use the proceeds and income of stocks, bonds, obligations, or other securities of any corporation or corporations, domestic or foreign, but only for the foregoing purposes, or some of them; and in general, to exercise any, all and every power for which a non-profit corporation known as a Foundation, organized under the provisions of the Michigan General Corporation Act for scientific, educational, and charitable purposes, all for the public welfare, can be authorized to exercise, but not any other power. No part of the activities of this corporation shall be the carrying on of propaganda or otherwise attempting to influence legislation.

Article III.

The location of the corporation is in the City of Dearborn, in the County of Wayne and State of Michigan.

The post office address of registered office in Michigan is Ford Engineering Laboratories, Dearborn, Michigan.

Article IV.

Said corporation is organized on a non-stock basis.

The amount of assets which said corporation possesses is:

Real property, none; personal property, $25,000.00 cash.

Said corporation is to be financed under the following general plan:

By contributions to it of funds and property absolutely or in trust for its purposes as herein stated and for no other purpose.

Article V.

The names and places of residence or business of each of the incorporators, are as follows:

Name.	Address.
Edsel B. Ford,	Grosse Pointe Shores, Michigan.
Burt J. Craig,	19595 Canterbury Road, Detroit, Michigan.
Clifford B. Longley,	440 University Place, Grosse Pointe, Michigan.

Article VI.

The names and addresses of the first named Board of Trustees are as follows:

Name.	Address.
Edsel B. Ford,	Grosse Pointe Shores, Michigan.
Burt J. Craig,	19595 Canterbury Road, Detroit, Michigan.
Clifford B. Longley,	440 University Place, Grosse Pointe, Michigan.

Article VII.

This being a benevolent corporation, its term is unlimited and in perpetuity.

Article VIII.

Additional members may be admitted to this corporation at any meeting of its members, upon the vote, or written assent incorporated in the minutes of the meeting, of not less than 2/3 of its existing members, or by the Board of Trustees with the written assent incorporated in the minutes of the meeting of the Board of not less than 2/3 of all the existing members, provided, however, that there shall never at any time be more than 9 members. Membership or any interest in this corporation shall not be assignable inter vivos by any members, nor shall membership or any interest in this corporation pass up any personal representative, heir or devisee. Membership of any member shall cease upon his death or resignation, or upon adoption at a meeting of members of a resolution assented to by the vote, or written assent incorporated in the minutes of the meeting, of not less than 2/3 of all of the members, not less than 10 days notice of intent to present such resolution to the meeting for action having first been given to all members either personally or by mailing to their respective last addresses appearing in the records of the corporation.

Article IX.

All of the property of this corporation and accumulations thereof shall be held and administered to effectuate its purposes and to serve the general welfare of the people.

Immediately following the organization of the foundation, Henry Ford, Clara Ford, and Edsel Ford all signed codicils to their wills, leaving their nonvoting Ford Motor Company stock to the foundation and their voting stock to their respective family beneficiaries.

During 1936, Henry and Edsel each gave sufficient shares of nonvoting stock to the foundation to permit the foundation to donate $115,000 to Henry Ford Hospital in Detroit and $935,000 to the Edison Institute in Dearborn. While Ford Motor Company officials and family members were on the foundation board of trustees, donations were made largely to domestic charities. Until Edsel died in 1943, a total of more than $1 million had been given each year to a list of twenty-seven domestic organizations, with the exception of a small amount to United China Relief. Of the total of $8,592,167 given during the same eight-year period, an amount of $6,822,000 was given to the Edison Institute. With Edsel's death, Henry Ford II and Benson Ford became members of the board of trustees.

In 1950, following the deaths of Henry and Clara Ford and the infusion of another $500 million or so, the foundation ceased operating as a local philanthropy in the state of Michigan and expanded to become an international foundation with headquarters in New York. With millions and millions to spend, the foundation leadership team of Paul Hoffman and Robert Maynard Hutchins became engaged in broad foreign as well as domestic projects of the type normally handled by the federal government. A ditty credited to Hutchins goes as follows:

> How firm a Foundation we saints of the Lord
> Have built on the faith of our excellent Ford . . .
> How firm a foundation; we've three times the dough
> And ten times the brains that any other can show.

About this time, the board of trustees was enlarged to fifteen members, with most of the new members being "liberals." Henry Ford Hospital in Detroit received a grant of $13.6 million in 1950 to build a diagnostic clinic. And, as was intended in the first place, education grants prevailed during the succeeding years. But rather than anything being given to a conservative institution such as the Edison Institute in Michigan, such grants were more likely to be for avant-garde projects in foreign countries. In 1955, however, a domestic educational grant of $260 million was donated to help raise the salaries of teachers in all 630 private, regionally accredited, four-year colleges and universities in the United States. That gift was at the time the largest in the history of American philanthropy.

Also in 1955, Ford Motor Company decided to permit its stock to be sold to the public. The Ford Foundation then offered its 10.2 million shares for sale and obtained $640,725,445, which was invested in other securities. This move provided diversification for the foundation's investments and at the same time to an extent absolved the Ford Motor Company and its harassed automotive dealers from blame for the questionable manner in which the Ford Foundation's money was being

The Ford Foundation

Henry Ford II in January 1966, about the time McGeorge Bundy was appointed president of the Ford Foundation in New York. (833.139739.12)

spent. Automotive customers did not know that the company and the foundation were not the same. At that point, Henry Ford II resigned as chairman of the foundation but stayed on as a member of the board of trustees.

In 1966, when McGeorge Bundy, a John F. Kennedy associate, was appointed the new president of the foundation, its headquarters were moved into lavish accommodations at 320 East Forty-third Street in New York, and the projects became politically motivated. At that time, the Ford Foundation was said to be the most politically active foundation in the United States. With added foreign offices and 1,500 employees, Bundy began overspending the foundation's income by more than $100 million a year.

Henry Ford II was very much involved in the welfare of Detroit. The 1967 Detroit riots led him to become a member of New Detroit Committee. His experience in dealing with the real and serious problems in Detroit led him to realize that the foundation's spending under Bundy's leadership was a tremendous waste and of very little value toward solving America's basic problems. It was only after a lengthy struggle with Bundy and convincing the majority of trustees one by one that he was able to arrange a grant of $100 million to Detroit's Henry Ford Hospital in 1973.

In early December 1976, after attending a foundation meeting in New York, Henry Ford II remarked, "I don't think I can stand this much longer. This place is a madhouse." In a particularly scathing letter dated December 11, 1976, to Alexander Heard, chairman of the board, he stated, "After 33 years I have come to the point where I have said all there is to say. I think it is time for me to step aside and, accordingly, I wish to resign from the Board effective immediately." Other criticisms in the letter included:

> The diffuse array of enterprises upon which the Foundation has embarked in recent years is almost a guarantee that few people anywhere will share a common perception of what the Foundation is all about, how its mission serves society. . . .
>
> The Foundation exists and thrives on the fruits of our economic system. The dividends of competitive enterprise make it all possible. A significant portion of the abundance created by U.S. business enables the Foundation and like institutions to carry on their work. In effect, the Foundation is a creature of capitalism — a statement that I'm sure would be shocking to many professional staff people in the field of philanthropy. It is hard to discern recognition of this fact in anything the Foundation does.

In a reply to Floyd L. Haight, a Dearborn citizen, concerning the letter of resignation, Henry Ford II wrote on January 25, 1977, as follows:

> Thank you for your comments on my resignation from the Board of Trustees of the Ford Foundation.
>
> I hope that the views I expressed at the time will cause some rethinking of staff policies and programs. The Foundation is an organization with vast potential for service to society here and in many other parts of the world, but I believe that it must, at the same time, help serve the economic system out of which it was created.
> Best Regards
> Henry Ford II

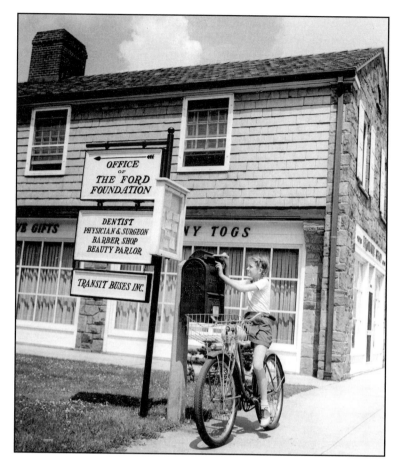

The Dearborn office
of the Ford
Foundation in the
early 1940s, when
the Springwells Park
subdivision at
Rotunda Drive and
Greenfield Road was
under development
by the foundation.
(833.82804.18)

Henry Ford II admitted that he had not been forceful enough in dealing with the foundation from the start and that it had been a mistake to let the foundation get out of Ford family hands. He told his secretary, Walter Hayes, "I didn't have the guts or the experience to scream or yell and tell them, 'Over my dead body.' That's what I should have done." Invited to address a Ford Foundation banquet in New York on December 8, 1977, he presented a speech of a more friendly nature, which began:

> I am very proud and grateful to be your guest this evening. It has been traditional, I know, to honor former trustees in this way. On the other hand, the manner of my leaving the foundation was not at all in keeping with tradition. I did not intend to burn any bridges behind me, and your invitation to be here tonight tells me that I am still in good grace and that you have not seriously considered renaming the foundation.

Today, the Ford Foundation still has its main offices in New York, with other offices in Africa, Asia, Latin America, and Russia. It has given billions of dollars in grants and loans. Its present goals are to:

Strengthen democratic values
Reduce poverty and injustice
Promote international cooperation
Advance human achievement

Under the presidency of Susan Vail Berresford, the foundation is again becoming cognizant of its founders. In December 1998, a grant of $500,000 was offered to the University of Michigan–Dearborn to maintain the historic structure and establish educational programs at Fair Lane, the Dearborn residence of Henry and Clara Ford. In presenting the grant, vice president Barry D. Gaberman stated that "although he did not know precisely why the foundation never contributed to the Henry Ford Estate in the past, the agency has been busy with its mission to advance human welfare and human rights to fifty nations around the world." The Ford Foundation is still thought to be the largest nonprofit agency in the United States, having provided more than $10 billion in grants and loans.

References

Accession 384, Box 1, L. J. Thompson Papers. Benson Ford Research Center, HFM & GV.

"Even Giving Takes Neat Financial Footwork." *Business Week,* January 14, 1961.

Foundation Reporter, 27th ed. Rockville, Md.: Taft Group, 1996, p. 432.

Hayes, Walter. *Henry: A Life of Henry Ford II.* New York: Grove Weidenfield, 1990.

Hibbs, Ben. "Mr. Ford's Busy Billions." *Saturday Evening Post,* March 16, 1963.

Moley, Raymond. "The Ford Revolution." *Newsweek,* January 9, 1956.

Young, Warren R. "The Remarkable Ford Foundation." *Life Magazine,* September 21, 1962.

Part V
Humanitarian Efforts

Henry Ford was a humanitarian of note, both in principle and in practice. He grew up a common person and remained at heart a common person throughout his life. His slogan was "Help the other fellow," and in practice he did just that. By helping, he meant giving the down-and-out an opportunity — giving them work to support themselves, not just a handout. The Henry Ford Trade School prepared thousands of disadvantaged boys for responsible positions as tool and die makers. He advised the adventuresome to go into business for themselves and proceeded to help many of them get started.

Very little of this aspect of Ford's personality has been appreciated by the public at large. Public opinion has been distorted by tales of men being worked to death in the Highland Park factories. But workers were free to leave, and some did. The majority stayed, however, to work at "Ford's" and were proud to wear a Ford badge. It is true that at the Rouge plant, as Henry Ford aged, his subordinates began to seize power in the factories, causing working conditions to become extremely difficult for employees. The United Auto Workers were then needed to improve the situation.

36
Fordism: An Economic Philosophy

Although Henry Ford spoke but a few words at a time, and those seldom in public, he was an evangelist — by demonstration rather than talk. Ford demonstrated an economic philosophy that appealed to millions of people worldwide, including numerous heads of states as diverse as capitalistic and communistic, totalitarian and democratic.

The economic philosophy demonstrated by Henry Ford was known as Fordism. It is not to be confused with the same term as applied by labor unions in relation to severe working conditions sometimes found in Ford Motor Company and other manufacturing plants of the period. Ford's economic philosophy as recognized by economists is ably described as follows by Feliks Tamm, who is credited with developing for the U.S. government the well-known Government Economic Indicators by which the country's economic health is judged. Since retiring from government work, Tamm has been conducting seminars in economics at the University of Maryland and Columbia University. Tamm's explanation of Ford's economic philosophy follows.

Fordism as Scientific Principle

Historians have given credit to Henry Ford as a developer of practicable automobile models and as an innovator and organizer of novel and efficient production processes (e.g., assembly line). These achievements pertain to technology, engineering, and management and describe Ford as a technocrat. But Ford also deserves credit for his socioeconomic concerns and even for his contribution to economic theory.

In fact, a combination of Ford's socioeconomic factors and technological characteristics had given rise to a special subject matter principle that was included in the business administration curriculum of the University of Frankfurt/Main in Germany. Since I was a student of business administration in that university from 1946 to 1950, I was well familiarized with that specific subject matter. The

Published previously in *The Ford Legend,* Vol. V, No. 3, 1996.

principle in question entailed a combination of two basically related economic processes, mass production and mass consumption, and was termed *Fordismus*.

With respect to economic theory, it makes good sense that mass production (i.e., supply schedule) be counterbalanced by mass consumption (i.e., demand schedule). As a practical proposition, mass production of a product is economically feasible only if it is met with mass consumption of the same product. Obviously, the term *Fordism* assumes that mass consumption or effective demand of automobiles (i.e., desire plus purchasing power) has to be promoted by the same positive action. It was believed that Ford did just that by charging reasonably low prices for his automobiles and promoting availability of cheap consumer loans and automobile service facilities. Because of his high regard for the principle of competition, he would, in some instances, help to finance the establishment of an across-the-street competitor for the service station he originally had helped to set up.

The assessment of the above characteristics has seemed to suggest that Ford was an adherent of the purchasing power theory of economic development. In fact, he had been deemed one of the leading proponents of that theory. A liberal wage policy in Ford business enterprises was said to offer proof of Ford's belief that a maintenance of high income levels not only is a good business policy but also helps to achieve a high level of general prosperity.

A few years later, doing my graduate work at the University of Nebraska and Columbia University, I was surprised to discover that the term *Fordism* was virtually unknown in American economic thought. Although the major encyclopedias carry *Fordism* as a term, its definition relates to the assembly line rather than to an interaction between mass production and mass consumption.

I had forgotten all about Fordism until about twenty years after my student days in Frankfurt, when I visited the Henry Ford Museum near Detroit. Two pieces of writing, displayed in a showcase, reminded me of my past study. There was a letter by Ford to his payroll department, instruction that the wages of Ford's personnel be doubled beginning at a certain time. Further, a different typewritten page, signed by Ford, expressed astonishment that each and every Ford employee does not yet own an automobile. Appropriate managers were to investigate that matter and to make arrangements for purchases on credit, if necessary.

Apparently, the theoreticians of the major American universities' economics departments were unaware of Ford's economic policy decisions unless they had failed to arrive at proper theoretical conclusions. As for me, I was reassured by the evidence that the term *Fordism* represents worthwhile economic principle and does honor to the man who was instrumental for its creation. Moreover, there is positive evidence that the industrialist, whom Thorstein Veblen would have called a captain of industry, is a true contributor to the purchasing power theory of economics. After all, written evidence in the museum indicates that Ford spent lots of his own money to enhance the purchasing power of a specific group of consumers. How many other theorists can give such a proof of conviction in their theoretical abstractions?

In today's perspective, the purchasing power of consumers, even anticipation of its change, may trigger off a boom or a bust. The major manifestation of purchasing power of consumers, retail sales, constitutes approximately 60 percent of the gross national product. In view of these considerations, Ford showed real pioneering spirit in puzzling out the functioning of the twentieth-century economy. By the same token, he could be said to have demonstrated vision with regard to the developments ahead of his own times.

During the Great Depression of the 1930s, it was the opinion of business in general that wages would have to be lowered, or at least held at the level where they were, for businesses to survive. This attitude on the part of business was, of course, very upsetting to labor unions.

In early February 1935, Matthew Woll, a vice president of the American Federation of Labor in Washington, sent a letter to Henry Ford asking for his opinion about workers' wages. On February 15, Ford replied as follows:

> In reply to your recent letter may I say at once that I have in nowise changed my mind concerning high wages. Unless the worker in American industry is enabled to use and enjoy the products of industry, the natural balance cannot be maintained. Our only market is our people. I believe that wages will continue to go higher not as the result of politics or from purely humanitarian motives, but as a result of the kind of management that will enable men to earn more. You understand, of course, that inexperienced or short-sighted management does not create the conditions in which men can earn more. Industry cannot pay men what they do not earn, but it can create methods by which men, with the same effort, or even less, can earn more and so receive more. In my opinion, absentee ownership in industry is one of the chief obstacles to higher wages, for two reasons: it imposes an extra tax on an industry in the form of unearned dividends, and it will not or cannot give the same attentive care to conditions that ownership and a regard for the good name of the business and the product can give.
>
> Industry as yet is in a crude stage, but the opportunities for skilled employment will tend steadily to increase rather than decrease. As industry advances — and that is the only direction in which it can go — the number of skilled men employed in making the machinery that in turn makes the machinery, that in turn makes the things which people use to earn their living, will greatly increase. That is, the incentive to skillful work will become ever a larger factor. In these classifications wages will go to higher rates than we have yet seen, with consequent increases for men in the lower classifications.
>
> I do not believe that production costs are ever really decreased by

reducing wages, but I have known higher wages usually to bring lower costs.

> Trusting that this answers your question, I am
> Yours sincerely
> Henry Ford

Woll was pleased with Ford's remarks and replied on March 1, 1935:

> I deeply appreciate your courtesy in replying to my letter on the question of high wages. You have come to occupy such an important place in the industrial leadership of the United States that I feel that your uncompromising position on this question will be of great assistance in clarifying the public mind on this important subject.
>
> It seemed to me that in the interests of public enlightenment a copy of your letter, together with my inquiry, should be given to the press, and I have taken the liberty of releasing it on February 28.
>
> With kind regards, I am
> Sincerely yours,
> Matthew Woll

Newspapers across the country on February 29 did publish at least excerpts from Ford's letter. The *Detroit Free Press*, for example, used the headline "Ford Still Favors High Wage Scales, Doesn't Believe Cuts Reduce Costs." Ford's explanation of the role of management was repeated word for word in this newspaper's coverage, but Ford's second paragraph forecasting labor's future need for highly motivated skilled workers was completely deleted. At that time, such a scenario was no doubt difficult to visualize. Ford's early prediction of what we now accept to be a crucial labor problem was indeed remarkable.

References

"Ford Still Favors High Wage Scales." *Detroit Free Press*, February 28, 1935.

Private communication from Feliks Tamm, Fort Washington, Md., September 1990.

37

The Sociological Department

When Henry Ford in 1908 was satisfied that he had an almost perfectly designed automobile in his Model T and was already rapidly outgrowing the assembly capabilities of his Piquette plant, he moved at once to build the huge Highland Park factory. Ford wanted the entire manufacturing as well as assembly operations to be carried out in this one giant plant. The architect of the new plant was to be Albert Kahn, William B. Mayo would become chief power engineer, and Edsel Ford, now out of school, would join the Ford executives.

As part of this Ford Motor Company expansion program, the Keim Steel Mills of Buffalo, New York, were purchased in 1911. This company, managed by John R. Lee and William H. Smith, was a manufacturer of pressed steel parts for the automotive industry. Ford needed parts such as frames and axle housings for the Model T, and Ford also wanted the managing team of Lee and Smith. Along with Lee and Smith also came John Findlater and William S. Knudsen. Lee, in particular, as general manager of Keim Steel Mills, had impressed Ford as being not only strong but also "frank, friendly, and fair."

Ford Motor Company then had no particular labor policy. There were dozens of wage classifications, modified daily according to circumstances. Walking with Edsel through the factory one day, Henry was greatly embarrassed when they witnessed two workers fighting. He realized that there must be something very wrong in his shop to cause such a confrontation between two of his employees. It would be Ford's British friend, Percival Perry, who would suggest a labor policy.

Percival Lea Dewhurst Perry had been selling Ford cars in Britain since 1904. After visiting the Fords twice in Detroit, he had made agreements not only to sell but also to build Ford vehicles at Trafford Park outside Manchester. The Perrys in 1912 invited the Fords to England for a visit. Spending a week at the Perry residence, Ford was told of Perry's experiences with workers at his plant at Manchester during the previous year. Perry had been concerned about the welfare of his workers — their living conditions and the low pay they were receiving in the rather lucrative automobile business. In 1911, workers at Manchester had been receiving only sixpence half-penny an hour for a

Ford Motor Company executives in Henry Ford's office at Highland Park in 1913. *Top row from left:* Charles Hartner, Henry Ford, Fred Diehl, Frank Klingensmith, John R. Lee, E. J. Hickie, and Charles E. Sorensen. *Middle row from left:* Peter E. Martin, Gus Degener, C. Harold Wills, John Wandersee, and Frank Kulick. *Bottom row from left:* Edward Gray, Joseph Galamb, Edsel B. Ford, and Charles Meida. That year, Henry was fifty years old and Edsel only twenty. (P.833.243)

fifty-six-hour week. Perry had raised his minimum wage to one shilling threepence per hour, resulting in better production as well as a better standard of living for his workers. Perry was convinced that good pay by the hour produced better results than the piecework pay in most factories. Ford respected Perry's judgment.

In 1913, John R. Lee was given responsibility for personnel at the Highland Park plant. Between 1911 and 1913, there had been high labor turnover because of the insistence on utmost efficiency from each workman on every job assigned and the power of any hot-headed foreman to fire a man on the spot. Under Lee, foremen were no longer allowed to fire workers indiscriminately. Lee also introduced reforms such as better lighting, better safety precautionary measures, and superb hospital facilities. Pay scales were adjusted to be somewhat more equitable, and year-end bonuses linked to company profits were distributed.

The personnel office, now under Lee's direction, was given wide authority over hiring, pay increases, and discharges. The rule: "No man was to be discharged until every possible effort had been made, and every means exhausted, toward lifting him up to the requirements of the Company, and to the equal of his fellow men." Dr. J. E. Mead, head of the plant hospital, found appropriate work for deaf, blind, and disabled applicants. A group of employees who had contracted tuberculosis were housed at Ford's expense in a "cottage" near the Highland Park factory and given light outside work while doctors monitored their health to ensure that the work they were doing was not detrimental to their health. These combined remedies, spearheaded by Lee, drastically reduced employee turnover.

One thing that Lee had realized during his days at Keim Steel Mills was that workers' home lives to a considerable extent controlled their attitudes at work. When the Ford Motor Company board of directors, under pressure from Ford, raised employee wages to five dollars for an eight-hour day in January 1914, there were guidelines to be followed by those workers who were to receive the high wages. Each employee, according to the rules, "must show himself sober, saving, steady, industrious and must satisfy the superintendent and staff that his money will not be wasted in riotous living." Single men as well as white-collar and female workers were not included at the start of the program. A new Sociological Department was organized under Lee's direction to take responsibility for determining eligibility of each employee seeking the higher pay. Starting with a staff of thirty, teams of investigators were trained to make inquiries concerning the living conditions in the thousands of households occupied by Ford employees. Lee's staff reached nearly 150 at the peak of its activities.

This writer, as a child of five, was at home when a Ford investigator called at the house and interviewed my mother. Besides asking a few questions and glancing about the room, there was no further intrusion. My father was then at work in Highland Park. My parents felt the visit was a benevolent gesture on the part of Ford Motor Company. Some have termed Ford's employee personnel involvements too paternalistic. Ford has stated that he did not consider himself paternalistic but more properly "fraternalistic."

The chief criticism of the five-dollar wage at that time was from other manufacturers across the country who felt it impossible to pay the same wages offered by Ford. The question of Ford's invasion of privacy in determining eligibility for the high wage was not pursued. It was well

Ford workers gathered on the lawn in front of the Highland Park plant, where they were taught the English language during 1914. The men are sitting at tables, and each teacher is using an easel. The five-dollar day had attracted thousands of immigrant employees. (0.4547)

known that Ford was trying to improve family life by encouraging family stability, home ownership, and the budgeting of income. Free legal services were offered to protect employees from unscrupulous real estate agents and retailers. Ford was so intent on his employees enjoying their extra pay to the fullest that he soon opened the first Ford Commissary next to the pay office at Highland Park to provide groceries, meats, and clothing at wholesale prices. Ford also hoped each of his employees would own and enjoy an automobile. He is said to have remarked to a friend, "Well, you know when you pay men well, you can talk to them."

The number of employees at Highland Park doubled in the two years following the five-dollar-day announcement. Many of the new employees could not speak or read English. To assist them, classes were held at the factory with instruction by plant employees who had had teaching experience. These sessions were held outside working hours, and the instructors worked without extra pay. Enrollment reached more than 2,200, with 150 instructors. Students representing fifty-five nationalities attended lessons for an average of six to eight months to

Henry Ford Trade School students leaving their school building (with awnings) adjacent to the Highland Park plant in May 1927. The school was organized in 1916 and flourished for thirty-six years. (833.49096)

complete the course. Upon graduation, students were presented with diplomas that were accepted by the U.S. district officials at Detroit entitling the holders to their first papers without further examination. As many as 6,000 foreign-born Ford employees celebrated Americanization Day at Detroit's City Hall at one time. The classes, arranged by the Sociological Department, continued until 1915 and helped provide Ford Motor Company with a relatively stable and appreciative workforce.

Under the auspices of the Sociological Department, the first of the famous Henry Ford Trade Schools for boys officially opened adjacent to the Highland Park factory on October 5, 1916. The school was designed to offer boys of poor families an opportunity to pursue a course of study that would provide cash as well as an industrial arts education. Many of the students had no fathers and instead of attending high school would have had to work full-time to support their families. The training these boys received in Henry Ford Trade School qualified them for the most demanding industrial responsibilities. It was not uncommon for Henry Ford Trade School graduates to organize and operate sizable manufacturing companies of their own.

Dr. Samuel S. Marquis, an Episcopalian clergyman and religious counselor to the Ford family, had offered to join Lee in the Sociological Department during 1915. Ford was elated and remarked, "I want you, Mark, to put Jesus Christ in my factory." Marquis worked with Lee until Lee left Ford Motor Company in the spring of 1919. That spring

Henry Ford with
Samuel Marquis
in 1915, when
Marquis was asked to
work with John R.
Lee in the Ford
Motor Company
Sociological
Department.
(833.2849)

had been a period of turmoil. Henry Ford had left Ford Motor Company in the hands of Edsel and had threatened his stockholders with a highly competitive automobile in order to convince them that they should sell their Ford Motor Company stock. Along with C. Harold Wills, Ford's automotive engineer since 1899, Lee left the company to develop a town on the St. Clair River. Wills manufactured the Wills St. Claire automobile, the "Molybdenum Car," and Lee incorporated and developed the community of Marysville.

Marquis successfully carried on the work of the Sociological Department at Highland Park with only minor changes. But as the much larger Rouge plant near Dearborn, headed by Charles E. Sorensen, began to demand Henry's attention, and Highland Park employees were being transferred by the thousand to Dearborn, Marquis found that Sorensen did not want a Sociological Department at the Rouge because he was convinced it would interfere with production. And Ford, to Marquis's astonishment, sided with Sorensen. By 1920, Ford was apparently losing faith in the benefits of benevolence to his workers. Personnel responsibilities at the Rouge plant were to be handled by Harry H. Bennett. Marquis resigned on January 25, 1921, and in disgust wrote a book in 1923 rather critical of Ford's modus operandi.

References

Accession 63, Marquis 1915–1923. Benson Ford Research Center, HFM & GV.

Accession 293, Marquis 1914–1923. Benson Ford Research Center, HFM & GV.

Boyle, Kevin, and Victoria Getis. *Muddy Boots and Ragged Aprons: Images of the Working Class in Detroit 1920–1930.* Detroit: Wayne State University Press, 1998.

Gaft, Samuel. *The Henry Ford Trade School.* Ann Arbor, Mich.: University of Michigan Press, 1998.

Marquis, Samuel S. *Henry Ford: An Interpretation.* Boston: Little, Brown, 1923.

Nevins, Allan. *Ford: The Times, the Man, the Company.* New York: Scribner's, 1954.

Nevins, Allan, and Frank Ernest Hill. *Ford: Expansion and Challenge, 1915–1932.* New York: Scribner's, 1957.

38
Detroit's Henry Ford Hospital

Of all the medical facilities sponsored by Henry Ford, the largest by far was Henry Ford Hospital of Detroit, a gigantic hospital to serve the general public. In his factories, of course, there were hundreds of small first-aid stations to treat minor injuries to his workers, and in his larger manufacturing plants such as the Rouge in Dearborn and Dagenham in England, he provided spacious hospital quarters manned by a variety of specialists to take care of both minor and major medical problems suffered by his employees.

Henry Ford Hospital had its beginnings on September 15, 1915, after a group of influential Detroiters in 1914 had organized the Detroit General Hospital Association, of which Henry Ford had been a major contributor. Progress on the planning and funding of the project began to lag, and Ford became impatient. He offered to pay back the previous donors an amount of $600,000 and build the hospital himself. This arrangement was agreed upon and implemented. Ford then instructed his general secretary, Ernest Liebold, to build and staff the Henry Ford Hospital.

Liebold studied other medical institutions, consulted noted doctors including the Mayo brothers, and formulated the basic plans for an outstanding hospital structure and medical organization. Liebold hired architects and contractors, managed completion of the building, hired doctors, and instituted several innovative features not only in the building's structure but also in the hospital's organization and operation.

Built with 486 private rooms, the institution operated as a "closed hospital" with doctors on salary. The hospital charged low fixed fees not related to the patient's income as was then customary. The American Medical Society was greatly disturbed to have a hospital operating in such a manner, but it was Ford's choice. A nucleus of young doctors was hired from Johns Hopkins University, with Dr. Frank M. Sladen becoming chief of medicine and Dr. Roy D. McClure chief of surgery.

The first occupants of the hospital were, very surprisingly, a group of about 100 derelicts, alcoholics, and drug addicts. Emergency cots, bedding, and food were hastily supplied. Detroit's city lodging houses and missions had been overtaxed. Ford realized, however, that he himself was considerably responsible for the problem because he had offered his workers such high wages that men were coming to Detroit in droves from far and wide to obtain employment in his factory. There was not sufficient work for all, and many of these men were not capable of employment. The hospital supplied medical treatment for about 600 men; in all, some 3,600 homeless were given temporary shelter. Only a few could be given jobs; many were instead given railroad fare home.

After the United States had entered World War I, Henry Ford Hospital, which had cost Ford approximately $4.5 million by then, was turned over to the government on November 25, 1918. As U.S. Army General Hospital No. 36, it treated 2,188 soldiers; of these, approximately 1,498 were from overseas. The hospital was returned to Ford for private use in July 1919. It started out with two main departments, internal medicine and surgery, and subdivisions were gradually established in various specialized fields. The number of doctors was increased rapidly until, in addition to clinical practice and medical research, a third major endeavor became the training of physicians and surgeons.

Hospital statistics during 1929 indicate that 132,669 patients had been registered to that date. Daily registrations were averaging 59 patients. Inpatients averaged 418 a day, yielding a 90-percent room occupancy and the consumption of 1,199 meals daily. Surgical operations averaged 23 a day, of which 2 were births. There were also 702 outpatients a day. All of this activity was managed by 694 employees, including 125 doctors and 100 nurses.

On January 28, 1925, the Henry Ford Hospital School of Nursing and Hygiene was organized, with nursing students housed in the elegant Clara Ford Nursing Home. Clara Ford was on the board of trustees and took an active interest in the school. The nursing students had their own glee club and dramatic club, their own tennis courts, archery range, basketball league, swimming team, and facilities for baseball and badminton. These activities were recorded in their yearbook, *Sonah*. With a resident director and six nursing instructors, the first class of sixty-nine nurses graduated in 1927. Henry Ford Hospital nurses were routinely offered free summer vacation trips on the Ford ore boats plying the Great Lakes.

A Convalescent School was operated by the hospital's pediatrics department. The hospital was convinced that young inpatients, in particular, recovered from their ailments more quickly if they were actively occupied. On the pediatrics floor were a classroom, a playroom, a craft room, a woodworking room, and a library and reading room to accommodate both bedridden and ambulatory children. There were games, lessons in music and art, and stories at least twice a day. Braille was taught to some, while movies were shown to others. Nature studies were held outdoors, and roof play areas were provided. Convalescent

Henry Ford Hospital as it appeared from the air about 1940. The high power-house stack is seen toward the back of the complex. The open-air balconies recall the manner in which tuberculosis patients were treated in the early days. (B.34140)

School records for 1945 list thirteen parties, eight movies, two magic shows, two musicals, and three worship programs in addition to Sunday school.

During Henry Ford's lifetime, $16,525,000 was invested in land, buildings, and hospital equipment. By 1947, the year of Ford's death, there were 1,600 professional and nonprofessional employees working for his nonprofit corporation. Whenever Ford became aware that friends or acquaintances were in need of medical care, he would see that they were treated at his Detroit hospital. Many schoolchildren in south-eastern Michigan, in particular, were given free medical attention and treatment. From his plantation in Georgia, his mining locations in West Virginia, and his lumber towns in upper Michigan, children often were provided transportation and hospitalization. A blind and physically handicapped schoolgirl from Georgia, for example, was treated for more

A classroom at
Henry Ford Hospital
Convalescent School
in April 1934.
Note the bed
patients in the rear
of the classroom.
(0.19344)

than a year at Henry Ford Hospital. To add to the girl's comfort, Ford installed a doorway to an adjoining room where her mother stayed during the entire period.

In May 1947, Edsel Ford's children established the Edsel B. Ford Institute for Medical Research in a separate building on the hospital grounds as a memorial to their father. Research in biology and physics, in particular, was considered basic to progress in medicine. The biology department staff was headed by Dr. O. H. Gaebler, and under him were chiefs of nutrition and metabolism, bio-organic chemistry, and enzyme chemistry. The physics department was headed by Dr. H. L. Watson, with research associates in the fields of x-ray diffractometry, nuclear radiation, and electronic microscopy. Staff accomplishments were announced at national scientific meetings and in many cases utilized in Henry Ford Hospital practice. When the Ford Foundation granted a $100 million donation in 1973, the Edsel B. Ford Institute for Medical

Research was absorbed into a combined education and research organization named the Henry Ford Health Sciences Center.

The grandchildren of Henry Ford have continued to provide major financial support for the hospital. But by the 1970s, to answer the growing health needs of the greater community, a development office was established to obtain help from additional individual and corporation donors. Today, Henry Ford Health System owns six hospitals outright, five other hospitals are managed by the system as joint ventures, and more than thirty ambulatory care clinics are operated across southeastern Michigan. In addition, the Henry Ford Health System provides health services to several large corporations in the Detroit area. There are now more than 1,000 physicians employed directly by the medical group and another 1,200 affiliated as private practice physicians. At least 800 resident interns and fellows are in training at Henry Ford Health System Hospitals.

References

Accession 1, Box 1, Fair Lane Papers. Benson Ford Research Center, HFM & GV.

Accession 65, E. G. Liebold Reminiscences. Benson Ford Research Center, HFM & GV.

Accession 168, Box 1, Henry Ford Hospital Convalescent School. Benson Ford Research Center, HFM & GV.

Accession 168, Boxes 58–61, Henry Ford Hospital Auditing Records. Benson Ford Research Center, HFM & GV.

Accession 924, Box 1, Henry Ford Hospital Publications. Benson Ford Research Center, HFM & GV.

Henry Ford Hospital—Information for Patients. Detroit: Henry Ford Hospital, 1947.

Henry Ford Hospital School of Nursing and Hygiene, 1925–50. Detroit: Henry Ford Hospital, 1950.

MacLean, Basil C. "Henry Ford Hospital—A Study of Growth." Henry Ford Hospital Library & Archives, 1949.

Painter, Patricia Scollard. *The First 75 Years.* Detroit: Henry Ford Health System, 1997.

Sladen, Frank J. "Background and Purpose of the Edsel B. Ford Institute for Medical Research." *Henry Ford Hospital Bulletin*, Vol. 6, March 1958.

39
Letters from the Past

Henry Ford was publicly chastised for his lack of knowledge of American history during the *Chicago Tribune* trial of 1919. Ford had made a statement during the trial that history as taught in textbooks was "bunk" and that textbook history dealt primarily with monarchs and wars, not the lives of ordinary people. Ford's disgust with the proceedings of the *Tribune* trial are thought to have induced him to seek a better method of teaching American history by demonstrating how life was lived by ordinary people in days gone by.

He began in 1919 by restoring his family homestead and furnishing it with as many of the original household items as he could find, in the process pestering his younger brother William's family for items they possessed, for they were the last of the Ford family to occupy the home. He also began seriously collecting the types of farm equipment he himself had used as a boy.

Ford's developing interest in America's past led him to buy and restore the Wayside Inn near South Sudbury, Massachusetts, in 1923. The inn needed to be furnished properly. Ford's agents initiated a search throughout New England for early American objects in wholesale quantity. What was not suitable for restoration of the inn was shipped on to Dearborn, where Ford had been collecting steam engines, carriages, and clocks, items he especially appreciated, and storing them in an abandoned tractor plant. By 1924, he was inviting acquaintances to his Dearborn "museum," located now in his new Engineering Laboratory, which had replaced the tractor plant. On the Fourth of July that year, he and Mrs. Ford personally paraded their antique carriages on the streets of Dearborn.

But to teach living history adequately, a much larger concept was developing in Ford's mind. With thousands of acres at his disposal, he selected a parcel of land alongside the main Detroit-Chicago railroad and adjacent to both his Engineering Laboratory and his mile-square Ford Airport, an expanse large enough to accommodate not only an enormous museum but also a historical village of a hundred buildings or more.

Encouraging Henry Ford was Thomas Edison, who promised to donate thousands of historical items related to his multitude of nineteenth-century inventions at Menlo Park, New Jersey, and also his complete private laboratory from Fort Myers, Florida. And with the knowledge that Ford was interested in "old stuff," hundreds of individuals throughout the United States and in Canada, Europe, and South and Central America were shipping him whatever objects they thought would tickle his fancy. Gifts, together with items Ford's agents and Ford automobile dealers were gathering in his behalf, were more than enough to fill his museum and his village buildings.

During 1928 and 1929, when Ford was collecting buildings and furnishings for what became known as Henry Ford Museum & Greenfield Village, he enlisted the help of countless elderly people. As he gathered antiques by the boxcar load from various portions of the United States, he realized that he would need detailed information about why and how these items were used in the past. Because the museum and village were to be used as an educational institution — the Edison Institute — each item would need to be properly identified and its proper use explained.

Ford himself was familiar with rural living back to about 1867, but beyond that, he depended on the recollections of older people. Museum assistants H. M. Cordell and J. A. Humberstone were instructed to prepare a questionnaire to be sent to people between seventy-five and ninety years old in order to obtain true records of how people lived before his time; Ford was then sixty-five. The method of selecting names of those to receive questionnaires is not clear, but some were sent a questionnaire because they had offered an item of antiquity to Ford. Others lived in relatively large nursing homes; one group of respondents resided at the Three-Quarters Century Club in Battle Creek, Michigan.

The number of questionnaires sent is not known, but a legacy of 112 replies is contained in four boxes in the Benson Ford Research Center of Henry Ford Museum & Greenfield Village (Accession EI-132). These are from both women and men with birthdates ranging from about 1830 to 1860. The replies came from twenty-three states and the District of Columbia. Some replies are handwritten, and some are typed; lengths vary from a scribbling on the back of the two-page questionnaire to an eighty-six-page, three-part manuscript. There is considerable redundancy from one to another because the questions were the same for all respondents. The questions are quite inconsistent, some being very specific and some very general. Some respondents, as might be expected, followed the questions on the questionnaire very precisely; others seemingly ignored the questionnaire in telling their stories in their own way to Ford.

Letters thanking the respondents for answering the questionnaire were mailed by Cordell and Humberstone. It is very unlikely that the answers to the questionnaires were read by Ford himself. Cordell, besides being a museum administrator, was also a relative of Ford, being the son of Thomasine, the youngest daughter of Henry's aunt Nancy Ford. Cordell was especially interested in antique lighting devices and was working on a book covering that subject. Cordell is said to have lost his position at the museum because he refused a donation from a party who turned out to be a friend of Clara Ford. Humberstone then took over the questionnaire correspondence.

The following is an example of a questionnaire response, from Mrs. S. G. Bressler of Philadelphia:

S. G. Bressler
2714 North 12th Street
Philadelphia, Pa.

Perhaps you will be so kind as to aid us in getting together certain information for Mr. Ford's historical records. Your courtesy will be greatly appreciated and your name, of course, not used unless with your consent, in any future publication issued by the museum. Not everyone will be able to answer all the questions; but most of them are answerable. If age has rendered this task too difficult, a daughter or grandchild may act as amanuensis and take it down for you. Take as long as you wish but please don't put it off. Answer each question in order, and minutely; this record will be extremely important and will play its part in history. If you have any daguerreotypes, ambrotypes, or old time photographs, we shall be delighted to have them as accompaniments to your article. Send the completed article to Henry Ford, Attention: H. M. Cordell, Dearborn, Michigan.

QUESTIONNAIRE

1. Name. Age. Birthplace.
    Mrs. S. G. Bressler (nee Elizabeth Christ)
    87 next birthday
    Born May 7, 1843

    Pine Grove Township, Pennsylvania. Now Schuylkill County. At one time Schuylkill County was part of Berks County. The town or village Pine Grove was close by to our land. It takes its name from the large white pine trees which made a beautiful grove when the early Pioneers came into the locality to settle there.

2. Description of childhood: (A) What you remember of your home and its furnishings; describe each room, even to the smallest article. (B) Your schooldays; books used, pens, copybooks and so forth. (C) Children's games played. (D) Your teacher and his or her methods and any interesting incidents remembered.

    (A) The house I was born in was a log house, built by my Grandfather, who was a lawyer or "Squire" and surveyor. He was well-to-do but lost all he had by accepting Continental Money. My father being the youngest, did not get any education on account of the failure, but the others already had

Mrs. S. G. Bressler (née Elizabeth Christ), born May 7, 1843, in a photograph she sent to Henry Ford in answer to the 1929 history questionnaire. (99.0.1.1)

their education. There is a record in Berks County where Justice Christ administered the oath of allegiance to the soldiers of the Revolution. There was a very large open fire-place. The upstairs was one large room with 5 large post beds of cherry wood, 5 straight back chairs and two large chests. One large table. The downstairs had 3 rooms. One room was the bed room for father and mother. One a living room. There were pictures on the wall of Washington and Jefferson and Philadelphia; a cherry-wood desk; 2 rock-ers and 6 chairs and a two-wing table. The other room was the kitchen. Here was the fireplace and a large wood stove. Wood was the only fuel. It had a large board table with benches on either side and could feed 14 at one time. We had home-made carpet in all the rooms except the kitchen. (B) The school was 2 miles away. I went 3 terms, the term was 3 months, but on account of the deep snow and severe weather I only had about 6 weeks to the term. The term was December, January and February. The book I had was Cobb's No. 1, from which I was taught to read and spell. The teacher taught each one separately as they were all ages and sizes. The pen was made of a goose feather. My father made my copy-book of paper and the teacher wrote the letters at the top and I copied them from that. (C) The only game I can remember was tag around the school-house. As to toilet, the boys used one side, the girls the other. (D) As to punishment, the boys got "licked with a hickory stick," the girls were put into the loft for an hour or so. The teacher was an old man, his name was Sinklenton Hikes. He preached liberty, freedom for the individual and equality before the law for all men. He was a Jefferson Democrat in politics.

3. Do you remember any tales of home life and customs told you by your parents and grandparents that will describe the life of their day?

I never saw my grandparents, as I was the youngest of 9, and this pleasure did not come to me.

There are a few things I remember my mother telling me, one about the indians coming to the home and that they never did any harm. Another thing I remember mother told me they were all busy in harvest time when grandfather was sent home from the Revolutionary War because he had taken turberculosis (consumption we called it that time) and that one of the neighbors then went in his place and was shot, but not killed. Grandfather did not get well, but died soon after returning from the War.

My father and mother were both good horse-back riders. Everybody had to be, or walk. When they went visiting they took their knife and fork along because not everybody had enough knives and forks to go around.

My father, Jonathan Christ, hauled the first anthracite coal ever taken out of this county with mules on cars running on wooden rails from Lawberry, or Lorberry, to the Union Canal Dock at Pine Grove. As a coal contractor he had 65 head of mules and horses.

4. Your duties around home; chores, evening employment; social diversions such as singing, parties, games, log-rollings, charivaris, customs at marriages, funerals, birthdays, and other celebrations; kind of fancy-work done by the girls and grown-ups, and the tools used. Dates that feather wreaths, hair wreaths and trinkets, wreaths of wool flowers and wreaths made of seeds, were made.

The girls were taught housekeeping, how to make butter, milking, during the evening we would knit stockings and make quilts. There were no musical instruments of any account except the band in town, which we could hear on our farm. In wintertime we had a lot of snow and since we lived in the mountains, we made sleds of boards and slid down the hills, and had lots of fun in these winter sports. The parties we had were on New Years, when the New Year Shooters would come around and wish us a Happy New Year. Then we would make supper and have cider. No marriage license required in those days, we went to a minister and were married. The funerals were largely attended. The coffin was made by the local cabinet-maker and taken to burial on a two horse wagon. No herse, or dead wagon, in my time at home. The girls knit lace and did embrordary work and made all our own finery. Our people never made whigs or hair wreaths, we wore our hair natural, used no paint or powder, but plenty of home-made soap. Flower wreaths were made from colored paper for decoration purposes around the living room.

5. Give detailed description of lighting methods of your early years or what was told you of earlier days; what sorts of lamps or candles or pine chips; how fires were kindled and kept through the night. Your remembrance of early matches, of the burning fluids; of the first use of kerosene and your first impression of it and the use of glass chimneys on lamps; the same with the introduction of the electric light, the telegraph and the telephone. Amusing or instructive anecdotes will be welcome.

We had grease lights and tallow lights, and lard lights — the lard lights we called "Lutzers" which was used to go to the Barn. The fires burned out during the night and were rekindled in the morning with flint, finally we got matches to make fire with. The first kerosene light I had after I was married about 3 years. The first impression was a pleasure. I liked them much better than tallow lights. We had small candlesticks with candles in them which stood on the mantel.

About the middle of the 1800's there appeared mantel candle sets of three pieces, two single sticks for the mantel ends and a three-candle piece for the mantel center. These were made of brass, on a marble base and the base was of various designs, some of them being a bee-hive, a soldier in mail, Paul & Virginia, man and woman in old fashioned dress, etc. etc. All were hung with glass pendants. Can you tell us your memories of these; at what date you saw them or of their purchase?

I cannot answer this question. We did not live near a large city and these things did not come through to the smaller towns. At least not where we lived.

6. Early recollections of (A) The country doctor, medicines, early surgery, etc.; also of the dentist. (B) Traveling peddlers. (C) Mail and its delivery. (D) Transportation and methods of travel. (E) Churchgoing and activities connected therewith; choirs, methods of paying the minister, church socials, etc. (F) Elections and the torch-light processions or accompanying illuminations.

As to doctor, my uncle, Jacob Christ, was the county doctor. He carried all his medicine with him on horseback. He set broken bones and amputated limbs and did all surgery at that time, also "pulled" teeth with a hook, but did no filling.

There were peddlers of all kinds. They were respected and honest. They sold all kinds of merchandise. Some of them had their store in the towns.

Travel was on foot, by horseback or by wagon or stage and finally by the Union Canal to Reading and Philadelphia.

We went to Church every 4 weeks — ours was the Reformed Church, followers of Ulrich Zwingley of Switzerland, who was a friend of Calvin. The church holiday was strictly observed, when there was one, we did not have many — Christmas and Easter were about the principle ones. We had no choir, my father was fore-singer, i.e. lead the singing. The preacher preached at several churches and got $50.00 per year and hay and food and farm products. He also worked his own land.

Father was a Jefferson Democrat and was elected Supervisor and took great interest in politics but I do not recall much of it, except that it always snowed on election day and I would stand by the window to watch him come riding home on our black stallion which was named "Rock."

7. Dress of men, women and children. Whatever you can recollect of the different parts of their costume and personal adornment. Use of bears' grease and tallow.

The men had frock coats, very wide pants and boots and white shirts and the boys wore "half-shoes." The stockings were wool and were all knit by the girls. The hats were broad brim soft felt. The women had tight waists, very full skirts with hoops and very long. The little girls had tight waists, and very long, full skirts. The boys had long pants buttoned by suspenders. The boys had little round felt hats.

Your face was your fortune then, there was little personal adornment, everybody knew who you was and none was needed, because nobody could be deceived, which is the object of all adornment.

We did not like bear meat and did not bother with the grease. Tallow was used for candles and for medical purposes, making salve, and greasing boots.

8. Farming implements and methods of farming in your day. Describe as many implements as possible and what you can recollect of the introduction of new inventions in the line of reapers, mowers, seeders, threshers, fanning mills, etc. Dairying and other farm activities. Describe the different washing machines you have seen.

We had horses, plow and harrow, and did the farming mostly by hand. The mowing was done with "Syckles" or "Sythe" by hand. Seed was sewn by hand with a bag over the shoulder. Thrashing was done with sticks tied on ropes. Washing done by hand on an oak wash board.

9. Going into town; exchange of produce for store goods; credit systems, etc.

When the horses were busy on other work we walked to town. Sometimes we would ride. Farm products were exchanged for merchandise at the General Store. The credit system was simple because everybody knew everybody else. Settlement was by the year generally. Money did not figure much in any transaction because it was no good, and because it was not necessary. The trade balance was always about even each year. There was no bank in our community.

10. Do you remember the introduction of the sewing machine? Did your folks subscribe to Godey's or Peterson's Magazine and what effect did they have on country and town life?

Yes I remember the introduction of the sewing machine. I also bought one. It was much talked about and people would walk miles to see one in operation.

We did not know anything of Godey's or Peterson's Magazine.

11. Tell about daguerreotypes and your personal experience in having them made; also the days of the modern photograph. If you can spare any old daguerreotypes or old photographs we shall be delighted to have them for our records.

I remember Daguerreotypes. It was a novelty. The photographer traveled in a wagon. His wagon looked like a little house. He had no horses of his own. The Tavern Keeper took his horses to move the little studio from place to place. We had some made for fun and out of curiosity.

12. Anything you can remember about old time roads, toll-gates and methods of taking toll; plank roads and their upkeep, early roadside inns or hotels and any interesting stories in connection therewith.

The roads were mere trails compared with present roads. Toll gates were like the gates at railroad crossings. You paid as you went through. Plank roads were considered great but they did not last long, because they required too much repairs to be of value. As a rule a Tavern was located at the cross roads every 6 or eight miles. Whiskey was sold for 3 cents a gill. Beer was uncommon — not used much. At that time, as now, worthless, weak men got drunk, while good men did not get drunk.

13. Fire-fighting in your district at different periods.

Fire fighting was done with buckets from a well or spring in chain gangs, handing filled buckets on to next man and empty buckets back again. Nearly always the fire fighting was useless as everything usually burned down, and all was lost.

14. Music and dancing; old customs, including singing schools, choirs, country dances, and the approximate dates when the seraphina, the dulcimer, the melodeon, the jew's-harp, the organ were used. Amusing or instructive incidents will be welcome. What were the names of some of the popular songs in your young days?

Not many musical instruments, but plenty of violins, and dancing at the taverns. I do not know much of it because I was not allowed to dance.

There were singing schools too, but the weather was generally so severe I could not go, and besides I was not so deeply interested by nature in any music . . . at least not at that time.

15. Anything else of interest that may not have been mentioned above, that may occur to you. This is an opportunity to do your part

in passing invaluable information to posterity. Things that may seem of little importance to you are, on the contrary, of the greatest importance in a record of this kind.

The most important thing of my younger days was the Civil War, and so much has already been told and written that to add more of the same thing will be of little or no value.

The most unexpected and the most wonderful change that I can think of at this moment is the change in the religious views of the people. When I was a little girl, nearly everything that is done now, as a matter of course, was considered a sin. The beautiful and healthful dresses of the girls of the present time would have been condemned as a sin when I was a little girl. The preachers preached Hell Fire then. They do not do it now. The preachers spoke as though they had a commission of authority handed to them direct from God Almighty, and those who did not believe that the preachers' word was God's Law (or pretend to believe it) were condemned without question. The preachers' interpretation of the Bible or of God's Law was the only correct view — all others were condemned. This change came quickly and suddenly. After the Centennial one could notice that the change was in process. The last War seemed to help to make it complete.

The morals of the people, however, have not changed. The people in my childhood were no better or worse than now, and the people of the present are no better or worse than when I was a girl. They are, and were, just people — sometimes following the wrong leaders, sometimes following the right leaders. But their morals were the same then as now.

16. At what date were the old time paper window curtains used? Those were in colored designs and we believe were bought by the yard.

When I was a little girl my mother bought paper at the store and made paper window curtains. The finished curtain was not sold then that I remember, but later on we could buy them ready to put on. We did not buy them by the yard. They came in rolls and in a variety of colors and were sold by the roll. A roll had enough paper for about 4 windows.

40
Quest for Alcohol Fuels

By 1916, the Model T had been a tremendous success, and the Fordson tractor was on its way. This was the year the Fords moved into Fair Lane and the Henry Ford & Son partnership was established. This partnership included not only tractor manufacturing operations but also the Henry Ford & Son Laboratories at Fair Lane, already engaged in "medical, botanical, and chemical research." Between 1916 and 1919, in particular, records indicate a multitude of experiments at Fair Lane attempting to find the ideal botanical source of ethanol for use as a motor fuel.

Only four months following the establishment of Henry Ford & Son Laboratories, Henry Ford was interviewed by the *Detroit News* concerning his views of the future. Portions of the interview also were published in the December 15, 1916, issue of the *Western Brewer*, to which Ford was a subscriber. He had subscribed to the *Western Brewer* in order to obtain the *Brewers Hand Book,* which had a complete list of all brewers and brewmasters in the United States. The following excerpts from Ford's interview illustrate his thinking at that time.

> "Michigan has voted for state-wide prohibition, but the 60 brewing plants in the state need not be abandoned," said Henry Ford to the *News* today. "Millions of dollars are invested in these plants. Economically it would be a shameful waste to have them become idle. But there is no reason why they should become so. Every standard brewing plant can be transformed from a brewery into a distillery for manufacturing denatured alcohol for use in automobiles or other internal combustion engines."
>
> By practical experimentation carried on during the last 18 months in the Henry Ford & Son laboratories and on the Ford farm in Dearborn, Mr. Ford has proved these two things:
>
> 1. That denatured alcohol can be used successfully as a fuel for the gas engine in automobiles and tractors.
>
> 2. That denatured alcohol can be manufactured and marketed at a price that will permit its general use as a gas engine fuel.
>
> After a long study of breweries and their methods by Mr. Ford and his engineers, he has come to the conclusion that all a standard

brewery plant needs, to be transformed from a brewery to a distillery, is the addition of a continuous still. And with raw material on every hand, the same amount of labor, no tax and in unlimited market, the denatured alcohol business will be as profitable for the brewery as the manufacture of beer. Mr. Ford's demonstrations are considered the beginning of a revolution in the use of liquid fuels in industry. They are conducted by J. B. Dailey, Ford research engineer, under Mr. Ford's personal supervision. So successful have been the small laboratory tests and the use of alcohol thus produced in cars and tractors on the Ford farm that Mr. Ford will shortly erect a larger experimental still for producing denatured alcohol on a large scale demonstrating its possibilities as a new industry in Michigan.

"There's simply no two ways about this fuel question," Mr. Ford said, as he turned from his desk in the Henry Ford & Son Laboratories in Dearborn. "Gasoline is going — alcohol is coming. It is coming to stay, too, for it's in unlimited supply. And we might as well get ready for it now. All the world is waiting for a substitute for gasoline. When that is gone, there will be no more gasoline, and long before that time, the price of gasoline will have risen to a point where it will be too expensive to burn as a motor fuel. The day is not far distant when, for every one of those barrels of gasoline, a barrel of alcohol must be substituted.

"Using alcohol in an ordinary Ford car, we are able to get 15 percent more power than with the present gasoline, although the mileage covered was not quite so high. The raw materials we have used in the laboratories in producing alcohol cheaply are various kinds of grains and vegetable substances. Tests were made with corn and wheat. Then we tried potatoes, grapes, cherries, peaches, currants, strawberries and many other kinds of small fruits. Carrots, turnips, beets, sugar cane and wood were also used. We also found that the wastes from canneries — such as apple peels and cherry pits, the waste from sugar factories and vegetable tops, usually thrown away on the farm — were surprisingly high in alcohol value.

"One of the best materials we found were cornstalks. These were ground up, mashed and boiled, and produced a very high percentage. An acre of cornstalks will produce 100 gallons of alcohol — some cornstalks would produce 50 percent more. Then the distiller can turn around and sell his waste back to the farmer for cattle food. Nothing has been taken from it but the alcohol — all the nitrogenous matter is still there, to go back to the soil as fertilizer. Again, we can import from Germany a kind of alcohol potato and make our barren, sandy acres in the north yield abundantly. These potatoes are not good to eat. They are large, like our beet, and the inside is reddish and juicy and very obnoxious in taste and odor. But they yield a wonderful amount of alcohol."

As mentioned in the interview, the man responsible for the experiments conducted for Henry Ford was John B. (Jack) Dailey, who had worked in the electrical department of Ford Motor Company at

Henry Ford and his engineers gathered around the first Fordson tractor being shipped overseas from Dearborn during World War I. Among them is Jack Dailey, the alcohol project engineer, leaning against the rear wheel of the tractor. Others, clockwise from Dailey, are Roy Bryant, Henry Ford, Eugene Farkas, Charles Sorensen, Ernest Kanzler, Frank McCormick, Otto Rheinhart, Louis Scott, Mead Bricker, Dick Crowel, Bredo Berghoff, George Brubaker, John Moore, and John Crawford (with his arm on the tractor radiator). The event took place in October 1917. (B.34935)

Highland Park and was, according to Ernest Liebold, Ford's secretary, "the type of man who had various ideas about things, and I think probably convinced Mr. Ford that there were a great many things he might do." Between 1916 and 1919, Ford's secretaries and Dailey answered the many letters sent to Ford concerning the laboratory's progress in alternative fuels for cars and tractors. Following the article in the *Detroit News*, Ford received dozens of letters of inquiry from brewing companies, government agencies, and Southern land agents. These are now in Accession 62, Box 77, of the Benson Ford Research Center. Following are excerpts from some of the more interesting letters:

Arlington, Florida, 7/24/17

I wish to call your attention to the possibility of producing sixty million barrels of crude alcohol on available lands now lying idle here in the state of Florida alone. The plant which is best suited for the production of crude alcohol is the Japanese sugar cane which . . . will yield as high as sixty barrels of crude alcohol to the acre. It would cost in the neighborhood of $150,000,000 to get a million acres of land into shape, but if the product can be marketed for $8 a barrel, there would be plenty of money in the crop to pay all running expenses and 25% dividend on the stock. I am ready to offer you my services for the pay and allowance of a common soldier in the regular army.

Fort Myers, Florida, 3/30/17

In compliance with your request of me I have shipped you twelve gallons of our cane syrup by express, and trust you will receive the shipment in good order. The syrup in the tall, unlabeled gallon cans was made from cane on the lower Gulf Coast of Lee County, and the other six gallons in labeled cans is made from cane produced inland. If you should want to try syrup as made from cane grown in the muck soils of the Everglade, I can secure it for you, and it is different.

Everglades Sugar & Land Co.
Miami, Florida, 11/12/17

[To Herbert Hoover, copy to Ford] Inasmuch as the gasoline situation seems to be growing acute would it not be well to consider submitting some special legislation to the next session of Congress, eliminating all of the red tape now connected with the manufacture of alcohol for fuel and power purposes? By removing all restrictions, millions of tons of waste vegetable products could be converted into alcohol for fuel and power purposes at low cost, and small stills could be operated in almost every part of the union. As you are no doubt aware, alcohol is already being used extensively in Europe as a motor fuel.

Everglades Sugar & Land Co.
Miami, Florida, 11/27/17

[Letter to Ford] I have received a communication from Mr. Hoover's department reading as follows: ". . . the matter referred to is one for the attention of Congress, as we have no power to legislate along the lines suggested."

Louisville, Kentucky, 12/13/17

You are necessarily much interested in the production of denatured alcohol and in cheapening the cost to consumers. I believe I could suggest to you how this could be done in Louisville, from sorghum juice, the advantages being: First, the low price at which distilling plants could be bought at the present time. Second, the surrounding country is especially adapted to the cultivation of sorghum. Third, the topography of the country is such that the juice could be brought to the distillery at a minimum cost.

Tallahassee, Florida, 10/16/17

Will you kindly have information sent to me regarding your success growing "alcohol potatoes?" And also please let me know if you will let me have some seed, and on what terms.

This answer to the "alcohol potato" letter was typical of many:

Inasmuch as Mr. Ford's experiments in connection with potatoes for industrial alcohol have not been completed we are not in a position to give you any definite information at this time. As soon as detailed information is available we shall be glad to advise you.

One of the last alcohol letters in the Ford archival file was written by Liebold on October 13, 1919:

Mifflin Chemical Corporation, Philadelphia

Your letter of September 27th received. In answer to your inquiry, we desire to advise that the question of commercial production of alcohol has been carried on by us in experimental work for the past five or six years and, while active work in this connection has ceased during the past month or six weeks, we nevertheless have been able to convince ourselves that the question is practical if properly conducted.

Negotiations with the Internal Revenue Service to operate a still became very complicated. As late as May 1918, it was necessary to explain to the IRS that the twenty-gallon experimental still then being operated belonged to Henry Ford and not to Henry Ford & Son. The still was located in a building on Michigan Avenue with no street number. This was likely Ford's "Water Works" building constructed in 1914.

It is conceivable that Ford, on his yachting trip to Cuba in early March 1917, was exploring the practicality of using sugar cane as a source of alcohol. His visit with Marscho Faschio, who was associated with sugar mills outside Havana, could have had that specific purpose. When Ford was visiting Thomas Edison in Florida, the two men visited a Florida sugar plantation on the shores of Lake Okeechobee. In July 1922, Ford had an option to buy 9,400 acres of cypress forest land in Lee County, southern Florida, near Deep Lake and the huge Gulf Sugar Corporation's tract.

By 1924, Ford's forestry operations in Iron Mountain, Michigan, were distilling wood chips by the ton into a variety of organic compounds including alcohols. These were sold as by-products, as was the carbon residue which was pressed into "Briquettes." A small replica of the Iron Mountain wood destructive distillation plant was constructed in Greenfield Village in 1929. With this apparatus, numerous vegetables, fruits, grains, and seeds were chemically dissected to determine the value of their constituents. These experiments culminated in Ford's selection of the soybean as the plant of greatest value.

As with a good many of Henry Ford's efforts — such as railroads, radio, and water power — government interference was his nemesis. Ford's attempt to promote ethanol as a motor fuel was hampered considerably by the various national and state statutes of Prohibition. Only now is the federal government awakening to the dire need for a renewable supply of energy. Ford had offered a solution to this problem back in 1916.

References

Accession 62, Box 77. Benson Ford Research Center, HFM & GV.

Accession 65, Ernest G. Liebold Reminiscences. Benson Ford Research Center, HFM & GV.

Accession 65, William B. Mayo Reminiscences. Benson Ford Research Center, HFM & GV.

Accession 65, Charles Voorhess Reminiscences. Benson Ford Research Center, HFM & GV.

41

Cooperative Farmers Association

Henry Ford grew up a farmer's son. His father gave him an eighty-acre farm of his own when he was twenty-four, a year before he was married. In 1902, although he was working in the automobile business in Detroit, he purchased the Ford family homestead and began planting crops and raising cattle on it. His 1908 Model T automobile was designed primarily with farmers' needs in mind. And with farmers as a major market for the car, he was very concerned about farmers' prosperity. Throughout his life, he was always watching out for the welfare of the farmer.

With Model T profits, Ford began buying hundreds of acres of farm land in the Dearborn area. On these farms, he demonstrated how he thought farms should be operated for maximal benefit to the farmer. In April 1915, Ford was sending telegrams to various Michigan legislators and to Governor Woodbridge Ferris advocating passage of Senate Bill 335, which prohibited charging unlawful interest on loans by bankers to farmers. When Ford's Model T was selling in record numbers in 1923, the *New York Times* announced: "Ford Plans to Raise More Efficient Cow." The cow would be a dual-purpose creature with the milk-producing characteristics of the Holstein or Jersey and the beefy lines of the Hereford or Black Angus.

Ford believed that the farmer should be an independent businessman, that, using modern farm machinery, including, of course, the Fordson tractor, he would prosper through thick and thin. During the post-World War I depression period, when farmers were begging for help, Ford's suggestion was more efficient production, not aid from bankers. He did not want bankers in control of the farmer's business. In his *Dearborn Independent* in July 1922, he published an article headlined "The Perversion of the Farm Loan System: Co-operative Democracy Inverted into Bureaucratic Oligarchy." In it, he stressed the inadequacy of the Federal Farm Loan Bureau in serving farmers' needs.

Well known as a benevolent and wealthy farmer, concerned with the farmer's welfare, Ford was besieged with requests from individual farmers throughout the United States for financial help. A large bloc of farmers dominated the "Ford for President" movement, which reached its peak in 1923. Ford, convinced by his wife, Clara, and by Thomas Edison that he should not become a politician, withdrew from the race, giving his support to Calvin Coolidge.

One of the possible cures for the ills of agriculture was the farm cooperative. Many cooperatives were beneficial in raising the price of farm produce by consolidating and improving production, together with aggressive promotional marketing. Sunkist oranges and Diamond walnuts are good examples. Ford was well aware that cooperatives could be helpful if managed primarily for the full benefit of the farmer. He took exception, however, to cooperatives that used their farmers to enrich their business managers. Ford learned that a large group of such cooperatives was managed by one man, Aaron Sapiro.

In April 1924, Ford allowed the first of a series of scathing articles to be published in the *Dearborn Independent* accusing Sapiro of cheating the farmers. These articles induced Sapiro to sue Ford for defamation of character, asking for $1 million in damages. The suit came to trial in Detroit in March 1927. After a bitter legal battle, the case was declared a mistrial; Ford retracted his statements concerning Sapiro and publicly apologized.

The thousands of acres of Ford Farms in Dearborn and elsewhere in southeastern Michigan were owned and operated by Ford himself. They were not truly cooperative farms. More than fifty resident farmers, together with other hired help, worked for wages on farms in the Macon and Tecumseh areas under the direction of Ford and his assistants, Edward Clark, Fred "Big Fritz" Loskowski, and Raymond Dahlinger. A large grain elevator in Dearborn made and sold flour from the vast wheat acreage, while other crops and livestock were marketed mainly at Detroit public markets.

During the Great Depression, however, Ford did permit organization of a large area of his own farm land as a cooperative. This land stretched from eight miles south of the town of Tecumseh to six miles north of Macon, an area encompassing the townships of Tecumseh, Raisin, and Macon — the bulk of Lenawee County and a portion of Washtenaw County. The constitution and bylaws of this only cooperative known to have been managed by Ford read as follows:

ARTICLE I. NAME.
The name of this Association shall be:
FORD'S COOPERATIVE FARMERS ASSOCIATION.

ARTICLE II. PURPOSE OF THE ASSOCIATION.
The purpose of this Association shall be to conduct general cooperative farming on the Ford farms in Macon, Tecumseh and Raisin Townships, Lenawee County, Michigan. The members of the Association shall cooperate and work together in the farming operations and agricultural pursuits which are to be conducted, and any and

all acts deemed necessary to such purposes by the Board of Trustees shall be considered within the purposes of the Association.

ARTICLE III. MEMBERSHIP.

Section 1.

The membership of this Association shall be restricted to men actively engaged in farm operations or agricultural pursuits on the Ford Farms, who have been admitted to membership by the Board of Trustees, and who shall have subscribed at or prior to admission, to the Constitution and By-Laws of the Association.

Section 2.

The Board of Trustees shall have the power to suspend any member, and after a hearing by the Board, to expel such member or members, whenever such suspension or expulsion is considered by not less than four trustees to be for the best interest of the Association. Any member expelled shall be given reasonable compensation for his interest, computed from date of last distribution of funds by the Association.

ARTICLE IV. OFFICERS AND THEIR DUTIES.

Section 1.

The Officers of the Association shall be seven trustees, elected individually by majority vote of the members immediately after adoption of this Constitution, and annually thereafter on the first Tuesday in February; Provided, however, that at any time by a majority vote of the members, two trustees may be elected to serve for a period of three years; and by a similar vote, two trustees may be elected to serve for a period of two years.

Section 2.

The Board of Trustees may designate one or more members as Chairman, President, or by any other name, to conduct the executive and administrative affairs of the Association. Members so designated shall have the powers vested in them by the Board, and shall serve at the will of the Board.

Section 3.

The entire management of the affairs of the Association shall be vested in the Board of Trustees.

ARTICLE V. PLACE OF MEETING.

The meetings of the Association and Board of Trustees shall be held at such time and place as are fixed by a majority of the Board of Trustees, or by any officer designated by the Board to call such meetings.

ARTICLE VI. VOTING.

The privilege of voting shall be limited to active members of the Association, each of whom shall be entitled to one vote. Proxies for voting shall be in writing, and shall be limited in effect to one meeting, unless proxy expressly otherwise provides.

ARTICLE VII. AMENDMENTS.

This Constitution may be amended by a two-thirds vote of the members; but no amendment shall be voted upon until the regular meeting next following the meeting at which the proposal is presented.

BY-LAWS.

ARTICLE I. MEETINGS OF THE ASSOCIATION.

Section 1.

Annual meetings for the election of Trustees shall be held here-after on the first Tuesday in February of each year, at such place as may be designated by the Board of Trustees; and notice of such meetings shall be given in writing to each member of the Association at least ten days prior to such meetings.

Section 2.

Regular meetings shall be held on the first Tuesday of each month, and special meetings shall be held at any time, upon not less than two days' notice given by the Board of Trustees or any member designated by the Board as executive officer.

Section 3.

Meetings of the Board of Trustees shall be held on the first Tuesday of each month, either in connection with regular meetings of the members or immediately following meeting of the members.

ARTICLE II. QUORUM.

Section 1.

A majority of the Board of Trustees shall be a quorum for the transaction of ordinary business. For the transaction of extraordinary business, the full Board shall meet.

Section 2.

A majority of the members of the Association shall constitute a quorum.

ARTICLE III. RULES AND REGULATIONS.

Each member of the Association agrees to abide by the following:

1. There shall be no smoking on the premises of the cooperative farmers.

2. The working day shall consist of ten working hours, with one hour for noon intermission. Work is to start at seven o'clock a.m. The Board of Trustees may change these hours as seasons or conditions require.

3. Arguments, if any, shall be settled at the meetings of the Association or the Board of Trustees, and not during working hours.

4. Any member injured while at work on the cooperative farms, upon furnishing proof, shall have his doctor bills paid out of the Association funds.

5. Any member of the Association appearing on the job intoxicated may be expelled immediately.

6. Members of the Association not residing on lands farmed may be allowed Ten Dollars ($10.00) per month as and for rent of outside property.

7. Each member agrees to prevent or keep cut all weeds around the farm buildings and the roads running through said farms.

8. Members of the Association may have their automobiles repaired

The harvesting of soybeans in 1932 on the Ford Cooperative Farms was highly mechanized. This Oliver combine attached to a Fordson-powered tractor cuts, threshes, and stores the harvested beans in its high-level bin until a truck drives alongside to collect and haul the beans to the mill in Saline. Soybeans usually were harvested in the fall but could be harvested with snow on the ground. (188.8193)

at the Association's garage, at the rate of Fifty Cents (50¢) per hour, which shall be charged to the individual's account.

9. Each member of the Association shall be limited to the sum of Fifty-Two Dollars ($52.00) per month for withdrawals or purchases of gasoline, clothing, groceries, etc. from the Association commissary store, etc. Amounts in excess of this specified sum must be paid for in cash.

10. Members of the Association may purchase gas and oil at the Cooperative Pump One Cent (1¢) per gallon of gasoline and One Cent (1¢) per quart of oil into a fund, to cover the cost of handling same.

11. Income of the Association from the sale of produce of every kind shall be paid into and kept in a fund which shall be divided among the members at least once each year. Division shall be equal among the members, after adjustment and equalization of the benefits distributed prior to the division of income.

These by-laws may be amended at any time by a vote of a majority of the members.

AGREEMENT WITH RESPECT TO PROPERTY, ETC.

Each member of the Association agrees to the following:

1. All farm machinery and farm equipment furnished by Mr. Henry Ford shall be appraised by three men, one of whom shall be a Ford representative, one of whom shall be chosen by the Association, and these two shall designate the third man.

2. Depreciation on farm machinery and equipment shall be deemed to be ten percent (10%) per annum of the appraised value.

3. All tools of the Association that become worn out or broken shall be replaced or repaired by the Association.

4. The fire protection at the garage and buildings on the Ford farms shall meet with the approval of a Ford representative.

5. The Ford farms shall rotate crops so that each parcel of said farms will be properly fertilized at least once every four years.

6. Wood to be cut on the Ford farms shall be selected by a Ford representative.

7. The Association shall maintain the blacksmith shop, owned by Mr. Henry Ford.

8. The Association shall furnish the labor necessary for all fencing of the premises and repair of buildings, it being understood that fencing materials and materials for repair of buildings will be furnished by Ford.

9. Each member of the Association shall cooperate with the Ford representative.

10. The Association shall maintain at least one hundred head of cattle, two teams of horses, a herd of sheep and hogs, and poultry flocks of suitable size for the farming operations being conducted.

Although members of the association were paying taxes for use of the farm acreage and rent of about ten to fifteen dollars per month for their houses, Ford was losing money because he was furnishing materials to keep his fences and buildings in repair. About 400 Fordson tractors owned by Ford Motor Company were turned over to the cooperative association to be used by association employees. Other agricultural implements in large numbers were also furnished by Ford. His general secretary, Ernest Liebold, had difficulty explaining the reason for such excessive farm losses to the Internal Revenue Service.

During this period, a major farm crop was soybeans, which were trucked to the Ford Saline and Milan processing plants. Wheat could be taken to Ford's flour mill in Dearborn. Hay, straw, and vegetables were sold on the open market. There were horses and cattle on some of the farms. The board of the association decided which farms were to plant

This is Henry Ford's water-driven soybean mill at Saline, Michigan, not only where cooperative farmers could bring their beans but also where independent farmers of southern Michigan and northern Ohio were encouraged to have their beans processed. During 1940, some 700 farmers used these facilities to process more than 200,000 bushels of soybeans. The beans were flaked in the tall four-story mill, while in the lower building to the left, the soy oil was extracted. (188.23330)

grains and which would operate as dairy farms, pig farms, or chicken farms, all part of the cooperative. Dozens of boys were hired during the summer to hoe weeds from the soybean fields.

Prices received by the association during that Depression period were not high. Some examples:

Timothy hay, $10 per ton	Potatoes, 50 cents per bushel
Clover hay, $16 per ton	Wheat, 45 cents per bushel
Sweet clover seed, $3 per bushel	Musty wheat, $10 per ton
Alfalfa hay, $18 per ton	Buckwheat, 90 cents per cwt.
Baled straw, $6 per ton	Soybeans, 50 cents per bushel
Mangels, $3 per ton	Ear corn, 33 cents per bushel
Turnips, 50 cents per bushel	Extracted honey, 6 cents per pound

The soybean oil extraction equipment employed at Saline. The process of separating soybean oil from the flaked bean was devised by Ford personnel in 1931 and is still in widespread use. The oil in the flaked bean is dissolved in a hydrocarbon such as hexane as it traverses the inclined tube, leaving the meal without its oil. The hexane is then boiled off the oil and recovered, leaving the oil for use in a large variety of commercial products. The remaining meal, with its high protein content, provides a valuable source for still other commercial products. (189.13315)

Association members could buy groceries and other household needs from the Ford Commissary at essentially wholesale prices. And children of association members attended schools well supported by Ford.

When Ford's soybean operations were at their peak in about 1939, other farmers in the region, who were not members of the Ford cooperative, also used the Saline and Milan soybean processing plants. More than 700 farmers within a 200-mile radius were growing soybeans on 22,588 acres from seed furnished by Ford, and an additional 15,624 acres were seeded by Ford under contract. The Saline plant alone could extract oil from 140,000 bushels of soybeans per year. Most of the balance of the crop was retained for seed the following year.

World War II was to bring the demise of Ford's Cooperative Farmers Association. Beginning in 1941, members could get work in defense plants providing considerably greater income. Association wages were about $2.50 per day, less than half of what was paid in the factories. Many of the farmers, however, stayed to work directly for Ford and his assistants as they had before the organization of the association.

In July 1944, when Ford was losing his health, it was decided that all of the southeastern Michigan Ford Farms should be turned over to Ford Motor Company. After complete inventories had been taken, the farms were offered for sale for cash. A few of the farmers living on the land were able to buy outright the property they had been occupying, but most could not. A letter to Clara Ford from a farmer's wife pleading for a means of staying on the farm they had worked for many years is quite distressing. Mrs. Ford could not help so many.

But even today, many of the farms in the Macon and Tecumseh areas maintain the manicured appearance of the Ford Farms of yesterday. Characteristic features are a picture-perfect white farmhouse, implement shed, and garage, bordered by a tight wire fence with round white fenceposts. The surrounding yellow and green fields stretch for nearly a half mile, perfectly flat and almost treeless.

References

Accession 23, Box 10, Ford Farms. Benson Ford Research Center, HFM & GV.

Accession 48, Aaron Sapiro Case. Benson Ford Research Center, HFM & GV.

Accession 65, F. W. Loskowski Reminiscences. Benson Ford Research Center, HFM & GV.

Accession 272, Box 7, Ford, Henry—Farming. Benson Ford Research Center, HFM & GV.

Accession 285, Boxes 2134, 2665, Sale of Lands. Benson Ford Research Center, HFM & GV.

Accession 572, No. 3862, Farming 9.12. Benson Ford Research Center, HFM & GV.

Bryan, Ford R. *Beyond the Model T.* Detroit: Wayne State University Press, 1990.

"Ford Opens Soy Bean Demonstration Plant," news release by N. W. Ayer & Son, August 8, 1938.

Interview with Michael Papp of Macon, Michigan, former member of the Ford Cooperative Farmers Association, July 1986.

Vertical File, Ford Farms. Benson Ford Research Center, HFM & GV.

Wik, Reynold W. *Henry Ford and Grassroots America.* Ann Arbor, Mich.: University of Michigan Press, 1972.

42
Two Camps for Boys

On June 15, 1940, newspapers announced, "Henry Ford today launched a 'National Youth Movement' of his own."

To 25,000 other industrialists and manufacturers in all parts of the United States, he mailed a letter pointing out the opportunity open to every employer of labor to help in solving what he saw as the greatest national problem, youth unemployment:

Dear Sir:

Of all problems confronting our country today, the gravest is that centering about our millions of unemployed youth.

To an extent far too sparsely recognized, the future character of our American government, institutions and ideals — perhaps their very existence — depends on what is done with the problem TODAY.

As I see it, this is peculiarly and particularly a problem for American business and industrial management — for only they can approach it CONSTRUCTIVELY.

Municipal, State and other agencies cannot attack it effectively. Their measures are temporary; they can do nothing of substantial and lasting good. All their projects tend to decrease youth's initiative and stultify self-reliance. That is unwholesome both for you and the nation.

Only widespread action by private business and industrial management can do the job effectively and CONSTRUCTIVELY—that is, on a basis such that youth retains its self-respect, is given hope and is started toward a life of usefulness and good citizenship.

I have a deep faith that, if American management, great and small, everywhere, will do its bit, each business and industry doing what it can to make opportunity for youth to get started, the problem will vanish.

Yours sincerely,
Henry Ford

With each letter went a booklet explaining Ford's ideas on how to meet the situation constructively and the results he had attained at Camp Legion and Camp Willow Run, at Dearborn and Ypsilanti, Michigan, respectively. Details of camp operations are given in this twenty-three-page booklet. To these youth camps, one in its third, the

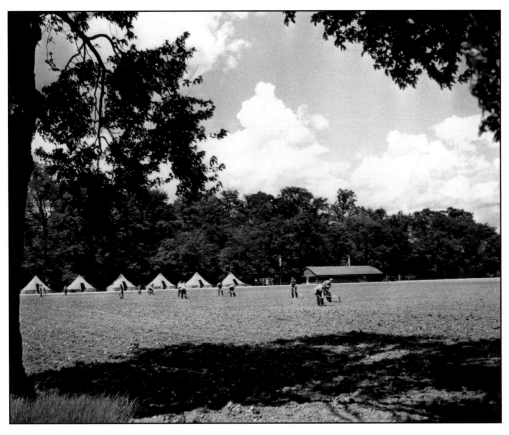

Boys working in one of the farm fields at Dearborn Camp Legion on an early summer day in 1938. Boys bunked in the tents seen at the left. The building to the right was their mess hall. (188.23415)

other in its second year, Ford gave his personal, daily attention. "I'd rather do this than anything else I know of," he told reporters.

Explaining the need for widespread action, the booklet says:

> It has been estimated that more than 2,000,000 boys in this country are out of school and out of work. A generation of youngsters, through no fault of its own, is at loose ends. Some, from particularly needy families, have been unable to finish school. Some have finished — and then spent months getting the idea that the world has no place for them.
>
> These boys need a chance to get started. They need to be given faith in the American way of life, given a reason to look forward to citizenship.

If it is impossible for industry to absorb all of them at once, there is something else that can be done. It is one of the most constructive things that could possibly be done.

They can be given a chance to work for a while close to the soil. In this way, they can gain in health, gain in self-reliance and self-respect, earn something and learn something. They can learn what city boys and town boys, especially, need to know: that the ultimate resource of this nation, or any nation, is its land.

Business can do it. It would be a fine thing if business were to accept it as a social responsibility. Whether it is done by individual business men, by a co-operative group or by a community, it needs to be done.

At both Camp Legion and Camp Willow Run is a group of 65 boys. Before coming to camp, all were unemployed. Most of them are sons of dead or disabled veterans. Each group has a 320-acre tract provided by Mr. Ford to work on. They are taught the fundamentals of agriculture and plant, cultivate and harvest many kinds of garden crops. The products are sold at wayside stands. From the revenue the camp operating expenses are paid. The boys sleep in tents, having their meals in a special mess-hall and each receives $2.00 per day. At the end of the season the cash balance remaining after payment of operating expenses is divided among the boys equally. Last season each boy received $128.00 in addition to his wages.

The boys govern themselves and maintain camp discipline through officers chosen from their own number. After the season ends, those who wish may enter the Henry Ford Trade School, or get jobs in Ford factories.

Letters to Ford show appreciation; one letter, for example, dated June 6, 1940, reads in part:

> May we, grateful parents, thank you for what you are doing for our boy, Leon Irish, and other boys at your camps, and the opportunity

The produce stand on Michigan Avenue in Dearborn where Camp Legion boys sold vegetable crops they had grown. Their fields were plowed by Ford tractors, but the boys did a lot of hoeing. (0.13854)

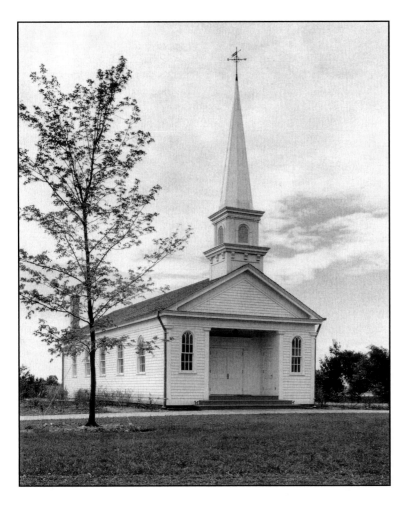

The chapel at the Willow Run Camp for Boys photographed about 1940, just before the property was claimed as a site for the Willow Run bomber plant. (188.27803)

you are giving them to be useful to themselves and to others, and to thank God for His goodness and mercies daily. You don't know what you mean to those boys; you stand for everything that's fine, good and honest, not only to those boys, but to everybody, everywhere, wherever the name of Ford is known, and because of your goodness God has blessed you.

> Sincerely,
> Mr. and Mrs. Leon Irish

Although the two Ford camps for boys started together in the summer of 1938, in the midst of the Great Depression, the building of the massive Willow Run bomber plant and airfield in 1940 interrupted the boys' farming operations at Ypsilanti. And by April 1944, returning veterans of World War II were found in need of rehabilitation and preparation for jobs in industry. With enthusiastic support from the

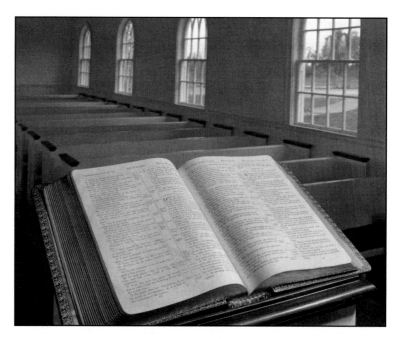

Interior of Willow Run Chapel. The Bible, not incidentally, is opened to Proverbs, Chapters 7, 8, and 9. The column heading on the left page is "A Young Man Led Astray." The boys conducted their own nondenominational Christian services. Henry Ford was not inclined to hire an ordained minister. (188.27800)

American Legion, Ford proceeded to upgrade his facilities at Camp Legion in Dearborn to accommodate as many as 120 veterans, giving them training similar to that provided in the Henry Ford Trade Schools.

References

Accession 285, Box 2277, Henry Ford Office. Benson Ford Research Center, HFM & GV.

Twork, Eva O'Neal. "Henry Ford's Camp Legion." *Dearborn Historian*, Spring 1994.

43

Georgia Experiments

By 1924, Henry Ford had manufactured 10 million Model T automobiles and had time and money to do just about anything he enjoyed doing. Just why he would at that time choose a project involving the little town of Ways Station, Georgia, is not clear. Ways Station was a railroad stop on both the Seaboard Air Line and Atlantic Coast Line railroads about seventeen miles south of Savannah. The town was named after a prominent early resident. It is said that Ford's friend John Burroughs, when passing the coastal area of Georgia on Ford's yacht, the *Sialia*, in 1917, had mentioned the area south of Savannah as being good for birding. A more likely reason for Ford's choice might have been to have a project site for the winter months in a climate less humid than was the Fords' winter home in Fort Myers, Florida, and where there would be plenty of land for agricultural experimentation.

Ford responded to a letter in December 1924 from Savannah real estate agent R. L. Cooper, who offered for sale the plantations of Strathy Hall, Cherry Hill, and Richmond near the town of Ways Station. Cooper was directed by Ford to buy not only the three plantations but also additional land along the Ogeechee River known as Bryan Neck. Over the next ten years, Ford acquired approximately 70,000 acres of mostly wooded land. The first publicized explanation of why he was purchasing so much land was that it would be used for Fordson tractor testing. Another reason, more probable but never admitted by Ford, was that the land would be used to grow rubber-producing plants. Throughout Ford's ownership, however, lumber was the chief product obtained from the land.

Although he did not announce them as such, Ford's objectives in retrospect were (1) to gainfully employ the men of the community at worthwhile endeavors, (2) to improve the health of families in the community, and (3) to provide educational facilities for the entire community. In short, the popular occupation of moonshining would be eliminated from Ford properties and more useful work provided, a health clinic would be supported by Ford to control diseases rampant in the community, and equal education for black and white children would be provided by consolidated schools with bus transportation for students.

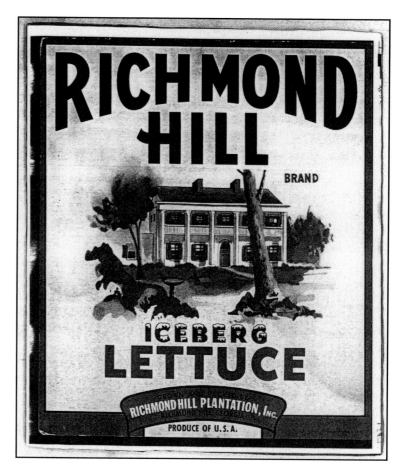

Henry and Clara Ford did not spend much time at Ways until 1937, when they occupied a new home built on the Richmond plantation site. Their usual residence time was from January through March each year. To operate the Ford Farms, as the property was called, John F. Gregory was put in charge. With a population of nearly as many blacks as whites and the number of Ford employees reaching 800, Gregory treated them all fairly; otherwise, Ford would have fired him.

The main source of employment at Ways was Ford's sawmill, planing mill, carpenter shop, and dry kilns. Trees covering 46,000 acres of Ford land were available. Large tree trunks were converted to lumber, smaller trees and limbs into plywood. Operation of the sawmill and planing mill made it possible to build a church, three large school buildings, a town hall, a post office, a fire station, a commissary, and later two subdivisions of prefabricated homes. The subdivisions consisted of Blueberry Village with 49 lots and homes and Richmond Hill with 125

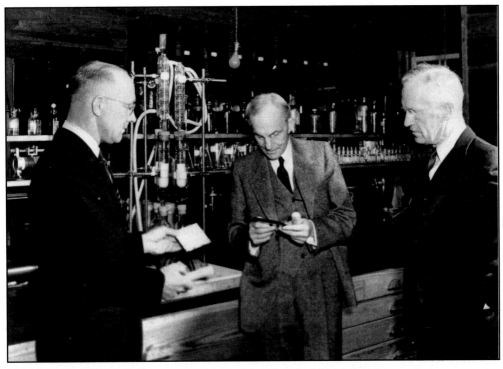

Dr. H. G. Ukkelberg, agricultural chemist, shows Henry Ford some samples of plastic tile made from wood wastes in Ford's research laboratory at Ways, Georgia. Ukkelberg previously had worked for Thomas Edison at Fort Myers, Florida. Standing at right is Jack Gregory, Ford's manager of Ford Farms at Ways. (0-4447-c)

lots and homes. Each home cost about $3,500, and they were rented to employees for ten to fifteen dollars a month. The carpenter shop for a time built coffins, church pews, house furniture, school desks, and such things. It also built *Little Lula*, a twenty-eight-foot cabin cruiser powered by two V-8 automobile engines, and later sold millwork such as window and door frames to lumberyards.

Ford gave special attention to Harry G. Ukkelberg, who had previously worked for Thomas Edison at Fort Myers and was now with Ford at Ways. His work for Edison had been finding a domestic plant from which rubber could be commercially extracted. Ukkelberg's work in the Ways Research Laboratory had the broad purpose of finding industrial uses for agricultural products and by-products. His first assignment, however, was to devise a plan for reclaiming the old antebellum rice fields along the Ogeechee River. The abandoned rice fields provided the

One of the several one-room schools for black children near Ways, Georgia, at the time Henry Ford was buying the property on which they were located. These primitive schools were abandoned when Ford opened the George Washington Carver School in 1940. (P.B.35145)

proper nutrients for growing lettuce. For ten years, the old Cherry Hill rice field marsh produced lettuce as a very successful commercial crop. In one year, 8,400 cases were sold at a profit of $12,122. To prevent spoilage in shipment, an ice plant was built and ice sold to the railroads for refrigeration.

Ford's interest in plant culture was far-reaching. Approximately 2,000 acres were cleared for experimental farming. The success George Washington Carver had had with peanuts was no doubt on his mind. The growing of almost all common vegetables was tried in the Georgia soil. Crops producing oils such as soybeans, tung, perilla, and chia were grown and their oils tested for useful properties. Fiber crops such as ramie were tested for strength. Gum trees were found useful for producing rayon; some of the experimental rayon was knitted into men's socks.

A lignocellulose plastic tile was made mainly from sawdust and corn cobs. Potato culls were converted into alcohol to be used in tractor fuel.

Animal husbandry was not of primary interest to Ford. However, he did investigate the physical properties of the wool of black sheep as compared to the wool of white sheep, and he tolerated a few oxen on the premises to recall past history. But tractors outnumbered horses by far. Both Ford and Carver firmly believed that plants, rather than meat or cow's milk, should feed humanity.

One of the early Ford projects at Ways was to rid the community of disease. The small, privately subsidized health clinic was supported entirely by Ford beginning in 1931. To prevent malaria, he began to have swamps drained to reduce the number of mosquitoes, but it was a slow process. In 1936, an estimated 50 to 75 percent of the population in the Ways area suffered from malaria. An army of seventeen nurses was assigned to canvass the community, take blood samples, and administer the new drug atabrine, thus bringing malaria under control. Hookworm had created another epidemic, at one point affecting an estimated 90 percent of the population. Medication along with needed improvements in sanitation essentially eliminated that disease in the Ways area. The clinic also conducted immunization programs for

Georgia Experiments

The George Washington Carver School was built to consolidate six outlying black school districts from which pupils were brought by bus. (0.6519)

The first-grade class of the George Washington Carver School in 1940. The children are all identified on the back of the original photograph. Standing in the back row to the left of center is Henry Ford in the light suit between two of the teachers. To the right of center are Ford's secretary, Frank Campsall, another teacher, and Jack Gregory. (P.0.19689)

typhoid, smallpox, and diphtheria and later provided for the schoolchildren, in particular, numerous examinations, prescriptions, x-rays, and minor surgeries. At times, Ford would send patients to Henry Ford Hospital in Detroit at his own expense. One Ways patient resided there for a year.

Good schools for the community were among Ford's primary objectives. Beginning in 1937, he not only built new school buildings for the white students but also insisted on providing equal educational opportunity for black students. School integration was not allowed by law in Georgia. On Ford properties were six dilapidated one-room school buildings for black students. Ford built a new building for them in Ways, naming it the George Washington Carver School. Carver dedicated the building on March 13, 1940. The Carver School opened with an enrollment of 150 students in the first seven grades; gradually, twelve grades and more than 300 students were enrolled. Ford buses carried the children from their homes to the new school, and textbooks were furnished without cost to the students. Evening adult classes in reading, writing, and arithmetic also were taught in the Carver School, and its Parent Teachers Association established a fund for students who wanted to attend college. Three members of the first graduating class of the Carver School earned degrees at Savannah State College.

As part of the educational program, a 100-acre forest area was cleared as a farm for Carver School students to operate. Children were asked to help clear the land of twigs and stones after the trees had been removed. All boys in the fourth grade and above were trained to operate a tractor. The boys operated the farm as a business, selling the

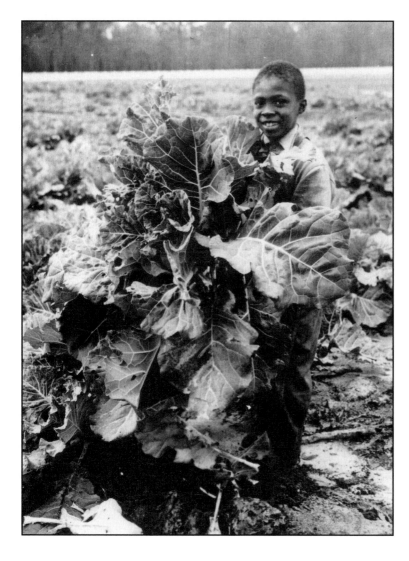

A boy picks collards, a type of cabbage, on the 100-acre vegetable farm operated by students of the George Washington Carver School at Ways, Georgia. This boy will receive a share of the profits. (0-6593)

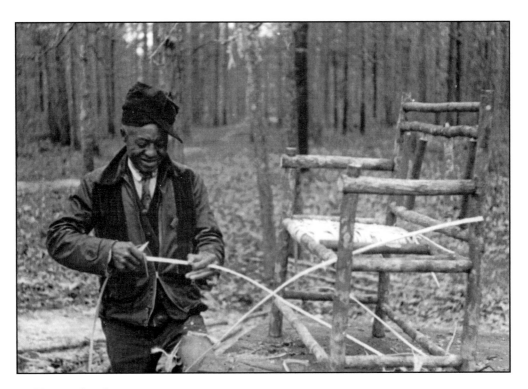

Ways resident Lee Slocum, previously on welfare, was employed by Henry Ford to teach basket weaving to students. (0.6586)

produce, keeping records, and each year making a profit that was divided among them at the end of the season.

With World War II in the offing, Ways operations became somewhat restricted. Some of the land was relegated to the government for Fort Stewart. Wartime regulations restricting equipment, fuel, and experimental work limited progress at Ways. In 1941, Ford's losses in Georgia were $400,000. That same year, the people of Ways petitioned the U.S. Postal Department and the two railroads to change the name of Ways Station to Richmond Hill, the name of the home of the Fords. On May 1, 1941, the name change took effect.

In 1943, Edsel Ford died, and Henry Ford again took over the presidency of Ford Motor Company. He was not well either mentally or physically and could no longer concentrate on operations at Richmond Hill. Clara Ford retained an interest, however. Costs of development and building programs at Richmond Hill Plantation as calculated at Dearborn in 1944 amounted to $2,198,852. Operating costs were another matter. In 1946, Gregory was dismissed by Clara, who substituted Ray Newman from the Michigan farms to operate the Georgia farms. Newman's orders were to cut down overhead and show a profit. The schools alone had cost nearly half a million dollars in operating expenses. Schools then were either closed or turned over to the county.

Many employees were dismissed. Henry Ford II, Henry's grandson, was essentially in charge and eliminated any operation under his control that was losing money. His grandfather had lost nearly $4 million on Richmond Hill operations.

Henry Ford died on April 7, 1947, Clara Ford in September 1950. Their wills left their personal property to the Ford Foundation. On May 11, 1951, as a finale, it seems, the sawmill burned down, with the loss of many of the remaining jobs and capital value of $275,890. Henry's grandson Benson Ford announced the complete discontinuance of operations in a letter to employees dated September 6, 1951. The Ford properties, with the exception of the Ford residence, were sold by the Ford Foundation to the Southern Kraft Timberland Corporation, which in turn sold it the following year to the International Paper Company.

The era of Henry Ford at Richmond Hill was over. As summarized by Dr. C. F. Holton, director of the Ways Station Health Clinic, "Henry Ford by means of his health clinic, his schools, and employment, has changed the population from a sickly, suspicious, illiterate and under-nourished group, into one of the healthiest communities in Georgia."

References

Accession 65, Dr. C. F. Holton Reminiscences. Benson Ford Research Center, HFM & GV.

Accession 65, Ray Newman Reminiscences. Benson Ford Research Center, HFM & GV.

Accession 65, H. G. Ukkelberg Reminiscences. Benson Ford Research Center, HFM & GV.

Bryan, Ford R. *Beyond the Model T.* Detroit: Wayne State University Press, 1997.

———. "Guide to the Records of Richmond Hill Plantation, Richmond Hill, Georgia 1925–1952." Benson Ford Research Center, HFM & GV, 1983.

Gregory, Edna R. "Ways Station–Richmond Hill." *Savannah Morning News,* December 7, 1941.

Long, F. Leslie. "Ukkelberg Remembered." *Richmond Hill Area News,* November 6, 1986.

Long, Franklin Leslie, and Lucy Bunce Long. *The Henry Ford Era at Richmond Hill, Georgia,* 1998. (Self-published.)

Rogers, George A., and R. F. Saunders, Jr. "Henry Ford at Richmond Hill, Georgia." *Atlanta Historical Society Journal,* Spring 1980.

44
Ford and the Disabled

As early as 1911, when John R. Lee joined the Ford Motor Company as manager of personnel, Henry Ford began paying particular attention to the assimilation of disabled people into the workforce. It is said that at that time, no man applying for work at the Ford factory was rejected because of his physical condition. He was examined after he was hired, not before. At that early period, there were on file 957 disabled men at work. Of these, 10 were totally blind, 207 were blind in one eye, 37 were deaf and dumb, and 234 had only one foot or leg. Appropriate work was found for them at regular wages.

In 1919, following the casualties of World War I, it was reported that Ford Motor Company had 670 operations in Ford plants performed by legless men and 2,637 performed by one-legged men. Two of these operations were adapted to armless men, 715 to one-armed men, and 10 to those who were blind. By October 1925, Henry and Clara Ford had given $10,000 to the American Foundation for the Blind.

The following letter was written on March 15, 1929, by Helen Keller of Forest Hills, New York:

Dear Mr. and Mrs. Ford:

I wonder if you realize what your friendship means to the blind.

As an example of its great influence for good, may I ask you to read the folder that accompanies this letter? In it, you will read of despair turned into hope, and defeat into victory for sightless men and women who long for usefulness, but do not know how, or in what direction, to take their first steps.

I wish there were new and beautiful words to thank you for the impetus you are giving the Foundation which is near to my heart.

With happy faith in your continued interest and friendship towards the sightless, I am,

Sincerely yours,
Helen Keller

Previously published in *The Ford Legend,* Spring 1998.

Helen Keller, counselor on international relations of the American Foundation for the Blind. Keller was born at Tuscumbia, Alabama, on June 27, 1880, and was both deaf and blind at age nineteen months. She authored *The Story of My Life* in 1902, "Optimism" (an essay) in 1903, *The World I Live In* in 1908, and *The Song of the Stone Wall* in 1910. She died on June 1, 1968. (Photograph courtesy of Helen Keller International.)

In a February 1929 letter referring to the efficiency of blind men working at Ford Motor Company, Ford's secretary H. M. Cordell named specific jobs in motor assembly, the gasket department, and the valve bushing department, which resulted in efficiencies of from 75 to 100 percent compared with men who had their sight. By the time of World War II, great advances had been made in the art of fitting the disabled man to industrial work. It was proved that disabled workers, in appropriate jobs, had equal or better production rates and fewer accidents than average workers in full possession of their physical faculties.

Dr. Frederick Searle, superintendent of the Ford Industrial Schools, stated in July 1943:

Daily more than 1200 persons, blind or with seriously impaired vision, enter the Rouge Plant, work their shift and go to their homes as do normal men having earned an equal amount in wages. One hundred fifty three deaf mutes; fifteen men in wheel chairs with both

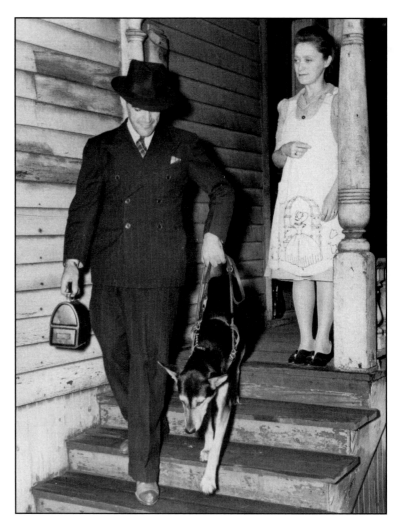

Sylvester Ripkowski and his leader dog, Blackie, leaving their home in Detroit
for work at the Rouge plant in October 1942. The dog will lead him to a nearby
bus stop, where a Ford-built bus will pick them up. Ripkowski may or may not
know that his house needs a coat of paint; his wife undoubtedly does.
(P.833.77082-6)

legs amputated; one with both hands gone; and one hundred thirty
seven minus a hand or a whole arm work regularly and as efficiently
as men who are favored physically. These men ask no odds and are
given none when work suited to their abilities is found.

In June 1944, the American Foundation for the Blind in New York
City awarded the Migel Medal to Henry Ford. The presentation was

scheduled for June 15 in New York. Ford then was over eighty years old and not well enough to travel. So Henry Ford II offered to accept the medal for his grandfather. The award had been established in 1937 by M. C. Migel, president of the foundation. The awards committee in 1944 included Migel and Helen Keller, who had referred to the foundation in her 1929 letter to the Fords. Announcement of the award was made by Dr. Robert B. Irwin, sightless executive director of the foundation, in these words:

> The Ford Motor Company has been a pioneer in finding industrial processes which can be performed satisfactorily by blind people seeking employment. Mr. Ford's example of providing employment to these people and keeping them at work during prosperity and depression has reopened to the blind the doors of many another manufacturing concern, which have found blind employees practicable when properly placed.

Helen Keller's presentation speech was as follows:

> There has glowed in my heart these many years a thrillingly beautiful memory of the mighty impetus which your family and Detroit gave to the campaign for the blind of America. Since, to our deep regret, your grandfather could not come to New York, it is a privilege for me to

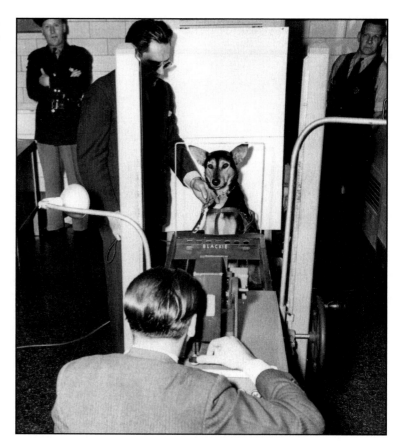

Mug shots are
necessary for photo
identification
badges.
(P.833.77082-6)

convey to him through you the American Foundation's Award for
Distinguished Service.

Truly the service of the Ford Motor Company to the blind is
unique in the annals of handicapped humanity. What a dream it was
when your grandfather first gave voice to an enlightened attitude
towards physically impaired persons who could work, and let the blind
enter his great plants not out of charity but because of their productive abilities! Profoundly we honor him for the vision with which he
looked behind their marred eyes and saw the living spirit that creates,
and for the humane policy that the Ford Company continues to this
day. Henry Ford has confirmed the new philosophy that the only
genuine rehabilitation is opportunity for the blind to develop their
usefulness.

Henry Ford II accepted the Migel Medal with these remarks:

It is with great pride and pleasure that I come here today to accept on
behalf of my grandfather this great honor you have chosen to bestow
upon him.

Will Ripkowski be able to handle this job? All, including Blackie, are apprehensive. Ripkowski does go to work at that spot, and Blackie is given a cushion under the bench for his comfort during the long working day. (P.833-77082)

The policy of the Ford Motor Company to give equal opportunity for work to all, including those who do not have the full use of their physical facilities, was determined many years ago by my grandfather. His reasoning was sound. Sentiment or pity had little to do with it. My grandfather is a kindly man but he also is a very practical man and his success has been the result of the opportunity which only America can give. He believes all should have that opportunity.

In connection with the furtherance of that policy, my father once said: "Our company has for a long time believed in and practiced the utilization of physically impaired workers. . . . We do not regard such employment as charity or altruism. All our handicapped workers give full value for their wages, and their tasks are carried out with absolutely no allowances of special considerations. Our real assistance

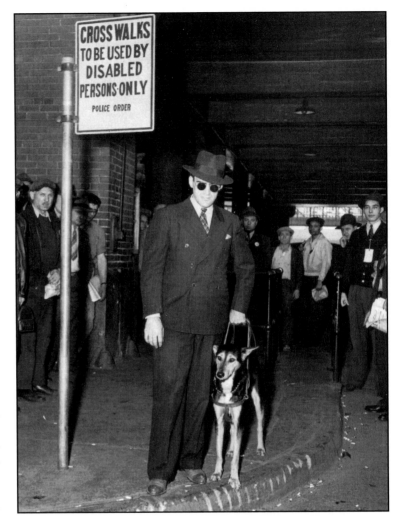

With the day's work over, Blackie keeps Ripkowski on the curb at Gate 4 of the Rouge plant while he watches intently for the light to turn green so they can cross busy Miller Road to the bus terminal. (P.833.77082-14)

to them has been merely the discovery of tasks which would develop their usefulness."

There are 26 totally blind and 98 partially blind persons working for victory in our plant. There are interesting stories connected with many of these people. But mostly they are not spectacular stories. These are simple people, assigned to full jobs in a large scheme of building those tools by which victory is being forged.

Each morning at the River Rouge plant in Dearborn, Michigan, a firmly stepping man gets off a bus at Gate Four. Ahead of him, wearing the now-familiar special leader dog strap, is a strong German Police dog. The man is Sylvester Ripkowski, who does a full day's work each day for the Ford Motor Company. The dog pauses at the curb, then cautiously steps down and guides his master across the

With a friendly glance back toward his friend the photographer, Blackie leads Ripkowski onto the bus to go home. (833.77082-10)

street and through the archway. Confidently the dog leads the man through several buildings and finally stops in front of a familiar bench. The dog curls up on a pallet underneath and the man goes to work. That's all there is to it, but it is symbolic of what can be done if there is the will to work in spite of any and all obstacles.

There are other interesting stories — such as the one concerning 43-year-old Harvey Carson whose job is to file to precise smoothness small steel stampings. When Carson applied for work it was found he lived in Boyne Falls, some miles away. The problem of transportation was paramount. So the company hired a neighbor of Carson's at another job. Now he gets to and from work easily and is happy at his job.

And there are cases where the blind have been hired along with relatives to make their transportation and other problems easier. There is Thomas Gibson who was hired last year. He does a wrapping and packing job in the stock department. When his job is finished, his sister, who was hired with him, places them on a conveyor belt which carries them where they are needed. Thomas Gibson is both blind and deaf. His only means of communication is through a special code which he and his sister have worked out and carry on by tapping the palms of their hands.

333

Over the Blue Network at Dearborn Inn on October 26, 1942, Blackie explains to the nation the responsibilities of the canine population during wartime. Blackie is being interviewed by Earl Goodwin of the Ford News Bureau. (833.77133-C)

These incidents, as I have said, are not in themselves spectacular. But the Ford Motor Company is proud to have these people as part of its team. They are good workers and happy ones. In their minds and hearts there is the same indomitable courage which is dynamically typified by the noble contribution of Miss Keller to our time.

This policy of ours is by no means a temporary expedient. We intend to follow it. In the world of tomorrow there will be jobs for all who want to work.

So, in the name of my grandfather, I accept this Migel Medal with great pleasure.

Today, Helen Keller Worldwide, with world headquarters in New York City, is carrying on the work of the American Foundation for the Blind. As one of the largest U.S.-based international blindness prevention organizations, it states that more than 35 million men, women, and children in the world are blind and that 80 percent of all blindness can be prevented.

References

Accession 285, Box 340, Correspondence, Helen Keller. Benson Ford Research Center, HFM & GV.

Accession 285, Box 615, Correspondence, Helen Keller to Mr. and Mrs. Ford, 1929. Benson Ford Research Center, HFM & GV.

Bryan, Ford R. "Early Ford Medical Facilities." *Beyond the Model T*. Detroit: Wayne State University Press, 1997.

"Ford and the Handicapped." *The Ford Legend,* Spring 1998.

"Henry Ford Honored for Giving Aid to Blind." *New York Times,* June 16, 1944.

"Human Reconversion: A Challenge of 1945." United Business Service, Boston, December 30, 1944.

Searle, Frederick E. "Use of Handicapped Workers." Speech presented at Silver Bay Industrial Conference, New York, July 29, 1943.

45
Did You Hear from Mr. Ford?

Henry Ford's general policy was to answer every letter written to him. It was good public relations. On one occasion at least, however, he is said to have observed a secretary working on a stack of letters and to have pushed the stack into a wastebasket. Ford received letters literally by the thousands. Many of these are filed in the archives of the Benson Ford Research Center of Henry Ford Museum & Greenfield Village. Letters received during 1925 alone, for example, fill thirty-four boxes arranged alphabetically by sender's name, averaging more than a boxful for each letter of the alphabet.

'To answer all of these letters, Ford had secretaries who sorted them by general subject and in nearly every case picked what was considered the best form letter with which to reply. Incoming letters could be subdivided into such categories as:

> Employment requests (the largest category)
> Offers of investment
> Congratulatory letters on the Ford car
> Complaints concerning the Ford car
> Congratulatory letters on Henry Ford's success
> Requests for autographs and photographs

During 1924 and 1925, most of the letters were answered by V. L. Shevlin, an assistant secretary to Henry Ford, from an office in Highland Park, Michigan.

If you were to write concerning a job at Ford Motor Company, you would likely get one of a group of six or more form letters in reply. If an applicant lived in Detroit or lower Michigan and had reasonable qualifications, this most encouraging reply was quite standard:

Dear Sir:

This will acknowledge receipt of your letter of recent date.

We have forwarded your application for employment to the proper department for attention and you will undoubtedly hear from them in the event they are in need of anyone at the present time.

Very truly yours,

If the applicant inquired about a job for the second time, or repeatedly, the following reply was used:

Dear Sir:

Replying to your favor of recent date, we wish to advise that there is nothing further we can say concerning employment other than that we will retain your application in our files for consideration should there by any developments along this line.

Very truly yours,

If the applicant was from out of state or a typical applicant with little to recommend him, the following reply was used most frequently:

Dear Sir:

Your letter of recent date, addressed to Mr. Ford, has been handed the writer for reply.

At the present time we have nothing in the way of employment we could offer a person of your capabilities.

We will, however, retain your application in our files for future consideration should anything develop along this line.

Very truly yours,

If the applicant was from a location where there was a Ford branch plant, the following reply was used:

Dear Sir:

Replying to your favor of recent date, we regret to advise that as we have absolutely nothing to do with employment conditions at our branches, it will be necessary for you to communicate with them direct.

We are sorry we cannot assist you in the way desired.

Yours very truly,

If the applicant was from a foreign country, such as England, the following reply might be used:

Dear Sir:

Replying to your favor of recent date, we wish to advise that as the Ford Motor Company of England, Ltd., and the Ford Motor Company here are separate and distinct organizations, your application for employment will have to be sent to them direct.

Regretting that we cannot be of some assistance to you in this regard, we are,

Very truly yours,

If the correspondent, for example, wrote in meticulous handwriting from Leavenworth Penitentiary in Kansas, was soon to be released, wanted work, was qualified as an accountant, but admitted being guilty of forgery, he received the following form letter:

> Dear Sir:
>
> The fact that this company has given men who have made a mistake an opportunity to make good, brings to our office a great many applications for work. It is impossible for us to give favorable consideration to the large number of requests made of us. We are very sorry that for this reason we cannot promise you employment.
>
> Very truly yours,

In reading a hundred or so of the letters to Ford, one finds that those of most job applicants are of a routine nature simply asking for any kind of work. A few describe such lofty expectations that the request is ridiculous, and, on the other hand, some reveal a pathetic sense of need. A surprising number of letters are from wives and mothers of men who are unemployed. It appears, however, that a form letter was used routinely regardless of the circumstances described.

If the correspondent proposed an investment opportunity for Ford, this reply was used:

> Dear Sir:
>
> Replying to your favor of recent date, addressed to Mr. Ford, we wish to advise that as he never makes investments of any kind, it will be impossible for us to favor you with the advice requested.
>
> Regretting we cannot be of some assistance to you in this regard, we are,
>
> Very truly yours,

If the correspondent was an eleven-year-old child, for example, had made up a poem about a Ford car, and wished her "papa" was able to get a Ford car, she received this form letter:

> Dear Madam:
>
> We wish, on behalf of Mr. Ford, to acknowledge receipt of and thank you very much for your favor of recent date.
>
> We assure you that the sentiment expressed is greatly appreciated.
>
> Very truly yours,

If the correspondent had a complaint about a Ford car, he would receive the following letter:

> Dear Sir:
>
> This will acknowledge receipt of your favor of recent date, addressed to Mr. Ford.

As the Ford Motor Company has not sold cars at retail for a number of years, it will be necessary for you to get in touch with an authorized Ford dealer who will do everything in his power to be of good service to you.

Regretting our inability to be of some assistance to you in this regard, we are,

Very truly yours,

If the correspondent inquired concerning manufacturing methods or machinery, this form letter was used:

Dear Sir:

I have your favor of recent date, addressed to Mr. Ford, and am forwarding, under separate cover, a copy of "The Ford Industries" which should give you the desired information.

Thanking you for your interest in Mr. Ford, I am,

Very truly yours,

Finally, if the correspondent asked for an autograph, a photograph, or other favor from Henry Ford, the following reply was standard:

Dear Sir:

We wish, on behalf of Mr. Ford, to acknowledge receipt of your favor of recent date.

As Mr. Ford is absent from the office, and the time of his return is most indefinite, we regret that we cannot favor you in the way desired.

Very truly yours,

In years following 1925, many more form letters were used and signed by Henry Ford's secretaries, C. A. Zahnow, Frank Campsall, and H. R. Waddell. More than fifty such form letters, in addition to those used to answer letters addressed to Henry Ford, were used to respond to typical letters addressed to Clara Ford, B. B. Lovett, and the Henry Ford Museum. It is interesting that sixty years ago, the Henry Ford Museum was using a form letter that read in part:

We wish to thank you for the opportunity to acquire _____ which you have submitted for our consideration. However, at the present time, the space available in the Museum will not permit us to make further additions to this collection. We regret that we are unable to take advantage of your offer.

References

Accession 62-2, Boxes 306–7, Highland Park, 1925. Benson Ford Research Center, HFM & GV.

Accession 292, Box 47, Henry Ford Office — Miscellaneous. Benson Ford Research Center, HFM & GV.

Part VI
Luxuries

By the time the Model T was on the market in 1908, Henry and Clara Ford were becoming wealthy. They had been renting small apartments in Detroit since 1891, and finally, in 1908, they built their first home for themselves in Detroit at 66 Edison Avenue. This house was quite adequate for their small family but would not be classed as luxurious. Ford was then investing heavily in farm land at Dearborn, where they built a small clapboard bungalow as a private retreat in 1910, but he and Clara did not succumb to exceptionally luxurious tastes until 1914, when the Fair Lane residence was conceived and Henry was more than fifty years old.

Model T profits accounted for essentially all of the Ford luxuries dating from Fair Lane in 1915 to the Richmond Hill mansion in the early 1930s. Henry and Clara were both involved in all of them, although Clara felt particularly responsible for the Fair Lane residence and Richmond Hill. Henry liked being at the Mangoes in Florida because Thomas Edison was there. Clara was particularly fond of sailing on the yacht Sialia *and made greater use of the* Fair Lane *railroad car than did Henry. And whereas Henry was inclined to consider vacation at the remote Huron Mountain Cabin a waste of his time, Clara loved living in the wilderness.*

46
Fair Lane Mansion

Henry, Clara, and Edsel Ford were living very comfortably on Edison Avenue in Detroit when the Selden patent suit was settled in favor of Ford at New York in January 1911. This was a great relief to Ford and to the Ford Motor Company, who had been trying to free themselves from Selden's automotive patent since 1903. In October 1911, Clara's mother, Martha, a staunch supporter of Henry and frequent guest of the Fords, died at the Bryant homestead. Clara loved her mother, who often spoke of the town of Warwick, England, where she had been born and lived until she was eight years old before coming to America with her father, William Bench.

Following Edsel's completion of school in the summer of 1912, the Fords took their first trip abroad. On this combined business and pleasure trip, both Henry and Clara planned to seek out their family roots. In England, they visited Warwick and found the home where Clara's mother had lived as a child. Later, in Ireland, they concentrated on County Cork. In Cork City, Henry found the street where his foster grandfather had lived as a boy and, in the Irish countryside, the small farm with dry-stone cottage near the little town of Ballinascarthy where his father had lived as a boy.

The street in Cork City, the boyhood home of Henry's grandfather Patrick Ahern, had in early days been the lane people took to get to the city's fairgrounds and was named Fair Lane. Henry's grandfather had often told of the early pleasures of Fair Lane. Henry knew no other grandfather. Patrick lived with Henry's family and was Henry's pal during the first eighteen years of Henry's life. The name of Fair Lane meant much to Henry. That was where the birds sang sweetest, and Henry had been taught those bird calls by his grandfather.

Ford might not have agreed to the abrupt raise of factory pay to five dollars a day at Ford Motor Company in January 1914 if he had known the effect it would have on his family life. His home on Edison Avenue close to the factory was immediately besieged with workers clamoring for jobs. The Fords no longer had the privacy they desired. They already had decided against moving out of Detroit to Grosse Pointe, where other wealthy business families resided, in favor of Dearborn, where

their old-time friends were living. They had purchased hundreds of acres in the Dearborn area and picked a location they owned on the Rouge River known as the Black Farm, where they would build a home much more opulent than their Edison Avenue residence in Detroit.

Henry Ford may have approached Frank Lloyd Wright in 1909 concerning a new home, thinking his house on Edison Avenue was much too modest. Only three blocks away, his business partner, Childe Harold Wills, was planning to build an elaborate home designed by Wright's protégé, Marion Mahony. But because Wright temporarily left the country at that time, his architectural business was turned over to Van Holst and Fyfe of Chicago. Without written contracts, Ford arranged in 1912 to employ Van Holst and Fyfe as architects and Frank Goddard of Detroit as contractor to build a residence in Dearborn at a cost not to exceed $250,000.

Preliminary work began in July 1913, but plans were so elaborate and expenses so much more than expected that Ford terminated the work of both Van Holst and Fyfe and Frank Goddard in February 1914. It was Clara Ford who found a Pittsburgh construction manager, W. H. Van Tine, to act as both architect and contractor for a home to be known as Fair Lane. Henry seems not to have found fault with Van Tine. Was it because Van Tine was Clara's choice? Expenses incurred by Van Tine would accumulate to more than $1 million with barely a whimper from Henry.

Ford's chief interest was in the powerhouse he would build. On the Black Farm purchased in July 1909, he had built a dam on the Rouge River and a small power plant. Ford now wanted a much larger one. In 1913, his new power plant, designed by Mark A. Replogie, was equipped with two Leffel water-driven turbines and two electric generators to supply 110 kilowatts of direct power. For its day, it was exceedingly efficient. Housed in a four-story building and costing $244,000, the powerhouse was dedicated by Ford's friend Thomas Edison on October 28, 1914.

On a warm day in the summer of 1923, Clara and Henry Ford pose for their photographer, George Ebling. Clara was especially proud of her peony garden in the background, and two of Henry's birdhouses are part of the scene. (P.O.5985)

All during 1914, the Fords were living at their Edison Avenue home. It wasn't until February 1915 that they moved to the Ten Eyck house on their property less than a mile from the ongoing construction of Fair Lane. There Clara could oversee the work being done. The Edison Avenue home was not completely vacated until June 1915.

During the 1914–15 construction of Fair Lane under Van Tine's direction, from 500 to 800 artisans and craftsmen were employed. The stonework exterior of both residence and powerhouse is of Marblehead Buff limestone obtained from the Kelly Island Lime & Transport Company of Cleveland, Ohio. The house was to contain 31,770 square feet of floor space, divided into fifty-six rooms. Included were swimming pool, bowling alley, field room, kitchen, service and storage rooms, seven bedrooms, and fifteen baths. The swimming pool (now a restaurant), bowling alley, billiard room, and par-three golf fairway on the grounds were amenities included for the benefit of Edsel, then twenty-one, who lived at Fair Lane less than two years before he married Eleanor Clay and moved to Detroit.

The building's gray outer walls, 18 to 24 inches thick, and inner partitions averaging 14 inches thick, together with heavy carved oak and walnut interior trim and many massive fireplaces, present a somewhat oppressive atmosphere. Clara later had some of the dark interior paneling painted in light colors, and both Henry and Clara were inclined to use rooms well lighted by outside windows. The sun parlor facing the river was a favorite.

Between October 1915 and February 1916, carpeting for Fair Lane was ordered by Van Tine from B. Altman of New York. On one list are fifty-four rugs, eight floor mats, two jardinieres, and several pillows. The rugs ranged in cost from $131 to $6,375, the former being a brown rush basement porch carpet. Total cost of rugs amounted to $57,105. All were

Clara Ford cutting iris blossoms for display in the house. This is on May 27, 1939, she is in her English garden, and George Ebling has been asked to record the scene. (188.71369)

approved by Clara before Altman received its pay. Clara turned down only one item, a piece of linoleum. Yards and yards of linens, brocades, tapestries, silks, and velvets were supplied by such stores as John Wanamaker, Gimbel Brothers, and Arnold Constable of New York and Carson Pirie Scott, Marshall Field, and Mandel Brothers of Chicago.

Building of the greenhouses was Clara's responsibility. She dealt with the Willens Construction Company, which bid $6,850 for three greenhouses, each 83 feet long and 20 feet wide, which were attached to the south side of the powerhouse. In March 1919, Clara also was dealing with Jens Jensen of Chicago. Jensen, the renowned Danish horticulturist and landscape artist, was employed to convert the Black Farm yard and adjoining fields, meadows, and woodlands into a beautiful natural setting for the residence. Many visitors to Fair Lane are convinced that Jensen's contribution was more significant than the architecture of the residence itself. Added to the premises in due time were gatehouse, servant cottages, pony barns, peacock and chicken houses, boathouse, and grandchildren's playhouse. Altogether the cost of Fair Lane is estimated to have been in the neighborhood of $3 million. Ford, about the time of its completion, asked his resident engineer, Charles Voorhess, "Don't you think a fellow is a darn fool for building a place like this?"

Both Henry and Clara enjoyed the privacy of the outdoors surrounding Fair Lane. Both were interested in plants and wildlife. Clara's chief interest was in flower gardening. She had been elected president of the Dearborn Garden Club in June 1914. While at Fair Lane, she belonged to numerous garden organizations, the most important to her being the Woman's National Farm and Garden Association. Close to the residence, she planted and cared for a peony garden, an iris garden, an English garden, a rock garden, and a trail garden. At considerable distance north of the house was her mammoth rose garden.

A memo in Clara's handwriting states, "Started rose garden in 1926." She was in touch during February 1926 with Harriett R. Foote, "Rosarian" of Marblehead, Massachusetts, who became consultant and designer of the spectacular rose garden at Fair Lane for which Clara became famous. Foote was also a supplier of rose bushes for such gardens and that year was sending 650 climbers to Clara at $1.25 each. The rose garden developed by Clara and Foote became five acres in size, holding at least 10,000 plants of 300 varieties.

In March 1929, the American Rose Society and its hundreds of members were invited to see Clara's rose garden. She was particular about whom she invited to see her gardens and much preferred fully dedicated groups rather than the "curiosity kind," as she called them. Clara received many letters complimenting her on her gardens, and she seemed to have saved every one. Articles describing her gardens were

A view of Clara Ford's 5-acre rose garden with approximately 10,000 plants. This photograph is taken from in front of the Pergola looking toward the Summer House to the south. Some distance beyond the Summer House is the Fair Lane residence. (0.5967)

published in well-known national magazines; one in 1930 described the rose garden as the "most elaborate garden devoted to roses on the continent of North America." Color photographs costing Clara ten dollars each were furnished to magazines for publication.

Henry Ford, on the other hand, was especially interested in birds at Fair Lane. He had placed hundreds of birdhouses about the premises before the residence was built. In addition to sponsoring a project with the Michigan Audubon Society, Ford, with the help of Edison, was sponsoring the Weeks-McLean Migratory Bird Bill, which was passed by Congress in 1913. This bill gave the U.S. Department of Agriculture power to protect migratory and insectivorous birds in their flights from one habitat to another. On their visit to England, the Fords had been convinced that English songbirds possessed a more delightful melody than their American counterparts. In early 1913, Henry made arrangements with the Shackleton Apiary in London for the importation of 600 pairs of English songbirds, including finches, skylarks, linnets, blackbirds, nuthatches, grosbeaks, warblers, thrushes, cardinals, jays, bluebirds, and many more. The birds were released on the grounds of the Black Farm (now Fair Lane) before dawn on April 16, 1913. It was disappointing, however, that the great majority of these birds soon vanished from sight.

Ford's inside hobbies at Fair Lane were carried forth on the top floor of the powerhouse, where he had a drafting room and light mechanical equipment. Also in the large garage on the ground floor of the powerhouse, automotive experiments were conducted. Between the powerhouse and the residence was a 300-foot utility and pedestrian tunnel. Clara's inside hobby was cooking. She was an excellent cook in the English tradition of her mother, and cooks not meeting her exact requirements were promptly dismissed. Henry supervised powerhouse personnel, while Clara supervised the maid, butler, houseman, cook, and at least two cleaning ladies at the residence. She also supervised the head gardener and often the men working for him. Both Henry and Clara had their own chauffeurs. Only the maid and the butler lived in the residence with the Fords. The extensive grounds were well fenced and guarded by a gatehouse at the road entrance.

The Fair Lane gardening staff was the largest group. A list of workmen reporting to Alfons DeCaluwe, head gardener, in 1930 is as follows:

John McIntyre — Working in greenhouse
Joe Waldi — Working in vegetable garden
Walter Scott — Working in English & Blue garden
Jay Allen — Working on trail gardens
Ed Suter — Working in rock garden
Clarence Schofosky — Working in rose garden
Alfred Miller — Working in rose garden
Joe Kodra — Watering in rose garden
Woodrow Bannister — Running sprinkler on lawns
Otto Sakriska — Cutting grass
Edward Deo — Cutting grass
Charles Rigdon — Cleaning lawns and driveways
Clarence Ross — Cleaning lawns and driveways
Henry Millman — Peony & experimental gardens
Al Sommers — Cleaning shrubbery
Charles Schick — Cleaning shrubbery
Leo Borsay — Helping out on odd jobs

With the exception of Clara Ford's relatives and the Ford grandchildren, there were few overnight visitors at Fair Lane. Clara's garden-

The somewhat fortresslike front of the Fair Lane mansion in Dearborn as it appeared in 1951, following Clara Ford's death. When the house was built in 1915, it was on North Dearborn Road, a public thoroughfare. But because the Fords by then owned the land on both sides of the road for a distance of a mile or more, they were permitted to restrict the road to use as their private entrance. (P.833.101694)

ing friends and gardening groups comprised the majority of daytime visitors. The Fords were away from Fair Lane a lot of the time. Their homes in Fort Myers, Florida, and Richmond Hill, Georgia, occupied their midwinter months, and during August they were either at their summer home at Harbor Beach on Lake Huron or their Huron Mountain home near Lake Superior. They could travel in privacy on their own railway car, yacht, or lake freighter.

The Fords could afford to be big spenders. Henry spent on a much larger scale than Clara, with losses in the millions on farming, schools,

A view of the Fair Lane mansion as seen from the woods across the river in 1953. The same Indiana limestone of which the residence is built also lines the banks of the river. To the far left can be seen the entrance to the underground boathouse where Clara kept her electric boat, the *Callie B.* (0.1185-A)

and various Ford Motor Company employee benefits. Clara's expenditures were likely to be orders of magnitude less and directed more toward local causes. Although their personal lifestyle did not change measurably, both were relatively generous during the Great Depression.

Henry was in somewhat poor health, both physically and mentally, following a slight stroke in 1939. When Edsel died in 1943, Henry became noticeably less capable, and Clara began looking after him. Clara's secretary, H. Rex Waddell, adroitly handled Henry's personal correspondence so that people were not aware of his condition. When Henry died on April 7, 1947, Fair Lane, which had been in joint ownership, then belonged to Clara. It was very well maintained during the rest of her life. Fair Lane

In January 1950, Clara was suffering from a mild heart condition and was in Henry Ford Hospital for six weeks. Although she had invited the Garden Club of America to meet at Greenfield Village for luncheon in May, she was unable to be present as hostess. The wives of Edsel and Benson Ford greeted the 535 attendees. Five thousand roses were used as decorations at Lovett Hall in Greenfield Village. When the delegates were brought to Fair Lane to see Clara's gardens, she waved to her guests from a wheelchair in her second-floor bedroom.

Clara Ford died of heart failure at age eighty-four on September 29, 1950. She was buried next to Henry in the Ford Cemetery on Joy Road near Greenfield Road in Detroit. At Fair Lane, domestic employees to whom separate residences had been provided were asked to leave the premises by mid-October. The maid and the butler, however, were allowed to remain at Fair Lane as caretakers for eleven more months.

The Fair Lane estate, consisting of 1,346 acres, was left by Clara to her four grandchildren, Henry, Benson, Josephine, and William. They, in turn, in March 1951, granted the estate to the Ford Motor Company. The Ford grandchildren had their pick of Fair Lane furnishings, but they took very little. The bulk of the furnishings were shipped off to be auctioned to the public by Parke-Benet Galleries of New York in October 1951. Clara's jewelry was auctioned separately in a Parke-Benet sale in November 1952. As part of the housecleaning process at Fair Lane, some 2,000 mementoes and personal belongings accumulated over the years by Henry and Clara and stored at Fair Lane were donated to Henry Ford Museum.

Ford Motor Company used the empty Fair Lane residence to house the Ford Archives. These materials consisted of myriad papers which filled the closets at Fair Lane, together with the Henry Ford Office Papers from the Ford Engineering Laboratory. During the years these materials were being classified, several books and reminiscences relating to the Fords and the Ford Motor Company were produced.

In December 1956, the year Ford Motor Company went public, the Fair Lane residence, with 210 acres, was given to the University of Michigan to be used as a new Dearborn campus. A cash gift of $6.5 million was also given to the university for construction of academic buildings. The Ford Archives were moved to the Ford Rotunda and then, following the disastrous Rotunda fire, to the Edison Institute (Henry Ford Museum & Greenfield Village), where they now reside. Fair Lane, now furnished to an extent as it was during occupancy by Henry and Clara Ford, is open to the public for tours and is also used as a conference center and nature study area for the benefit of university faculty and students.

References

Accession 1, Boxes 1–187, Fair Lane Papers. Benson Ford Research Center, HFM & GV.

Accession 1, Box 35, Copies of November 6, 1914, Bill of Complaint; April 25, 1916, Joint and Several Answers of Frank H. Goddard; and February 17, 1922, Satisfaction of Final Decree. Benson Ford Research Center, HFM & GV.

Accession 1, Box 35, Ernest Liebold's memorandum regarding Van Tine. Benson Ford Research Center, HFM & GV.

Accession 65, Ernest Liebold Reminiscences, 1951. Benson Ford Research Center, HFM & GV.

Accession 65, Mr. and Mrs. Lewis Simpson Reminiscences, 1951. Benson Ford Research Center, HFM & GV.

Accession 99.1.1804, Circa 1911 rendering by Wright associate Taylor Wooley described as the earliest known architectural rendering for Henry Ford's home Fair Lane. Benson Ford Research Center, HFM & GV.

Accession 587, Box 48, Office of Henry & Clara Ford Estate, L. J. Thompson. Benson Ford Research Center, HFM & GV.

Accession 588, Boxes 1–6, Estate of Clara J. Ford. Benson Ford Research Center, HFM & GV.

Patterson, Ronald O. "The Mystery behind Wrightian Influence in the Ford Fairlane Home." May 20, 1973. Accession 1129. Benson Ford Research Center, HFM & GV.

Van Zanten, David T. "The Early Work of Marion Mahony Griffin." *Prairie School Review,* Vol. 3, No. 2, 1966.

47
The Mangoes

The Ford and Edison families were not particularly close until 1914, when John and Emily Burroughs and Henry and Clara Ford were invited by Thomas and Mina Edison to visit them at their Fort Myers home known as Seminole Lodge. At that time, Edison was developing a battery and starter system for the Model T car. The three couples, together with the Edisons' son Charles and his fiancée, had an enjoyable outing exploring the Everglades. The Fords that year were building Fair Lane in Dearborn but did not have a winter home. They were very favorably impressed with the climate of Florida and the relaxed atmosphere of the little town of Fort Myers.

Edison had owned Seminole Lodge back in 1886, when he married Mina Miller, his second wife, and they spent their honeymoon there. Every winter, the Edisons spent several months at Fort Myers. Next to the Edisons', a fourteen-room gray-shingled bungalow had been built in 1911. This house had been named the Mangoes.

A letter dated March 7, 1916, from Robert W. Smith, president of the Robert W. Smith Corporation of New York City, to Henry Ford reads as follows:

> I have just placed my winter home, "The Mangoes," at Fort Myers, Florida, on the market and it occurs to me that as you have visited Mr. Edison there and have seen this property which is the next adjoining property southwest or on the down river side, you might be interested in it either for yourself or some of your friends. A description of the property in brief is as follows:
>
> The property immediately adjoins the winter home of Mr. Thomas A. Edison, and in the variety of its trees and other features is very similar, in fact, the two properties were formerly one and were developed together. My plot has a frontage on MacGregor Boulevard of 177 feet and depth of about 450 feet to the Caloosahatchee Bay and the deed covers riparian rights to the channel one quarter of a mile or more out in the river.
>
> On this plot there are about 150 bearing grape fruit trees and 50 orange trees most of the latter having recently been budded to the best varieties of oranges and should come into bearing next year. Besides the above there are mangoe trees, pawpaws, lemons, limes, guavas,

tangerines, coconuts, bananas, etc., etc., and on the vegetable plot, all the seasonable vegetables can be raised.

The house is the best built structure in Fort Myers. It happened that when I took my superintendent to Fort Myers to build the house about five years ago, we arrived just in time to witness a tornado which tore things up pretty generally and my superintendent promptly doubled all framing timbers of the house so that it is very heavy in construction. The house contains a very large living room with a 4 ft open fire place, dining-room, butler's pantry, kitchen and a bathroom on the first floor, besides two very large porches, and a kitchen porch on which are the laundry tubs; and on the second floor there are four large sleeping rooms, a very large bathroom and a sleeping porch facing the river, a large trunk room, an abundance of closet room throughout the house and besides this there is a large attic. The house is equipped with a very complete and efficient hot water heating system, electric lights, Venetian windows on the first floor, hard wood floors, tapestry wall coverings, beamed ceilings in the living room and dining room, and is furnished complete. There is also a garage built in style to match the house with accommodations for a good sized car, a sleeping room for chauffeur or servant, a pump room, a tool room and storeroom overhead. There is a splendid 100 foot well, equipped with gasoline pumping engine and tank which supplies water under pressure to the house. The house also has a fire hose system one hose on each floor. For complete up to date equipment I believe that the place has not its equal in Fort Myers and is located as it is within fifteen minutes walk of the heart of the town and beautifully situated on the banks of the Caloosahatchee Bay. I know of no more ideal location.

If you would be interested in this property I would be glad to go into the matter more fully with you. I am sending herewith two photographs which I will be glad to have you return if you are not interested.

Very truly yours,
Robert W. Smith

Ford's assistant secretary, C. S. Anderson, sent this reply to Smith on March 13, 1916:

Your letter to Mr. Ford of March 7th, bringing to his attention the fact you have recently placed your winter home the Mangoes at Ft Myers, Fla on the market, has been referred to the writer for attention.

Mr. Ford would not be interested in property of this kind as he does not visit Florida enough to warrant a purchase there. We thank you, however, for having brought this to our attention.

Very truly yours,
C. S. Anderson

Correspondence from Ford's general secretary, Ernest Liebold, to Smith on April 13 asking the price resulted in Smith's real estate agent,

The Fords camping with the Edisons and John Burroughs in the Everglades of Florida in February 1914. This trip sparked Henry's interest in Florida as a winter retreat. (P.0.755)

James Hutton of Fort Myers, setting a price of $25,000 on April 20. On May 26, by telegram, $20,000 was offered by Ford's secretary, Anderson. Hutton, on May 27, wired that he could accept $22,500. Ford would not budge, and Hutton, on May 31, accepted a price of $20,000 on behalf of Smith. Months were involved in examining the abstract of title, utilizing a lawyer in Jacksonville recommended by the Jacksonville Ford dealer as being knowledgeable in Florida state law. Smith became impatient with the long wait for his money. The check for $20,000 was sent to him on August 10, 1916. Final settlement with both Henry's and Clara's names on the deed is recorded as December 20, 1916.

By October, Killian Melber of Melber Floral Company of Fort Myers was hired by the Fords to be responsible for having the orchard properly fertilized, pruned, and sprayed. An inventory of furnishings found that there was a scarcity of bedding, dishes, and silverware. Furnishings did not at all meet Clara's standards. There is little evidence that the Fords stayed there during the winter of 1916–17. In October 1917, Hutton wrote to Liebold as follows:

The restored Fort Myers, Florida, residence once owned by the Fords and known as the Mangoes. The home fronts MacGregor Boulevard facing south, and the backyard extends to the Caloosahatchee River, where there is a dock. The Mangoes, immediately adjacent to the Edison home, was used regularly by the Fords as a winter home from the time of its purchase in 1916 to 1931, when Thomas Edison died. The Fords finally sold the home in 1945. In this 1997 photograph, most of the tropical shrubbery and citrus so appealing to the Fords in the early days no longer appears. The city of Fort Myers now owns the Ford home, and it is maintained as a public museum along with the Edison home. (Photograph courtesy of Jim Niccum.)

Mrs. Alfred G. Vanderbilt has written, through her agents, for accommodations here in Fort Myers for the winter. It occurred to me that if Ford does not expect to be down this winter he might be willing to lease his place for one season, and if so, I wish you would advise me.

In November 1917, Melber sent a shipment of three boxes of grapefruit and two boxes of oranges to Clara and another similar shipment in December. Clara was very concerned about the poor condition of the fruit upon its arrival in Dearborn. Melber tried to explain the reasons for the imperfections in the citrus fruit, and Liebold repeatedly specified to Melber the necessary manner of shipment to prevent spoilage. Clara enjoyed her citrus, and the fruit from her orchard at the Mangoes was to be a continuing problem until the property was sold thirty years later.

For the next fifteen years, the Fords and the Edisons spent a portion of their winters side by side. The Edisons, however, spent a more lengthy period at Fort Myers than did the Fords. Edison had his own laboratory across MacGregor Boulevard where he could work. Ford had no such laboratory on his property and kept constantly in touch with his business in Dearborn. The Fords usually limited their stay to little more than the month of February. Most appealing to them both were the exotic trees on the property, which had not been noted in Smith's description. Described by a botanist, they included:

> a giant Mallaluca Lucadendorn, probably one of the largest in the area. Beside it is the Ficus Exotica, with its amazing maze of roots. And then there is the large Banyan tree. There is a magnificent night blooming Cereus, that blooms almost suddenly under an October moon. And the fragrance of the Jasmines and Cabbage Palms are seasonal delights. In certain seasons there is lush bloom on the Jolia and the Vanilla Orchid.

Although she was at the Mangoes but a short time each year, Clara Ford took great interest in the grounds, gardens, and orchards. She was very fond of citrus fruits, and whenever she complained in the least about arthritis, Henry would accuse her of drinking too much orange juice. She also took charge of interior furnishings. The bills from the Robb & Stucky Company, a Fort Myers dealer in "Furniture, Rugs and Victrolas," list items of furniture, window shades, drapes, slip covers, and a refrigerator, all charged to Mrs. Henry Ford. Clara must have refurnished the entire house. An undated "list of material for Florida" includes the following:

6 rattan chairs	1 small mirror
1 rattan couch	1 small table
2 lawn seats, rustic	1 swivel chair
2 beds	1 drafting table
2 bed rails	1 drafting table base
1 dresser	1 drafting tools
2 dresser glasses	1 small rocking chair
1 dresser glass	1 folding bed
1 glass top table	2 large mats
1 dresser	1 bundle small mats
1 small table	2 sets bed springs
1 dressing table	2 mattresses
1 writing desk	4 bed rails
3 bbls. dishes	3 electric floor lamps

2 plain mattresses	2 beds
2 box mattresses	1 cedar chest
1 clock	1 bunch rag rugs
1 mirror	2 nail pullers
1 rocking chair	1 siding chisel
4 dining room chairs	1 crt. curtain poles
4 table stands	7 pkgs. chair cushions
1 umbrella	1 melodeon
1 lawn table	4 lawn chairs

In January 1918, the house was ready for occupation by the Fords. That same month, Melber had installed for them a "Buckeye" Triplex Electric Pump on the well to replace the pump powered by the gasoline engine. That May, a bid of $450 to paint the house was offered to Liebold, who responded, "figure entirely out of proportion, therefore suggest leaving the matter stand."

In June 1922, an additional 35 feet of property frontage was purchased from Charles W. Stribling for $13,500. In February 1929, Clara was dealing with the Thomas A. Esling Company of Detroit. She was having them supply to Fort Myers:

37 pair glass curtains of 40" ecru marquisette made to slip on rod with plain hems & heading
4 pair hangings and 4 valances and dressing table skirt of green stripe cretonne and 1 small pad covering the cretonne
1²/₃ yards plain chintz for dressing table top
10⅝ yards cretonne for screen
9 pair hangings of warp print complete with painted pole, rings, brackets and ends
Hardware: 168 brass rod
6 pair small brackets
30 pair large brackets
6 slip covers of green linen print for owner's cushions
1 swing cushion covered in green stripe
4 down pillows covered in stripe
6 down pillows covered in linen

The above order was priced at $892.77.

The Fords had been using their private railroad car, the *Fair Lane,* to travel to and from Fort Myers. On the *Fair Lane,* they brought a sizable supply of foods. The following list was labeled "Shipped to Florida on *Fair Lane"* and dated February 1, 1930:

8 Broilers	12 Quarts Milk
2 Hens	6 Quarts Cream
2 Capons	4 Quarts Buttermilk
6 Wild Ducks	15 Dozen Eggs
5 Pheasants	1 Dressed Ham

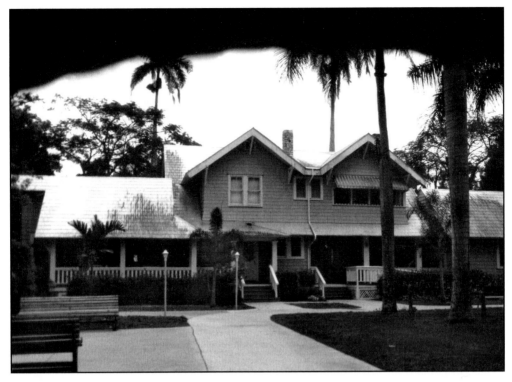

The rear of the Ford winter home in Fort Myers, Florida, as it appeared in 1997. (Photograph courtesy of Jim Niccum.)

10# Butter in Crocks	2 Pork Loins
12# Butter in 1# packages	2 Spare Ribs
10# Cottage Cheese	25 Pork Sausages

At about two-day intervals between February 6 and March 1, eleven express shipments from Dearborn replenished these same items. During the winter of 1930–31, Henry Ford was hurrying to develop the V-8 engine for his car. In order to keep abreast of its progress, he had two of his engineers bring prototypes of the new engine from Dearborn to Fort Myers, together with a portable dynamometer, to test the engines. It is said that the two Ford engineers stayed in Ford's "guest house" while in Fort Myers.

By 1931, the Fords had engaged Frank M. Stout of the Home Insurance Agency in Fort Myers as overseer of their property. A note in Clara's handwriting reads:

For Mr. Stout.

Clear out walk from front door, make far end as wide as part near house. Clean out furns and growth on both sides of Mango trees as I explained to you. Take away flower bed on south side of little pump house, and plant clump of bamboo. Take vegetable garden away from

At Fort Myers about 1920, the Fords appear to have Thomas Edison as their guest on the enclosed veranda of the Mangoes. Clara has in her lap a copy of *The Spur*, a magazine of arts and decoration. (0.1346)

present place, and replace with grass in garden next to the Edison fence, plant 2 or 3 rows carrots, 2 rows onions, half row parsley.

Flowers — do not plant verbenas, carnations, salvia, in fact plant only calendula nasturtions. I should like a small bed of pansies if you can find a place where they will be likely to grow.

Plant the driveway just the same, only not so much pink, more dusty miller.

Kitchen sink only 2 years old. Plumber says ruined by grape fruit.

On August 12, 1931, Stout sent the following letter to Frank Campsall at Henry Ford's office:

The following work outlined by Mrs. Ford has been completed: the Fern and Bryophyllum bed at the left hand side of the front porch has been cut back and the path widened going to the Edison grounds.

The path leading from porch to front sidewalk between the mango trees has been widened and greatly improved by trimming back the fern.

Pandanus on left side going from house to small gate has been cut back.

The small flower bed on the street side of the pump house has been taken out and the pump house will be shielded from view by a clump of bamboo planted immediately in front.

Also the garden has been disposed of and has been planted over with grass. The only thing remaining here is the Papaya trees.

The Bohemia tree that formerly stood on the left front side of the house about half way to the front walk has been moved over to the right side of the grove where it has more light and is doing fine.

In addition to the above, I have had the driveway gate widened and a new approach built so that it is level with the street.

Thomas Edison died at Orange, New Jersey, on October 21, 1931, and the Fords never again spent winters at the Mangoes. Stout continued to oversee the property and had the same trouble as Melber in getting citrus fruits to Dearborn in a manner that pleased Clara. From July 1938 until the property was sold, the Mangoes was rented under Stout's supervision.

On August 22, 1944, Lewis Conant, then occupant of the Mangoes, wrote this letter to Henry Ford:

As you know we have had a disastrous hurricane strike Fort Myers last Wednesday night and I thought you might be interested to know how your property here went through it.

The worst of the storm ran from about ten o'clock Wednesday night to about noon Thursday, with high winds, seas, and water after that. Your house here was undamaged, we boarded up the french windows and the water in the river came up to about one hundred feet of the house. The large mango tree next to the servants wing crashed and just missed the house but took down our electric wires, several smaller trees were blown down and nearly all the fruit is gone. Your sea wall stood up but is badly washed out behind it. The two royals in front of the house stood up unexpectedly. We were without water, gas, phone for two days and are still without the electric service.

Mrs. Edison's pier is nearly all gone and the RELIANCE, Mr. Edison's electric launch that you planned to take to Detroit was washed away and is down the beach about a mile a total wreck. I went down this morning and salvaged the wheel and shaft. You have all the electric equipment at Detroit.

Mrs. Edison fared worse than you did, most of her wall is gone, part of her house damaged by falling trees and about thirty five of her best trees are gone. Mr. Edison's Lab across the street just lost some of the roofing.

Very sincerely yours,
Lewis Conant

In February 1945, F. A. Thomson, a Ford accountant, visited the Fort Myers property. In talking to a caretaker, O. Underwood, and to the tenant, Conant, he found the premises in good physical condition but not in good financial condition. In addition to taxes of $600 annually, there were three people being paid for caretaking and only one paying rent. (Conant paid $45 per month.) The Fords were losing $1,690 annually. From real estate agent Edna F. Grady, Thomson learned that sale of the property would bring $15,000 to $20,000. In August 1945, the year the Fords sold off much of their other personal property, the Mangoes was sold to Thomas M. Biggar for $20,000.

Much more recently, in 1988, the Mangoes was sold to the city of Fort Myers for $1.5 million and is now part of the Edison-Ford Winter Estates, operated by the city as a museum.

References

Accession 1, Box 43, Fair Lane Papers. Benson Ford Research Center, HFM & GV.

Accession 62, Boxes 13, 47, 88, Henry Ford Office. Benson Ford Research Center, HFM & GV.

Accession 587, Box 13, Office of Henry and Clara Ford Estate. Benson Ford Research Center, HFM & GV.

Accession 884, Box 1, L. J. Thompson Papers. Benson Ford Research Center, HFM & GV.

48
The Yacht *Sialia*

When Henry Ford was planning the Rouge complex in 1916–17, he was studying the supply situation in regard to iron ore, coal, and limestone. With the Rouge River being dredged to allow ships to bring supplies by water, he had an interest in the availability of these raw materials from foreign countries as well as from the United States. One considerable source of iron ore and coal was in Cuba.

Ford wanted to investigate the Cuban supply situation personally but, being wary of using public transportation for the trip, asked William B. Mayo, his chief engineer, to find an oceangoing yacht with which he could make the trip in privacy. Mayo is likely to have suggested the trip inasmuch as he was well acquainted with Cuba, having sold steam power plants to sugar plantation owners before joining Ford Motor Company. Mayo searched the East Coast for several weeks to find a suitable vessel and finally located one in New York named the *Sialia*, which had been owned by James K. Stewart of Chicago, partner in the Stewart-Warner Speedometer Company. The ship was seaworthy, having crossed the Atlantic more than once and sailed the Caribbean on several occasions. She had been on a cruise in Norway when World War I erupted.

The *Sialia* was purchased by Ford on January 20, 1917, for $250,000. Ford, a bird lover, kept the name *Sialia* for the ship because it is the ornithological name for the Eastern Bluebird of the United States — the "Bluebird of Happiness." The blue bird on a yellow background became the house flag of the *Sialia* and became the official pennant of the Ford Motor Company fleet.

The *Sialia* was designed by Henry G. Gielow of Gielow and Orr in New York and was built in 1913 by Pusey and Jones in Wilmington, Delaware. It was a twin-screw steel schooner with clipper-style bow and overhung stern. Its triple expansion oil-fired steam turbines of 1,250 horsepower were built by Harlan and Hollinsworth, also of Wilmington. Its fuel capacity of 150 tons gave it a cruising radius of

---

Previously published in the *Dearborn Historian*, Vol. 29, No. 2, 1989.

6,000 miles, greater than any yacht of the *Sialia's* dimensions. But with a cruising speed of only 14 knots and a top speed of 16 knots, it was no racer. Length overall was 202 feet, 7 inches, with beam of 27 feet; gross tonnage was 552. A one-kilowatt Telefunken wireless system was installed by Atlantic Communication Company on February 3, 1917, and rented to Ford for $53 a month.

The *Sialia* had been decorated by Seessel, Inc., of New York. The interior finish was of hardwoods. For the owner and guests, there were five double and four single staterooms accommodating fourteen people or more, in addition to quarters for officers and crew. The 119-foot deck house also contained saloon, dining room, and smoking room.

This was Ford's first yacht. He did not belong to a yacht club and had no intention of joining one. Registering a yacht with the government without association with a club was rather unique, it seems.

The yacht was berthed at Brooklyn, New York, when Ford took possession on February 16, 1917. By February 21, barely a month following purchase, the Fords and their guests were starting their first trip on the *Sialia* — their trip to Cuba, which is fairly well documented. The guests from Dearborn included William B. Mayo and the family of George Brubaker. Brubaker was the husband of Clara Ford's sister Eva. With the Brubakers were their daughters Grace and Bernice. In their private railroad car, the Fords next picked up John Burroughs at Roxbury, New York, and proceeded by rail to Charleston, South Carolina, where they all embarked for the cruise. S. J. Presser, captain of the *Sialia*, had brought the ship down from New York.

After two days at sea, the party stopped very briefly at the Harvey Firestone residence on the east coast of Florida. From there, they sailed around the tip of Florida, reaching Fort Myers on February 27, where their motor launch took them to Thomas Edison's home on the Caloosahatchee River. Then it was off to Havana, where they arrived on March 1, when Burroughs wrote as follows in his diary:

> Our boat is anchored near where the *Maine* was sunk. Our wireless keeps us posted on the news. Every night, over our heads, here in the dark air, darts and shoots all the important news, no one the wiser except as it is revealed by this instrument. A network of pulsing lines overhead which our senses are too dull to apprehend. It is such a mystery and magic as the ages of superstition and ignorance never dreamed of. The news is typed on a sheet of paper and given to Mr. Ford. This is the news you get the next morning.

With the *Sialia* anchored in Havana Harbor, the businessmen, with Ford automobiles at their disposal, visited coffee and sugar plantations, including those of Mayo's friend Marscho Faschio and a man named Pelayo. Staying on the ship a good deal, Burroughs paid close attention

A nice view of the *Sialia* in open water with pennants flying. The masts supported radio aerial wires rather than sails. Between 1917 and 1929, Henry and Clara Ford used the vessel to cruise the Great Lakes, the Atlantic coast, and the Caribbean. Clara was the one who wanted the yacht. Henry said, "OK, if you never ask what the thing costs." He knew that having a yacht would be very expensive; also, his stomach did not do at all well on the water. (P.0.4981)

to the radio telegraph for news of his ailing wife at home in Roxbury. The ladies, with power launch at their disposal and private automobiles on shore, toured Havana and its outskirts.

The *Sialia* left Havana on March 6, 1917. On the return trip, a violent storm arose, sending the ship into such pitching that it is said none of the guests could remain on their feet with the exception of little two-year-old Bernice with her very low center of gravity. While cruising the Caribbean, the *Sialia* was ordered to report for inspection by the Naval Reserve Forces. A letter dated March 5, 1917, indicated the ship had been enrolled for Naval Coast Defense. Ford could do nothing but agree to release the *Sialia* whenever needed for the war. After reaching Charleston, the party disembarked, returning home again by train. Presser and crew returned the ship to New York. As soon as Ford and his guests had left the ship, Ernest Liebold, Ford's keeper of the exchequer, ordered Presser to reduce the crew considerably. This trip to Cuba seems not to have resulted in either iron ore or coal being shipped to the Rouge plant from Cuba. Later on, however, Ford did purchase exceptionally high-grade iron ore for his Rouge furnaces from South America and Africa.

After about two weeks in New York, the *Sialia* was brought by way

While Henry Ford and William Mayo attended to business in Cuba, John Burroughs (far left), Clara, her sister Eva Brubaker, and Eva's two daughters, Grace and Bernice, spent much of their time onshore in Havana. (0.33)

of Québec and the St. Lawrence Seaway to Cleveland for repairs, arriving on May 12, 1917. The following letter from Liebold to the secretary of the Navy explains the situation at that time:

Hon. Josephus Daniels
Secretary of the Navy
Washington, D.C.

My dear Mr. Daniels:

I have your telegram of the 15th in answer to my inquiry of the 11th. On May 12th I wired the U S Navy Special Board for Patrol Vessels as follows:

"Mr Ford authorizes immediate release Steam Yacht *Sialia* for sale to you at actual cost. Vessel now at Cleveland for repairs. To whom will we assign insurance policies and when will you take possession? Wire answer immediately."

We had previously ordered the boat from New York to Halifax where Mr. Ford expected to load the Tractor patents and models and with five or six of our men, she was to be sent to England, but while awaiting orders at Halifax, the Canadian Government furnished transportation on one of their troop ships, which was convoyed to England. The vessel was therefore ordered to Detroit in the event that we might wish to make further shipments of material to England.

However, in going through the canals, the Yacht broke a propeller shaft coupling and the Captain was instructed to proceed to Cleveland under slow speed, where she is now in dry dock undergoing repairs.

The actual cost to Mr. Ford was $260,000, but we understand that the Board has appraised her at $220,000. Mr. Ford is indeed very glad to be of service and awaiting your further commands, I am,

Very truly tours,
E. G. Liebold

On May 25, 1917, the *Sialia* left Cleveland for the ocean and its wartime service. So after just one trip on his first yacht, Ford lost it to the Navy without its having ever reached Detroit or Dearborn.

Exactly one month after the Armistice, the Navy announced plans for the sale of groups of ships, including U.S.S. *Sialia*, SP-54. It was not until April 1920, however, that Ford seemed to take an interest in buying it back. The original *Sialia* was found to be in poor repair, having been abused and neglected and with several expensive items missing, such as propellers, motor launch, and wireless. Daniels, in this letter, instructs his commandant to release the vessel to Ford:

April 13, 1920
From: The Secretary of the Navy
To: Commandant, Sixth Naval District
Subject: "*SIALIA*" S.P.-543-sale of.

Enclosures: Two copies of Bill of Sale

1. Mr. Henry Ford, Detroit, Michigan, the former owner of the "*SIALIA*" has agreed in negotiations with the Board of Review to repurchase the "*SIALIA*" at a cost of one hundred and sixty-eight thousand, five hundred dollars ($168,500.00). Enclosed herewith you will find two copies of Bill of Sale which, when completed in all respects, will constitute your authority to deliver the "*SIALIA*" to him.

2. It is understood that all radio, ordnance equipment and listening devices, if any are installed, will be removed from this vessel before delivery.

3. You are requested to communicate with the owner direct and it is the desire of the Navy Department that the transfer should be completed at as early a date as practicable. The actual date of the transfer should be inserted in the blanks on the last line of the Bill of Sale.

Josephus Daniels.

The ship was released by the Navy on April 20, 1920, and certificate of ownership mailed to the new master, Captain Perry E. Stakes, on May 4. Propellers were found in California and the motor launch located during May and returned to Ford.

The *Sialia* had to be brought from Brooklyn Navy Yard back to Detroit, where a dock was leased at 1524 East Jefferson Avenue. In late May 1920, Sidney Houghton, a naval designer, started work refurbishing the *Sialia* at a cost of approximately $150,000. As soon as refurbishing was complete, Ford took Edsel, Liebold, Mayo, Clarence Avery, and other Ford Motor Company men on the *Sialia* to Escanaba on Lake Michigan to inspect mine and forest properties he had just purchased in Michigan's Upper Peninsula. Between August 1 and August 13 of that same summer, the *Sialia* was at Seal Harbor, Maine, summer home of the Edsel Fords. Other trips to Seal Harbor were taken during subsequent summers. Frequent family excursions were made between Detroit and Lake St. Clair. The *Sialia,* usually berthed at the Rouge plant, picked up guests at the foot of East Grand Boulevard for the outings. Henry's sister Margaret Ruddiman and her daughter Catherine, together with Thomasine Gardner and other members of the Gardner family, were treated to a cruise to the Ford cottage at Harbor Beach on Lake Huron during the summer of 1920.

Ford was never quite satisfied with the speed of the *Sialia* with its twin steam-turbine engines. Three years after he had repurchased it from the Navy, he bought the giant cargo ships the *Henry Ford II* and the *Benson Ford* in 1924. He was very satisfied with these. These huge carriers had each been fitted with a rather unique opposed-piston diesel engine. Ford decided he would like diesels of smaller size but similar design in the *Sialia.* So the yacht was taken to the Sun Shipbuilding and Drydock Company at Chester, Pennsylvania, in 1925, cut in two, and a 21-foot section added amidships, after which twin diesels were installed. This major operation on the *Sialia* is said to have cost Ford $1 million. The sad result was that the *Sialia* was a bit slower than before.

The *Sialia* seems not to have been used as much by the Fords as one might have expected. The Fords began to use their big ore carriers for trips on the Great Lakes. Henry, in particular, enjoyed vacationing on the mighty freighters, and the *Sialia* pennant was seen on the big ships whenever the owner was aboard.

In June 1929, Ford sold the *Sialia* to the A. N. Andrews Investment Corporation in New York City. In 1938, ownership was in the name of Eleanor U. Andrews of Freestone Castle, Greenwich, Connecticut. The *Sialia* next became the *Yankee Clipper* when, in 1938, she was sold to the Clipper Line in Philadelphia. It had gone into commercial use. The U.S. Navy again commandeered the vessel in 1941, naming it the U.S.S. *Coral.* It was sold by the Navy in July 1947, to John J. Duane of Quincy, Massachusetts, and his company scrapped it in Quincy in 1948 at age thirty-five after having served in two world wars.

The yacht *Sialia* docked at its home port at the Rouge plant in Dearborn. In the background are the mighty Hulett unloaders and Mead-Morrison transfer bridges which unload the Ford lake freighters that bring ore, limestone, and coal to the plant. (P.188.7884)

In order to have a boat of some kind for his personal use, Ford had purchased in April 1919 a gasoline yacht named *Widgeon,* which was renamed *Sialia II* by Ford. This boat was kept by Ford until April 1920, when the original *Sialia* was repurchased from the Navy. The *Sialia II* was sold to a Dr. H. Torrey of Detroit for $95,000 in May 1920 and renamed *Tamarack.*

Ford had still another yacht, which he bought in 1935. Its name was *Truant.* It had been owned by Truman H. Newberry, secretary of the Navy under Theodore Roosevelt and later a U.S. senator from Michigan. The *Truant,* a 138-foot yacht built in 1892, was richly appointed in teakwood and mahogany. Samuel Insull had bought it in 1926, but after his vast utilities empire began to crumble, he sold it to the Naval Militia in Chicago, where it was used to train Naval Reserves. It was transferred to the Sea Scouts in 1933 for training cruises. Ford purchased the ship from the Sea Scouts in 1935. After extensive over-hauling, he donated the *Truant* in July 1941 to the Sixth Naval Training Station in Chicago, where his grandson Henry Ford II was in training. At Chicago, it was again used as a Naval training ship.

References

Accession 62, Box 30. Benson Ford Research Center, HFM & GV.

Accession 284, Box 26. Benson Ford Research Center, HFM & GV.

Accession 384, Box 1, L. J. Thompson Papers. Benson Ford Research Center, HFM & GV.

49
The Railway Car *Fair Lane*

Following the institution of the five-dollar day in 1914, Henry Ford found it increasingly difficult to travel without immediate recognition by the public and constant annoyance by reporters. Traveling locally by automobile, he could maintain a modicum of privacy, but for long trips he needed some other form of private conveyance. For travel on water, he purchased the steam yacht *Sialia* in 1917. For land travel privacy, he arranged on February 18, 1920, with the Pullman Company for the purchase of a private railroad car to be named *Fair Lane*. By then, Ford also had decided to purchase his own railroad — the Detroit, Toledo & Ironton — in which he obtained controlling interest on July 9, 1920.

Ford was anxious to have the *Fair Lane* private car by September 1920 in order to travel by rail to Michigan's Upper Peninsula and examine his recently purchased Michigan Iron, Land & Lumber Company holdings. Response from the Pullman manufacturing department was: "we will use our endeavor to do this, but we cannot guarantee to do so under the present labor and materials." Arrangements were that Pullman would prepare general specifications and drawings and deliver at the earliest practicable date on the basis of cost of labor and materials, including 150 percent on direct labor for overhead or shop expense, plus 20 percent for profit. Payment was to be 25 percent paid when the car was "laid down," 25 percent when the car was "in paint," and the balance of the calculated price when the car was completed.

The *Fair Lane* was delivered to Dearborn from Pullman's Kensington, Illinois, shops on June 23, 1921, at a cost of $159,000. This price was higher than Ford had anticipated. Pullman justified the high price in a letter to Ford:

> When considering the cost of this car you must take into consideration the quality of material, designs of interior finish, and class of workmanship, demanded by your designer, Mr. Houghton. In this respect, this is without doubt, one of the most elegant and expensive design of car we have ever built, as are also some of the materials, such as Monel roofing, walnut interior finish with specially matched veneering, made to order. Window curtain material with back to match draperies, etc.

Henry and Clara Ford's private railroad car, the *Fair Lane*. The 82-foot-long all-steel car weighing 100 tons was built by the Pullman Company in 1920-21 at a cost of $159,000. The interior was designed by Sidney Houghton of London, who also designed the interior of the yacht *Sialia*. The *Fair Lane* was used by the Fords from 1921 to 1942, when it was given up because of limitations on the use of private railroad cars during World War II. Although sold in 1942, it has found its way back to Dearborn and the Henry Ford Museum. (U.78777)

Much of the delay in delivery was caused by the interior furnishings being designed by Sidney Houghton, who was traveling between his New York and London offices seeking exotic materials for Clara Ford to approve before installation by the Pullman Company. At times, Houghton's whereabouts were not known, and Clara was slow in making her decisions. Houghton and Clara had worked together before when the *Sialia* was being furnished.

The *Fair Lane* was 82 feet long, 10 feet wide, and 14 feet high, and it weighed 100 tons. Construction was of steel with an attractive rear observation platform. It was equipped to accommodate eight passengers together with attending cook and porter. In addition to relatively spacious sleeping quarters, there was a kitchen, a dining room seating eight, and, toward the end of the car, a comfortable observation lounge.

To stock the *Fair Lane* for passenger travel, Clara compiled a list of 230 items of crockery, 144 items of glassware, 169 pieces of silverware, 38 pantry items, and 79 types of kitchen utensils including 28 pans. The list would service a hotel of modest size. Table linens numbered 189, with 10 caps and jackets for cooks and 15 jackets for waiters. Sleeping linens numbered 266, including 80 each of sheets and pillow slips. The linens were intentionally labeled *Fairlane* rather than *Fair Lane*, perhaps to discourage theft.

Between trips, the *Fair Lane* was housed in a train shed on a Michigan Central siding next to Ford's flour mill on Oakwood Boulevard in Dearborn. The first trip from Dearborn was by way of the Wabash Railway to Decatur, Alabama, on the Tennessee River, where Henry Ford was attempting to gain control of Muscle Shoals. The voucher, dated June 28, 1921, for the round trip was $730.08. Other trips during that first year included one to Boston and return; two round trips to Iron Mountain, Michigan; two trips to and from Walling, Nutall, and Kenova, West Virginia; a trip to Washington, D.C.; and four round trips to New York City. The railroads charged Ford $11,130 to haul the *Fair Lane* on these trips during 1921.

Charges made by the various railroads for hauling a private car depended on several factors. The basic charge for moving the empty car without passengers was equal to 10 passenger fares. The car and passengers attached to a regularly scheduled train called for the fare of 25 passengers. If the car and its passengers were moved as a special train, cost was that of 125 passengers. The *Fair Lane* was most often attached to a regularly scheduled train such as the *Detroiter* going to New York or the *Wolverine* coming back from New York. On a single trip, more than one railroad was often involved. The New York Central, with its tracks in Dearborn, arranged passage for each entire trip. On a trip from Dearborn to Ways Station, Georgia, the New York Central would haul the car from Dearborn to Cincinnati, the Southern Railway from Cincinnati to Atlanta, the Central of Georgia from Atlanta to Savannah, and either the Atlantic Coast Line or the Seaboard Air Line from Savannah to Ways Station. The trip to and from Dearborn to Ways Station in 1940, for example, going by way of Washington, cost $896 going down and $1,117 coming back. Included in the return fare was the cost of "parking" the car on a siding at Ways for forty-three days.

In comparison with the *Sialia*, however, the *Fair Lane* was much less expensive both in initial cost and especially in operating costs. Ford never complained about the cost of the *Fair Lane* as he often did about the cost of the *Sialia*. His complaints about *Sialia* expenses were not heard by Clara, however, who liked her luxuries.

Ernest Liebold, Ford's secretary, handled nearly all of the correspondence between Ford and the Pullman Company. On December 26, 1922, Liebold notified the Pullman people concerning "vibration in riding in Mr. Ford's private car." After sending the car to Kensington for inspection, Pullman's response was:

> beg to advise that upon going over this car we found some of the wheels slid flat and a number of pedestal bolts as well as center plate bolts loose, all of which causes would contribute to the trouble experienced on this car when brakes were applied. On cars in Railroad service these features are ordinarily looked after by the yards forces while cars are laying over in terminals, but I presume you have had this car stored in your own yards or sheds and as a result these features were overlooked.

In March 1923, Liebold wrote as follows to the Pullman Company:

> Mr. Ford is contemplating the construction of a new private car. He seems to be of the opinion that he would have it built somewhat longer than the one he is using at present and would like very much to know the maximum length of Pullman cars that have been built.
>
> I would like to have you submit designs or drawings of such cars if you still have them.
>
> Very truly yours,
> E. G. Liebold

It seems, however, that Ford temporarily gave up the idea of a longer private car and went on using the *Fair Lane*.

The *Fair Lane* continued to be used for both business and recreation. Edsel Ford as well as Henry used the car often to conduct Ford Motor Company business in Washington, New York, and elsewhere. Clara used the *Fair Lane* frequently to shop in New York with her Dearborn friends, and trips were made to Ellsworth, Maine, the closest railroad station to the Edsel Ford "Skylands" home on Mount Desert Island. Henry and Clara used the car to travel south in January to their Mangoes winter home in Fort Myers, Florida, and later, when they built their new Richmond winter home at Ways Station, Georgia, the *Fair Lane* was often parked on the railroad siding through the months of February and March.

Clara, in particular, enjoyed traveling by rail to New York. In the early days, Henry and Clara together were often escorted around the city and taken to various attractions by their friends the Gaston Plantiffs. Gaston was manager of the eastern sales district for Ford Motor Company. Henry, however, did not like to go to New York, where he was sure to be recognized. So Clara often planned trips there with a few of her friends from Dearborn. Quite often, these were her nieces, daughters of her brother Roy Bryant. Clara would have the *Fair Lane* parked at Mott Haven Yards connected with Grand Central Station, and a Ford Motor Company driver was assigned to take her and her friends from place to place according to her wishes. Clara was not recognized by the public, she shopped freely, and occasionally she met Mina Edison or Idabelle Firestone at one of the stores.

When Clara stayed in New York for several days, she would register at a hotel such as the Biltmore or the Ritz-Carlton under an assumed name and would go in and out freely without recognition. She had several standing accounts with New York stores, purchasing her clothing, for example, from Stein & Blaine, stationery from Tiffany, and jewelry from Cartier. Clara was well known in these New York establishments, and she purchased expensive items several times each year.

In March 1929, a Pullman car inspection engineer rode from Detroit to the Pullman yards at Chicago on the *Fair Lane*. He reported the need for no fewer than twenty-two major repairs and in addition recommended: "Exterior of *Fair Lane* should receive color coat of varnish and two varnish coats as condition will soon be such shape as to require this work." The car was kept at the Pullman yards two weeks for the work to be done; the bill was $7,719.95.

In May 1929, Henry Ford was preparing for Light's Golden Jubilee to honor Thomas Edison on October 21, 1929. For this event, he wanted a nineteenth-century railroad passenger coach and questioned the Pullman Company concerning drawings and photographs describing vintage cars. These were sent to Ford, with an offer to build him such a car. He did not deal with Pullman, however, but instead found an old wooden coach in Maine and had it beautifully restored by his own workmen in Dearborn.

By the mid-1930s, Pullman passenger cars were being air conditioned, while the *Fair Lane* had only its original fans. Edsel Ford inquired of Pullman concerning the design of an air-conditioning system for the *Fair Lane*. The cost of their recommended system would have been $12,000. However, a letter from Liebold to Pullman-Standard Car Manufacturing Company in October 1935 reads as follows:

> Referring to your letter of September 21st, with quotation on specifications for air conditioning of Mr. Ford's private car "Fair Lane."
>
> In discussing this matter further, Mr. Ford is of the opinion that he might consider building a new private car. The "Fair Lane" Mr. Ford feels is rather small for his use and would therefore like to know if you would submit floor plans of a car showing additional space sufficient for another room.
>
> Awaiting your reply,
> E. G. Liebold

Drawings dated December 30, 1935, were submitted to Ford, and Edsel soon gave up trying to have the *Fair Lane* air conditioned.

No new *Fair Lane* was built, and it was Clara who was most disappointed when, in 1942, private cars such as the *Fair Lane* were no longer allowed because of rigid war restrictions. That year, Henry, Clara, and their servants took the *Fair Lane* on February 28 to Richmond Hill by way of Berry, Georgia, and returned to Dearborn by way of Tuskegee, Alabama, on March 19. It was Clara who took the *Fair Lane* on its last trip as their private car. Again, it was to New York, on April 26, for a four-day shopping trip. For the Fords, the *Fair Lane* had traveled on more than 400 journeys between 1921 and 1942, with each and every trip's date, destination, and charges recorded. Cost of parking the *Fair Lane* in New York at Mott Haven Storage, for example, had increased from $2.59 per day in 1921 to $7.17 per day in 1942.

Ford knew the *Fair Lane* was in poor mechanical condition, and he told Liebold to sell it for $25,000. It was sold to St. Louis Southwestern Railway Lines in November 1942 for executive use. Subsequently, it was first modernized, then neglected, and wound up in very poor condition at a Cherokee resort at Tahlequah, Oklahoma. From there, it was rescued by Detroiter Richard P. Kughn, who had it fully restored and returned to Detroit. On December 11, 1996, Mr. and Mrs. Kughn donated the restored *Fair Lane* to Henry Ford Museum & Greenfield Village. So now, the *Fair Lane*, in all its elegance, is back home within just a few car lengths of its twenty-year car-shed location in Dearborn.

References

Accession 1, Box 103, *Fair Lane* Papers. Benson Ford Research Center, HFM & GV.

Accession 285, Boxes 15, 38, 144, 1043, 1949, Henry Ford Office Papers. Benson Ford Research Center, HFM & GV.

Accession 384, Box 1, L. J. Thompson Papers. Benson Ford Research Center, HFM & GV.

Accession 587, Box 12, Office of Henry and Clara Ford Estate. Benson Ford Research Center, HFM & GV.

Vertical File, Railroads—*Fair Lane* Pullman Car. Benson Ford Research Center, HFM & GV.

50
Wayside Inn

Prior to Henry Wadsworth Longfellow's poem *Tales of a Wayside Inn,* this structure was known as the Red Horse Tavern. To quote from the famous poem, "And half effaced by rain and shine, the Red Horse prances on the sign." Built in 1683 by David Howe, the inn was originally called Howe Tavern. After David's death, his son Ezekiel Howe in 1746 gave the inn the name Red Horse Tavern. The property remained somewhat neglected but still in the possession of the Howe family until 1897, when it was sold to Edward Lemon of Malden, Massachusetts, who refurbished the building and again opened it to the public.

Lemon died in 1920. Although his wife kept the house, she was hoping that someone would buy the place from her and continue the inn's old traditions as a hostelry. L. Loring Brooks, a near neighbor, was able to interest some prominent Boston people in the idea. Eight individuals, including Charles W. Iliot, Henry Cabot Lodge, Mrs. Nathaniel Thayer, and Dr. Myles Standish, decided to issue invitations to two hundred other prominent people throughout the United States, asking them to become shareholders in a trust to acquire and hold the Wayside Inn. On November 2, 1922, Henry Ford received a letter from Brooks containing the following solicitation:

> Mrs. Lemon, the present proprietress and landlady of the Wayside Inn, South Sudbury, Mass., informed me that you called at the Inn with Mrs. Ford last week.
>
> A trust has been formed — the Wayside Inn Trust — for the purpose of taking over the Inn, preserving its historical side and also having Mr. Robert P. Packett of Franconia, New Hampshire — a famous inkeeper — as manager. I am taking the liberty of sending you under separate cover by registered mail papers on this trust.
>
> I am sorry that I could not have met you and Mrs. Ford while you were at the Inn. I live on the hill opposite the Inn in the summer and have recently come to town for the winter months.
>
> We have received a large number of letters from historical societies approving our plan. They believe the Inn should be continued to be run as an inn and not as a museum. If action had not been taken, it would undoubtedly have gone into a road house or an antique shop, and surely as Wayside Inn is known all over the United States through

The restored Wayside Inn at South Sudbury, Massachusetts, as it appeared about 1926. The inn became the headquarters for collecting antiques not only to refurbish the inn itself but also for the museum at Dearborn. Wayside Inn is now a nonprofit educational and charitable trust, the original trust having been established by Henry and Clara Ford in 1946. (P.0.3352)

Longfellow's *Tales of a Wayside Inn,* that would have been sacrilege.

We would like very much to have you and Mrs. Ford take an interest with us in this, say twenty-five or fifty shares. It will help you and you can feel that you were one of the others who made the saving of the Inn a success.

The trust runs for practically twenty years and the stockholder has no liability. It was drawn up very carefully by prominent lawyers here in Boston. I am also enclosing a list of names of some of the people who have subscribed.

Yours sincerely,
L. Loring Brooks

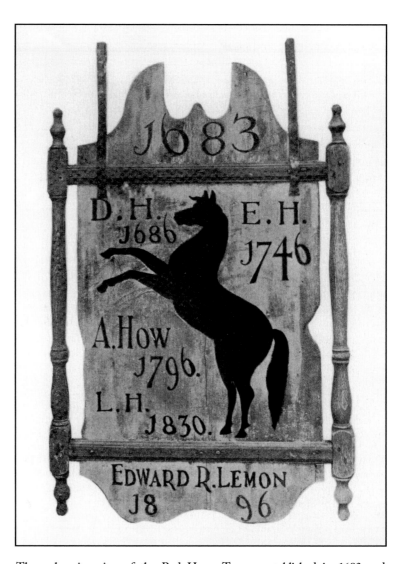

The welcoming sign of the Red Horse Tavern, established in 1683 and operated by four generations of the Howe family. Henry Ford bought the inn from the estate of Edward R. Lemon, who had purchased it in 1896. The inn began to be called the Wayside Inn after Longfellow had written *Tales of a Wayside Inn*.

There is no record of the Fords having bought stock in the Wayside Inn Trust.

It is said that Clara Ford was the one who "saved" Wayside Inn. Henry Ford was not yet into antiques. He was, however, for some reason very interested in the history of the Howe family. He had had his fill of minor stockholders and was not inclined to be a minor stockholder himself. In whatever endeavor, he wanted to be completely in charge, Clara, of course, being agreeable.

Records show that in 1923, Henry and Clara acquired Wayside Inn and 90 acres of land in Sudbury, Massachusetts, from Cora Lemon for $65,000. Closely following that transaction, the Fords purchased seventeen parcels in Framingham, sixteen parcels in Marlborough, and fifty-five more parcels in Sudbury, totaling 2,666.92 acres. The added acreage was not only for the inn but also for Ford's planned farms and schools. In front of the inn ran the old Boston Post Road with its heavy traffic. With permission, Ford proceeded to build a new stretch of roadway a mile long to provide a bypass for vehicular traffic. The new road cost him $330,831.01 and was presented to the state for one dollar.

Although they were in Dearborn, the Fords kept in very close touch with activities at Wayside. Frank Campsall, their personal secretary, was staying at the inn during 1923 and reporting on operations. In a letter to Ford dated July 21, 1923, he mentions:

> Have been thinking a good deal what is best to have the Inn continued as — that is, principally the dining feature. They very seldom, since I've been here, have over a dozen or so meals to serve, outside of the people who run the Inn. They charge $2.50 for chicken dinner, $1.50 for cold meat dinner, which is about the same as the chicken only they have cold ham, and $1.00 for tea. Prices seem high . . .

Henry's interest in antiquities began in earnest with Wayside Inn. He assigned W. W. Taylor as his full-time agent to find items suitable for refurnishing the inn. Taylor loved his work, covered all of New England, and purchased way beyond what was required for just the inn. Old objects were stored in barns near the inn, and much of the surplus was taken to the Cambridge plant of Ford Motor Company, where it was transshipped to the Fordson tractor plant in Dearborn. Clara would not have any of it in her home at Fair Lane. She is said to have told Henry that he should have his own museum in Dearborn. When Ford automobile dealers learned of his apparent obsession with antiques, they made the matter much worse by sending all sorts of old-fashioned relics to their esteemed employer.

One of the items Henry needed for his inn was the old Red Horse Tavern sign which had graced the entrance to the premises back in the days of Longfellow. Finally, the historic sign was found to be in the attic of Edward A. Huebener of Dorchester, Massachusetts. Huebener refused to sell to Ford's agents but offered to give the sign to Ford free of charge if Ford, in person, would pay him a visit. The sign being sufficiently important to Ford, he did make the trip east to meet Huebener.

After a bit of casual conversation, Huebener gladly tossed the historic sign into the trunk of Ford's limousine and agreed to accept something later from him in exchange.

Within a matter of days, Huebener wrote to Ford asking for his personal check for one cent as his price for the sign, promising to cash the check so that Ford's no doubt sizable bank account could be balanced. Ford must have felt the sign was well worth the asking price, for he promptly signed a personal check on February 28, 1924, for exactly one cent, drawn on his own account at the Dearborn State Bank, a bank Ford owned.

Huebener photocopied Ford's check and kept the original until July 24, 1924, when, in order to keep the billionaire's account balanced, he endorsed it and turned it in to the First National Bank of Boston. The canceled check was returned to the Dearborn State Bank, then to Henry Ford, and was saved with hundreds of other canceled checks at Fair Lane, the Ford home.

Utilization of the land for farming at Wayside was begun at once. During the fall of 1923, oxen was tried for plowing, and the following April, a nice pair of four-year-old Durham oxen was purchased for $200. Farther from the inn, Fordson tractors were in use. The inn had been remodeled room by room and reopened for business by February 1924. The Fords had converted a woodshed attached to the inn for facilities for their own private use. During the summer of 1924, while the Fords were entertaining the Edisons and the Firestones at Wayside Inn, the men went to Plymouth, Vermont, to visit President Coolidge. The president presented Ford with an old wooden sap bucket. After that, well-wishers from across the country began sending sap buckets of every shape and size to Ford in Dearborn.

Ford also had ideas about how children should be educated. One of his most publicized school projects at Wayside was the reconstruction in

Copy of the canceled check Henry Ford wrote to Edward Huebener in the amount of $.01.

Henry and Clara Ford greet students on the opening day in 1927 of the reconstructed Redstone School, "The Little Red Schoolhouse." As part of the ceremony, Mary's little lamb, with fleece as white as snow, was also a participant. (P.0.17627)

1926 of the Redstone School, originally built in 1798 in Sterling, Massachusetts. Ford operated the school primarily for the benefit of children of his Wayside employees. This was the Little Red Schoolhouse associated with the poem "Mary Had a Little Lamb." Ford's interest in both children and history was demonstrated when he insisted that the scene with Mary and her lamb be reenacted on the Redstone School grounds on the day the school opened. With about sixteen students, this school operated at Wayside from 1927 until 1951, accommodating grades one through four. In the fall of 1930, in order for the Redstone pupils to continue their education, Ford restored the 1849 Southwest School and offered grades five through eight. From Southwest, these pupils next attended Sudbury High School.

The picturesque old stone gristmill on the grounds of Wayside Inn in Massachusetts as it appeared in 1933 restored by Henry Ford. With machinery built by the Campbell Water Wheel Company of Philadelphia, the mill ground wheat, corn, and buckwheat on the two millstones, and the products were sold to the public in Ford's store nearby. At the inn, guests were served bread, pastry, and cakes made from the flour ground at the mill. (P.0.19816)

The largest and most beneficial school project at Wayside was the Wayside Inn Boys School, begun in 1928. Involving about thirty boys between the ages of sixteen and eighteen who had been wards of the state, the school was designed as a boarding school to provide an education while making each student financially independent. A scholarship of between $400 and $500 per year, paid monthly and based on the boy's own budget, was adjusted according to age, class, and performance. For this stipend, students were to attend standard high school academic classes as well as accomplish work assignments as required in the various Wayside industries. In 1931, the school was enlarged to fifty boys. With an academic faculty of seven and with the assistance of some eighty members of the Wayside staff, the majority of the boys were helped tremendously in supporting themselves.

The Wayside community was to be self-supporting. In addition to the inn, there were field crops of fruits, vegetables, and grains and a roadside market to sell the produce. There was a sawmill, a blacksmith shop, and an unusually attractive operating gristmill. In 1924, Ford had started building the gristmill near the site of a previous mill. He obtained four large millstones from France, which, when employed with eighteenth-century milling machinery and an overshot water wheel, produced a gristmill appearing as it might have during the American Revolution. The mill was in operation by 1929.

There was a chapel, named Martha-Mary Chapel after the mothers of Clara and Henry, respectively. The chapel was similar in appearance to six other Martha-Mary Chapels built by the Fords at various locations in the United States. As were the others, this chapel was nondenominational, with daily exercises conducted by the students of the schools. A local writer remarked: "Did you ever go to a church where the minister was under sixteen and the guest speaker was six? Where there was no creed? No collection? Where service was held on weekdays and not on Sunday?"

The innkeeper, Earl J. Boyer, maintained a daily diary which he sent to the Fords in Dearborn each week, as also did W. W. Taylor while he was searching for antiques throughout New England. The inn diaries reported names of important guests who stopped at the inn, names of employees and their wages, problems arising and their solution, menus being served to Wayside guests, and the beauty of summer flowers.

Clara was especially interested in the flower gardens. It was her primary hobby wherever she lived. Her second hobby was food and cooking, making it essential for her to approve the menus used at Wayside Inn.

Copied from Wayside Inn diaries are these two menus:

THANKSGIVING DINNER
1926

Consomme

Celery   Olives   Salted Nuts   Mints

Home Made Jelly   Cranberry Sauce

Roast Hen Turkey with Stuffing

Mashed Potatoes   French Spinach
Buttered Onions   Baked Squash

Hearts of Lettuce with Russian Dressing

Old-fashioned Plum Pudding with Cream Sauce

Pumpkin Pie   Mince Pie

Tea   Coffee   Cider

December 25th, Christmas Day

Tomato Soup

Celery   Olives   Nuts   Mints

Cranberry Sauce

Roast Stuffed Turkey

Glazed Sweet Potatoes   Mashed Turnip

Mashed White Potatoes   Green Peas

Asparagus Salad

Plum Pudding with Cream Sauce

Mince Pie   Squash Pie

Coffee   Tea   Cider

Wayside Inn was remarkably successful as long as Henry Ford was alive and pumping money into it. When he wanted to do something, he didn't pay much attention to costs. When he became feeble toward the end of World War II, and costs were revealed to Clara and Henry Ford II, the Wayside property needed to be reassessed. Losses during 1944 are recorded as $165,391.79. Since 1923, losses totaling $2,848,187.27 had been reported to the Internal Revenue Service. The inn lost more than $686,000, the farms more than $1,364,000, and the schools more than $797,000.

In July 1945, Clara Ford was notified that Ford attorneys had created the Wayside Inn Corporation under the trusteeship of Henry Ford II, B. J. Craig (treasurer of Ford Motor Company), and Frank Campsall. Deeds to the Wayside Inn property were to be turned over by Henry and Clara to the corporation. The message closed with, "The corporation would be operated by Ford Motor Company, of course, under your direction if you wish." Little by little, most of the farm land was sold until only 300 acres immediately surrounding the inn remained.

With the death of Henry Ford in April 1947, the Wayside Boys School was closed. From 1946 through 1950, when Henry Ford II, Benson, and William Clay Ford were on the Ford Foundation board, the foundation had subsidized Wayside Inn to the extent of $150,000. In 1950, Clara Ford died. By 1952, William Clay Ford was president of the Wayside Inn Corporation board, and Donald K. David, president of the Ford Foundation, was on the same board. The inn was kept open and operating until December 22, 1955, when a disheartening fire almost completely destroyed it.

After much deliberation and planning by a Wayside Inn Committee, on October 10, 1956, William Clay Ford requested of David the support of the Ford Foundation in restoring the inn. The foundation agreed to a donation of $500,000 for the building's restoration. In 1957, William Clay Ford announced that six members of the board of trustees of the National Trust for Historic Preservation would

Clara and Henry Ford sitting by a fireplace in their historic Wayside Inn, built in 1686 near South Sudbury, Massachusetts. The photograph was taken about 1925, when Henry's agents were busy scouring New England for antiques, some of which became furnishings for the restoration of Wayside Inn and some of which were sent on to Dearborn, where Ford was amassing his early American museum. (P.0.1061)

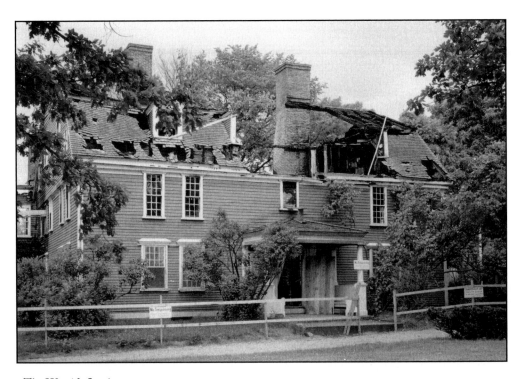

The Wayside Inn in July 1956, following the disastrous fire of the preceding December and before restoration work had begun. (P.B.12844)

be added to the Wayside Inn board. Concurrently, the National Trust accepted the responsibility for completing the restoration of the inn and administering the property. The inn reopened under the jurisdiction of the National Trust in June 1958. Wayside Inn is now designated a National Historic Site operating as both an inn and a museum.

References

Accession 1, Boxes 124–27, Fair Lane Papers. Benson Ford Research Center, HFM & GV.

Accession 23, Boxes 7, 17, Henry Ford Office. Benson Ford Research Center, HFM & GV.

Accession 111, Boxes 1–38, Wayside Inn General (Diaries). Benson Ford Research Center, HFM & GV.

Accession 292, Boxes 1–29, Frank Campsall Papers. Benson Ford Research Center, HFM & GV.

Accession 921, Box 6, William Clay Ford Papers. Benson Ford Research Center, HFM & GV.

Garfield, Curtis F., and Alison R. Ridley. *As Ancient Is This Hostelry: The Story of the Wayside Inn.* Sudbury, Mass.: Porcupine Enterprises, 1988.

51
Botsford Tavern

Botsford Tavern operated for nearly 160 years on Grand River Avenue in Farmington, Michigan. Built in 1836 by Orrin Weston, it began to be run as a tavern in 1841. Known in its early days as Sixteen-Mile House, as measured from downtown Detroit, it began serving farmers and drovers and was an official stop for the stage coach. Over the trail northwest from Detroit, the tavern was half a day's journey on horseback and a full day's trip with wagon and team. The tavern became the property of Milton G. Botsford in 1860, and Sixteen-Mile House then became known as Botsford Tavern.

Henry and Clara Ford were both bitten by the nostalgia bug during the 1920s. Henry, in particular, after he had been accused in court of not knowing history, vowed to demonstrate history by means of historical artifacts, and a means of displaying them was necessary. He needed buildings. The Ford Homestead in 1920 was first to be filled with historically accurate objects. In 1923, it was the Wayside Inn at Sudbury, Massachusetts. Remembering their youthful gaiety dancing at Botsford Tavern, both Henry and Clara agreed that it would be fun to resurrect those days, try to live them over.

In June 1924, for $100,000, Henry and Clara Ford acquired Botsford Tavern and approximately 33 acres of land from Frank P. Botsford, son of Milton G. Botsford. Thirty other small parcels surrounding the tavern property also were acquired at that time. Grand River Avenue was then being widened to carry heavy traffic, making it advisable to move the tavern back 300 feet from the widened road. With purchase of the extra land, together with extensive improvements in the properties, the investment became $602,243.07.

Within the next two years, the Fords had restored and refurnished Botsford Tavern to suit their own tastes. Largely from the surplus of antiques collected in New England for Wayside Inn, they transformed the tavern's appearance to recall the early and middle 1800s. The outward construction of the building was maintained much in its original form. Interior arrangements were modified somewhat. Both Henry and Clara Ford became personally involved in choosing furniture, carpeting, wallpaper, window treatments, and decorative items. The

The exterior of Botsford Tavern in June 1925, after it had been moved back from the road, now with an addition to the rear of the building and equipped with a new front drive and landscaping. (0.5589)

furniture they chose was simple and inexpensive in style, and much of the carpeting was of woven or hooked rag placed on painted wooden floors. Windows were neatly draped in muslin. The simple, comparatively uncluttered rooms of the Botsford Tavern as restored by the Fords were meant to illustrate the lifestyle of plain Midwestern people during the Victorian era.

Beginning with the Great Depression, neither the Botsford Tavern nor Ford's Dearborn Inn could meet expenses on its own. Occasionally, Henry and Clara would entertain their friends at the tavern. But at times, Botsford Tavern was closed for several months. By 1931, the Oakwood Hotel Company, a subsidiary of Ford Motor Company, had been formed, with Edsel Ford as president and offices at Ford Motor Company headquarters on Schaefer Road in Dearborn. In 1934, Henry and Clara Ford agreed to lease Botsford Tavern together with furnishings and equipment to the Oakwood Hotel Company for a term of five years for payment of one dollar. An agreement already had been made between the Oakwood Hotel Company and the L. G. Treadway Service Corporation, a hotel operating company, to manage both the Dearborn Inn and the Botsford Tavern.

Botsford Tavern operating losses charged to the Oakwood Hotel Company for 1934 were reported as $3,550. In the dining room in

1935, the hostess was being paid $150 per month, cooks $75, and part-time waitresses averaged $25 per month. With operating expenses of $17,480 and receipts of $12,428, losses in 1935 were $5,052. Losses during 1936 were $5,543. Cash advances from Ford Motor Company (Oakwood Hotel Company) were making up the losses. The L. G. Treadway Service Corporation was in 1936 suggesting ways to improve business:

1. An appropriation of $400 to $600 for newspaper advertising.

2. Use of the Ziegler Cottage on Botsford property to sell loomed products made in Greenfield Village and duplicate antiques from the Ford Museum.

3. A team of horses and sled to be kept at the Tavern this winter for use of guests at a fee.

One corner of the Botsford Tavern parlor as it appeared in 1926. This room is much more stylish and expensive in appearance than the others in the tavern. It was in the parlor that the owner entertained personal friends. A picture of Henry Wadsworth Longfellow hangs on the wall above the organ. At the opposite end of the room, curtained windows bracket a large ornately framed mirror. In the center of the parlor is a heavy square table holding an album. (0.11611)

Botsford Tavern   In November 1938, the following letter was sent to B. J. Craig, secretary of Ford Motor Company, by Treadway's resident manager of Botsford Tavern:

Dear Mr. Craig:

The bank account of Botsford Tavern is again at a low state, and after the December 5th payroll will be practically cleaned out, and I would appreciate it if you would make arrangements for a $2,000 advance to Botsford Tavern sometime early in December.

Trusting that this can be arranged, I am

Yours very truly,
John Packard
Resident Manager

The warm end of the tap room at Botsford Tavern as it appeared in 1935. Liquor bottles in a variety of shapes and colors line the shelves behind the bar table. Although the original fireplaces remained in use in major areas of the building, steam heat had been added to nearly all rooms in 1925. (188.74204)

THE FARE

AT THE

Botsford Tavern

WHERE 19TH CENTURY HOSPITALITY PRESIDES

Dinner $1.50

Chilled Fruit Cocktail   Tomato Juice   Cranberry Juice
Grapefruit Juice   Pineapple Juice   One-half Florida Grapefruit

Celery   Olives   Assorted Relishes

Consomme   or   Soup

One-half Broiled Spring Chicken
Two Broiled French Lamb Chops
Filet Mignon Steak
Baked Sugar Cured Ham

Vegetables: -- Peas, Asparagus, Creamed Potatoes, French Fried Potatoes

Salads: -- Hearts of Lettuce, Jellied Vegetable Salad,
Stuffed Pear, Fruit Salad

Dressings: -- French, Mayonnaise, Thousand Island

Desserts: -- Special Botsford Ice Cream, Strawberry Sundae,
Butterscotch Sundae, Cakes, Coffee

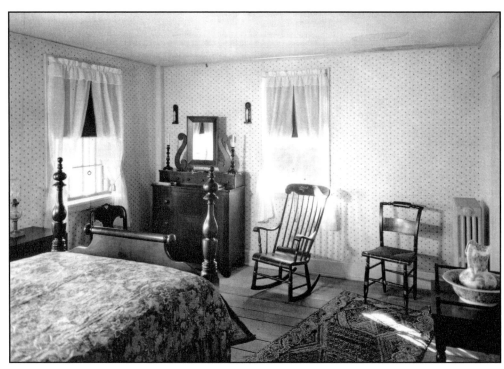

A typical bedroom at Botsford Tavern in 1925. Plain and simple, with four-poster bed, mirrored dresser, wooden chairs, small loose carpets on pinewood floors, a kerosene lamp, washbowl and pitcher — along with steam heat. This corner room is no doubt slightly larger than some along the front and side of the building. (0.11262)

Notes scrawled on the letter indicate that only $1,000 was sent, with a notation "Total Advances to Date — $27,000." That same year, C. B. Longley, a Ford attorney, had been inquiring about other hotel management companies. One being considered was the management company in charge of the Book Cadillac Hotel in Detroit. The L. G. Treadway Service Corporation terminated its service to Botsford Tavern on December 1, 1938, and Robert E. Hamilton of the Dearborn Inn assumed its management.

Dated February 17, 1939, the following letter was sent from the tavern's hostess to Clara Ford:

My dear Mrs. Ford,
    This is to say goodbye and to tell you how sincerely sorry I am that I may not see you to do so. I would like you to know that we will

always recall our four years at Botsford Tavern with regard and affection and that we are grateful to you and Mr. Ford for making them possible.

This sweet old place has been a pleasant home to us and we are grieved to leave it. With every good wish to you both, I am,

Faithfully yours,
Antoinette F. Shaw

On June 13, 1939, this letter was sent to Henry Ford's secretary, Frank Campsall:

Dear Mr. Campsall:

Relative to inquiry regarding Botsford Tavern we made a change in the management of Botsford Tavern on March 1st. Mr. and Mrs. Frank Shaw, who had been there since 1934, were replaced by Mrs. Lorna Clark who took over the duties of hostess on March 1st.

The policy of the tavern has not been greatly changed except that we now serve people for luncheon, teas and dinners without reservations. This has increased the business somewhat. The type of menu also has been changed, and we are attaching two sample menus of luncheon and dinners. In addition to the attached menus we also serve New England Breakfasts to parties at $.75 to $1.00 per person, and, of course, the special Botsford Tea for late afternoon is still very popular at $.75 per person.

Mrs. Clark has proved to me that she is a very charming person, and in my opinion is doing an excellent job in her new work.

If there are any other details that you would like, please advise me.

Sincerely yours,
Robert E. Hamilton
Manager

On April 1, 1939, the following "assignment" was made:

For valuable consideration receipt of which is acknowledged, THE OAKWOOD HOTEL COMPANY, a Michigan Corporation, hereby assigns to SEABOARD PROPERTIES COMPANY, a Delaware Corporation, its interests in the Lease Agreement dated September 22, 1934, by and between Henry Ford and Clara J. Ford, Lessors, and the OAKWOOD HOTEL COMPANY, Lessee, and which Lease Agreement covered certain lands and buildings in the SE 1/4 of section 36, T I N, R 9 E, Oakland County, Michigan, known as "BOTSFORD TAVERN."

THE SEABOARD PROPERTIES COMPANY agrees to fulfill all of the obligations on the part of the Lessee in the said lease to be performed.

The above was signed by John Crawford, representing the Oakwood Hotel Company, and Herman L. Moekle, representing Seaboard Properties Company. Both of these men worked for Edsel Ford at Ford Motor Company. Although Seaboard Properties was now

The ballroom on the second floor of Botsford Tavern. This was where Henry and Clara Ford had danced back in the 1880s. Until Lovett Hall was built at Greenfield Village in 1937, the Fords occasionally invited their friends to dances in this ballroom. Henry's musicians provided the music. The dance floor is said to be cushioned with springs to make dancing more enjoyable. (188.74224)

to fulfill the requirements of the lease, it did not own the tavern. It was not until July 1944, when Henry and Clara were disposing of much of their personal property, that Botsford Tavern was conveyed to Seaboard Properties Company for $229,050.49.

Clara, following Henry's death, must have inquired about Botsford Tavern. Hamilton, in July 1948, wrote to H. R. Waddell, Clara's secretary, providing the names of all full-time dining-room employees and their rates of pay. Quoting from the letter:

For your information Botsford Inn had a net profit last year of $4,263.00. This was the net figure after paying all real estate taxes, government income taxes, and other expenses. On the same basis in 1946 we had a net profit of $6,115.00. We consider this very good at this place because of their unusual expenses and the fact that we have no other revenue except their food — there are no sleeping rooms or bar revenues.

After Clara Ford died in September 1950, the Botsford Inn was sold together with its furnishings to the John Anhut family of Detroit, who successfully operated the inn for many years. In 1963, the inn was designated a State Historic Site. Recently, however, it has again fallen on hard times and at present is closed to the public.

References

Accession 1, Box 123, Fair Lane Papers. Benson Ford Research Center, HFM & GV.

Accession 33, Boxes 37, 38, Auditing Records. Benson Ford Research Center, HFM & GV.

Accession 384, Box 1, L. J. Thompson Papers. Benson Ford Research Center, HFM & GV.

Cordell, Harold M., Reminiscences. Benson Ford Research Center, HFM & GV.

Cutler, Edward J., Reminiscences. Benson Ford Research Center, HFM & GV.

"Henry Ford's Latest Antique." *Country Life*, September 1928.

Lewis, David L. *The Public Image of Henry Ford*. Detroit: Wayne State University Press, 1976.

"A Mid-West Victorian Inn." *The Mentor,* June 1929.

Nevins, Allan, and Frank Ernest Hill. *Ford: Expansion and Challenge: 1915–1932*. New York: Scribner's, 1957.

"A Victorian Tavern." *Antiques*, December 1926.

52
Dearborn Country Club

In 1923, the Ford Engineering Laboratory, being built on Oakwood Boulevard and housing Henry Ford's private office, established Dearborn rather than Highland Park as headquarters of Ford Motor Company.

Most of Henry Ford's top executives would now have their offices either at the Engineering Laboratory or at the nearby Rouge plant. Dearborn had been Ford's hometown since birth, and most of his close friends were there. Should the hometown of Henry Ford be second-class? Should Dearborn bow down to the "Pointes" or to the "Hills" in rank? Ford thought not! He wanted his friends and employees to have the best, and he could afford it. He was making and selling 9,000 automobiles a day, more than 2 million a year. These were boom times.

Some say he did it for his old friends who lived in Dearborn. Some say it was for his company executives. It was certainly not for himself — he never played a game of golf. He is said to have once hit a golf ball and in the process hit a girl in the head with the ball. He had no further interest in the game.

The Fords made their wishes known to Ernest Liebold, general secretary to Henry Ford. According to Liebold, he was told by Ford, "Now, you have somebody lay out that golf club. I don't want any professionals or any of these high-class fellows. We want to lay out a good practical golf club that anybody and everybody can use." There was to be no smoking or drinking of liquor, and food menus were to be simple and reasonable. Apparently, Ford did not intend to have golf professionals at the club, but other minds eventually prevailed, and David Robertson was later engaged as golf instructor.

Edsel Ford, then president of Ford Motor Company and living in Detroit, pitched in to help. He helped Liebold in arranging for Donald Ross, designer of Detroit Golf Club, to lay out the course on 163 acres of Ford-owned land on the east side of Military Road south of Ford Road. The land had been purchased by Ford in 1909 at a cost of $71,434.03.

Previously published in the *Dearborn Historian*, Vol. 30, No. 1, 1990.

Dearborn Country Club under construction in November 1924. The architect was Albert Kahn, and the builder was the Otto Misch Company. (P.0.19116)

The course would consist of eighteen holes covering a distance of 6,659 yards (3.78 miles). It was laid out so that the sun would never be directly in a player's eyes, always at an angle of at least 60 degrees.

For a clubhouse, Ford commissioned Albert Kahn, who had designed several factories and office buildings for Ford. Clara Ford was interested in the design of the clubhouse and suggested that it be built of logs, but after some attempt, her suggestion was found impractical. Instead, it was to be of Old English timbered construction. Clara did collect the antique English furnishings, however. A bill dated January 25, 1925, for furniture and tapestries purchased from Harry J. Dean Company of Detroit amounted to $9,084. The clubhouse is said to have cost the Fords about $250,000.

Ford Motor Company employees William Smith and B. R. Brown supervised construction of the clubhouse by the Otto Misch Company. Ray Dahlinger, head of Ford Farms, was in charge of landscaping the course according to Ross's plans. This job of constructing sand traps, bunkers, greens, and tees was quite in contrast to Dahlinger's other responsibility at that time of providing a perfectly level field for the Ford Airport. Dahlinger had about fifty workers building the golf course.

The course was ready in the spring of 1925, but the clubhouse with its locker rooms, dining room, and grand ballroom was not completed until that fall. Corporation papers had been filed by Clifford B. Longley in March 1925 over the signatures of Ernest Kanzler, George Brubaker, R. L. Welborn, Herman Kalmbach, R. D. McClure, and W. H. Smith. On May 2, 1925, the club petitioned the Detroit District Golf Association and the United States Golf Association for membership.

397

On April 3, 1925, the first applications for membership were received. First in line was Clyde M. Ford, mayor of Dearborn, followed by twenty more Dearborn men. A week later, applications from Detroiters were accepted. There were Ford Motor Company employees among them, but employees did not dominate the list.

A summer 1925 roster of club members shows a total of 135, of which about two-thirds had used the greens during June and July of that summer. One party had played the course seventy-six times, and Henry Ford is recorded as having admitted two guests during the two months. Club initiation fee was $100; dues were $38 per quarter; greens fee was $2. Meals (table d'hôte) were $1 for breakfast, $1.50 for lunch, and $2 for dinner.

In September 1925, the first board of governors was appointed, with Louis W. Howe, chairman; Henry A. Haigh, vice chairman; Harry A. Snow, secretary; Herman Kalmbach, treasurer; and William H. Smith. John S. Rummer was hired as manager and Mrs. Rummer as housekeeper. Rummer reported to the board of governors, who in turn were controlled by Liebold, who obtained his instructions from Henry Ford.

The first meal served in the dining room was on September 29, 1925, when Henry and Clara Ford entertained Mr. and Mrs. Louis Ives. Dining-room check number 1, for the party of four, amounted to $6 and was signed with a flourish by Henry Ford.

The first official formal function at the club was an invitational dinner dance for forty couples on October 30, 1925, hosted by Henry and Clara Ford. At this full-tails and white-tie affair, Ford Motor Company executives accounted for about half of the guests, and a quarter were doctors, several from Henry Ford Hospital. The names of many

The clubhouse of Dearborn Country Club as it appeared on November 6, 1927. (P.189.4963)

BREAKFAST

____

FRUITS AND PRESERVES

Grape Fruit (half) .25   Orange .15. Sliced .25

Stewed Prunes .20   Bananas with Cream .30

Orange Juice .35

Orange Marmalade .30   Strawberry Jam .30

Currant Jelly .30

CEREALS, CAKES

Oatmeal .25   Shredded Wheat .25   Corn Flakes .25

Grape Nuts .25   Kelloggs Bran .25

Puffed Rice .25   Puffed Wheat .25

Dry or Buttered Toast .15

Wheat Cakes .30   Waffles .40

EGGS AND OMELETTES

Boiled (2) .30, Poached on Toast .10, Fried (2) .10, Shirred (2) .40

Scrambled (3) .50, Omelette Plain .50, Omelette with Tomatoes .75

Omelette with Kidney .75, Ham and Eggs .75, Bacon and Eggs .75

GRILLED

Lamb Chop (1) .40   Pork Chop (1) .35   Breakfast Sausage .40

Broiled Ham .60   Broiled Bacon .60

Kippered Herring .40   Soused Filet of Mackerel .40

POTATOES

American Fried .20   Hashed Brown .25   Hashed Cream .30

COFFEE, TEA

Coffee. small pot .15, for two .25

English Breakfast Tea, Orange Pekoe, Ceylon Green .15

A July 1925 Dearborn Country Club menu.

A rear view of the Dearborn Country Club clubhouse as it faces the golf course. The date is October 14, 1925, and landscaping is well under way. (189.3107)

Raymond C. Dahlinger, with his Henry Ford Farm workers, was in charge of landscaping the Dearborn Country Club golf course and the clubhouse grounds. (833.78084)

of Ford's old Dearborn friends were conspicuously missing. A wholesome dinner followed by an evening of vigorous old-fashioned dancing clearly demonstrated that the Fords obtained more pleasure from dancing than from playing golf. Benjamin Lovett had arrived in town, and all of Dearborn soon would be dancing to Ford's musicians.

Under Ford, the club was obviously destined to lose money. With the luxuries of expensive chinaware, custom woven Irish linens, Monel metal kitchenware to prepare expensive foods, and hired help paid at high factory wages, the board of governors soon found inappropriate losses. A statement by the board for the period May 1927 to June 1928 divulges a loss of $70,000. Recommendations by the board included the possibilities of (1) increasing membership, (2) raising dues, (3) serving less costly foods, (4) restricting guests, (5) closing the clubhouse during winter months, and (6) renting the second-floor rooms to employees. But Ford continued to cover the losses. Even during the Depression of the 1930s, the Dearborn Club survived when many others in the Detroit area failed and were closed.

And Liebold had his problems. In addition to his project's losing money, which was contrary to his principles of management, Liebold found Ford's rules regarding smoking and drinking impossible to enforce fully. In one instance, when Ford became aware of the sale of cigars and cigarettes on the premises, Liebold was angrily instructed to burn the entire lot of tobacco in one big bonfire. Of course, members then brought their own narcotics so that the club environment became

A formal dance party held in the ballroom of the Dearborn Country Club on November 24, 1931. (189.9206)

quite obnoxious to Clara Ford in particular. The sight of women smoking cigarettes was especially intolerable to Clara. Other than financially, the Fords did not patronize the club to any great extent.

Ford's brothers, John and William, were less than enthusiastic about the club. John did not join, and Will, although a member, seems to have seldom used the facilities. In fact, Will was sometimes well in arrears in his dues, as were several others much of the time. In extreme cases, delinquent accounts were turned over to attorney Clifford B. Longley for collection. Ford's sister Margaret Ruddiman and her daughter were given memberships to the club by Henry. Some of the Bryants were active club members during this early period.

In March 1944, Henry and Clara Ford transferred the country club property to Seaboard Properties Company, a corporation owned by the Ford family. Members of the club at that time arranged to lease the club property from Seaboard on a yearly basis until 1952, when the members voted to raise funds to purchase the club for $300,000, subject to a substantial mortgage. On August 15, 1959, the mortgage was paid off and burned with much jubilation. In addition to what Henry Ford had provided, the club now has a swimming pool, air conditioning, and watered fairways.

References

Accession 65, E. G. Liebold Reminiscences. Benson Ford Research Center, HFM & GV.

Accession 292, Boxes 32–33, Henry Ford Office (Miscellaneous Files of Frank Campsall). Benson Ford Research Center, HFM & GV.

Files of the Dearborn Historical Museum.

53
Richmond Hill

At the time Henry Ford decided to purchase the Richmond Hill plantation along with several other antebellum plantations near Ways Station, Georgia, in December 1924, the winter home of the Fords was next door to that of the Thomas Edisons in Fort Myers, Florida. Ford and Edison were very close friends, and Ford managed to get to Fort Myers to see his friend for a week or so every year. After Edison died in 1931, the Fords seldom returned to Fort Myers, although they continued to maintain their house there until it was sold in 1945.

Among the properties considered by Ford in Georgia was Saint Catherine's Island, 25,000 acres, one of several islands along Georgia's Atlantic coast. The New York agent described it as:

> the ancestral residence of Button Gwinnett, one of the signers of the Declaration of Independence, and some six or eight guest houses formerly slave huts, a harbor on the west side of the island second to none on the Atlantic Coast, and last but not least it affords wonderful deer, turkey and duck shooting as well as marvelous fishing, yachting, etc.

Ford offered $750,000, which was declined because the asking price was $1 million. Later, when the island was offered for $750,000, Ford declined.

The Fords seemed to pay little attention to their Georgia properties until February 1930, when, on their way to Fort Myers, they parked their private railroad car for two days at Ways Station. On March 31 of that same year, the Fords made a separate trip from Dearborn to Savannah, paying for two days of additional engine rental at Savannah and parking their private car for two days at Ways before returning to Dearborn on April 6. In late March 1931, when returning from Fort Myers, the Fords again parked their car at Ways for two days. There is no record of the Fords traveling south in the winters of 1932 or 1933, but they spent three weeks in Fort Myers during the winter of 1934.

In preparation for a vacation at Ways in 1935, Ford's secretary, Frank Campsall, wrote the following instructions to property manager J. F. Gregory:

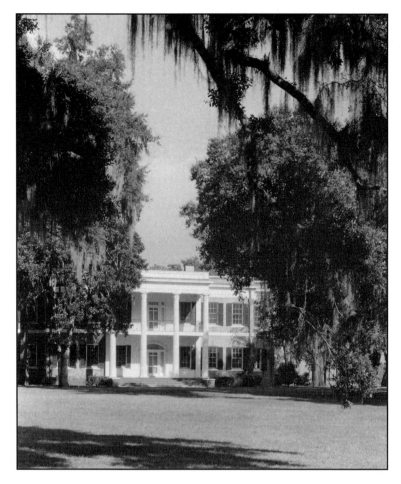

A front view of the
Richmond Hill
residence. At times,
the Fords would
bring their Dearborn
musicians to
Richmond Hill, and
old-fashioned dances
would be held on this
front lawn.
(P.0.5628)

Dear Mr. Gregory:

Will you kindly arrange to have the Cherry Hill House thoroughly cleaned and the house well warmed as Mr. and Mrs. Ford plan on coming down, probably between February 17 and 20 for a stay of two or three weeks, or more. Have plenty of fuel ready.

It will not be necessary to arrange for any extra help as the two boys on the private car will be available as well as Mrs. Ford's maid. The writer will also accompany them.

Our present plans are to leave here on February 15 for New York where we may spend two or three days and from there proceed south. This information, of course, is to be kept confidential.

Very truly yours,
Frank Campsall

The restored Cherry Hill house was being used that year as a temporary residence for the Fords and their private staff. Near Cherry

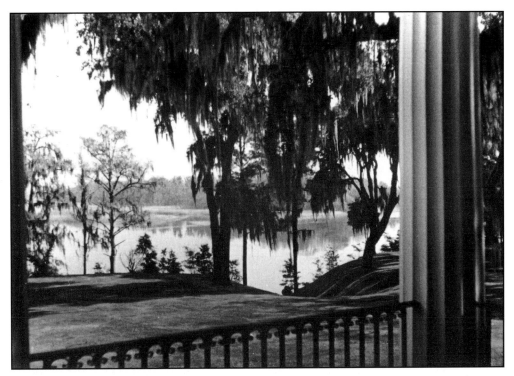

A view from the veranda of the Richmond Hill residence facing the Ogeechee River and land owned by the Fords on the opposite side of the river. (P.O.6568)

Hill was the antebellum site of the old Richmond plantation house on the Great Ogeechee River. Clara had chosen this site with its rows of ancient live oaks as a suitable location for the elegant Southern mansion of her dreams.

The Fords had examined a few Southern mansions for architectural ideas. The one in which they were particularly interested was the Hermitage on the northern outskirts of Savannah. Although it had been a beautiful building in its day, by 1934 it was in extreme disrepair. But the bricks of which it was built were particularly attractive, and the Fords decided to buy the buildings on the property for its bricks and move the bricks to the Richmond site at Ways. At the same time, two of the small Hermitage slave quarters, built of the same brick, were dismantled and reerected in Greenfield Village at Dearborn. Also at Dearborn, Clara was having a model built of the home she was planning at Richmond. The model was fitted with miniature furniture of the exact type she planned to use. Drawings of the Richmond house and topographical blueprints of the grounds had been prepared by architect Robert O. Derrick of Detroit. The local architect was Cletus William Bergen of Savannah.

The Fords were at Ways again in February 1936, and they stayed for forty-eight days. Visitors that year included Doctors Sladen and

McClure of Henry Ford Hospital in Detroit and Clara's friend Ellen Plantiff of New York. That spring, Clara, among piles of Hermitage brick, was marking off the dimensions of her Richmond house and turning the first sod in preparation for construction. She was very impatient concerning progress on her house, and the Fords were back at Ways for a few days in November to keep things moving properly.

Most of the furnishings for the Richmond home were taken from the Henry Ford Museum and the Fair Lane residence in Dearborn. Furniture sent to Ways from the museum on December 12, 1936, included:

> Chippendale, tip-top, table. Walnut with inlaid satinwood
> 8-sided, mahogany, tip-top, pedestal table attributed to Phyfe
> Dutch marquetree miniature cabinet
> Phyfe mahogany work table with drop leafs
> Small serving table with pierced metal border
> Martha Washington curly maple work table
> Hepplewhite walnut work table
> Duncan Phyfe dining table
> Floral pattern rug 20' x 22'
> Heavy deep colored rug with border 14' x 17'
> Faded floral pattern rug 10' x 17'
> Three-bordered rug, deep blue background 8' x 16'

Another list of items packed in the museum on January 15, 1937, included:

> Five wicker side chairs
> Four wicker arm chairs
> One small whatnot
> One washstand — ivory
> One stool — ivory
> One chest of drawers — ivory
> One armchair — ivory
> One pair bedends, head — ivory
> One pair bedends, foot — ivory
> One mirror for bureau — ivory
> One blackwalnut wood box
> Four lawn chairs
> Two lawn chairs with foot rests
> One sofa
> One small step-ladder
> One six-panel fire screen
> One five-panel fire screen
> One bureau
> One dresser
> Sewing machine
> Two sets of two each, bedrails

A view of one end of the living room at Richmond Hill about 1940, as it was when Clara Ford was entertaining her friends from Savannah. (P.0.2064)

A packing list, dated January 18, 1937, made up at Fair Lane, describes more than a hundred small items to be taken to Richmond by Truck No. 1. These included kitchen utensils, glassware, chinaware, linens, books, bedposts and rails, mattresses, and armchairs. Truck No. 2 was to take a similar load with more lawn chairs, sofas, lamps, and a box of fruit. Some of these furnishings may have been used at the Cherry Hill residence at Ways.

The Fords left Dearborn for Ways on the *Fair Lane* on January 19 and stayed this time for seventy-nine days, not returning to Dearborn until April 12. Campsall had stayed in Dearborn. Ford's chauffeur, Rufus S. Wilson, wrote weekly letters to Campsall apprising him of the situation at Ways:

Jan. 28, 1937
Dear Mr. Campsall,

The Boss is quite restless & doesn't know what to do first. He is with Gregory most of the time & I am driving Mrs. Ford. He hasn't been in the office at Cherry Hill five minutes since he has been here.

He called Mr. Bennett & Edsel last night about 8 P.M. & was quite upset about Mr. Sorensen building barricades & fences at the Rouge. Otherwise he is fine. I think he is a lot better than he was. I will write you again & let you know if he quiets down.

Mrs. Ford is a lot better than she was when she got here. She told Mrs. Dahlinger her rheumatism didn't hurt her a bit today. She is well pleased with the new house but awful anxious to get moved in. They are still staying at Cherry Hill.

Yours truly,
R. S. Wilson

P.S. The hotel is nowhere near done & the Boss has put Kanack in charge & is pushing it himself.

Feb. 1, 1937
Dear Mr. Campsall:

Mr. Ford is feeling fine and I think he is much better than he was when he got here. He rides around a lot with Mr. Gregory but he doesn't seem to be so nervous & irritable.

Mrs. Ford's rheumatism is giving her quite a bit of trouble. I think she will be better when she gets in the new house so she won't have to move around so much.

A view of the dining room at Richmond Hill about 1940. Chairs and table were likely from the Henry Ford Museum in Dearborn. (P.0.2068)

They will probably move into their house about Wednesday or Thursday. Both of them are terribly anxious to get moved.

The weather is 56 degrees, cloudy & raining a little today. Mr. & Mrs. Dahlinger are still here. I don't know when they are leaving.

The hotel should be completed in about 3 or 4 weeks. The Boss is pushing it quite strong.

Yours truly
R. S. Wilson

Feb. 13, 1937
Mr. Frank Campsall:

You spoke of some letters being held up. If there are any, Mr. Ford must have them as I have nothing in the office.

Mrs. Ford hasn't been out much this week but says that she is feeling lots better.

The Boss is 100% better, as he has slowed up a lot & is taking more rest than he did when he first got here. Since Edsel has been here they haven't moved five miles from the house. They have breakfast at 9:00, lunch at 1:00 & dinner at about 6:00 so you see they haven't much time for traveling. I think Edsel is leaving tonight.

Mr. & Mrs. Dahlinger are still here & don't know when they are leaving.

Everything is fine & everyone is on their toes as the Boss is sure pushing everything.

Very truly yours,
R. S. Wilson

Feb. 22, 1937
Mr. Frank Campsall:

Jack Gregory has been in the hospital since last Sat. & is quite sick. The doctor told him he would have to stay in for a week. They say he has the Flu.

Mrs. Ford is quite well but is staying off her feet as much as possible. She goes around the house in a wheel chair.

Mr. Ford is well & is resting more than I have ever known him to. He was out & around 5 hours today & that is quite unusual for him. We are going to Macon tomorrow to see one of his friends.

We are getting quite a colony of Dearbornites in Ways. I suppose Lovett will turn it on down here. I would like to put him in the Bunk house with his gang.

The Boss hasn't definitely decided when you are coming down but hinted that it would be about March first.

As ever,
Yours truly
R. S. Wilson

Signing the guest register at Richmond during February and March 1937 were:

Edsel Bryant Ford
                       Eleanor Clay Ford
                       Frances Ann Bryant (Clara's niece)
                       E. R. Bryant (Clara's brother)
                       Katharine Bryant (Clara's sister-in-law)
                       S. W. Raymond (Clara's brother-in-law)
                       Mrs. S. W. Raymond (Clara's sister)
                       Stanley Ruddiman (friend of the Fords)
                       Camille Ruddiman (friend of the Fords)

Henry and Clara were back at Ways from January 26 until March 24, 1938. By this time, the Community House, built by Ford for girls' home economics instruction, had been completed. The upper floor was a ballroom for instruction in old-fashioned dancing. In early March, the Fords organized a dancing party with Benjamin Lovett and Ford's Dearborn orchestra furnishing the music. Approximately one hundred guests were invited from Savannah. The guest list consisted of nearly all married couples, including nine doctors, a mayor, a judge, and two colonels. Ways inhabitants seemed not to be among the guests.

Savannah was prompt in responding. The Hibernian Society of Savannah invited the Fords to its 126th anniversary on March 17 at the DeSoto Hotel, but Clara's instructions to Campsall were, "Just say that Mr. Ford is sorry, but will be impossible to attend." The Fords also were invited to hear Grace Moore at the Savannah Municipal Auditorium on March 22. The mayor offered his private box, third from the stage on the left, which accommodated eight people. A note in Clara's handwriting reads, "Please say to the Mayor we will not be able to accept for the 22nd as we are leaving next week." The Fords left Ways on March 25, having been in Ways two months. They needed to be back in Dearborn, where the Wilbur Wright Celebration was being planned at Greenfield Village for April 16.

After a trial round-trip inspection run to Kalamazoo on January 10, 1939, the *Fair Lane* was off to Ways with the Fords on board January 29. One of Clara's social events that year was a buffet supper catered by Savannah Kitchens on February 21, 1939. A total of eighty-six guests consumed 350 sandwiches, 100 cheese biscuits, sponge cakes, creole kisses, almond crescents, salted pecans, pickles, fruits, coffee, and chocolate. Clara paid Alice S. Heyward $83.80 for catering the event.

On their return from Ways on March 16, the Fords traveled by way of Natchez, Mississippi, accepting the invitation of Mrs. George M. D. Kelly of the Natchez Garden Club to join its Pilgrimage Tour. The Fords stayed with the Kellys at Melrose. The following September, Ethel Kelly wrote to Henry:

> We consider that you and Mrs. Ford have been the outstanding guests
> to Natchez during the entire eight years since the origin of the

Henry Ford, standing in the rear and facing the camera, with his Dearborn orchestra providing the music for old-fashioned dancing in front of the mansion at Richmond Hill. Playing instruments are "Little Billy," "Perry," "Baxter," and "Castel." Other photographs taken on the same occasion show young people, perhaps students, dancing on the lawn. (0.2079)

Pilgrimage, and knowing your appreciation of lovely old things we naturally feel that an expression of your approval will add great prestige to our project. We have never before made this request of anyone.

The *Fair Lane* was parked at Ways from February 15, 1940, until April 1. The major event that winter was the visit of George Washington Carver, who at Ford's invitation came from Tuskegee Institute to dedicate the Carver Consolidated School at Ways on March 15, 1940. Clara was busy arranging for a shipment of grapefruit and oranges to Ways from their Florida property at Fort Myers, also for twelve Japanese quince shrubs to be sent from Dearborn to Ways and for a crate of Puerto Rican pineapples to be expressed on the *Orange Blossom Special* from Edgewater, New Jersey.

In mid-March, a hurried trip by auto was taken to Florida. With Robert Rankin, Clara's driver; Rufus Wilson, Henry's driver; and Campsall, the party left Ways on March 16. It was said to have been Mrs. Ford's trip. On the way, Campsall told a reporter: "I don't know where we are going. Mrs. Ford instructs the chauffeur after they get into the car. They never make hotel reservations in advance." Henry and Clara with one of the drivers rode in a large Lincoln, Campsall and the spare driver in a new Lincoln Zephyr. They stayed the first night in St. Augustine at the Marion Hotel. On the entire trip, the party registered under Campsall's name. Stopping the next day at Hobe Sound, Henry and Clara visited with Edsel and slept that night on Edsel's boat, while the "boys" stayed at a hotel. They drove on to Fort Myers the next day and talked with the Conants, who rented the Mangoes from the Fords. The real purpose of the trip was for Clara to see her brother Fred Bryant, who was ill at Dunedin. On the way back, with stops at the Bok Tower and Marineland, they again stopped at St. Augustine, returning to Ways after a trip of 1,340 miles. The Fords left Ways for Dearborn about a week later.

During the winter of 1941, the Fords were in Ways from January 28 until March 10. Clara had become acquainted with an elderly black woman named Janie Lewis who had once been a slave and lived in a small, dilapidated house several miles south of Ways. The Fords in a way adopted her, building her a new house next to her old one and insisting that she live in it. Arrangements were made for her support for the rest of her life.

By 1941, the townspeople of Ways wanted to show their appreciation for the advantages the Fords had provided their community. By negotiating with the two railroads and the U.S. Post Office Department, they were able to change the name of Ways to Richmond Hill on May 1, 1941, in honor of the Fords. But otherwise, progress at Richmond Hill was taking a turn for the worse because of restrictions brought about by World War II. The following year in May was the last time the Fords could use the *Fair Lane,* their private railroad car. By 1942, they were in Ways only for the first nineteen days of March. On their return trip, they went by way of Tuskegee Institute to visit with Carver.

The Fords went to Richmond Hill each winter by rented private rail car for the next five years, until 1947, the year Henry died. During this period, Henry, because of Edsel's death in 1943, had heavy Ford Motor Company responsibilities and was in poor physical and mental condition. When he died in 1947, Clara tried to continue the Richmond Hill operations but found them much more costly than she had expected. To lower cost, she discharged many employees, including Gregory, and cut school expenses. Clara died on September 29, 1950. A devastating fire destroyed the Richmond Hill sawmill on May 11, 1951, and meant the end of the Ford era at Richmond Hill. Clara had willed her property to the Ford Foundation, which immediately sold all but her mansion to Southern Kraft Timberland Corporation.

Furnishings from the Richmond Hill residence were shipped to Dearborn and, along with Clara's Fair Lane furniture, were auctioned by Parke-Benet Galleries in New York. The residence was put on the market by the Ford Foundation in July 1951 but not sold until February 1961, for $250,000. Gradually, the house deteriorated until about 1975, when it was restored somewhat as a community center with the surrounding grounds developed as golf courses. In 1980, the house was opened to the public as a restaurant. An extensive renewal of the entire property was undertaken in 1981 by Dr. Gaith Pharaon, a Saudi Arabian businessman. Now in excellent condition, the entire 1,800 acres and mansion have become the property of Sterling Bluff Association, which purchased it in March 1998 for $47 million, promising to develop an exclusive community of expensive winter homes for wealthy Easterners. Clara would be very pleased.

References

Accession 1, Box 43, Fair Lane Papers. Benson Ford Research Center, HFM & GV.

Accession 285, Box 2568, Henry Ford Office. Benson Ford Research Center, HFM & GV.

Accession 292, Box 30, Henry Ford Office. Benson Ford Research Center, HFM & GV.

Accession 587, Boxes 68–71, Office of Henry Ford and Clara Ford. Benson Ford Research Center, HFM & GV.

Bryan, Ford R. "Guide to the Records of Richmond Hill Plantation, Georgia 1925-1952." Benson Ford Research Center, HFM & GV, 1983.

Lewis, David L. "Ford at Richmond Hill." *Cars & Parts*, September 1973.

———. "New Lease on Life." *Detroit Free Press*, March 23, 1975.

Long, Franklin Leslie, and Lucy Bunce Long. *The Henry Ford Era at Richmond Hill, Georgia.* Self-published. Richmond Hill, Georgia, 1998.

54
Huron Mountain Club

People living in Dearborn sixty to seventy years ago read in the newspapers each summer of the annual trip of Henry and Clara Ford to their summer home in the Huron Mountains. Their "cabin" at the Huron Mountain Club was approximately forty miles north of Marquette, Michigan, several miles beyond the small town of Big Bay.

The region in which the Huron Mountain Club was situated comprised a group of granitic mountains, rugged but not lofty, interspersed with lakes and streams. Over nearly all of the club area stood the primeval forest. Some of the slopes and crests were bare, but in the main the land was heavily timbered with hardwoods and hemlocks. Good stands of pine, maple, cedar, basswood, and birch joined in the array.

The Huron Mountain Shooting and Fishing Club was organized in 1889 by twelve charter members headed by Horatio Seymour, Jr., of Marquette. Several wealthy Detroiters, including the lumber baron Truman H. Newberry, were among these charter members. According to a report of the club's Conservation Committee, "The Huron Mountain Club was originally founded and has since been maintained by a group of men and women of different interests and occupations who have found a common bond in the few months of every year spent at the Club. This bond is their love of the still unspoiled natural beauty of the place."

The originally issued soliciting circular described the club as having 9,000 acres, including six lakes in the heart of the Huron Mountains, with the proposal of making the region a hunting and fishing park. A clubhouse was to be built and lakes and streams stocked with fish. It was to be a stock corporation with shares of stock at $100 and a maximum of five shares per individual.

At the time the club was formed in 1889, steamboat transportation was provided twice a week between Marquette and Houghton with stops along Lake Superior including Big Bay. A $2,313 clubhouse was built in 1893 on Pine River. The charge for board and room at the club-

Previously published in the *Dearborn Historian*, Vol. 32, No. 3, 1992.

The Ford cabin at the Huron Mountain Club north of Marquette in Michigan's Upper Peninsula. This was Clara's favorite summer resort. Dozens of photographs show her feeding the deer that roamed the woods and came to the door for some tasty morsel. Clara's personal maid, Rosa Buhler, is said to have greatly enjoyed taking an early-morning swim in the frigid waters of Lake Superior each morning. Henry seems not to have especially relished living in such solitude in the woods, and neither Henry nor Clara participated a great deal in social events at the club. (0.2847)

house was a dollar a day per person. The club had no license to sell alcoholic drinks in the early years, but members could provide their own.

There was to be no shooting during the summer months, but in the fall, deer, grouse, ducks, geese, and bear were fair game. The killing of loons, hedgehogs, chipmunks, and such "small but picturesque and harmless game" was discouraged. The "plucking of rare flowers, the uprooting of ferns and the needless mutilation of trees and shrubs" were frowned upon. Without charge, rowboats were made available on Pine, Trout, Rush, and Ives Lakes, with guides available, if desired, for two dollars a day. Powerboats were not permitted on the inland lakes, and auto roads were not opened into the forests.

In 1901, scheduled steamboat transportation was discontinued because it was losing money, and the sand road from Marquette to Big Bay required two days to negotiate by horse and carriage. But in 1906, a railroad was built to Big Bay, and the club was revived. In 1914, a post office was established, and by 1917, automobiles and a better road became the method of getting from Marquette to the club. By the 1920s, fifty families had built cabins in the woods and along rivers and lakes. Until that time, conditions had been quite primitive. No telephone service was provided to the cabins, each cabin had its pump, each fireplace its crane and kettle, and a portable tub was an item of everyday equipment.

In the early 1920s, Henry Ford had purchased a good portion of the timber of the Upper Peninsula of Michigan including a large portion of Baraga County, which shared the Huron Mountain area with Marquette County. So Ford had plenty of lumber just across the peninsula with which to build a cabin. In fact, he helped other Detroiters at the club by providing them with lumber from his Pequaming mill. The town of Pequaming and thousands of adjoining acres had been purchased by Ford from Dan Hebard, the town's founder, in 1923.

By 1929, the majority of the seventy-four family members were Detroiters, with almost as many from Chicago. Other cities represented included Cleveland, Philadelphia, Pittsburgh, and smaller cities in Michigan, Illinois, Pennsylvania, New York, Massachusetts, and Iowa, plus one family from California. That year of 1929 witnessed the change in club structure from a stock corporation to a cooperative with all members having equal status. In May 1929, when Hebard was president of the club, Henry and Clara Ford joined.

The Fords, of course, wanted a private cabin, and no cabin could be erected on club property without authority of the board of directors and adherence to club specifications. From archival records, it appears the Fords may have restored an existing cabin at Huron Mountain Club. No previous owner is recorded, but many of the cabins were passed from generation to generation. Membership in the club was often inherited.

Robert O. Derrick, Inc., of Detroit was chosen by the Fords as architect for their cabin. A letter dated December 9, 1929, from Derrick indicated that the cabin would accommodate twelve people. The Fords apparently had not yet been to the location. The general contractor for building the cabin was J. H. Godwin of Marquette. Godwin had been recommended by the club manager for having built other cabins to proper specifications as established by the club's board of directors. The cost of building a cabin was higher there than it would have been in Detroit because of the cost of board and lodging for the workmen.

A letter from Derrick to Clara Ford estimated that the cabin would be ready for occupancy by August 1930. Some furnishings were

Interior of the Ford Huron Mountain cabin. This well-furnished living room features a beamed ceiling, natural stone fireplace, rustic furniture, chintz-covered sofa and chairs, and a rag carpet. Lighting was by electricity as well as fireplace. Following Henry's death in 1947, Clara continued to spend Augusts here, bringing friends and relatives to keep her company. (0.8543)

purchased by Mrs. Ford from Tonella & Rupp of Marquette in May 1930. Bills were received from Godwin as late as July 1931, however.

According to published by-laws, some of the rules at Huron Mountain Club, when the Fords joined, were as follows:

Annual dues to be $250.
Only one cabin and one rowboat per homesite.
Tradesmen and guides hireable at the Clubhouse.
No tips are to be given directly to Club employees.
Members are to contribute to an annual Employee Fund.
Car storage at Club: $1/day, $5/week, $15/month.

No automobile is to be parked behind a cabin.
Train, Marquette to Big Bay: Leaves 9:45 a.m.; Arrives 11:35 a.m.
Club autos to Big Bay: $2/person; $1.50/trunk.
Clubhouse summer rates $6/day/person; winter $7/day.
Gun license must be obtained from Club manager.
No loaded firearms during closed game season.

It was said that "pastimes imported from the city — golf, tennis, croquet, trapshooting, even equestrianship — have held at best no more than a partial and temporary interest. The wilderness is the thing. Hunting with the camera has long been a pursuit of a few, with trophies which adorn every cabin."

The Fords most often visited the Huron Mountain Club in late summer. A favorite mode of transportation was ore boat from Dearborn to Marquette. These mammoth carriers plied constantly between the Rouge plant and the Marquette and Duluth ore docks. The ships had luxurious passenger quarters, and when the Fords were not on board, guests were invited aboard for vacation trips. Henry Ford Hospital nurses dominated the list. The Fords would debark at Marquette with their staff and drive in private automobiles the forty miles to the club.

There is little indication that the Fords became greatly involved in official club activities. Neither of them became an officer of the club, although Henry did serve on the land committee and furnished machinery for a well-equipped repair shop at the club. There is likewise little evidence that the Fords did much hunting or fishing at the Huron Mountain Club.

Henry Ford seems to have spent considerable time in Big Bay. The reminiscences of Archie Fleury, who operated the telephone office at Big Bay, tell of long conversations with him. Ford was being besieged by reporters and deluged with unwanted phone calls and telegrams, and he enjoyed the game of being somewhere he was not expected to be.

Ford loved the little town of Big Bay — so much that in 1943, at age eighty, he bought the town. This included fifty-two houses, the large lumber mill, and the hotel. He spent several millions restoring the mill and employee homes, and another half million restoring the hotel in which he maintained a seldom-used private suite for himself and Clara. The hotel also served as a vacation headquarters for numerous friends who worked at Ford Motor Company and Henry Ford Hospital.

The Big Bay properties, including the cabin at Huron Mountain Club, were overseen by F. J. Johnson, Ford's Upper Peninsula properties manager. One letter from Johnson tells of three cabins having burned to the ground at the club during the winter and nothing but snow damage to the Ford cabin.

After Henry Ford's death in 1947, "Mrs. Henry Ford" is listed as the club member. After Clara's death in 1950, the Big Bay properties

were offered for sale and sold in 1951. About that same time, the Ford
membership and cabin at the Huron Mountain Club were transferred
to the J. W. O'Boyle family of Texas oil wealth. Edsel Ford was not
living, and the grandchildren were apparently not interested in wilderness life. Today, the hotel at Big Bay operates as the Thunder Bay Inn.
The old sawmill structure at Big Bay still stands and is said to be undergoing renovation by its present owner, Emerson Fleury.

Recent reports indicate the Huron Mountain Club occupies some
24,000 acres and still has only fifty cabins. A Huron Mountain Club
Wildlife Foundation has been created, and the area teems with naturalists from universities investigating forest and wildlife conditions in that
relatively pristine environment. The foundation was involved in the
transfer of four timber wolves from Minnesota to upper Michigan.

At times, the U.S. government advocates that the club be converted
to a national park, but members have been able to convince those advocates that the area is not suitable for mass recreation because it is too
cold, has too few beaches, and is too far from centers of population. And
as for preservation, the club is doing fine.

References

Accession 23, Box 5. Benson Ford Research Center, HFM & GV.

Accession 65, Archie Fleury Reminiscences. Benson Ford Research Center,
HFM & GV.

"The Book of Huron Mountain." Report of the Conservation Committee,
Huron Mountain Club, 1929.

McNulty, Dorothy J. "Money Enhancing Nature." *Detroit Free Press,* February
18, 1975.

Rydholm, C. Fred. *Superior Heartland: A Backwoods History.* Private publication,
1989.

55

Henry Ford in Sculpture

Henry Ford's likeness is represented in a variety of media. Commonplace are simple two-dimensional photographs, which exist by the thousands. Coins and medallions honoring Ford have been distributed by the hundreds. Three-dimensional relief plaques, busts, and statues are less abundant.

Recorded as property of Henry Ford Museum are several busts and bas-relief plaques that are not on display and are presumed to be in storage. These are very sketchily described in the records as follows:

Accession 00.771, Pine bust of Henry Ford.
Accession 29.1327, Sculpture — Henry Ford.
Accession 34.231, Sculpture — Henry Ford — Maker: J. C. Marxen, Omaha, Nebraska, woodcarving made from likeness in 1931 catalog.
Accession 34.307, Bust — Silk; Lacquer — Henry Ford — Maker: Fachian Children's Home, China.
Accession 35.256, Bust — Marble — Henry Ford — Maker: Mario Trafeli, Detroit, Michigan, 1924.
Accession 37.650, Bust — White Marble — Henry Ford — Height 15 inches.
Accession 40.28, Plaque — Carved Wood bas-relief — Henry Ford — Maker: Facchina Plinio, Udine, Italy.
Accession 41.91, Bust — Gilt Finished — Henry Ford — Maker: Bonnie Bean — Bust Height 19 inches.
Accession 44.75, Plaque — Large white composition bas-relief — Henry Ford — Plaque Height 17 inches, Width 22 inches.
Accession 51.13, Bust — Small Plaster — Henry Ford — Maker: Mario Trafeli. Object corresponds to 35.256.

The great majority of busts and statues of Henry Ford are, of course, not in the Henry Ford Museum but are scattered worldwide, mainly in the United States but also in England and quite likely in Russia, Brazil, and Australia. A few of the outstanding busts and statues of Ford are described on the following pages, arranged chronologically according to date of execution.

An early bust of Henry Ford was one that employees at the Highland Park plant of Ford Motor Company planned in 1914 as a gift

to him for display in the factory. This was considerably prior to the
announcement of the five-dollar day in January 1915. C. S. Pietro, who
had previously made a bust of J. P. Morgan, was commissioned by the
employees to make one of Ford. Because Pietro's studio was in New
York City, the problem was to induce Ford to make the necessary trip to
New York. He only consented provided that they would also have a bust
made of his wife, "in appreciation of the self-denial and the big help
given during the years when he was struggling for success." Both busts
were finished and placed on display for the first time at Pietro's studio
at 402 Fifth Avenue on January 14, 1915. What became of these two
busts following that first display is not known.

A life-size bust of Henry Ford was initiated in 1934 by Hans
Wollner, a German sculptor living in Detroit. Correspondence with
Ford's secretary, Ernest Liebold, indicates that Wollner would have
liked to have worked with Ford personally instead of using "sculptogra-
phy" as suggested by Liebold. Wollner would have liked to have the bust
displayed at the "Century of Progress" in Chicago during the summer of
1934. The following letter from Wollner to Edsel Ford relates the early
history of the bust:

Henry Ford in
Sculpture

The original clay model
of Hans Wollner's
bust of Henry Ford,
completed in 1937 and
photographed by Wollner
in his studio. (0.19825)

October 25th, 1935
Dear Mr. Edsel Ford:

About a year ago I made a bust of your father, Mr. Henry Ford, and dedicated it to him through Mr. Liebold. This bust was made of my own accord entirely according to pictures and photographs which Mr. Liebold brought me on several occasions. While Mr. Liebold was at my home, he rendered his opinion and even Mr. Bacon who came with him helped me as much as possible.

After I finally delivered the bust, Mr. Liebold wrote me a very nice letter of acknowledgment saying that he considered the bust one of the finest of Henry Ford.

But I am not satisfied with it as yet, because I did not have a chance to compare my work with the model.

As I have mentioned, I have never seen Mr. Henry Ford, and it would be absolutely necessary to see him, perhaps just for a few minutes, as I could then put on those last finishing touches which are so important.

I might add that Mr. Henry Ford himself is not fond of sitting, or even too modest to be interested in having one made, but I believe you would be, and hope that with your help we can finish it up.

One of the six copies of the Wollner bust now resides in the library of the Henry Ford Museum's Research Center. (Photograph by the author.)

Hoping you will see the matter in exactly the way it is meant, I remain

Respectfully,
H. Wollner

There seems to be no specific record of Wollner's original bust reaching Ford or the Henry Ford Museum. But in 1963, the centennial year of Ford's birth, the Henry Ford Trade School Alumni Association obtained permission to use Wollner's original bust to cast six bronze duplicates of the original. These in turn were donated by the association to institutions bearing the name of Henry Ford. Included were Henry Ford Hospital, Henry Ford Community College, Henry Ford Centennial Library, Ford Motor Company, and Henry Ford High School; one copy was given to the National Portrait Gallery in Washington, D.C. The Edison Institute, under its name at that time, did not qualify, but the bust given to the Ford Motor Company in 1963 was eventually given to the Henry Ford Museum about 1980 and now resides in its Research Center.

Irving R. Bacon, Ford's personal artist whose paintings decorate the walls of Henry Ford Museum, was asked by Ford in 1943 to prepare a bust. Bacon had had no experience in sculpture and conferred with a local Swedish sculptor for guidance. The bust was to be life-size in clay, as used by the automotive stylists working near him in the Ford Engineering Laboratory. Bacon took great pains to prepare a perfect likeness of Ford, and Ford found the bust very satisfactory. But Bacon and others felt that such a great man should have a much more impressive bust in his honor. So, using the smaller bust as his model, Bacon next prepared three busts of giant proportions — four feet high and three feet wide. Although the original life-size bust had a bronze finish, each of the giant busts was given an individual finish — one was iron, one bronze, and one marble. One of the three giant busts is now at Fair Lane, the Ford residence in Dearborn; another is at the Jerome-Duncan

Ford dealership near Detroit. Whereabouts of the third giant bust are unknown.

Commissioned shortly after the death of Henry Ford in 1947, a statue in his honor was unveiled at the Dagenham, England, plant of Ford Motor Company on October 14, 1948. The statue was unveiled by Lord Airedale, at that time chairman of Ford Motor Company, Ltd. Attending the ceremony was C. W. Dyson-Smith, the sculptor. This statue was recently used as the pattern for two more, one located at the Ford Research and Development Center at Dunton, England, and one at the Ford Training and Development Center in Dearborn.

In 1968, the Interservice Club Council of Dearborn appointed a Henry Ford Statue Committee to conduct a fund-raising campaign for the purpose of establishing a suitable memorial to Ford. Margaret W.

One of Irving Bacon's life-size busts of Henry Ford on display in Henry Ford Museum in 1963. (P.0.6712)

Henry Ford in Sculpture

Above is one of the three giant Bacon busts of Henry Ford now located in the showroom of the Ford Jerome-Duncan dealership in Sterling Heights, just north of Detroit. Richard Duncan, who established a Ford car museum in connection with the dealership, photographed the bust in his museum in 1997. (Photograph courtesy of Richard Duncan.)

Statue of Henry Ford by C. W. Dyson-Smith, 1948. (P.188.74768)

426

Ference, wife of Ford Motor Company's vice president of research, was chosen as chairperson of the committee. The noted sculptor Marshall Maynard Fredericks of Birmingham, Michigan, known for his many exquisite monumental sculptures throughout the United States and abroad, was selected to design and execute the statue. Funds were collected by letters of solicitation, posters, canisters, and special events. Schoolchildren in particular became enthusiastic donors. The memorial was dedicated on June 8, 1975, with Edsel B. Ford II acknowledging the gift as a representative of the Ford family.

This beautiful monument consists of a free-standing, life-size bronze statue of Ford, augmented by four dioramic bronze reliefs all mounted on dark green marble. The memorial is located near the west end of the Henry Ford Centennial Library, which faces Michigan Avenue in Dearborn. The memorial, being placed perpendicular to the avenue, is very inconspicuous, however, and many Dearborn residents,

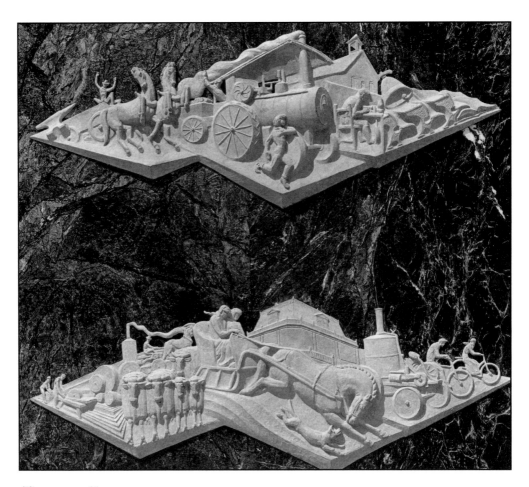

The upper and lower bronze reliefs to the left of the Fredericks statue of Ford. (Photograph courtesy of Marshall M. Fredericks Studios.)

even those using the library, are unaware of the statue's existence now that there are small trees and shrubs around it.

To the left of the statue, the upper bronze relief depicts Ford during his childhood. It shows an anvil, horses and wagon, the steam traction engine that inspired him to be a mechanic, Ford as a youth sitting at a bench repairing a watch, and the Scotch Settlement School where he obtained his elementary education.

In the lower bronze relief to the left of the statue are Ford as a young man timbering and cutting lumber; with his fiancée, Clara, riding in a sleigh; the Square House he helped build; the steam threshing engine he operated; and Henry bicycling with Clara.

To the right of the Fredericks statue of Ford, the lower bronze relief shows many of the vehicles Ford created, including his first tractor, his first car with him driving, the Model T, his first truck, his first commer-

cial car, and two of his famous racing cars, including "Old 999" with himself at the wheel.

The upper right bronze relief shows some of the buildings historically important to the Ford empire, including the first Ford world headquarters, Ford's first little workshop on Bagley Avenue in Detroit, the Piquette plant where the Model T was developed, the famous Ford Rotunda, the new world headquarters of Ford Motor Company, and a manufacturing plant with a row of various Ford-related vehicles.

A copper bust of Ford is mounted on the Thomas MacFarlane Biggar Memorial to Henry Ford in front of the Ford residence on MacGregor Avenue in Fort Myers, Florida. The residence, known as the Mangoes, is now part of Edison-Ford Winter Estates, a museum operated by the city of Fort Myers. Biggar purchased the home from Henry and Clara Ford in 1945 and erected the memorial in 1985. On

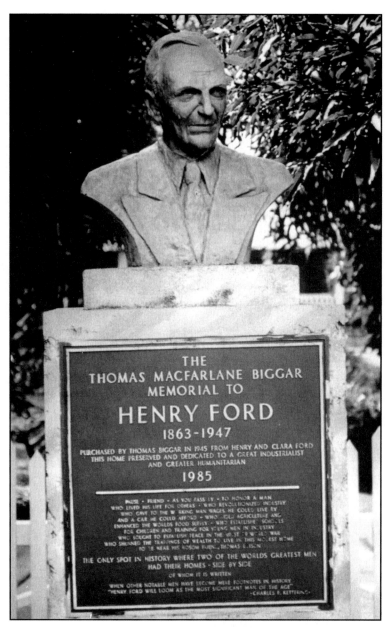

The Thomas MacFarlane Biggar Memorial to Henry Ford in front of the Ford
residence in Fort Myers, Florida. (Photograph courtesy of Arnold L. Sarlo.)

Uncommon Friends by Donald Wilkins, Fort Myers, Florida. In the background is the Caloosahatchee River Bridge. (Photograph courtesy of Arnold L. Sarlo.)

A bust of Henry Ford by Dorothy Spradley, Richmond Hill, Georgia, 1991. (Photograph courtesy of Richard B. Folsom.)

A 1998 bronze duplicate of the Henry Ford statue by Dyson-Smith in
Dagenham, England, in the courtyard of the Ford Motor Company Training
and Development Center at Dearborn, Michigan. (Photograph courtesy of
Joshua Kristal, *Monday Morning News*, Detroit.)

John Jensen's statue of Henry Ford, Richmond Hill, Georgia, 1999. Shown are Richard R. Davis *(left)*, mayor of Richmond Hill, and Jensen *(right)*. (Photograph courtesy of Robert Morris, *Savannah News-Press.)*

the memorial plaque are the statements "This home preserved and dedicated to a great industrialist" and "The only spot in history where two of the world's greatest men had their homes — side by side."

In a work known as *Uncommon Friends,* the three Vagabonds — Thomas Edison, Harvey Firestone, and Henry Ford — are depicted in a sculpture grouping that shows them relaxing by the pool in Centennial Park in downtown Fort Myers, Florida. Each gentleman is outfitted in a three-piece cast aluminum suit designed and executed by Fort Myers sculptor Donald J. Wilkins. The project, commissioned in 1988 and still under construction, also will include a copper alligator and her babies, manatees, frogs, turtles, and water lilies — all lighted at night.

On May 4, 1991, Mayor Richard R. Davis of Richmond Hill, Georgia, unveiled a memorial to Henry Ford consisting of a life-size bust mounted on a granite base. The sculptor was Dorothy Spradley of the Savannah College Department of Art and Design. As part of the unveiling ceremony, the song "I'll Take You Home Again Kathleen" was sung by Margaret Glynn Aliffi, who, as a student, had sung this song for Ford at chapel service in Richmond Hill fifty years earlier.

A bronze statue, a duplicate of the one by Dyson-Smith in Dagenham, England, was dedicated on January 21, 1998, in the courtyard of the Ford Motor Company Training and Development Center at

Dearborn. Edsel Ford II, great-grandson of Henry Ford, after unveiling the statue, stated: "At eighty years old, Henry Ford said that anyone who stops learning is old, whether eighty or twenty. Those who keep learning stay young."

The city of Richmond Hill, Georgia, unveiled a life-sized clay statue of Henry Ford in its city hall foyer on August 29, 1999. The statue was produced by John Jensen, art professor of Armstrong Atlantic State University. The statue rests on a marble base and shows Ford wearing a gray suit, white shirt, purple tie, and gold cuff links. As part of the ceremony, Professor David L. Lewis of the University of Michigan delivered an address.

As a memorial to Henry Ford, the people of Ballinascarthy, Ireland, on September 3, 2000, unveiled a full-sized stainless-steel replica of a Model T Ford as a "Millennium Project." Quentin Keohane designed the memorial base of stone, and Kevin Holland produced the Model T. Both architect and sculptor are natives of Ballinascarthy, the little town

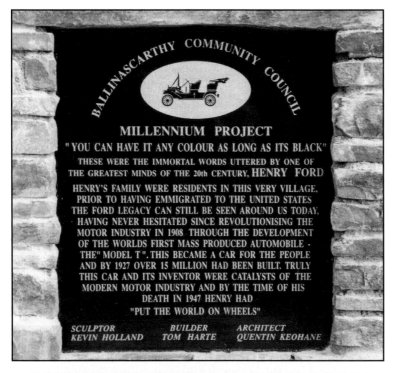

Memorial plaque honoring Henry Ford in Ballinascarthy, Ireland, near the homesite of Ford's ancestors. (Photograph courtesy of Dan Holland.)

Hazel Ford Buttimer, Ballinascarthy resident, presenting a Model T souvenir to Kevin Holland, sculptor of the Model T replica. (Photograph courtesy of Dan Holland.)

nearest the homesite of Henry Ford's ancestors. Major speakers at the unveiling included Robert Clark, West Cork Ford dealer, and Edwin J. Nolan, chairman of Henry Ford & Son, Limited.

The several works of sculpture described here, each created in honor of Henry Ford, are certainly far from a complete assembly. Before this book is printed, other sculptures will be called to our attention. As for other types of memorials to Ford, the number of buildings, streets, and automobiles attest that perhaps he has more commemorative objects carrying his name than any other human being.

References

Accession 65, Irving Bacon Reminiscences. Benson Ford Research Center, HFM & GV.

Accession 284, Box 30, Folder U (Underwood). Benson Ford Research Center, HFM & GV.

Accession 285, Box 1849, Hans Wollner correspondence. Benson Ford Research Center, HFM & GV.

Cassidy, Eddie. "Village Makes Dazzling Four-wheel Tribute to Legendary Car Maker." *Irish Examiner*, September 4, 2000.

"Dedication of the Henry Ford Statue." Henry Ford Centennial Library, Dearborn, June 8, 1975.

"Ford Dedicates Training Center." *U.S. Auto Scene*, January 21, 1998.

"Henry Ford Makes Artful Return to Richmond Hill." *Savannah Morning News*, August 30, 1999.

"The Henry Ford Millennium Project." *The Ford Legend*, Spring 2001.

"An Inspiration to All Who Pass By . . ." *Ford Times*, November–December 1948, p. 17.

Lewis, David L. "Ford Nomenclature." *The Ford Legend*, Summer 1998.

Lewis, David L., and Carolyn Navarre. "A Statue for Henry Ford." *Model "T" Times*, July–August 1970.

"Sculptor Was Local; Images Were Global." *Detroit Free Press*, April 6, 1998.

Index